MW01142093

BLAIR & KIRSTEN ALEXANDER
4918 LA-HAL-DA AVE. N.E.
TACOMA, WA 98422

WASHINGTON STATE
TRAVELER'S
AFFORDABLE ACCOMMODATIONS

Choosing a place to stay is often like a puzzle. Fit your pieces together with the help of this guide to all types of lodgings for all types of travel.

Author
Elaine C. Ingle

Cottage Computer Publishing
P. O. Box 4704
Wenatchee, WA 98807

Library of Congress Cataloging in Publication
Ingle, Elaine C.
    Traveler's affordable accommodations, Washington
state : a comprehensive guide to affordable lodging
throughout Washington state / author,
Elaine C. Ingle.
    p. cm.
    Includes index.
    Preassigned LCCN: 95-70498.
    ISBN 0-9639064-1-0

1. Hotels--Washington (State)--Guidebooks. 2. Washington
   (State)--Guidebooks. I. Title

TX907.3.W37164 1995   647.94'79701
                              QBI95-1748

1st Edition: May, 1994
2nd Edition: October, 1995

Special Contributors:
                      Jean Riggs & J. Randall Riggs

             Cover Illustration & Graphic Design:
                      XL-ART - Kirk Dietrich

                                Printer:
                    Lambson Lithographics

                      San Juan Island photos:
                      Juniper Garver-Hume

DEDICATION

To "Jackal" Jean Riggs for her tenacious
work ethics and keen eye, many, many
thanks.

To Randy Riggs, my partner, for many hours
of hard work, understanding, and moral
support. This book could not have happened
without him.

To my daughter Trina Ingle-Cabreros for her
confidence, encouragement, and love.

INTRODUCTION

Traveler's Affordable Accommodations is written for all my fellow travelers who like their "creature comforts" away from home to be affordable.

The dictionary definition of **AFFORDABLE** is to have sufficient means for; to meet expenses without detriment to one's estate.

We all like a bargain and like to receive the best value for our buck. My means are modest, but now and then I also want to splurge, so at times I can "afford" a little more. I have expanded the scope of this book to include a variety of accommodations fit for vacation, business, and adventure travel.

One criteria for being mentioned in this book is to have lodgings, double occupancy, for less than $100 a night sometime during the year. Many places have high season rates that may not be considered "affordable", but during the off season the same accommodations may be reduced as much as 50% or more. Being aware of the bargains that are available will help you plan when to make your journey and where to stay.

The updated information in this guide was compiled from June, 1995 to September, 1995. Every attempt has been made to obtain accurate up-to-date rates. However, rates are subject to change so please confirm when making reservations or checking in.

No attempt has been made to rate any of the lodgings listed in this publication. Every attempt has been made to give you all the facts so you can do your own ratings. Have fun!

Elaine Ingle

Traveler's Affordable Accommodations

answers commonly asked questions.

- Up-to-date rates and other costs
- Number of rooms/cabins/units
- Number of nonsmoking rooms
- Directions
- Children welcome or adults only
- Pet policies and costs
- Morning coffee - in the room
  or provided in the lobby
- Breakfast provided
- Phone in room - cost per call
- Amenitites
- Shuttle services
- Parking areas and cost
  for Seattle & Spokane

Towns are listed alphabetically and lodgings are listed alphabetically within each town or area.

See the index for quick reference.

A special reference index on types of lodging, areas, and activities of interest is located at the back of the book.

Contents

OROVILLE

395

97

20 WINTHROP

COLVILLE

NEWPORT

ashington
Pass

OMAK

2

LEAVEN-
WORTH

CHELAN

COULEE DAM

SPOKANE

2

WENATCHEE

28

90

195

97

90

MOSES LAKE

395

WASHINGTON

PULLMAN

YAKIMA

CLARKS-
TON

12

TRI-CITIES

DAYTON

82

WALLA
WALLA

12

97

© 1995 Gray Mouse Graphics

0   25   50   75

Miles

Seasonal Rates: In many recreational areas there are two or more seasons, a peak season and off season. The low price referenced is for the off-season, the high price for the peak season.

Rates are subject to change.

Discounts: Many establishments give a variety of discounts. The prices quoted in this book are "rack" rates, the standard price with no discounts. Always inquire about discount rates that may apply to you - corporate, AAA, senior, off-season, handicap, military, group, mid-week, etc.

TYPES OF LODGINGS AVAILABLE

Motels and Hotels
Most "affordable" motels and hotels are privately owned. The chain motels/hotels that appear in this book are usually owned or operated by individuals. All rooms have private facilities unless otherwise noted. Most motels and hotels have a variety of discount rates.

Bed & Breakfasts
Bed and Breakfasts generally do not have coffee/tea making facilities, phones, or TVs in the room, but offer other unique features. Each location's facilities will be mentioned on an individual basis. For insurance purposes all bed and breakfasts' guest rooms are nonsmoking.

Hostels
Hostels are not just for students or young adults, and you don't have to be a member. They tend to foster an atmosphere of camaraderie and guests often share travel experiences.

Resorts and Lodges
Most resorts and lodges are destination areas and reservations should be made early. The accommodations may be cottages, cabins, houseboats, chalets, or lofts.

• ABERDEEN

(pop. 16,660) This seaport town is located on Grays Harbor, west of Olympia.

Visit the Aberdeen Museum of History, Aberdeen Trout Hatchery, and Grays Harbor Historical Seaport. A full scale replica of the 18th century vessel *Lady Washington* is open for tours when in port. Other points of interest are the canneries, log booms, and lighthouses.

Located in Grays Harbor County the sales/use/lodging taxes are 10.9%. Also see Cosmopolis and Hoquiam for lodging.

$30-$46   **CENTRAL PARK MOTEL,** 6504 Olympic Hwy, Aberdeen, WA 98520, phone 360-533-1210 or 1-800-927-1210. Nine units with two nonsmoking rooms available. Located in a beautiful rural area with restaurant, gas, and groceries approximately 1/2 mile away. Cable TV and telephones in each room. Automated wake-up calls available. There are two double rooms with two queen beds in each room, three rooms with queen beds, two with double beds, one with two doubles, and one family room. Five units have kitchenettes. Free coffee and other beverages every morning in the lobby. Children welcome, pets allowed with some restrictions. **Rates:** single $30; double $46; family room $46; no charge for extra person or local phone calls. Major credit cards accepted. **Directions:** approximately 5 miles west of Montesano and 5 miles east of Aberdeen on Hwy 12, south side of freeway.

LYTLE HOUSE BED & BREAKFAST - see Hoquiam.

$45-$95   **The NORDIC INN CONVENTION CENTER,** 1700 S. Boone St., Aberdeen, WA 98520, phone 360-533-0100 or 1-800-442-0101 (US & Canada). 66 rooms, 44 nonsmoking. Phones, TV, restaurant, and bar. No coffee/tea making facilities in the rooms, but there is a coffee shop. Remodeling plans include an indoor swimming pool and hot tub. Children welcome, pets allowed. **Rates:** single $45-$95; double $55-$95; local phone calls free; pet deposit of $25 and $5 per night; extra person $7. Major credit cards accepted. **Directions:** from Hwy 105 follow road to Westport, 2 blocks past South Shore Mall and 1 block past Grays Harbor College.

$45-$99 **OLYMPIC INN MOTEL**, 616 W. Heron St., Aberdeen, WA 98520, phone 360-533-4200, reservations 1-800-562-8618, fax 360-533-6223. This two level motel has 55 rooms, 41 nonsmoking. Phones, TV, fans, some microwaves, king or queen beds, and 3 kitchen units with basic cookware. No coffee/tea making facilities in the rooms, but available in the lobby. This two story motel has very spacious rooms and features soundproof brick construction. Wake-up service. Children 12 and under free, pets allowed. **Summer Rates:** *6/15 to 9/15 -* single room (1 bed) $45-$70; double (2 beds) $55-$75; family room (2 bedrooms) $74-$95; kitchen units $77-$99; pets $9 per night; extra person $9; local phone calls free. **Winter Rates:** $45-$77. Major credit cards accepted. **Directions:** from Hwy 12 go downtown and stay on Wishkah St. to Alder, make a left; 1 block on the left.

RED LION INN, 521 W. Wishkah St., Aberdeen, WA 98520, phone 360-532-5210, fax 360-533-8483, reservations 1-800-547-8010.

$36-$52 **THUNDERBIRD MOTEL**, 410 W. Wishkah St., Aberdeen WA 98520, phone 360-532-3153. Right on the main street in the center of town, this two story motel has 36 rooms, 23 nonsmoking. Phones, TV, ceiling fans, mini refrigerators, coffee making facilities, king, queen, and water beds. Outdoor hot tub. Children welcome, infants free. Pets allowed, no charge. **Rates:** single (1 person) $36; double (2 people, 1 bed) $46; double room (2 people) $47-$52; extra person $4; no charge for local phone calls. Major credit cards accepted. **Directions:** approaching from the south, cross over the bridge and turn left on Wishkah, in the center of town, on Hwy 101 northbound.

ACME see Bellingham or Deming for lodgings.

AIRWAY HEIGHTS see Spokane for lodgings.

AMANDA PARK see Lake Quinault.

ANACORTES (pop. 11,700) This seaport town is located on Fidalgo Island and is the gateway to the San Juan Islands.

(A-nuh-KOR-tez) is bounded on three sides by Puget Sound. It has marinas full of commercial and pleasure boats, and its deep water port accommodates ocean-going vessels. Fidalgo Island is the first of the San Juan Islands. Victoria B.C. is a 3 hour ferry ride to the west. The Cascade Mountains are a 2 hour drive to the east. Climate - temperate marine typical of Puget Sound. The weather is usually cool, seldom extremely hot or cold. Summers are dry; winters bring light rain.

Located in Skagit (SKA-jit) County, the sales taxes are 7.8% for lodging.

$75-$90 **ALBATROSS BED & BREAKFAST**, 5708 Kingsway West, Anacortes, WA 98221, phone 360-293-0677 or 1-800-622-8864. Four guest rooms in this 1927 Cape Cod style home. Rooms are graced with beautiful period wood finish, crystal chandeliers, king or queen beds, and private baths. Common areas feature a fireplace, library, TV, VCR, and stereo equipment. Also available are sight-seeing cruises aboard a 46 foot sailboat (3 hours - $35 per person) and bicycle rentals. Children permitted, outdoor smoking, kitchen privileges for "catch of the day", pets by arrangement. Hosts will assist guests in getting their car in line for the early morning ferry to Victoria, pamper them with a full breakfast, then transport them back to their car in time for departure. **Summer Rates:** *May to September* - double rooms $85-$90; children and extra person $5-$10; no charge for local calls. **Winter Rates:** $75-$80. Visa & MasterCard. **Directions:** from Mt. Vernon take Hwy 20 exit to Anacortes, from Commercial St. turn left on 12th. Continue 2 miles west on 12th, it becomes Oakes Ave., go straight at the ferry landing traffic light 1/2 mile to Skyline Way, turn left on Skyline Way, go two blocks to Kingsway, turn left.

$42-$125 **ANACORTES INN**, 3006 Commercial, Anacortes, WA 98221, phone 360-293-3153, fax 360-293-0209, reservations 1-800-327-7976. A total of 44 units, 33 nonsmoking. Cable TV, direct dial phones, refrigerators, microwaves, and coffee/tea making facilities in rooms. Five units offer fully equipped kitchens. Heated, outdoor swimming pool. Children 12 and under free, pets allowed in four rooms with advance arrangements. **Summer Rates:** *5/01 to 10/15* - $60-$82; jacuzzi room *July and August* $125; extra person $5; pets $10; kitchen units $5 extra; local phone calls free. **Winter Rates:** *10/16 to 4/31* - $42-$55; jacuzzi room $70. All major credit cards accepted. **Directions:** entering town from Hwy 20, turn right on Commercial. The Inn is between 32nd and 30th.

$45-$110 **CAP SANTE INN,** 906 9th St., Anacortes, WA 98221, phone 360-293-0602 or 1-800-852-0846. A total of 34 units, 18 nonsmoking. TV and direct dial phones, local calls free. Courtesy coffee and rolls provided in the lobby. Laundry facilities available. Children welcome, no pets. The Inn overlooks the marina and yacht harbor. Within walking distance of dining, marinas, and downtown shopping. Ten minutes to the ferry terminal. **Summer Rates:** *Memorial Day to 10/31* - double occupancy $64-$68; suite (6 person capacity) $110; extra person $5. **Winter Rates:** *11/01 to Memorial Day* - double occupancy $45-$50; suite $89. Major credit cards accepted. **Directions:** coming into town on Hwy 20 turn right on Avenue R and proceed to 9th St.

$53-$189 **FIDALGO COUNTRY INN,** 1250 Highway 20, Anacortes, WA 98221, phone 360-293-3494, fax 360-299-3297. All new facility, grand opening July 1995. A total of 50 units with 40 nonsmoking and 2 handicapped accessible. In-room amenities include phones, TV, and air conditioning. No coffee/tea making facilities in the rooms, but available in the lobby 24 hours, also a continental breakfast is provided. Fireplace and jacuzzi suites available. Seasonal outdoor pool and jacuzzi, meeting room for 50 people. Children 12 and under free, no pets. **Summer Rates:** *5/15 to 9/15* - single $59-$74; double (2 people) $69-$84; suites $129-$189. **Winter Rates:** prices reduced 10%. Most major credit cards accepted. **Directions:** from I-5 take Exit 230, Hwy 20, cross over bridge to Fidalgo Island, located at the intersection of Hwy 20 and Hwy 20 Spur, turn off to Oak Harbor.

$28-$65 **GATEWAY MOTEL,** 2019 Commercial Ave., Anacortes, WA 98221, phone 360-293-2655 or 1-800-428-7583. Total units 13, 4 nonsmoking, 5 non-equipped kitchenettes (4 have microwaves). TV and phones in rooms, local calls free. No coffee/tea making facilities in the rooms. Near laundromat, theater, restaurants, boat marina, and park. Free shuttle to bingo hall. Children free with parents, small pets by arrangement. **Summer Rates:** *6/5 to 9/31* - $40-$45; suite $50-$65. **Winter Rates:** $28-$34; suite $40-$55. MasterCard, Visa, & Discover. **Directions:** located on the corner of 21st & Commercial.

$65-$85 **HASTY PUDDING HOUSE BED & BREAKFAST,** 1312 8th St., Anacortes, WA 98221, phone 360-293-5773 or 1-800-368-5588. Four guest rooms, two with private facilities, two with shared. Coffee/tea making facilities in 2 rooms, full breakfast provided between 8 and 9 a.m. Children over 10 welcome, no pets. This 1913 craftsman style home is an antique lover's dream. Located on a quiet residential street and within walking distance to restaurants, shops, marina,

and park. Smoking permitted outside. **Rates:** double $65-$85; extra person $20. Most major credit cards accepted. **Directions:** from I-5 take Exit 230, Hwy 20, to Anacortes. In Anacortes, go north on Commercial Ave. to 8th, left on 8th, proceed 4 blocks.

Hasty Pudding House Bed & Breakfast

$48-$110 **ISLANDS INN & LA PETITE RESTAURANT**, 3401 Commercial, Anacortes, WA 98221, phone 360-293-4644. 36 rooms, 20 nonsmoking. Most rooms have views and a fireplace, some rooms have whirlpool bathtubs. Coffee makers and refrigerators in all the rooms, plus a complimentary "Dutch breakfast". Seasonal, heated outdoor pool and hot tub. Children are welcome, dogs allowed. La Petite Restaurant on the grounds is open for dinner Tuesday through Sunday 5:00 p.m. to 10:00 p.m. **Summer Rates:** *5/01 to 10/14* - single $65-$110; extra person $5; pet charge $5 per night. **Winter Rates:** $48-$85. Major credit cards. **Directions:** entering Anacortes on Commercial Ave., the Islands Inn is the first motel on the right side.

$55-$85 **MARINA INN**, 3300 Commercial, Anacortes, WA 98221, phone 360-293-1100. Total of 52 units, 37 nonsmoking, all with TV and phones, local calls free. No coffee/tea making facilities in the rooms, but available in the lobby at all times plus a continental breakfast. Eleven rooms have microwaves and refrigerators, but not equipped with cookware or dishes. Other amenities include an indoor hot tub, six jacuzzi rooms, and free guest laundry. View rooms of San Juan Islands, water, and Mt. Baker. Children 12 and under free, no pets.

Summer Rates: *6/16 to 9/31* - $65-$75; jacuzzi rooms $85; extra person $6. **Winter Rates:** $10 less. Major credit cards. **Directions:** follow Hwy 20 into Anacortes, the Marina Inn is 1 1/2 blocks on the left.

$40-$48 **NANTUCKET INN**, 3402 Commercial, Anacortes, WA 98221, phone 360-293-6007. Three guest rooms are available in this home which was built by a lumberman in 1925. Two rooms on the second floor have private facilities, one room on main floor has bath in the hall. The house is furnished with antiques, quilts, and lovely old things. Children welcome on a limited basis, no pets. House telephone may be used for local calls at no charge. Coffee is provided in the morning and La Petit Restaurant, across the street, is open from 7 a.m. to 10 a.m. for breakfast. **Rates:** single $40; double $48. No credit cards. **Directions:** Hwy 20 joins Commercial at 36th St., the Inn is on the left at 34th.

$70-$80 **OLD BROOK INN BED & BREAKFAST**, 530 Old Brook Lane, Anacortes, WA 98221, phone 360-293-4768. Two rooms are available in this wonderful getaway, nestled in a park-like setting where an ancient orchard once thrived. A babbling brook flows into a small pond with fishing possibilities. There are walking trails through the forest and an 18 hole golf course is one mile away. Both rooms have private facilities. The upstairs room sleeps four comfortably. There is an extensive library, ground floor deck, and the kitchen is open to guests. Continental breakfast provided. Children welcome on a limited basis, pets by arrangement. **Rates:** main floor room $70; upstairs room $80; extra person $10. Visa & MasterCard. **Directions:** from Hwy 20 going west, turn left at Sharpe's Corner at the Country Corner Restaurant, proceed for 1/4 mile, turn right on Old Brook Lane.

$30-$65 **SAN JUAN MOTEL**, 1103 6th St., Anacortes, WA 98221, phone 360-293-5105, fax 360-293-3024, reservations 1-800-533-8009. Three story motel with 29 units, 9 nonsmoking. In-room amenities include phones and TV with HBO. Free morning coffee in the office, and there are 20 units with kitchenettes (cookware not furnished). Within walking distance of restaurants. This motel has a great view of Mt. Baker and is within 10 minutes of the ferry. Children welcome, small dogs allowed. **Summer Rates:** based on number of people per room $35-$65; pets $5 per night; local phone calls 25¢. **Winter Rates:** $5 less per person. Major credit cards accepted. **Directions:** go through Anacortes to the last signal light, turn left, and proceed for one block, 6th St. & O Ave.

$47-$72 **SHIP HARBOR INN,** 5316 Ferry Terminal Rd., Anacortes, WA 98221, phone 360-293-5177, reservations 1-800-852-8568, Canada 1-800-235-8568. This is the closest motel to the ferry terminal with 20 lodge units and 6 cabins, 50% nonsmoking. In-room amenities include TV, phones, and some rooms have microwaves and refrigerators. The cabins have equipped kitchens. Morning coffee and a continental breakfast are provided in the office. Restaurants within walking distance. Children welcome - there is even a playground, pets allowed on a limited basis. Two rooms in the main building have fireplaces, balconies, and king beds. All rooms have a view of the ferry and San Juan Islands. **Rates:** single $47; double $72; suite $65; family room $72; extra person $4; local phone calls free. Major credit cards. **Directions:** take I-5 to Exit 230, proceed 20 miles west on Hwy 20 to Anacortes, follow Commercial Ave. to 12th St., turn left and go 3 miles.

$69-$89 **SUNSET BEACH BED & BREAKFAST,** 10 Sunset Beach, Anacortes, WA 98221, phone 360-293-5428 or 1-800-359-3448. Three guest rooms, one with private facilities, TV, and private entrance, two with shared facilities. All rooms are located on the main floor and have views of seven islands. Relax on the large deck at the house or the smaller deck by the water. No pets. Full breakfast served from 8 a.m. to 9 a.m., also ferry bag for early departures. Smoking permitted

outside. **Summer Rates:** $79-$89; extra person $25. **Winter Rates:** $69-$79. MasterCard, Visa , & Discover - $2 cash discount. **Directions:** in Anacortes follow signs to ferry, go past ferry one mile on Sunset Ave. to Washington Park, at entrance follow road two blocks to Puget Way.

$65-$90 **The INN AT BURG'S LANDING**, 8808 Villa Beach Rd., Anderson Island, WA 98303, phone 206-884-9185. A total of 4 rooms, two have private facilities and TV, two have shared facilities. Full breakfast provided. Children five and under free, no pets. This contemporary log homestead, built in 1987, offers spectacular views of Mt. Rainier, Puget Sound, and the Cascade Mountains. The Inn has a hot tub and a private beach. Area activities include beachcombing, scuba diving, tennis, and golf. Tour the island by bicycle or on foot. Shuttle provided to restaurant. **Rates:** double occupancy $65-$90; extra person $15. MasterCard & Visa. **Directions:** 100 yards east of the ferry landing on Villa Beach Road.

(pop. 4,555) is located 15 miles northeast of Everett, on the Stillaguamish River. It is three miles off I-5 at the intersection of Hwy 9 and Hwy 530.

$37-$56 **ARLINGTON MOTOR INN**, 2214 SR 530, P. O. Box 3387, Arlington, WA 98223, phone 360-652-9595. 42 rooms in this typical two story motel adjacent to I-5 at Exit 208, 20 nonsmoking rooms, 6 rooms with mini refrigerators. Phones, TV, and indoor hot tub. No coffee/tea making facilities in the rooms, but available in the lobby. Children welcome, pets allowed. **Rates:** single $37-$44; double $49-$51; family room $56; extra person $5; pets $20 refundable deposit, $10 first night, $5 consecutive nights; no charge for local phone calls. Major credit cards. **Directions:** just off I-5 at Exit 208.

$36-$75 **SMOKEY POINT MOTOR INN,** 17329 Smokey Point Dr., Arlington, WA 98223, phone 360-659-8561. 54 rooms, 50% nonsmoking. Phones, TV, AC, year-round heated pool, and jacuzzi. No coffee/tea making facilities in the rooms, but available in the lobby. The townhouse suites have kitchens with basic cookware and microwaves. Children 5 and under free, pets allowed. Within walking distance of shopping center and restaurants. **Rates:** single room (1 bed) $36-$41; double (2 beds) $49-$53; townhouse suites $75; extra person $5; pets $5 per night, deposit $20; no charge for local phone calls. Credit cards accepted. **Directions:** just off I-5 at Exit 206.

ASHFORD is located on State Road 706 going to Mt. Ranier from the west.

Settlers arrived in the Nisqually Valley in 1888. In the early 1900's three trains arrived daily to bring tourists to the newly established Mt. Rainier National Park. Mount Tahoma Trails has established hut-to-hut skiing on 80+ miles of groomed and ungroomed trails used from December to March.

Lodging and sales taxes equal 9.6%.

$65-$137 **ALEXANDER'S COUNTRY INN**, 37515 State Rd. 706 E., Ashford, WA 98304, phone 360-569-2300 or 1-800-654-7615 (US). 12 nonsmoking rooms, each with a unique personality and old-fashioned charm. Nine rooms have private facilities, three with shared. No phones or TV. In the evening guests mingle in the parlor by the fireplace as the innkeeper serves complimentary wine or enjoy the hot tub overlooking the trout pond. Children 8 and under free, no pets. A full country breakfast is provided to guests in the widely acclaimed restaurant. **Summer Rates:** *5/01 to 10/31* - double occupancy $82-$98; suites $137; extra person $15; taxes included. **Winter Rates:** $65-$82; suite $105; taxes included. Visa & MasterCard. **Directions:** one mile before the SW corner of Mt. Rainier National Park.

$60-$115 **The CABINS AT THE BERRY**, P. O. Box 176, Ashford, WA 98304, phone 360-569-2628. One log cabin and one rustic cottage, a year-round getaway in the forest. Smoking discouraged. Both units have full kitchens and wood heat from a cozy fireplace stove. The "Cabin" has an antique bathtub to view the evening stars through the bathroom skylight, 2 double beds, and 4 twin beds. The "Cottage" has a shower, one queen bed and 3 twin beds. Children welcome, pets okay, especially llamas. Check in at the Wild Berry Restaurant. **Rates:**

cabin: 1-2 people $60, 3-4 people $80, 5-8 people $115; cottage: 1-2 people $60, 3-5 people $70. MasterCard & Visa. **Directions:** in Elbe, go east on Hwy 706, through Ashford and continue another 5 miles east toward the Mt. Rainier National Park entrance. Located on the right side of the highway, 1 mile from the Nisqually entrance to the park.

$30-$50 **GATEWAY INN**, Route 706, Ashford, WA 98304, phone 360-569-2506. Eleven units with private facilities, 6 log cabins sleep up to 4 people. TV in the rooms and lounge. Fireplaces in the log cabins. No coffee/tea making facilities in the rooms, but a restaurant, bar, and coffee shop are on the grounds. Children 7 and under free, pets allowed. **Rates:** single $30; double $35-$50; extra person $5; pets $5; pay phone 25¢. MasterCard, Visa, & Amex. **Directions:** go 6 miles past Ashford on SR 706, just before the entrance to Mt. Rainier on the right side of the highway.

$60-$105 **GROWLY BEAR BED & BREAKFAST**, 37311 SR 706, P. O. Box 103, Ashford, WA 98304, phone 360-569-2339 or 1-800-700-2339. Two guest rooms, one with private bath and balcony; one with shared facilities. In a quiet, secluded location, this 1890 homestead mountain house is located one mile from the entrance to Mt. Rainier National Park. The house is surrounded by native shrubs, flowers, and tall evergreens. Full mountain breakfast with pastries from nearby Sweet Peaks Bakery; restaurants are located within walking distance. **Summer Rates:** *5/01to10/31* - $95 & $105; extra person $30. **Winter Rates:** $60 & $70. Visa, MasterCard, & Amex. **Directions:** one mile from Nisqually entrance to Mt. Rainier National Park, on State Road 706.

$45-$125 **JASMER'S BED & BREAKFAST & CABINS**, P. O. Box 347, Ashford, WA 98304, phone 360-569-2682. A total of 6 nonsmoking accommodations. Two guest rooms have private facilities, private entrances, microwave, refrigerator, and one room has a fireplace. A continental plus breakfast is provided at check in. Big Creek Cabin has a seasonal hot tub. The cabins are equipped with TV, VCR, woodstoves, fireplaces, and furnished kitchens. Children over 10 welcome, no pets. **Summer Rates:** B & B $75-$95; cabins year-round rates $90-$125; extra person $10. **Winter Rates:** B & B $45-$65. Visa & MasterCard. **Directions:** 6 miles west of Mt. Rainier National Park.

$59-$75 **The LODGE NEAR MT. RAINIER**, 38608 SR 706 E, P. O. Box 86, Ashford, WA 98304, phone 360-569-2312. Four cabins and 3 lodges, each have modern bathroom, kitchen, and a fireplace, no phones. Restaurant and bar within walking distance. Relax in tranquility with wildlife and evergreens at the foot of Mt. Rainier. Located on 16 acres, there is a multitude of activities year-round. Group accommodations are ideal for retreats, family reunions, church groups, etc. Children welcome, sorry no pets because of the wild animals. **Rates:** cabins sleep 2 to 4 people, $59-$75 for two; extra person $10. Lodges - capacity 12 to 25 people, $250-$375 per day. *Minimum stay of 2 nights on weekends and holidays.* Visa, Discover, & MasterCard. **Directions:** coming from the south along I-5 take Exit 68, go east on Hwy 12 to Morton. From the north on I-5 take Exit 142B toward Puyallup on Hwy 161. The Lodge is located 1/4 mile west of the Nisqually entrance to Mt. Rainier National Park on SR 706.

$55-$70 **MT. RAINIER COUNTRY CABINS**, P. O. Box H, Ashford, WA 98304, phone 360-569-2355. 10 cabins all have private facilities. Five cabins have coffee/tea making facilities, 6 cabins have kitchenettes and fireplaces. 900 feet from the entrance to Mt. Rainier National Park. Skiing, hiking, bicycling, and fishing nearby. Restaurants within walking distance. Children 2 and under free, pets allowed. **Summer Rates:** *7/04 to 10/31* - $65-$70; extra person $10; pets $10. **Winter Rates:** $55-$60. Visa & MasterCard. **Directions:** 5 miles past Ashford toward entrance to Mt. Rainier National Park.

$58-$118 **MT. RAINIER GUEST SERVICES**, P. O. Box 108, Ashford, WA 98304.

NATIONAL PARK INN at Longmire, phone 360-569-2411, reservations 360-569-2275. *Open year-round.* Located at the 2700 foot level of Mt. Rainier. This historic rustic lodge has been refurbished and offers 25 nonsmoking units. Seven units have shared facilities, 18 with private facilities. **Rates:** 1-2 people in rooms with shared facilities $58; private facilities $80; 2 bedroom units (1-3 people) $108. Major credit cards. **Directions:** 6 miles into the park from the southwest entrance.

PARADISE INN, phone 360-569-2275. Located at the 5400 foot level of Mt. Rainier, this lodge is *open from May 17th to noon October 2nd.* All 126 rooms are nonsmoking, 96 have private facilities and 30 have shared. This historic hotel was built in 1917 and remains much the same today. The large lobby was built with hand-hewn Alaskan cedar timbers. Children welcome, infants free. **Rates:** 1-2 people in rooms with shared facilities $62; private facilities $88; 2 bedroom units (1-3 people) $112; suites $112-$118. Major credit cards. **Directions:** 31 miles from Elbe.

$65-$95 **MOUNTAIN MEADOWS INN BED & BREAKFAST**, 28912 SR 706 East, Ashford, WA 98304, phone 360-569-2788. Originally a mill superintendent's home built in 1910, there are 5 rooms, each with private facilities. Children over 10 welcome, pets allowed by arrangement. TV in the living room, sauna available, and a model train museum. Full country breakfast cooked on an old fashioned wood cooking stove. The view from the spacious front porch in bygone days overlooked the booming sawmill town of National, no longer in existence. Today the view has been transformed to one of natural wild life habitat. **Summer Rates:** $75-$95; extra person $15. **Winter Rates:** $65-$85. Visa & MasterCard. **Directions:** 3/4 mile west of the Ashford post office on State Road 706 E., 6 miles from Mt. Rainier National Park Nisqually entrance.

Mountain Meadows Inn Bed & Breakfast

$50-$77 **NISQUALLY LODGE**, State Road 706, Ashford, WA 98304, phone 360-569-8804. 24 units, all non-smoking, TV, phones, and air conditioning. Each room is "mountain size". No coffee/tea making facilities in the rooms, but coffee and a continental breakfast are provided in the "Great Room". The lodge also has an outdoor hot tub. Children welcome, infants free, no pets. **Summer Rates:** *5/01 to 9/30* - $67-$77. **Winter Rates:** $50-$60. Visa, MasterCard, Diners, & Amex. **Directions:** 7 miles east of Elbe on SR 706, 1/2 mile east of Ashford, 5 miles before the national park entrance.

ASOTIN (uh-SOH-tin)

(pop. 1,039) is the gateway to Hells Canyon and is located on the Snake River in the southeast corner of the state. See Clarkston for lodging.

•AUBURN (pop. 33,280) is located between Seattle and Tacoma in the Green River Valley.

The city is just 15 miles from Sea Tac Airport. The city has 22 parks that support a wide spectrum of passive and active outdoor activities. Location of the Pacific Northwest Super Mall.

Sales taxes and lodging tax equals 11% for accommodations with 60 or more units, less than 60 units 8.2%.

$70-$75   **BLOMEEN HOUSE BED & BREAKFAST**, 324 B St. NE, Auburn, WA 98002, phone 206-939-3088. This 1912 Queen Anne style Victorian was Auburn's first hospital during World War I. There are 2 guest rooms available with separate or shared baths. The rooms are furnished with charming antiques and decorations. A large continental breakfast is provided. Children over 12 by arrangement, no pets. Smoking allowed on the verandah. **Rates:** double occupancy $70-$75. No credit cards. Cash, traveler's checks or personal checks. **Directions:** from I-5 take the Hwy 18 Exit, go to the Enumclaw/Auburn Exit, right on Auburn Way No. to downtown Main St., turn left, go to Auburn Ave., turn right, 2 blocks north of Auburn General Hospital.

Blomeen House Bed & Breakfast

$46-$54 **NENDELS INN AUBURN,** 102 15th St. NE, Auburn, WA 98002, phone 206-833-8007 or 1-800-547-0106. 35 rooms, 18 nonsmoking. Rooms have phones and remote control TV. 4 rooms have refrigerators and microwaves for an additional cost of $10. No coffee/tea making facilities in the rooms, but pastries and coffee are available in the lobby. Within walking distance of restaurants. Children welcome, pets allowed. **Rates:** single room $46; double room $54; pets $10. Major credit cards. **Directions:** east of SR 167, take the 15th NW Exit, second light on the right.

$66-$74 **PONY SOLDIER MOTOR INN Best Western,** 1521 D St. NE, Auburn, WA 98002, phone 206-939-5950, fax 206-735-4197, reservations 1-800-634-7669 (5) (21). 66 rooms, 70% nonsmoking. Phones and remote control TV with HBO. No coffee/tea making facilities in the rooms, but a continental breakfast is provided in the lobby. Sauna, outdoor pool, and spa. Within walking distance of restaurants. Children 12 and under free, small pets allowed. Next to municipal airport, one tie down space provided at the airport. **Rates:** single room $66-$69; double room $74; extra person $5; pets free; local phone calls free. Major credit cards. **Directions:** 1 mile east of Hwy 167 at "D" St. and 15th NW.

BAINBRIDGE ISLAND

(pop. 16,390) To reach Bainbridge Island, travel thirty minutes west by ferry from Seattle. It can also be accessed by bridge from Poulsbo.

The island is 4 miles wide, 12 miles long, and is the eastern gateway to the Olympic Peninsula.

Located in Kitsap County the sales/use taxes are 8.1%.

$50-$125 **BOMBAY HOUSE BED & BREAKFAST,** 8490 Beck Rd. NE, Bainbridge Island, WA 98110, phone 360-842-3926 or 1-800-598-3926. A hilltop location with views of the ferries and ships gliding through Rich Passage. This three story Victorian mansion was built by a master shipbuilder in 1907. Five guest rooms are available, 3 with private facilities, 2 with shared. One guest room on the main floor features a tin soaking tub in the center of the room. The Captain's suite, 2nd floor, covers the full front of the house. It has a wood stove, queen bed, futon couch, refrigerator, and water views. Expanded continental breakfast provided. Children over 6 welcome, no pets, no smoking in the house. One block from public transportation. Close to the beach, a country theater, and fine dining. **Rates:** single $50-$80; double $55-$85; suite $125; local phone calls free. Visa, MasterCard, Discover, & Amex. **Directions:** from the ferry, left on Winslow Way, right on Madison, left on Wyatt, right at "Y" in road, uphill 1 1/4 mile to elementary school, veer right down West Blakely, one block to house.

Bombay House Bed & Breakfast

$50-$80   **CEDAR MEADOWS BED & BREAKFAST,** 10411 Old Creosote Hill Rd., Bainbridge Island, WA 98110, **phone 360-842-5291.** Four nonsmoking rooms are available in this large cedar home. TV and phone in the King room. Four rooms share two bathrooms, private facility available on request. Cable TV & VCR in lounge, bikes, badminton, and croquet. Full breakfast provided, time flexible. Shuttle provided to and from ferry. Children welcome, no pets. Short walk to the water, 6 acres of wooded and open areas to watch the deer, raccoons and birds. Contact Karen Yearsley for brochure. **Rates:** single $50-$70; double $60-$80; extra person $10; local phone calls free. No credit cards. **Directions:** from the ferry turn left at 1st traffic light, right on Madison, go to next 4 way stop, turn left on Wyatt Way (road goes down a steep hill and curves left), get in left lane, follow sign to Eagledale. Go 2 miles, turn right on Taylor, take 1st left onto Old Creosote Hill Road. Cedar Meadows is the 2nd drive on the right at the top of the hill.

$69-$129 **ISLAND COUNTRY INN**, **920 Hildebrand Lane N.E., Bainbridge Island, WA 98110, phone 360-842-6861, reservations 1-800-842-8429, fax 360-842-9808.** A total of 46 rooms, 39 nonsmoking, and two handicapped accessible. In-room amenities include cable TV, phones, and private outside entrances. There are 6 equipped kitchen units and 14 deluxe rooms or suites. The deluxe rooms and suites are equipped with robes and coffee/tea making facilities. Two large suites also have fireplaces. A continental breakfast is provided. The nearest restaurant is half a block away, two blocks to public transportation. Children welcome, 14 years and younger free with parents, no pets. **Rates:** double occupancy $69-$129; extra person $5; local phone calls free. All major credit cards. **Directions:** from the ferry continue through the traffic light to the second light, turn left on High School Rd., then make an immediate left on Hildebrand Lane.

$75 **ROSE COTTAGE BED & BREAKFAST**, **11744 Olympic Terrace N.E., Bainbridge Island, WA 98110, phone 360-842-6248 or 1-800-842-6255.** There is one suite and one cottage available, both with private facilities. The cottage has a sitting room, dining nook, and Euro kitchen (coffee maker, fridge, and microwave), the refrigerator is stocked for a buffet continental breakfast. The suite has the same amenities as the cottage, plus a private hot tub room. Covered parking in the carport. Children welcome, no pets, and no smoking. **Rates:** double occupancy $75. MasterCard & Visa. **Directions:** from the ferry follow Hwy 305 four miles to Koura, turn left (west), go past golf course, turn right on Olympic Terrace.

The Rose Cottage Bed & Breakfast

$80 **The WEST BLAKELY INN,** 8494 Odd Fellows Road, Bainbridge Island, WA 98110, phone 360-842-1427 or 1-800-835-1427. This bed and breakfast has three spacious guest rooms, all with private facilities, queen beds, and phones. Once the Odd Fellows Hall (circa 1912), the Inn has been completely refurbished to retain its original style. Two rooms have cozy wood stoves and one room has 1,000 square feet! Bath house with jacuzzi; two blocks to the beach or State Park; full gourmet breakfast. Will shuttle to and from ferry by arrangement. Children 3 and older welcome, pets by arrangement, smoking permitted outside. **Rates:** double occupancy $80; extra person $20; local phone calls free. No credit cards. **Directions:** from the ferry turn left at 1st traffic light, right on Madison, go to next 4 way stop, turn left on Winslow Way to stop sign, turn right at Madison, left on Wyatt, proceed south on Blakely, go past grammar school, stay right to stop sign, at corner of W. Blakely and Oddfellows turn right.

BAY CENTER (pop. 300) is just a short distance in southwest Washington from the Pacific Ocean

$35-$50 **BLUE HERON RESTAURANT & MOTEL,** P. O. Box 377, Bay Center, WA 98527, phone 360-875-5130. Two large deluxe rooms with private facilities, TV, and phones. One furnished kitchen unit sleeps 8. Breakfast provided. The Blue Heron is one of the renowned eateries in the area with fresh seafood processed in its own Fish House. After filling one's self with fine food in this quaint community, stay in the motel across the street. Children welcome, pets by arrangement. **Rates:** $35-$40; kitchen unit $50; extra person $5; sales taxes 7.8%. MasterCard & Visa. **Directions:** from I-5 in Olympia take the Montesano Exit, follow Hwy 101 for 45 miles, turn at exit to Bay Center (between South Bend and Naselle) 1.5 miles off Hwy 101.

BEAVER is in the northwest corner of the state on Hwy 101, approximately 8 miles north of Forks.

$32-$75 **BEAR CREEK MOTEL**, P. O. Box 213, Beaver, WA 98305, phone 360-327-3660. 10 motel style units on the shores of the Sol Duc River, no nonsmoking units. One unit has a fully equipped kitchen. No coffee/tea making facilities in the rooms, but the restaurant is open from 5:00 a.m. to 9:00 p.m. daily. Mini grocery store, gift shop, and RV parking. Access to the river is at the state park just south of the motel. Children welcome, free with parents, pets allowed. **Summer Rates:** *5/15 to 9/15* - single (1 bed) $42; double (2 beds) $48; kitchen unit $75; pets $10; taxes 7.8%. **Winter Rates:** $32-$38, & $65. MasterCard & Visa. **Directions:** on Hwy 101, 14 miles northeast of Forks, 43 miles southwest of Port Angeles.

$65-$100 **EAGLE POINT INN BED & BREAKFAST**, P. O. Box 213, Beaver, WA 98305, phone 360-327-3236. This newly constructed log house has 3 nonsmoking rooms, all with private facilities. The Inn was built as a bed and breakfast. The innkeeper, Chris Christensen, has a flare for decorating with antiques. Phones available, large fireplace in the sitting room, dining room, one kitchen, and a hot tub for guests to use. Located on the Sol Duck River, there is fishing, hiking, eagle viewing, a firepit, and picnic shelter. Full breakfast is provided. This is a romantic getaway, therefore, no children or pets. **Summer Rates:** double $75-$100; taxes 7.8%. **Winter Rates:** $65-$75. MasterCard & Visa. **Directions:** on Hwy 101, just north of Forks, at milepost 202 turn onto Storman Norman Rd., go to the Y and take the right fork.

BELFAIR is approximately 40 miles north of Olympia on the southeastern hook of the Hood Canal.

$42-$65 **BELFAIR MOTEL**, NE 23322 Hwy 3, P. O. Box 1135, Belfair, WA 98528, phone 360-275-4485, fax 360-275-5443. This two story motel offers 28 rooms, 16 nonsmoking. Phones, queen beds, remote control basic cable TV, and six equipped kitchen units. No coffee/tea making facilities in the rooms, but available in the lobby. Restaurant within walking distance. Children two and under free, no pets. **Summer Rates:** *5/15 to 9/30* - single room $42-$46; double $51; kitchen units $59-$65; extra person $5; taxes 7.8%. MasterCard, Visa, Discover, & Amex. **Directions:** 1/2 mile south of town on Hwy 3; 28 miles from Shelton and 18 miles from Bremerton.

$65 **COUNTRY GARDEN INN BED & BREAKFAST**, NE 2790 Old Belfair Hwy., Belfair, WA 98528, phone 360-275-3683. Enjoy the decor of these three modern guest rooms, all with private facilities, guest robes, wood burning fireplaces, ceiling fans, and skylights. A truly relaxed atmosphere situated on the Union River. Hot tub, high tea first Saturday of each month, and 5 course dinners available in the winter months. The rooms are above the gift shop, separate from the main house, with a deck overlooking the herb gardens. Smoking is permitted on the outside decks. Muffins and coffee will be placed at your door at 7:30 a.m. and a full country breakfast is served at 9:30 a.m. Adults only, no pets. **Rates:** double occupancy $65; taxes 7.8%. Most major credit cards. **Directions:** about 3 miles north of Belfair.

BELLEVUE *(pop. 87,900) is east of Seattle between Lake Washington and Lake Sammamish.*

Once known only as a suburb of Seattle, Bellevue is now the fourth largest city in Washington. Busy and affluent, the streets appear to carry more luxury cars than anywhere else in the state. Bell Square is renown for shopping. Many high-tech companies, banks, and corporate offices occupy the modern skyscrapers and mirrored buildings.

Sales/use and lodging taxes for 60 or more units are 14%, less than 60 units 8.2%.

$60-$100 **BELLEVUE BED & BREAKFAST**, 830 100th Ave. SE, Bellevue, WA 98004, phone 206-453-1048. Private suite or two single rooms. The suite has two bedrooms, each with private bath. Large front room with cable TV and views of the city. Full breakfast with gourmet coffee, usually from 8 to 9 a.m., but can be flexible. Centrally located near Lake Washington. Children over 10 welcome, no pets, and no smoking. **Rates:** double occupancy $60; suite $100; 5th day free. MasterCard & Visa, personal checks or cash preferred. **Directions:** from I-90 exit at Bellevue Way, go 1 mile to SE 8th St., turn left and continue west to 100th Ave., turn left to 830 100th Ave., on the left.

$90-$100 **BELLEVUE INN Best Western**, 11211 Main St., Bellevue, WA 98004, phone 206-455-5240 or 1-800-421-8193. 180 units, 75% nonsmoking. In-room amenities include hairdryers, lighted make-up mirrors, coffee makers, TV, phone, and some units have refrigerators. Room service is available, outdoor pool, restaurant, and bar. Parking free. Children under 18 free with parents, no pets. **Rates:** single room $90; double room $100; local calls 60¢; extra person $5. Winter and commercial rates. Major credit cards. **Directions:** from Hwy 405 take Exit 12 west on SE 8th St., turn right on 112th and proceed to Main, on left side.

DAYS INN BELLEVUE, 3241 156th Ave. SE, Bellevue, WA 98007, phone 206-643-6644, fax 206-644-7279, reservations 1-800-329-7466.

$40-$45 **KANES MOTEL**, 14644 SE Eastgate Way, Bellevue, WA 98007, phone 206-746-8201 or 1-800-746-8201. 16 units, 9 nonsmoking rooms. In-room amenities include phones, TV, and 4 units have kitchenettes (dishes and cookware available on request). Morning coffee is available in the lobby; restaurants within walking distance; 2 blocks to public transportation. Children 10 and under free with parents, pets allowed. Close to shopping. One block from Bellevue Community College and Mormon Temple. **Rates:** single $40; double $45; kitchen units $45; pets $10; local phone calls free. Most credit cards accepted. **Directions:** from I-90 Exit 11A in Eastgate area; from the west Exit 11A, cross over the freeway (north), turn left on Eastgate, 1/2 block to motel.

RED LION INN, 818 112th Ave. NE, Bellevue, WA 98004, phone 206-455-1515, reservations 1-800-733-5466.

SILVER CLOUD INN, 10621 NE 12th St., Bellevue, WA 98004, phone 1-800-551-7207.

BELLINGHAM (pop. 52,179) is located 30 miles south of the Canadian border on I-5.

This seaport town is situated on several hills overlooking Bellingham Bay and the San Juan Islands. Western Washington University (9,000 students) dominates Sehome Hill overlooking the city.

Located in Whatcom County the sales/use taxes are 7.8%.

$60-$85   **A SECRET GARDEN BED & BREAKFAST**, 1807 Lakeway Dr., Bellingham, WA 98226, phone 360-671-5327 or 1-800-671-5327. Two nonsmoking rooms with private facilities are available in this charming elegant turn-of-the-century home with magnificent views overlooking Bellingham Bay. The Blue Room has a featherbed, the Rose Room suite has 3 rooms and sleeps five. TV is available and the parlor has a grand piano. A generous breakfast is provided. Children over 5 welcome, no pets. **Rates:** double occupancy - Blue Room $60; Rose Room $85; extra person $15. MasterCard & Visa. **Directions:** from I-5 take Exit 253 east on Lakeway Dr., cross street is Toledo.

$29-$69   **ALOHA MOTEL**, 315 N. Samish Way, Bellingham, WA 98225, phone 360-733-4900. Aloha means welcome. There are 29 rooms, 6 nonsmoking, and 2 kitchen units with basic cookware. Phones and TV with HBO. No coffee/tea making facilities in the rooms, but rolls and coffee are available in the lobby. Close to restaurants, mall, and the college. Children welcome, 12 and under free, pets allowed with a $5 refundable deposit. **Summer Rates:** single room (1 bed) $32-$38; double room $40; kitchen unit $40; apartment suite (3 beds, 3 people) $69; extra person $5; local phone calls free. **Winter Rates:** $3 less. MasterCard & Visa. **Directions:** from I-5 Exit 252 to Samish Way, go 1/2 mile to motel.

$40-$70   **BAY CITY MOTOR INN**, 116 N. Samish Way, Bellingham, WA 98225, phone 360-676-0332, reservations 1-800-538-8204. There are 51 rooms, 35 nonsmoking, and 1 kitchen unit with basic cookware. Phones, cable TV, AC, workout room, pool table, and 3 jacuzzi suites. No coffee/tea making facilities in the rooms, but donuts/muffins and coffee are available in the lobby. Children welcome, 12 and under free, no pets. **Rates:** single room $40-$45; double room $43-$50; kitchen unit $50; suites $70; extra person $5; local phone calls free. MasterCard & Visa. **Directions:** from I-5 Exit 252 and follow University signs to Samish Way.

$90-$150 **BIG TREES BED & BREAKFAST**, 4840 Fremont St., Bellingham, WA 98225, phone 360-647-2850. This charming period home, built in 1907 in the post-Victorian style, is nestled among old growth cedars and firs overlooking Lake Whatcom. Three rooms, two with private facilities. The rooms include TV, phones, beautiful hand stitched quilts, comfortable chairs, and featherbeds. Breakfasts are hearty and homemade. Children over 12 are welcome, no pets. **Rates:** double occupancy, Queen room $90; King room $110; family room $150; extra person $10; local phone calls free. MasterCard, Visa, or check. **Directions:** from I-5 take the Lakeway Exit east toward Lake Whatcom. From the Fred Meyer store, continue for 3 miles, Lakeway becomes Cable St., then Lake Whatcom Blvd. Take a right on Geneva, continue to Fremont, turn left and continue for 2 blocks.

$45-$95 **The CASTLE BED & BREAKFAST**, 1103 15th St., Bellingham, WA 98225, phone 360-676-0974. Four nonsmoking rooms available, all with private facilities. Phones in two rooms, TV in the lounge, plus a reading room. A full "healthy" breakfast is provided. Public transportation in front of the house. Within walking distance of

The Castle Bed & Breakfast

restaurants, entertainment, and shops. Excellent views of Bellingham Bay and the San Juan Islands can be seen from any guest room. The Castle offers old world grandeur, with museum quality furnishings and antique shop. Honeymoon suite with private bath. Theme rooms: Victorian, Oriental, and Middle East. **Rates:** single $45; doubles $85-$95; extra person $15; local phone calls free. Major credit cards accepted. **Directions:** high on a hill in the Fairhaven District, Exit 250 off of I-5, on 15th and Knox Ave.

$50-$60 **CIRCLE F BED & BREAKFAST**, 2399 Mt. Baker Hwy., Bellingham, WA 98226, phone 360-733-2509, fax 360-734-3816. This is an 1892 country home on a 300 acre working farm. There are 4 nonsmoking guest rooms, 1 with private facilities and 3 with shared. Three rooms on the second floor have double, queen, or twin beds, and shared facilities. The master bedroom has a private bath, queen bed, and crib. Fly fishermen have access to semi-private Squalicum Lake. Children are sure to enjoy the farm animals: cows, horses, pigs, chickens, dogs, and cats. No domestic pets, but horse lodging is available. A hearty farm breakfast is provided in the cozy turn-of-the-century farmhouse kitchen. **Rates:** double occupancy $50-$60; extra person $5; horse lodging $15. No credit cards. **Directions:** from I-5 take Exit 255 and proceed for 5 1/2 miles, Circle F Machine Shop and driveway on the right.

$45-$80 **COACHMAN INN**, 120 Samish Way, Bellingham, WA 98225, phone 360-671-9000 or 1-800-962-6641 (WA), or 1-800-543-5478 (Canada), fax 360-738-1984. 61 deluxe guest rooms, 40 are nonsmoking rooms, and one unit has a kitchenette. TV, phones, no coffee/tea making facilities in the rooms, but a continental breakfast is provided. There is a restaurant within walking distance. This home away from home is air-conditioned, has a warm, comfortable decor, indoor jacuzzi, sauna, and a heated outdoor pool. Children welcome, no pets. **Rates:** single room $45-$50; double room $55; suite $80; local phone calls free. Major credit cards accepted. **Directions:** coming from the north exit I-5 at Exit 253, take a left on Ellis St., proceed south to 120 Samish Way; from the south Exit 252, go west to Samish Way & turn right, proceed to 120 Samish Way.

COMFORT INN, 4282 Meridian St., Bellingham, WA 98226, phone 360-738-1100 or 1-800-221-2222.

DAYS INN, 125 E. Kellogg Rd., Bellingham, WA 98226, phone 360-671-6200 or 1-800-831-0187, fax 360-671-9491.

$50-$70 **DECANN HOUSE BED & BREAKFAST**, 2610 Eldridge Ave., Bellingham, WA 98225, phone 360-734-9172. Two nonsmoking rooms with private facilities. TV in lounge, pool table, games and puzzles available. Full breakfast provided. Public transportation in front of the house and shuttle provided to the airport, ferry, or bus. Children over 12 welcome, no pets. This large white Victorian house has a view of the islands, bay, and marina. Located one mile from downtown and the University. **Rates:** $50-$70; extra person $15; local phone calls free. No credit cards; checks and cash only. **Directions:** from I-5 take Lakeway Exit 235, go right on Lakeway, stay on main arterial, which will change to Holly as it goes through downtown and then becomes Eldridge Ave., DeCann House is on the right 2.3 miles from the freeway.

DeCann House Bed & Breakfast

$38-$45 **EVERGREEN MOTEL**, 1015 Samish Way, Bellingham, WA 98225, phone 360-734-7671, reservations 1-800-821-0016. This motel is off the main thoroughfare in a quiet location. 11 rooms, 2 nonsmoking. TV, phones, coffee/tea making facilities, and 9 kitchen units with basic cookware. Children welcome, under 12 free, no pets. Within walking distance of restaurant/bar. Public transportation next door. Close to Lake Padden. **Rates:** double room $45; suite $38-$42; extra person $5; phone calls 25¢. Visa, MasterCard, & Amex. **Directions:** from I-5 take Exit 252 - traveling north turn right off exit road, going south turn left off exit road.

HAMPTON INN, 3985 Bennett, Bellingham, WA 98225, phone 360-676-7700, reservations 1-800-426-7866.

HERITAGE INN Best Western, 151 E. McLeod Rd., Bellingham, WA 98226, phone 360-647-1912, reservations 1-800-528-1234.

$34-$58 **KEY MOTEL**, 212 N. Samish Way, Bellingham, WA 98225, phone 360-733-4060. A total of 40 rooms, 21 nonsmoking. All have TV and phones, no coffee/tea making facilities. Children 12 and under free, no pets. Sauna, hot tub, and outdoor pool. Shuttle provided to airport or ferry. Within walking distance of restaurant/bar. Public transportation across the street. Five minutes to downtown. Many parks, beaches, and movie theaters nearby. Golf course 5 minutes away and 1 hour to Mt. Baker ski area. **Rates:** single room $34-$56; double room or family room $42-$58; extra person $4; local phone calls free. Major credit cards accepted. **Directions:** from I-5 take Exit 252 - going north turn right, from south turn left onto Samish Way, proceed for 1 mile, across from McDonalds.

$36-$46 **LIONS INN**, 2419 Elm St., Bellingham, WA 98225, phone 360-733-2330. This motel is located in a quiet residential area and has a total of 15 rooms, 7 nonsmoking. All have TV, phones, coffee/tea making facilities, and mini refrigerators. Four units have kitchens with basic cookware. Children age 12 and under free, pets in designated rooms by arrangement. **Rates:** single room $36-$38; double room $42; kitchen units $46; extra person $3; local phone calls free. Visa & MasterCard. **Directions:** from I-5 take Exit 257 - from the south make a left and go under the freeway, follow Northwest Ave. for 1 1/2 miles, Northwest becomes Elm; from the north, Exit 257 right on to Northwest Ave.

$59-$74 **NORTH GARDEN INN BED & BREAKFAST**, 1014 N. Garden, Bellingham, WA 98225, phone 360-671-7828 or 1-800-922-6414 (US), 1-800-367-1676 (Canada). A Queen Anne Victorian house on the National Historic Register with 10 nonsmoking guest rooms available, 8 with private facilities, 2 with shared. Full breakfast served 7-9 a.m. weekdays, 8-10 a.m. on weekends. Close to WWU, 7 rooms have views of Bellingham Bay. TV in lounge. A Steinway grand piano adorns the entry. Children over 10 welcome, no pets. **Rates:** single room $59-$69; double room $64-$74; extra person $15; local phone calls free. Major credit cards accepted. **Directions:** from I-5 take Exit 253, right at stop sign, right at stoplight to Lakeway, Lakeway becomes Holly, 3 blocks on Holly, left on Garden.

$31-$95 **PARK MOTEL**, 101 N. Samish Way, Bellingham, WA 98225, phone 360-733-8280 or 1-800-732-1225. A total of 58 rooms, 46 are nonsmoking, one townhouse suite with fully equipped kitchen. TV and phones. No coffee/tea making facilities in the rooms, but a continental breakfast is provided from 6-11 a.m. and restaurants are within walking distance. Children under 12 free, no pets. Five minutes from downtown Bellingham, 45 minutes from Mt. Baker. **Summer Rates:** *6/01 to 8/31* - single room $40-$50; double room $45-$55; suite $85-$90; townhouse apt. $90-$95; extra person $5; local phone calls free. **Winter Rates:** $31-$85. Major credit cards accepted. **Directions:** from I-5 take Exit 252 to Samish Way.

QUALITY INN, 100 E. Kellogg Rd., Bellingham, WA 98226, phone 360-647-8000, or 1-800-900-4661, fax 360-647-8094.

RAMADA INN, 215 Samish Way, Bellingham, WA 98225, phone 360-6734-8830, or 1-800-2RAMADA.

$32-$50   **SHANGRI-LA DOWNTOWN MOTEL,** 611 E. Holly St., Bellingham, WA 98225, phone 360-733-7050. This two story motel has a total of 20 rooms, 4 nonsmoking. In-room amenities include TV and phones. Free morning coffee is available in the lobby. Two units have kitchens with basic cookware. Children welcome, small pets allowed. Near WWU, downtown shopping, and Alaska Ferry Terminal. **Rates:** single room (1 bed) $32-$38; double room (2 beds) $42; suite $50; family room $50; extra person $3; pets $5; local phone calls free. Lower winter rates. Major credit cards accepted. **Directions:** from I-5 take Exit 253, turn right, located 1/4 mile from exit.

$40   **SPRINGCREST FARMS BED & BREAKFAST,** 6058 Everson-Goshen Rd., Bellingham, WA 98226, phone 360-966-7272. Accommodations consist of two comfortable bedrooms with a private entrance and shared bath. One room has a double bed and the other has twin beds. This is an operating dairy farm with 70 cows and calves. Children welcome, two and under free, crib available. Nature trails and 1/4 mile from a fishing lake. Full farm style breakfast. Smoking permitted outdoors. **Rates:** $40; children age 3 and up $1 per year; local phone calls free. No credit cards; checks and cash only. **Directions:** from I-5 take Mt. Baker Hwy, Exit 255, proceed 4 miles, turn left on Everson Goshen Rd. 4 miles (10 miles from Bellingham, 7 miles east of Lynden).

TRAVELERS INN, 3750 Meridian St., Bellingham, WA 98225, phone 360-671-4600 or 1-800-633-8300.

VAL·U INN MOTEL, 805 Lakeway Dr., Bellingham, WA 98226, phone 360-671-9600, reservations 1-800-443-7777 (US), 1-800-451-7767 (Canada), fax 360-671-8323.

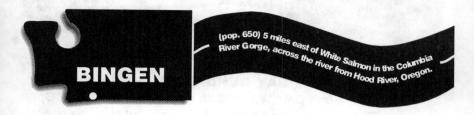

BINGEN (pop. 650) 5 miles east of White Salmon in the Columbia River Gorge, across the river from Hood River, Oregon.

(BIN-jin) is a popular place for boardsailors. This area offers year-round skiing at Mt. Hood, whitewater rafting, windsurfing, ancient petroglyphs, Stonehenge replica, Maryhill Art Museum, Bonneville Dam, the Gorge Scenic Highway, and many waterfalls.

Located in Klickitat County the sales/use taxes are 7%, the lowest in the state.

$11-$39 **The BINGEN SCHOOL INN BED & BREAKFAST**, Humboldt & Cedar Streets, Bingen, WA 98605, phone 509-493-3363. The Inn is a hostel type lodging with 6 private rooms and three dorm style rooms. TV in lounge, full indoor gym with weight room, basketball, volleyball, and rock climbing wall. There are limited cooking facilities. A restaurant on the grounds offers dinners in July and August. Shuttle is provided to the bus station, sailing sites, and airport by appointment. Children welcome, no pets. On-site windsurfing and mountain bike rentals, plus instructions. **Summer Rates:** *6/01 to 9/30* - private rooms, 2 people $39; dorm beds $11. **Winter Rates:** private rooms $29. Visa & MasterCard. **Directions:** in Bingen, follow Hwy 14 to Cedar Street, then go uphill (north) for 1 block.

$32-$43 **CITY CENTER MOTEL**, 210 West Stuben, Bingen, WA 98605, phone 509-493-2445. 9 motel rooms, one nonsmoking. All rooms have TV, and there are 4 kitchen units with basic cookware. No phones or coffee/tea making facilities in the rooms, but a bakery and espresso place are within walking distance. Adjacent to laundromat. This is basically a working man's motel that caters to fishermen and hunters. No parties. Children age 18 and under free with parents, no pets. **Rates:** single rooms $32; double $43; taxes included. Visa & MasterCard. **Directions:** in the center of town on Bingen's main street.

BIRCH BAY is located just 5 miles south of Blaine and the Canadian border. Enjoy clamming, crabbing, swimming, golfing, and exploring the tidal flats.

$60-$70 **BIRCH BAY BUNGALOWS**, 8226 Birch Bay Dr., Birch Bay, WA 98230, phone 360-371-2851. Open year-round. Three individual cottages on the beach that sleep six people, and have fully equipped kitchens. Hair salon on-site. Within walking distance to restaurants and water slides. Clam digging and shallow, safe swimming on private sandy beach. Children welcome, exotic caged birds allowed, no other pets. **Summer Rates:** $70 daily; $400 weekly; taxes included. **Winter Rates:** $60 per night. No credit cards. **Directions:** I-5 Exit 270, go west to Birch Bay, left at Harborview, right on Birch Bay Dr., proceed about 1 mile, on right side.

$50-$135 **DRIFTWOOD INN RESORT MOTEL & GIFT SHOPPE**, 7394 Birch Bay Dr., Birch Bay, WA 98230, phone 360-371-2620. Open year-round. 13 units - cottages, motel units, apartments, and condos. All have TV, kitchenettes with fridge, coffee pot, and microwave. Some units have fireplaces. Beach access, park, heated pool, and play area. Children welcome, small dogs allowed in the off-season for $7 a night. **Summer Rates:** *5/15 to 9/10* - single room $50; double room $65-$75; family room, 4 people $75; suite, sleeps up to 8 $125-$135; extra person $5; taxes 7.5%. **Winter Rates:** flexible. MasterCard, Visa, & Amex. **Directions:** 8 miles west of I-5, take Exit 266 west for 8 miles to Jackson, then right for 2 miles to Birch Bay Dr., left 3 blocks.

$75 **LANDLUBBER COTTAGES**, 8036 Birch Bay Dr., Birch Bay, WA 98230, phone 360-371-7200. Open year-round. Two 1 and 2 bedroom housekeeping cabins rent by the night or by the week. Three night minimum stay in summer. Both have equipped kitchens, linen, and TV. The two bedroom cabin sleeps six. Gift shop and espresso bar on the premises, close to market. Beach right across the street. **Summer Rates:** *7/01 to 9/01* - $75 per night; $495 per week. **Winter Rates:** flexible. Major credit cards. **Directions:** from I-5 take Exit 270, proceed west on the Birch Bay/Lynden Rd. to Harborview Rd., left on Harborview Rd. to Birch Bay, turn left at waterslides and go one block.

$50-$125 **TIDE FLATS,** 8124 Birch Bay Dr., Birch Bay, WA 98230, phone 360-371-7800. Six 1 and 2 bedroom suites with fully equipped kitchens, baths, and dining rooms. The more expensive units have water views. Smoking discouraged. Restaurant on the grounds. Children 5 and under free, no pets. **Summer Rates:** double occupancy $95-$125; extra person $12; taxes 7.5%. **Winter Rates:** $50-$75. MasterCard, Visa, & Amex. **Directions:** take Exit 270 off I-5 to the end of Birch Bay/Lynden Rd., turn left to water, turn right and proceed 2 and a half blocks.

BLAINE (pop. 2, 640) is located in the northwest corner of the state and is the port of entry for Canada when traveling on I-5.

Blaine and its sister city, Birch Bay, are ideally situated for virtually every kind of outdoor activity, both winter and summer. They are just an hour from Mt. Baker for downhill skiing, cross country skiing, snowshoeing, sledding, and climbing. In addition, the saltwater bay offers nonstop summer beach fun and peaceful winter solitude.

Located in Whatcom County the sales/use taxes are 7.8%.

$33-$60 **ANCHOR INN MOTEL,** 250 Cedar St., Blaine, WA 98231, phone 360-332-5539. The 13 rooms are all on one level, 10 nonsmoking. Phones and cable TV. No coffee/tea making facilities in the rooms, but there are 5 kitchen units with cookware available. All rooms have a bay view. Within walking distance of a restaurant. Children welcome, no pets. **Rates:** single (one bed) $33-$60; double (2 beds) $60; kitchen units $40-$55; extra person $5. MasterCard, Visa, Discover, & Amex. **Directions:** from the south, Exit 274, on Peace Portal Dr., 2 miles from exit; from the north cross the border and head for downtown on Peace Portal Dr., don't take the freeway, stay on the main road for 8 blocks.

$34-$42 **BAY SIDE MOTEL,** 340 Alder, P. O. Box 1529, Blaine, WA 98230, phone 360-332-5288. 24 rooms, 11 nonsmoking. Phones, TV, and outdoor pool. No coffee/tea making facilities in the rooms, but available in the lobby. One kitchen unit with basic cookware, fridge, and microwave. Within walking distance of a restaurant. Children 12 and under free, no pets. **Summer Rates:** single (one bed) $36;

double (2 beds) $42; kitchen unit $42; extra person $3. **Winter Rates:** $34-$38. MasterCard & Visa. **Directions:** from the south, Exit 274, 2 miles from exit; from the north cross the border and head for downtown, don't take the freeway, stay on the main road and proceed to the motel.

$10-$19 **BIRCH BAY AYH-HOSTEL**, 4639 Alderson Rd. #630, Blaine, WA 98230, phone 360-371-2180. *Closed October to March.* 14 nonsmoking rooms, 2 with private facilities, 12 with shared. Children welcome, no pets. This large hostel can accommodate individuals, families, and groups. All the sleeping rooms are small and homelike. The fully equipped kitchen and large common area provide an easy place for travelers of all ages and nationalities to meet, relax, and converse. Volleyball, badminton court, and sauna. Hostelers enjoy the tranquility they find here, as well as the proximity to the busy city of Vancouver, Canada. Guests receive a special discount on whale watching tours from Birch Bay. **Rates:** per night, members $10; nonmembers $13; couples room surcharge $6; under 18, with parent $5; local phone calls 25¢; taxes included. Visa & MasterCard. **Directions:** from the south, on I-5 take Exit 266, proceed on Grandview west 6 miles to Blaine Rd., go north 2 miles to Alderson Rd., go 1/2 mile to Bay Horizon County Park. From the north, Exit 270 from I-5, go 3 1/2 miles west on Birch Bay/Linden Rd., south 1 mile on Blaine Rd. to Alderson Rd., 1/2 mile to Bay Horizon County Park.

$33-$45 **MOTEL INTERNATIONAL**, 758 Peace Portal Dr., P. O. Box 446, Blaine, WA 98230, phone 360-332-8222. Typical two story motel with 22 rooms, 5 nonsmoking. Phones, TV, coffee making facilities in the rooms. Restaurant and bar on the premises, opens at 7 a.m. Children welcome, no pets. **Rates:** single (one bed) $33-$37; double (2 beds) $45; extra person $5; no charge for local phone calls; taxes included. MasterCard, Visa, & Amex. **Directions:** 1 1/2 miles from the border in the center of town.

$29-$37 **WEST VIEW MOTEL**, 1300 Peace Portal Dr., Blaine, WA 98230, phone 360-332-5501. 13 rooms, 2 nonsmoking and 6 equipped kitchen units. All rooms have TV, fridge, and microwave. Restaurant within walking distance. Picnic area with shade umbrellas, and there is a large field out back. Children welcome, no pets. **Rates:** single (one bed) $29-$33; double (2 beds) $37; extra person $4. MasterCard & Visa. **Directions:** from the south take Exit 274 off I-5, drive straight to the first motel; from the north take first Blaine Exit, go through town and around the bend.

BONNEY LAKE (pop. 7,860) see Puyallup for lodging.

BOTHELL (pop. 12,990) see North Seattle for lodging.

BOW is just north of Mount Vernon, see Mount Vernon for lodging.

BREMERTON (pop. 37,730) is located on the Kitsap Peninsula on the west coast of Puget Sound.

Located 11 miles from downtown Seattle by ferry, Bremerton is home to the Puget Sound Naval Shipyard.

Located in Kitsap (KIT-sap) County the sales/use taxes are 8.1%.

$57-$120 **BAYVIEW INN Best Western**, 5640 Kitsap Way, Bremerton, WA 98312, phone 360-373-9900 or 1-800-422-5017 (WA), nationally 1-800-528-1234. A total of 143 rooms, 40% nonsmoking. Phones, microwaves, refrigerators, TV with remote control. Coffee/tea making facilities in the rooms and available in the lobby. Continental breakfast provided Monday-Friday. Indoor pool, jacuzzi, restaurant, and bar. Health club next door free to guests. Children under 18 free with parents, no pets. Most rooms have balconies overlooking the bay. **Rates:** single room $57-$67; double room $62-$72; suite $79-$120; local calls free. Major credit cards accepted. **Directions:** from the ferry go right on Washington to 11th, follow 11th to Kitsap Way, then turn right and proceed for about 1 mile.

$39-$50 **DUNES MOTEL**, 3400 11th St., Bremerton, WA 98312, phone 360-377-0093 or 1-800-828-8238. A total of 64 rooms, with 34 nonsmoking rooms. Air-conditioned, phones, TV, most rooms have refrigerators. Coffee/tea making facilities in the rooms, 5 units have equipped kitchenettes. Free continental breakfast is provided seven days a week. Swim spa indoors, guest laundry, and video rentals. Children welcome, pets allowed. **Rates:** single room (1 bed) $39; double room $50; suite $45; extra person $5; pets (cat) $15 (dog) $20 per stay; local phone calls free. MasterCard, Visa, & Discover. **Directions:** from Hwy 3 take Kitsap Way Exit, turn right, proceed one mile, on right side.

$50-$77 **FLAGSHIP INN**, 4320 Kitsap Way, Bremerton, WA 98312, phone 360-479-6566 or 1-800-447-9396, fax 360-479-6745. 29 luxury rooms with private, full width balconies. Located on Oyster Bay. The Flagship Inn has 14 nonsmoking rooms. In-room amenities include 2 phones, remote control, cable TV with Showtime, VCR, refrigerator, and microwave. Morning coffee is available with a complimentary continental breakfast until 11:00 a.m., followed by home baked cookies, fruit, tea, and hot chocolate available 24 hours a day. Other amenities include video library rentals, seasonal outdoor pool, and free parking. Children 6 and under free, small dogs allowed. **Rates:** single room (1 bed) $50-$60; double room (2 beds) $65-$77; pets $6; local phone calls 35¢. Major credit cards accepted. **Directions:** from the ferry go right on Washington to 11th, follow 11th to Kitsap Way, turn right and proceed for about 3/4 mile.

$49-$60 **MIDWAY INN**, 2909 Wheaton Way, Bremerton, WA 98310, phone 360-479-2909, reservations 1-800-231-0575, fax 360-479-1576. A total of 60 rooms, 31 nonsmoking. Phones, remote control TVs, refrigerators, and air conditioning. In-room coffee and tea, 12 kitchenette units. A free continental breakfast is provided 7 days a week. Guest laundry and video rentals. Near good restaurants and shopping. Children welcome, small pets allowed. **Rates:** single room (1 queen bed) $49; double room (2 beds) $54; executive suite $60; extra person $7; pet fee $10 per stay; local phone calls free. Major credit cards accepted. **Directions:** from ferry turn right at Washington and follow to 11th, turn left on 11th to Warren, turn right and proceed 1/2 mile.

QUALITY INN AT OYSTER BAY, 4303 Kitsap Way, Bremerton, WA 98312, phone 360-405-1111, reservations 1-800-776-2291.

BREWSTER (pop. 1,635) is between Chelan and Omak on Hwy 97.

Agriculture plays a large part in the economy of the town which ships Washington fruit to locations all over the world. Brewster has a large river shore park featuring picnic facilities, tennis courts, a swimming pool, and a waterfront pathway.

Located in Okanogan County the sales/use taxes are 7.6%.

$58-$65 **APPLE AVENUE MOTEL**, P. O. Box 632, Brewster, WA 98812, phone 509-689-3000, fax 509-689-0400. This new 2 level motel has 17 units, 10 nonsmoking. The rooms have phones, TV, air conditioning, and refrigerators are available. Guests may use the Brewster Motel swimming pool. There are no coffee/tea making facilities in the room, but a continental breakfast is provided from 6:30 to 10:00 a.m. Children welcome, pets by arrangement. **Rates:** double occupancy $58-$65; extra person charge $5. Amex, Visa, & MasterCard. **Directions:** north of town on Hwy 97.

$34-$40 **BREWSTER MOTEL**, 806 Bridge St., Brewster, WA 98812, phone 509-689-2625. A total of 10 rooms, with one nonsmoking room. In-room amenities include phones and TV. No coffee/tea making facilities in the rooms, but 5 units have kitchens with basic cookware. Seasonal, outdoor swimming pool. Children welcome, pets allowed. One block from Columbia Cove Park, basketball court, tennis court, swimming, and boating. **Rates:** single room $34; double room $40, extra person $4; local phone calls free; pets free. Visa & MasterCard. **Directions:** Hwy 173 by the bridge, one mile from Hwy 97.

BRIDGEPORT (pop. 1,510) see Pateros or Brewster for lodging.

BRINNON is located on Hwy 101 on the Hood Canal, 37 miles south of Port Townsend.

This small town sits on the shores of the Hood Canal, 12 miles south of Quilcene. Visit the Whitney Gardens from May to June when the rhododendrons are in full bloom. Located in Jefferson County the sales/use taxes are 7.9%.

$35-$68 **BAYSHORE MOTEL**, 31503 Hwy 101, Brinnon, WA 98320, phone 360-796-4220 or 1-800-488-4230. Total of 12 units, and one apartment with kitchen, 6 nonsmoking. The rooms are large with queen or king beds and TV. No coffee/tea making facilities, but available in the office. Within walking distance of restaurant/bar. Children welcome, no pets. Scenic area in the Doseywallops Valley at the foot of the Olympic Mountains. The bay offers clamming and other beach activities. **Summer Rates:** single (1 bed) $40-$43; double (2 queen beds) $48; apartment $68; extra person $5. **Winter Rates:** $35-$63. Amex, Visa, & MasterCard. **Directions:** centrally located on Hwy 101.

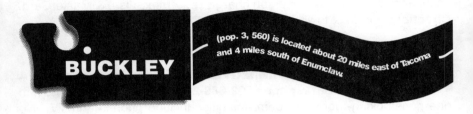

BUCKLEY (pop. 3, 560) is located about 20 miles east of Tacoma and 4 miles south of Enumclaw.

Buckley is an historical town with small town hospitality. Annual events include log show in June, arts and crafts fair in July, and antique rod and car show in August.
Located in King County the sales/use/lodging taxes are 11%.

$45-$90 **MOUNTAIN VIEW INN**, 29405 Hwy 410 East, Buckley, WA 98321, phone 360-829-1100, fax 360-829-9879, reservations 1-800-582-4111. Total of 41 rooms, 24 nonsmoking. All rooms have phones and TV with HBO. Jacuzzi suites available. No coffee/tea making facilities in the rooms, but a continental breakfast is provided in the lobby from 4:00 a.m. to 10:00 a.m. Outdoor pool, hot tub spa, and sauna. Restaurant within walking distance, close to shopping. Children 12 and under free, pets allowed. **Summer Rates:** 5/16 to 9/15 - single (1 bed) $50-$55; double $60; suites $75-$90; extra person $5; pets $10 first day, $5 each night after. **Winter Rates:** $5 less. Major credit cards. **Directions:** centrally located in downtown Buckley.

$30-$39 **WEST MAIN MOTOR INN**, 466 West Main, Buckley, WA 98321, phone 360-829-2400. Located in the heart of the Buckley Historical District. A total of 14 rooms, 7 nonsmoking available. In-room amenities include remote control TV with HBO. No coffee/tea making facilities in the rooms, but within walking distance of restaurants and grocery stores. Children 10 and under free, no pets. **Summer Rates:** single $33; double $39. **Winter Rates:** single $30; double $35. MasterCard & Visa. **Directions:** turn right off Hwy 410, go to the center of town, at 4th and Main.

BURLINGTON is just north of Mount Vernon and east of I-5. This small community is close to the North Cascade Highway and Mt. Baker ski area.

From I-5 take Exit 229 to the Pacific Edge Outlet Mall.
Located in Skagit County the sales/use taxes are 7.8%.

$50-$150 **COCUSA MOTEL**, 370 W. Rio Vista, Burlington, WA 98233, phone 360-757-6044, reservations 1-800-628-2257, fax 360-757-8618. Total of 61 units, 23 nonsmoking, and 2 handicap rooms. In-room amenities include phones, TV, and six units have equipped kitchenettes. Morning coffee and continental breakfast is available in the lobby from 6 to 10 a.m. Outdoor swimming pool. Restaurants within walking distance, close to tulip fields, 1 mile from Cascade Mall and Pacific Edge Outlet Center. Children welcome, no pets. **Rates:** single (1 bed) $50; double (2 beds) $55; honeymoon suite $150; family room $75; extra person $3; local phone calls free. Major credit cards. **Directions:** from I-5 take Exit 230, 1/2 mile east, visible from the freeway.

$35-$52 **STERLING MOTOR INN**, 866 S. Burlington, Burlington, WA 98233, phone 360-757-0071, fax 360-757-7906. Total of 35 units, 18 nonsmoking rooms. In-room amenities include phones and TV. No coffee/tea making facilities in the rooms, but seven units have kitchenettes. Chinese restaurant/bar open for lunch and dinner. Children welcome, 12 and under free, pets allowed. Close to shopping, ferry to San Juan Islands, North Cascade Hwy, Deception Pass, Chuckanut Dr., Mt. Baker Hwy, and other scenic areas. **Rates:** single $35-$46; double $45-$52; pets $6; extra person $5; local phone calls free. Major credit cards accepted. **Directions:** from I-5, take Exit 230, east 2 blocks to Burlington Blvd., 3 blocks south of Hwy 20.

CAMANO ISLAND is located east of Whidbey Island.

$75 **INN at BARNUM POINT,** 464 S. Barnum Rd., Camano Island, WA 98292, phone 360-387-2256 or 1-800-910-2256. Located on the beach, the Inn is a modern two story home and offers two spacious guest rooms. Each room has a queen bed, fireplace, down quilts, and its own bathroom. Both rooms are on the second floor and have a private entrance. A full breakfast includes home baked bread or rolls. Activities: bird watching, beach combing, observing sea lions, otters, or the deer in the orchard. Children welcome, no pets, and no smoking in the house. Restaurant 6 miles away. **Rates:** double occupancy $75; extra person $30; taxes 7.6%. MasterCard, Visa, Discover, & Amex. **Directions:** Exit 212 off I-5, follow Hwy 532 to E. Camano Dr., turn south, follow to Russell Rd., go east to Barnum Rd., follow to the end.

Inn at Barnum Point

$65-$75 **WILLCOX HOUSE BED & BREAKFAST,** 1462 E. Larkspur Lane, Camano Island, WA 98292, phone 360-629-4746. Victorian/country style home furnished with antiques. Four nonsmoking rooms, all with private facilities. Phone available on request. Full breakfast provided. Children 10 and older welcome, no pets. Quiet rural area with views of Mt. Baker and Skagit Bay. **Rates:** single $65; double $75; extra person $15; taxes 7.6%. Discover, Visa, & MasterCard. **Directions:** Exit 212 off I-5, follow Hwy 532 one mile west of Stanwood to Smith Rd., turn right and follow signs.

CAMAS see Vancouver for lodging.

CARLTON (pop. 50) is on Hwy 153, 18 miles south of Winthrop. Outdoor recreation includes hunting, fishing, river float trips, horseback riding, and hiking.

$42-$45 **COUNTRY TOWN MOTEL**, P. O. Box 297, Carlton, WA 98814, phone 509-997-3432. Located on the "Cascade Loop", this motel has 22 rooms all on one level. No designated nonsmoking rooms, but rooms are well ventilated. TV, coffee, and microwave in the lobby. Six units have equipped kitchens. Outdoor pool, hot tub, mini golf, horseshoes, and a recreation room with a pool table. Children welcome, small pets okay. R.V. parking with full hookups. **Summer Rates:** *6/01 to 10/31* - single room (1 bed) $42; double (2 beds) $45; kitchen units $45; extra person $3; pets $5; taxes 7.6%. **Winter Rates:** available. MasterCard & Visa. **Directions:** on Hwy 153, 18 miles south of Winthrop.

CARNATION see Snoqualmie for lodging.

CARSON is located 50 miles east of Vancouver in the Wind River District of the Columbia River Gorge.

Home of Carson Hot Mineral Springs Resort as well as the largest tree nursery on the west coast.

Located in Skamania (skuh-MAY-neeuh) County the sales/use taxes are 7%.

$35-$120 **CARSON HOT MINERAL SPRINGS RESORT**, P. O. Box 370, Carson, WA 98610, phone 509-427-8292. This rustic resort is a bohemian retreat open year-round. The original Hotel St. Martin was built in 1897 and the cabins around 1927. The hotel has 9 rooms with shared facilities; 12 cabins with toilet/sink; 2 housekeeping cabins with kitchens (no cookware), toilet/sink. There is one recently built hot tub suite that sleeps up to six people and has private facilities. The rooms are very Spartan, no TV or phones. The reason to come here is not the lodging, it's the incredible massages. Baths: men's and women's bathhouses have individual claw foot tubs. The baths take one hour and include a 20 minute soak in hot mineral water, a relaxing warm body wrap, and a shower. A bath attendant will assist you. Go for the full treatment and get the one hour massage after your bath to feel like a new person. Another reason for coming here is the great food at the restaurant in the hotel. Children under 5 free, pets by arrangement in cabins only. **Rates:** hotel $35; cabins $38-$43; hot tub suite $120; RV's $10-$13; tent space $5; bath $8; massage $32-$38. MasterCard & Visa. **Directions:** on Hwy 14 from the west, turn left at the Carson Junction 4 miles past Stevenson, proceed 1 mile into Carson, turn right and go 1 mile to the resort; from the east, turn right at Wind River Junction and proceed 1 1/4 miles to the resort.

Carson Hot Mineral Springs Resort

$35-$72 **COLUMBIA GORGE MOTEL,** Wind River Road, P. O. Box 777, Carson, WA 98610, phone 509-427-7777. Four deluxe "cottage style" units on three scenic acres with an additional four "motel style" units in the main building, all nonsmoking. Queen beds, TV, and coffee/tea making facilities. The cottages have kitchens with basic cookware and dishes. Gorge and mountain views, close to Carson Hot Springs and golf course. Within walking distance of restaurants. Children welcome, infants free, pets by arrangement. **Summer Rates:** motel units $50-$62; cottages $60-$72; extra person charge $6. **Winter Rates:** motel units $35; cottages $60. Amex and personal checks. **Directions:** from Hwy 14 turn at the Carson Junction and proceed for 1 mile.

CASHMERE

(pop. 2,530) is in the middle of the state on Hwy 2, just 12 miles from Wenatchee.

Home of the world famous Aplets & Cotlets, tours daily from May-Dec. Cashmere is situated along a popular rafting stretch of the Wenatchee River. A short distance away is Peshastin Pinnacles State Park, a well-known rock climbing area.

Located in Chelan County, the sales/use taxes are 8%.

$75-$80   **CASHMERE COUNTRY INN BED & BREAKFAST,** 5801 Pioneer Ave., Cashmere, WA 98815, **phone 509-782-4212, reservations 1-800-291-9144.** Built in 1907, this Victorian farmhouse has 5 guest rooms, all with private facilities. Guests are welcome to relax in the living room, curl up with a good book in the game room, or enjoy the pool and hot tub. Smoking is restricted to outdoor areas. The front porch is screened in and has wooden chairs for relaxing. Full gourmet breakfast. Adults only, no pets. **Rates:** *two night minimum on holidays and festival weekends* - double occupancy $75-$80. On selected dates in fall and spring the second night is half price. MasterCard, Visa, Amex, & personal checks. **Directions:** from Hwy 2 turn west into Cashmere, at the bridge with the apple boxes, follow Division St. thru town, this becomes Pioneer, on the left side of street just past the cemetery.

$36-$62   **CASHMERE'S VILLAGE INN MOTEL,** 229 Cottage Ave., Cashmere, WA 98815, phone 509-782-3522 or 1-800-793-3522. In the heart of Cashmere, the Inn offers friendly atmosphere and country charm with 21 units, 10 nonsmoking. Phones, TV, king and queen beds. No coffee/tea making facilities in the rooms, but available in the lobby. Microwaves and mini refrigerators in some of the units. Four restaurants within walking distance. Children welcome, infants free, no pets. **Summer Rates:** *two night minimum on holidays and festival weekends* - single room $44-$55; double rooms $50-$62; extra person $8.

Winter Rates: $36-$50. MasterCard, Visa, Amex, Discover, no personal checks. **Directions:** from Hwy 2 turn west into Cashmere, at the bridge with the apple boxes, turn left at first stop sign, proceed to the end of the block.

CASTLE • ROCK (pop. 2, 075) 48 miles north of Portland, 120 miles south of Seattle on I-5.

Castle Rock is west of I-5 at Exit 49, Mount St. Helens and the Spirit Lake Memorial Highway are east. Recreation: fishing for salmon or steelhead in the Cowlitz or Toutle Rivers; smelt dipping in the Cowlitz; boating in the rivers and Silver Lake; motorcycle races on weekends from May to September.

Located in Cowlitz (KOW-litz) County the sales/use/lodging taxes are 9.5%.

$29-$48 **MOTEL 7 WEST,** 120 Walsh Rd., Castle Rock, WA 98611, phone 360-274-7526. A total of 24 rooms, with 12 nonsmoking. Phones and cable TV in all the rooms. No coffee/tea making facilities in the rooms, but available in the lobby, and there is a restaurant next door. Children welcome, twelve and under free, pets allowed. **Seasonal Rates:** single room $29-$40; double room $40-$48; no charge for pets; local phone calls free. Major credit cards accepted. **Directions:** I-5 Exit 49, located on the left (north side) of the Spirit Lake Memorial Hwy.

$38-$48 **MOUNT ST. HELENS MOTEL,** 1340 Mt. St. Helens Way NE, Castle Rock, WA 98611, phone 360-274-6002, fax 360-274-7721. This two story motel has a total of 32 rooms, with 27 nonsmoking. All rooms have direct dial phones, cable TV, AC, and queen beds. No coffee/tea making facilities in the rooms, but available in the lobby. On site restaurant/bar, laundry facilities, and fitness center. Children welcome, small pets allowed in 3 rooms. Five miles to Mount St. Helens visitor center and 41 miles to the Coldwater visitor center. **Rates:** single room (1 bed) $38; double room (2 beds) $48; extra person $5; pet charge $6 per night; local phone calls free. Major credit cards accepted. **Directions:** from I-5, take Exit 49, located east of I-5.

$67-$98 **TIMBERLAND MOTOR INN**, 1271 Mt. St. Helens Way, Castle Rock, WA 98611, phone 360-274-6002. A total of 40 rooms, with 31 nonsmoking, and jacuzzi suites. In-room amenities include phones, TV, refrigerators, coffee/tea making facilities, king or queen beds. Some units have microwaves. Children welcome, infants free, small pets allowed. Several restaurants within walking distance. Close to Mount St. Helen's visitor center. **Rates:** single room (1 bed) $67-$74; double room (2 beds) $69-$77; suites $88-$98; extra person $5; pet charge $5; local phone calls free. Major credit cards accepted. **Directions:** from I-5, take Exit 49. Located on the left (north side) of the Spirit Lake Memorial Hwy.

CATHLAMET

(pop. 510) is located on the Columbia River on Hwy 4, about 25 miles west of Longview and 40 miles east of the Pacific Ocean.

(KATH-LA-muht) is an historic 1846 fishing and logging town dating back to the Hudson's Bay Company era. The name Cathlamet is derived from the Indian Tribe that once inhabited the area. Activities: golf, tennis, bicycling, boating, boardsailing, fishing, and touring the Julia Butler Hansen game refuge.

Located in Wahkiakum (wuh-KEYE-uh-kuhm) County the sales/use taxes are 7.5%.

$55-$85 **BRADLEY HOUSE COUNTRY KEEPER BED & BREAKFAST**, 61 Main St., P. O. Box 35, Cathlamet, WA 98612, phone 360-795-3030 or 1-800-551-1691. Four nonsmoking rooms, 2 with shared facilities, 2 with private facilities. No phones in the rooms, TV in the parlor. Children over 8 years old, no pets. Full breakfast provided, complimentary wine or sherry in late afternoon. Built in 1907, this elegant house was the home of a lumber baron. The atmosphere is quiet and relaxing. View the Columbia River from the front rooms. The rear rooms overlook the garden. Activities include cycling, golf, tennis, fishing, sailing, windsurfing, canoeing, browsing in shops, and visiting the museum. **Rates:** single room $55-$75; double room $65-$85; extra person $15. Visa & MasterCard. **Directions:** 1 1/2 blocks south of Hwy 4, 27 miles west of I-5 and 35 miles east of Hwy 101.

$45-$135 **GALLERY BED & BREAKFAST**, State Road 4, At Little Cape Horn, Cathlamet, WA 98612, phone 360-425-7395 or fax 360-425-1351. Five nonsmoking rooms, all rooms have toilets and sinks, 2 upstairs rooms share a shower/bath. The three rooms on the main floor all have private facilities and jacuzzi tubs. The house is adorned with fine art, paintings, and antiques. TV/VCR in large sitting room, outdoor jacuzzi spa on deck overlooking the Columbia River. Well-behaved children over 10 welcome. Some pets allowed, must check first. Reservations are necessary for the continental or gourmet breakfast. Two acres of flowers and trees with lots of wildlife - eagles, seals, and sea lions. Private beach. Art gallery is open to the public. **Rates:** $45-$135. No credit cards. **Directions:** on ocean beach highway (SR4), halfway between mile posts 41 and 42.

Gallery Bed & Breakfast at Little Cape Horn

$28-$33 **NASSA POINT MOTEL**, 851 East SR 4, Cathlamet, WA 98612, phone 360-795-3941. Six rooms, no non-smoking. TV, coffee/tea making facilities, and non-equipped kitchenettes. Children welcome, pets allowed at no charge. Located on the Columbia River, close to good fishing and windsurfing. Full service marina, historic homes tour, and golf three minutes away. **Rates:** single room $28; double room $33; extra person $3; public pay phone 25¢. Visa, MasterCard, & Discover. **Directions:** 3 miles east of Cathlamet on Hwy 4.

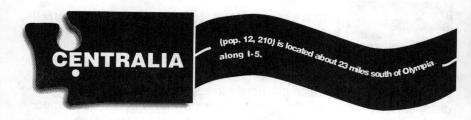

CENTRALIA (pop. 12, 210) is located about 23 miles south of Olympia along I-5.

(sen-TRAY-leeuh) is home to regional slow pitch tournaments, held every weekend from May through August. Shop at the Factory Outlet Mall.
Located in Lewis County the sales/use taxes are 7.7%.

$50-$65 CANDALITE MANSION BED & BREAKFAST,

402 N. Rock, Centralia, WA 98531, phone 360-736-4749 or 1-800-489-4749. This mansion was built in 1903 for a local lumber baron. The current owners have placed a candle in every window to welcome guests. There are six guest rooms to choose from with king, regular, or twin size beds. Two rooms have private facilities and 3 rooms share a large bathroom with a six foot jet bathtub and a large shower. All the rooms are on the second floor off a six foot wide hall. Game room and a parlor with a large fireplace. Full breakfasts include a variety of gourmet dishes. Adults only, no pets. This is a smoke free environment. **Rates:** double occupancy $50-$65; local phone calls free; taxes included. No credit cards. **Directions:** from I-5 take Exit 82, follow Harrison, it becomes Main, follow to N. Rock, turn left and proceed for 3 blocks.

$65-$85 CAVENESS HOUSE BED & BREAKFAST, 1011

Caveness Dr., Centralia, WA 98531, phone 360-330-5236. Three rooms on the second floor share two bathrooms. One room has twin beds, or choose the queen (with feather mattress) or double bed. All rooms have a coffee maker, and washstand with pitcher and bowl. Relax on the upstairs deck or verandah on the main floor. One acre of gardens, hot tub, double swing, horseshoes, and croquet. Close to factory outlet stores. Breakfast is a full continental, choice of juice or champagne, served on antique china with crystal and silver. Children by arrangement, no pets, smoking outside. **Rates:** double occupancy $65, $75, & $85; local phone calls free. No credit cards. **Directions:** from I-5 take Exit 82 west 3 blocks, turn left at light on Johnson Rd., to the end of the block and take a hard right onto Caveness Dr., turn left into driveway.

$40-$52 **FERRYMAN'S INN,** 1003 Eckerson Rd., Centralia, WA 98531, phone 360-330-2094. A total of 84 units, with 40 nonsmoking units. Phones, TV, six units have kitchens with basic cookware and dishes (2 nonsmoking). No coffee/tea making facilities in the rooms, but a continental breakfast is provided with fresh coffee in the lobby everyday. Children welcome, pets allowed. Restaurant within walking distance. Heated outdoor pool, indoor hot tub, and coin-operated laundry. Workout room off the property. Close to factory outlet stores. **Rates:** single room $40; double room $46; suite $52; extra person $5; pet charge $5; local phone calls free. Major credit cards accepted. **Directions:** Exit 82 off I-5, from the north take a left, go to second light take a left. Coming from the south, go right, take a left at the first light.

$40-$80 **HUNTLEY INN,** 702 W. Harrison, Centralia, WA 98531, phone 360-736-2875 or 1-800-448-5544-2-1, fax 360-736-2651. A total of 87 units, 50% nonsmoking. Phones, cable TV with HBO. No coffee/tea making facilities in the rooms, but a continental breakfast is provided in the lobby. Children 12 and under free, pets allowed. River and park behind motel. Restaurant within walking distance. Outdoor pool. **Rates:** single room $40-$48; double room (2 beds) $49; jacuzzi suites $80; extra person $4; pet charge $10 per stay; local phone calls free. Major credit cards. **Directions:** Exit 82 off I-5 to Harrison.

$35-$74 **LAKE SHORE MOTEL,** 1325 Lake Shore Dr., Centralia, WA 98531, phone 360-736-9344 or 1-800-600-8701. Two story motel with 34 units, 12 nonsmoking. Phones, cable TV with Showtime, and coffee/tea making facilities in the rooms. Children 16 and under free with parents, pets allowed. **Rates:** single room $35-$42; double room (2 beds) $43-$54; suite $60-$74; rollaway $6; no pet charge; local phone calls free. Major credit cards. **Directions:** take Exit 81 off I-5.

$27-$50 **The PARK MOTEL,** 1011 Belmont, Centralia, WA 98531, phone 360-736-9333. 32 rooms, 12 nonsmoking. Phones, cable TV with HBO. No coffee/tea making facilities in the rooms, but there are 4 equipped kitchen units available. Children welcome, infants free, pets allowed. Adjacent to Borst Park. **Seasonal Rates:** single room $27-$37; double room (2 beds) $38-$40; suite $45-$50; extra person $5; pet charge $3; local phone calls free. Major credit cards. **Directions:** Exit 82, one block west at the corner of Belmont and Harrison.

$33-$50 **PEPPERTREE MOTOR INN,** 1208 Alder St., Centralia, WA 98531, phone 360-736-1124. A total of 24 units, 8 nonsmoking. Phones, TV, AC, and kitchenettes with basic cookware. Children 10 and under free, pets allowed. Restaurant, bar, and coffee shop on the premises; also within walking distance of restaurants. One block to public transportation; close to factory outlet stores and antique mall. **Rates:** single room $33-$36; double room $35-$38; family room $42-$50; extra person $5; pets one time charge $5; no charge for local phone calls. MasterCard & Visa. **Directions:** Exit 81 off I-5.

CHEHALIS (pop. 6, 560) is located about 28 miles south of Olympia just off I-5. (chuh-HAY-lis)

$40-$95 **NENDELS**, 122 Interstate Avenue, Chehalis, WA 98532, phone 360-748-0101 or 1-800-648-7138. A total of 70 units, with 35 nonsmoking. All have queen beds, phones, and TV. The suite is available by reservation only during the summer. No coffee/tea making facilities in the rooms, but a continental breakfast is provided. Children 12 and under free, pets allowed. Restaurant within walking distance. Heated outdoor pool and hot tub. Close to restaurants, shopping, and two golf courses. **Summer Rates:** single room $45; double room $49; suite $95; extra person $5; local phone calls free; pets $5 per night; sales taxes 7.7%. **Winter Rates:** single $40; double $44; suite $95. Major credit cards accepted. **Directions:** Exit 76 off I-5, east side of freeway, visible from the exit.

$39-$50 **The RELAX INN**, 550 SW Parkland Dr., Chehalis, WA 98532, phone 360-748-8608. 29 units, 24 nonsmoking, all on the ground level. In-room amenities include phones, king or queen beds, and TV with Movie channel. Morning coffee is available with a continental breakfast in the lobby. Restaurant/lounge next door. Children welcome, pets allowed with a refundable deposit. 12 acre park with large pool and kiddy pool across the street. **Rates:** single room $39-$42; double room $47-$50; local phone calls free; sales taxes 7.7%. Amex, Discover, Visa, & MasterCard accepted. **Directions:** Exit 76 off I-5, two blocks east on 13th Street.

CHELAN see Lake Chelan.

CHENEY • is located about 14 miles southeast of Spokane.

(CHEE-nee) has a year-round population of 7,800 residents, with an additional 1,600 dormitory students during the academic year at Eastern Washington University.

Located in Spokane County the sales/use/lodging taxes are 10% for lodgings with 40 or more units.

$34-$38 **ROSEBROOK INN**, W. 304 First, Cheney, WA 99004, phone 509-235-6538, fax 509-235-9229. Four rooms, all with private facilities, cable TV, phones, and equipped kitchenettes with microwaves. Complimentary instant coffee and juice in the rooms. No designated nonsmoking rooms. Laundry facilities on the premises. Children 5 and under free, pets allowed. **Rates:** $34-$38; extra person $5; pets $10 refundable deposit; no charge for local phone calls. MasterCard, Visa, Amex, & Discover. **Directions:** follow 1st St. to the south end of town.

$35-$43 **WILLOW SPRINGS MOTEL**, 5 B St., Cheney, WA 99004, phone 509-235-5138, fax 509-235-4528. Located just 20 minutes from Spokane. This motel has 44 rooms, 22 nonsmoking. In-room amenities include phones, cable TV, and 12 units have kitchenettes with basic cookware. Morning coffee is available in the office. Adjacent restaurant/lounge. On weekends a continental breakfast is provided. Children 12 and under free, small pets allowed. **Rates:** single room $35; double room $41; family room with kitchen $43; extra person $4; pets $5 per night; no charge for local phone calls. Major credit cards accepted. **Directions:** located on the main street between 1st & B St.

CHEWELAH (pop. 1, 980) is located in the northeast corner of the state 45 miles north of Spokane.

(chuh-WEE-luh) is fast becoming one of the nations' retirement havens. There are numerous reasons why retirees would find Chewelah a favorable place to relocate. There are mountains on three sides of this beautiful valley and 49 Degrees North ski area is close by.

Located in Stevens County the sales/use taxes are 7.5%.

$34-$48 **49ER MOTEL & RV PARK**, Hwy 395, Chewelah, WA 99109, phone 509-935-8613. A total of 13 units, 2 nonsmoking. Phones, TV, and two units have kitchenettes with basic cookware. No coffee/tea making facilities in the rooms, but available in the lobby. Indoor swimming pool and jacuzzi. Children welcome, pets allowed by arrangement. **Rates:** single $34; double $38; 3 to 4 people $43-$48; local phone calls free; group rates available. Amex, Discover, Visa, & MasterCard. **Directions:** 10 miles from 49 Degrees North ski area, 3 miles from Chewelah golf course.

$36-$42 **NORDLIG MOTEL**, W. 101 Grant St., Chewelah, WA 99109, phone 509-935-6704. A total of 14 units, with 10 nonsmoking. Phones, TV, refrigerators, and coffee/tea making facilities in the rooms. Children welcome, pets allowed. **Rates:** single $36; double $42; extra person $5; rollaway $5; pets $3 one time charge; local phone calls free. Major credit cards. **Directions:** 1/2 block off Hwy 395 in a quiet, park-like setting.

CHINOOK (shi-NOOK) see Long Beach Peninsula.

CHINOOK PASS

is located west of Yakima on Hwy 410. This is a popular area for fishing, hunting, bicycling, 4-wheeling in the hills, and snowmobiling. See Naches for lodging.

CLARKSTON (pop. 6, 750) is located in the southeast corner of the state on the Snake River, just across the border from Lewiston, Idaho.

Clarkston is the hub for adventure trips into Hells Canyon. The Snake River offers many forms of recreation for all ages.

Located in Asotin County the sales/use taxes are 7%.

$25-$34 **ASTOR MOTEL**, 1201 Bridge St., Clarkston, WA 99403, phone 509-758-2509. A total of 8 units, with 1 nonsmoking unit. Phones, TV, no coffee/tea making facilities, but there are 3 kitchen units with basic cookware. Children welcome, pets allowed. **Rates:** single room $25-$28; double room $30-$34; extra person $5; kitchen units $130 per week; local phone calls free. Discover, Visa, & MasterCard. **Directions:** on Hwy 12 coming into town.

$26-$30 **GOLDEN KEY MOTEL**, 1376 Bridge St., Clarkston, WA 99403, phone 509-758-5566. 16 rooms with phones, TV, and outdoor pool. Two nonsmoking rooms. No coffee/tea making facilities in the rooms, but available in the lobby. Restaurant/bar within walking distance. Children under 5 years old free, pets allowed free. **Rate:** single $26; double $30; extra person $2; local phone calls 25¢; taxes included. Visa & MasterCard. **Directions:** 1 mile after crossing into Washington from Idaho, on right-hand side of road.

$32-$38 **HACIENDA LODGE,** 812 Bridge St., Clarkston, WA 99403, phone 509-758-5583, reservations only 1-800-600-5583. A total of 30 units, with 15 nonsmoking units. Phones, remote control cable TV, small refrigerators, AC, and coffee/tea facilities in the room. Children welcome, pets by arrangement. Within walking distance of the Snake River, parks, shopping, restaurants, and laundromat. The Hacienda is an older motel, but very clean and offers friendly, personal service. **Rates:** single room $32; double room $38; pet charge $5; local phone calls free. Major credit cards accepted. **Directions:** Hwy 12 in Clarkston.

$35-$80 **HIGHLAND HOUSE BED & BREAKFAST**, 707 Highland, Clarkston, WA 99403, phone 509-758-3126. This colonial style home, built in the late 1890's, has 5 nonsmoking rooms individually named after historical English counties. Three rooms have private facilities and 2 with shared. Coffee/tea making facilities in the rooms, full breakfast, dinner by arrangement. The rec room offers TV, darts, dominoes, and shove halfpenny (an old English board game). Shuttle provided to airport and river tour marinas. Children welcome, pets allowed. **Rates:** single room $35; double room $70; suite $80; local phone calls free. MasterCard & Visa. **Directions:** from Bridge St. turn south onto 6th, go past downtown shopping area, and turn right onto Highland, park at the corner of 7th and Highland.

Highland House Bed & Breakfast

QUALITY INN, 700 Port Drive, Clarkston, WA 99403, phone 509-758-9500, fax 509-758-5580, reservations 1-800-221-2222.

$55-$85 **RIVERTREE INN Best Western**, 1257 Bridge St., Clarkston, WA 99403, phone 509-758-9551 or 1-800-597-3621. A total of 61 units, with 34 nonsmoking units. Phones, TV, outdoor pool, sauna, workout room, hot tub, kitchenettes, and BBQ area. Children welcome, infants free, no pets. No coffee/tea making facilities in the rooms, but available in the lobby all hours. Restaurants and bar within walking distance. **Rates:** single room $55; double room $60; triple room (3 double beds, 6 people) $85; extra person $5; local phone calls free. Major credit cards. **Directions:** Hwy 12 is Clarkston's main street (Bridge Street), the Rivertree Inn is 12 blocks west of the interstate bridge.

$29-$38 **SUNSET MOTEL**, 1200 Bridge St., Clarkston, WA 99403, phone 509-758-2517, reservations only 1-800-845-5223. A total of 10 units, with 3 nonsmoking. Phones, TV, and covered parking. No coffee/tea facilities in the room. Two kitchen units, no cookware or dishes. Gas barbecue and picnic table available. Children under 12 free, dogs allowed, no cats. **Rates:** single room (1 bed) $29-$35;

double room (2 beds) $38; extra person $5; local phone calls free; taxes included. MasterCard, Visa, Amex, & Discover. **Directions:** Hwy 12 in Clarkston.

CLE ELUM

(pop. 1,780) is located 40 miles east of Snoqualmie Pass along I-90.

(klee-EL-uhm) is an Indian name meaning "swift water." The town is a popular place to begin rafting trips on the Yakima river. Cle Elum was founded as a mining town.
Located in Kittitas County the sales/use taxes are 7.5%.

$27-$40 **BONITA MOTEL,** 906 E. First St., Cle Elum, WA 98922, phone 509-674-2380. This older motel has 9 rooms that are nice, clean, and comfortable. 3 nonsmoking rooms. Phones, TV, no coffee/tea making facilities in the rooms, but one unit has an equipped kitchen. Children 12 and under free, some pets are allowed. Eight RV sites. **Rates:** single room (1 bed) $27-$32; double room (2 beds) $36-$40; local phone calls free. Visa & MasterCard. **Directions:** from the east take Exit 86 off I-90 and go west about a mile, south side of the main street; from the west, Exit 85 and drive through Cle Elum about 1 1/2 miles.

$40-$48 **CEDARS MOTEL,** 1001 E. First St., Cle Elum, WA 98922, phone 509-674-5535 or 1-800-431-5535. 32 units with phones and TV. No nonsmoking rooms. No coffee/tea making facilities in the rooms, but the Cottage Cafe next door is open 24 hours. Children 12 and under free, pets allowed. Large shady area in the front. Across the street from the Greyhound bus terminal. **Rates:** single room $40-$42; double room $44-$48; extra person $2; local phone calls free. Major credit cards accepted. **Directions:** from I-90 Exit 84 westbound; Exit 85 eastbound; on the main street next door to the Cottage Cafe.

$55 **MAMA VALLONE,** 302 W. First St., Cle Elum, WA 98922, phone 509-674-5174. Two rooms upstairs, both with private facilities and TV. No phones or coffee/tea making facilities in the rooms, but a continental breakfast is provided. Diner house downstairs open from 4:30-9:30 p.m. Children are welcome, but rooms are small and suitable for 2 people, no pets. This is a nonsmoking premises. **Rates:** double occupancy $55. Major credit cards accepted. **Directions:** from I-90 take Cle Elum Exit, Mama Vallone is located on the west end of the main street, First St.

Mama Vallone

$45-$115 **MOORE HOUSE BED & BREAKFAST**, 526 Marie Ave., P. O. Box 629, South Cle Elum, WA 98943, phone 509-674-5939 or 1-800-22-TWAIN. A total of 12 nonsmoking units range from economical to exquisite. This was once the bunkhouse for Milwaukee railroad crewmen. Six units have private facilities, 6 with shared. TV and coffee/tea making facilities in the cabooses (2) only. TV in lounge on request. Outdoor hot tub available year-round. Children welcome, no pets. Full breakfast is provided. The extensive collection of railroad memorabilia is very unique. The inn is located next to the Iron Horse State Park Trail (non-motorized), and is ideal for biking, strolling, and xc skiing. **Rates:** single room $45-$105; double room $55-$105; suite $115; family room $75-$115; extra person $10. MasterCard, Visa, & Amex. **Directions:** from I-90 take Exit 84, watch for turn-off to South Cle Elum, go under the I-90 overpass, turn right on Madison St., go 2 blocks, turn left, go about 4 blocks.

$30-$55　**MUS MOTEL**, 521 E. First St., Cle Elum, WA 98922, phone 509-674-2551. A total of 9 units, 3 nonsmoking. All rooms have TV, no coffee/tea making facilities, but 5 units have small equipped kitchens. Children welcome, pets allowed. Within walking distance of restaurants. Quiet, outdoor sitting and sunning area. **Rates:** single room (1 person) $30; double $45; suite $55. Visa & MasterCard. **Directions:** take Cle Elum Exit off I-90, midtown on the main street - one block from the famous Cle Elum Bakery.

$45-$55　**STEWART LODGE**, 805 W. First St., Cle Elum, WA 98922, phone 509-674-4548. A total of 36 rooms, 21 nonsmoking. All units have private facilities, TV, and phones. No coffee/tea making facilities in the rooms, but available in the lobby. Outdoor pool and spa. Children welcome, infants free, pets by arrangement. Quiet setting, view of the mountains. **Rates:** single room (1 person) $45; 2 people $50; double (2 beds) $55; extra person $5. Major credit cards. **Directions:** from I-90 going east, take Exit 84, on the left after exit; going west take Exit 85.

$45-$60　**THE LAST RESORT**, P.O. Box 532, Roslyn, WA 98941, phone 509-649-2222. A total of 12 rooms, 4 nonsmoking. The motel units have cable TV, mini-fridge, and wet bar. Children welcome, no pets. Restaurant and country store on the grounds. The Last Resort is located on the eastern slope of the Cascades and just a leisurely stroll away from beautiful Lake Cle Elum. Banquet facilities, catering services, pig roasts, storage rental, lodge & motel rooms, gas, RV hookups, and snowmobile repair. **Rates:** motel single $45; double $60. Visa & MasterCard. **Directions:** take Exit 80 off I-90 to Roslyn, follow State Road 903 seven miles west to Lake Cle Elum.

$40-$55　**TIMBER LODGE**, 301 W. First St., Cle Elum, WA 98922, phone 509-674-5966, fax 509-674-2737. A total of 29 rooms, 10 nonsmoking. Phones, TV, and air conditioning in every room. Indoor hot tub and 2 exercise bikes. No coffee/tea making facilities in the rooms, but available in the lobby. Small refrigerators and microwaves available. Children welcome, pets allowed. **Rates:** single room $40-$45; double room $50-$55; family room $53; no charge for local phone calls; fridge or microwave $4.50. MasterCard, Visa, & Amex. **Directions:** take Cle Elum Exit off I-90 - on the west end of town.

$38-$45 **WIND BLEW INN MOTEL,** HC 61 Box 10, Cle Elum, WA 98922, phone 509-674-2294. This newly reno-vated motel has taken on a western theme. There are 8 units with 2 nonsmoking rooms. No coffee/tea making facilities in the rooms, but 2 units have kitchenettes and coffee is provided in the office. The "bunkhouse" sleeps 2 to 6 people. Phones, TV, and outdoor picnic area. **Rates:** $38-$45. Discover, Visa & MasterCard. **Directions:** at the junction of Hwy 97 and Exit 85 from I-90, east side of Cle Elum on the main street.

CLINTON

is located on the south end of Whidbey Island, one hour north of Seattle. Use Exit 189 off I-5 to reach the Mukilteo ferry landing, take the Mukilteo ferry to Clinton. See Whidbey Island for lodging.

COLFAX • (pop. 2, 800) is located in the southeast corner of the state at the intersection of State Route 26 and U.S. Route 195. Spokane is an hours drive north.

Colfax is the gateway to the Palouse Empire and is the county seat of Whitman County. The topography consists of rolling hills and is recognized as one of the nation's largest producers of wheat, split peas, and lentils.

Located in Whitman County the sales/use taxes are 7.5%.

$31-$49 **SIESTA MOTEL,** S. Main & Thorn Streets, Colfax, WA 99111, phone 509-397-3417. A total of 18 rooms, 5 nonsmoking. Phones, TV, and AC. No coffee/tea making facilities in the rooms, but restaurants are within walking distance. Refrigerators in some rooms. Children 3 and under free, no pets allowed. **Rates:** single room (1 double bed) $31; single room (queen bed) $31-$35; 2 queen beds with fridge $49; local phone calls 50¢. Visa & MasterCard. **Directions:** on Colfax's main street, coming from Pullman it is the first motel on the right.

$28-$32 The **WHEEL INN MOTEL,** Rt. 1 Box 130-E, Colfax, WA 99111, phone 509-397-3195. A total of 9 rooms, no nonsmoking. Rooms have phones and cable TV. Outdoor pool. No coffee/tea making facilities in the rooms, but the restaurant on the premises is open from 6 a.m. to 10 p.m. Children welcome, pets allowed. **Rates:** single $28;

double $32; pets $50 refundable deposit. Credit cards accepted. **Directions:** 50 miles south of Spokane at the junction of Hwy 195 and Hwy 23.

COLVILLE (pop. 4, 500) is located 65 miles north of Spokane and 13 miles east of Lake Roosevelt.

(KAWL-vil) recorded history dates back to 1811 when caucasians began exploring the Columbia River for the Northwest Fur Company. This panoramic land has 4 definite seasons and many outdoor activities. There are over 80 miles of trails for cross country skiers in the Colville National Forest, as well as abundant hunting and fishing.

Located in Stevens County the sales/use taxes are 7.5%.

$35   **BEAVER LODGE,** 2430 Highway 20 E., Colville, WA 99114, phone 509-684-5657. Six cabins furnished with 2 double beds, woodstoves, a table and chairs. The kitchenettes include microwave, two burner hot plate, coldwater sink, and basic cookware. No private facilities in the cabins, bath house is close by. Located on Lake Gillette, there are RV hookups, tenting, grocery store, restaurant, and boat rentals. The restaurant opens at 7 a.m., but breakfast is limited. Children welcome, pets allowed. Open year-round. **Rates:** $35 per cabin; extra person $2.50 for over 4 people. Visa & MasterCard. **Directions:** from Spokane, take Hwy 395 to Colville. In Colville take Hwy 20 east for 25 miles.

$40-$95   **BENNY'S COLVILLE INN,** 915 S. Main, Colville, WA 99114, phone 509-684-2517 or 1-800-680-2517, fax 509-684-2546. A total of 106 rooms, 68 nonsmoking. Phones, TV, and AC. No coffee/tea making facilities in the rooms, but restaurants are within walking distance. Indoor pool and spa. Children 11 and under free, pets allowed. Suites have fireplaces and whirlpool tubs. Surrounded by excellent hunting, fishing, water skiing, hiking, and bicycling. Also, within one hours drive of two ski areas. **Rates:** single $40-$54; double $48-$62; suite $85-$95; extra person $6; local phone calls free. Amex, Visa, MasterCard, & Discover. **Directions:** on Hwy 395 at the south end of Colville, 65 miles north of Spokane and 55 miles south of Canada.

$32-$50 **DOWNTOWN MOTEL**, 369 S. Main, Colville, WA 99114, phone 509-684-2565. A total of 20 rooms, 3 nonsmoking, all with private facilities, TV, and phones. Some rooms have coffee/tea making facilities, 5 units have kitchens equipped with basic cookware. Children 5 and under free, some pets allowed, no cats. Downtown, close to all businesses. 12 miles from Lake Roosevelt for fishing and water sports. **Rates:** single $32-$45; double $37-$50; extra person $5; local phone calls free. **Directions:** 65 miles north of Spokane, 50 miles south of Canadian border, located on Main Street, Hwy 395.

$45-$55 **MAPLE AT SIXTH BED & BREAKFAST**, 407 E. 6th, Colville, WA 99114, phone 509-684-5251. Two nonsmoking rooms on the second floor share one bathroom. One room has a twin bed and the other a queen bed. The house has central air conditioning and is decorated with a mix of modern and antique collectibles. There is a sitting room equipped with a table and phone for pleasure or work. Breakfast is continental with homemade bakery goods. Children 4 years and older, pets by arrangement. **Rates:** single $45; double $55. No credit cards, personal checks or cash preferred. **Directions:** 3 blocks east of Main St. at the corner of 6th and Maple.

$65-$100 **MY PARENTS' ESTATE**, 719 Hwy 395, P. O. Box 724, Kettle Falls, WA 99141 , phone 509-738-6220.

My Parents' Estate Bed & Breakfast

Once the Providence nuns' convent, the house dates back to 1869. Completely renovated in 1983, it became a B & B in 1989. There are 3 rooms in the main house, a suite with efficiency kitchen, and a cottage - all have private facilities. The rooms are decorated with elegant turn-of-the-century furnishings. The estate covers 43 acres. 5 of the acres around the house include a rose garden, cemetery, large gazebo, 8 garages, half court gymnasium, and caretaker's house (the cottage). A full breakfast is served for guests in the main house. The cottage rents by the week or month. Children welcome in the cottage, no pets. Smoking outside only. **Rates:** single $65; double $75; suite $100. MasterCard & Visa. **Directions:** from Colville follow Hwy 395 for 7 miles, turn at the white rail fence, sign attached to the mail box.

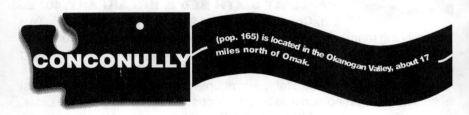

CONCONULLY (pop. 165) is located in the Okanogan Valley, about 17 miles north of Omak.

(KAHN-kah-NUHL-lee) is located on the Conconully Reservoir and offers year-round activities. Resorts in Conconully offer boat and/or canoe rentals, horseback riding, mountain bike rentals, RV parking, campsites, and laundromats. The only town in the state where you can snowmobile down Main Street.

Located in Okanogan County the sales/use taxes are 7.6%.

$25-$45 **CONCONULLY LAKE RESORT**, P. O. Box 131, Conconully, WA 98819, phone 509-826-0813. *Open from April 15 to November 15.* Four cabins and one apartment, one unit is nonsmoking. All cabins have fully equipped kitchens, 3 have private facilities. The small cabin's facilities are located 60' away. Apartment has microwave, no kitchen. Spectacular view of the lake from all the cabins. Boat rentals, convenience store, boat moorage, community barbecue pit, dock fishing, hiking, bike riding. One mile to town and restaurants. **Rates:** $25-$45. MasterCard & Visa. **Directions:** from Seattle take Hwy 97 to Omak, then follow signs to Conconully. Turn right at Herb's Market and Salmon Creek Inn, 1 mile northeast to resort - well marked.

$40 **CONCONULLY MOTEL**, P. O. Box 98, Conconully, WA 98819, phone 509-826-1610. Four rooms, no nonsmoking. All rooms have private facilities, TV, coffee/tea making facilities, and refrigerators. Restaurant across the street. Children 3 and under free, pets allowed with restrictions. **Rates:** double occupancy $40; extra person $5; pets free. Visa, MasterCard, & Discover. **Directions:** last motel on Main St.

$45-$55   **GIBSON'S NORTH FORK LODGE,** P. O. Box 205, Conconully, WA 98819, phone 509-826-1475. Two recently constructed two story cabins come with an upstairs balcony overlooking the creek. Both cabins have a fully equipped kitchen, upstairs bedroom, bathroom, linens, and color TV. One cabin sleeps 4, the other 8. Children 18 and under free with parents, pets allowed, no smoking indoors. Close to Conconully Lake and Conconully Reservoir for fishing, boating, or swimming. A year-round vacation area, xc ski or snowmobile out the front door in the winter. **Rates:** double occupancy $45 & $55; extra person $5; pets free. No credit cards. **Directions:** north end of Conconully, past the Forest Service building.

Gibson's North Fork Lodge

$55   **JACK'S R.V. PARK & MOTEL,** P. O. Box 98, Conconully, WA 98819, phone 509-826-0132. Six units, 4 nonsmoking. This new motel has fully equipped kitchens, heated outdoor pool, private decks to the creek, and TV. Pay phone available. Children 2 and under free, pets allowed. **Rates:** double occupancy $55; extra person $5; pets free. Visa, MasterCard, & Discover. **Directions:** on Main St.

CONCRETE (pop. 735) is located on Hwy 20 in the northwest corner of the state, about 32 miles east of I-5 and Mount Vernon. Baker Hot Springs is 20 miles north.

$40-$75 **BAKER LAKE RESORT**, P. O. Box 100, Concrete, WA 98237, phone 360-757-2262. *Open from April 15 to October 1st.* 10 rustic cabins on the lake, no nonsmoking, 6 with private facilities, 4 with shared. All cabins have equipped kitchens, gas heater, cooking stove, outdoor firepit, and picnic table. Guests furnish own linens and towels. The generator is turned off from 11 p.m. to 6:30 a.m., kerosene lamps are provided in the cabins. Baker Lake Resort is nestled between two glacier-fed creeks on the edge of Baker Lake. Boat ramp and moorage is available, also rental boats. Children welcome, pets allowed with restrictions. Less than 2 hours from Seattle or Vancouver, B.C. **Rates:** cabins (2 people) $40-$75; extra person $7; pets $2-$10; taxes 7.6%. *Minimum 2 nights on weekends, 3 nights on holidays.* MasterCard, Visa, & Discover. **Directions:** from I-5, just north of Mt. Vernon, take the North Cascades Hwy 20 east to milepost 82, then north on Baker Lake Rd. to milepost 20.

$40-$45 **NORTH CASCADE INN**, 4284 Hwy 20, Concrete, WA 98237, phone 360-853-8870 or 1-800-251-3054. 14 units, 7 nonsmoking, with TV and phones. No coffee/tea making facilities in the rooms, however, the Inn has a full service restaurant and lounge. Children 12 and under free, no pets. Shuttle provided to airport or town. The grandeur of the North Cascades and the beauty of the Upper Skagit River Valley surrounds the Inn every season. **Rates:** single $40; double $45; extra person $5; local phone calls free; taxes included. Visa & MasterCard. **Directions:** located 30 miles east of I-5 on Hwy 20 before Concrete.

CONNELL (pop. 2,600) is located 32 miles north of Pasco. (kah-NEL)

M & M MOTEL, 730 S. Columbia Ave., Connell, WA 99326, phone 509-234-8811.

$22-$35 **TUMBLEWEED MOTEL,** 433 S. Columbia Ave., P. O. Box 796, Connell, WA 99326, phone 509-234-2081. 29 rooms, 5 nonsmoking. TV, phones, outdoor pool. Free coffee/tea making facilities in the rooms. Children welcome, pets allowed. Within walking distance of a restaurant. **Rates:** single room $22-$26; double room $30-$35; no charge for local phone calls; taxes 7.5%. Diners, Amex, MasterCard, & Visa. **Directions:** on state highway 395, 30 miles north of Pasco, 43 miles south of Ritzville, first exit into Connell.

• CONWAY is located 5 miles south of Mt. Vernon at the mouth of the Skagit River.

$80-$95 **SOUTH FORK MOORAGE,** 2187 Mann Rd., Fir Island, Conway, WA 98238, phone 360-445-4803. Two guest houseboats, the "Karma" and the "Tea House", are on the Skagit River. Both unique lodgings for that special occasion. The "Karma" has leaded glass windows, a small wood burning fireplace, tiny kitchen, and a cozy sitting room. The "Tea House" has a fully equipped galley, full size shower, walk around deck, skylight, sleeps 4, and is all on one level. Looking out at the river gives this retreat a special ambiance. Children and pets by arrangement. 15 minutes from La Conner. **Rates:** double occupancy $80-$95; extra person charge $10; taxes of 7.5% included. No credit cards. **Directions:** south of Mt. Vernon on I-5 take Exit 221. Going north turn left, going south turn right, take next right to Fir Island Rd., cross bridge take left at Mann Rd., 1 mile on the left.

"The Tea House"

COPALIS BEACH

is located on the Pacific Ocean on Hwy 109, just north of Ocean Shores.

(koh-PAY-lis) Things to do: whale and seal watching from the jetty; fishing of all kinds: river, lake, surf, or charter boat; horseback ride, moped, or bicycle on the beach; kite flying; sandsculpture; and all the other wonderful beach activities.

Located in Grays Harbor County the sales/use/lodging taxes are 10.9%.

$53-$79   **BEACHWOOD RESORT**, Box 116, Copalis Beach, WA 98535, phone 360-289-2177. 18 units that will each accommodate 6 people. No nonsmoking units. Units have two double beds, plus rollaway bed in the living room, fireplaces, and TV. Complete kitchens with basic cooking utensils and dishes. Seven beach units. Play area with swings, slides, etc. Heated outdoor pool in season, mini golf, hot tub, and sauna. Half a mile to a restaurant, one block from public transportation. Children 12 and under free, pets allowed. **Summer Rates:** double occupancy $68-$79; $5 per pet; extra person $5; pay phone. **Winter Rates:** double occupancy $53-$65. MasterCard & Visa. **Directions:** 8 miles past Ocean Shores, on Hwy 109.

$36-$48   **DUNES RV RESORT & MOTEL**, Box 237, Copalis Beach, WA 98535, phone 360-289-3873. Five one bedroom units with hide-a-bed, TV, and fully outfitted kitchens. No nonsmoking units. Many things to do at this oceanfront resort. There is a large clam cleaning kitchen to use during the clam digging season, 32 RV sites, and 6 tent sites. Children 5 and under free, no pets in motel. Restaurant within walking distance. Shuttle provided to Aberdeen and Ocean Shores, 150 yards to public transportation. **Summer Rates:** 5/15 to 9/15, holidays & clam tides - double occupancy $48; extra person 16 years and older $5, under 16 years, $2; pets $2. **Winter Rates:** double occupancy $36. Major credit cards. **Directions:** take Hwy 109 from Aberdeen, located at mile marker 20.5, 3041 SR109.

$62-$120   **IRON SPRINGS RESORT**, P. O. Box 207, Copalis Beach, WA 98535, phone 360-276-4230, fax 360-276-4365. Open year-round, the 28 accommodations are ultra-modern, spacious, and home-like. Each individual cottage is nestled among the weathered spruce trees. Fireplaces, fully equipped kitchens, and a panoramic view of the ocean. There are also studio apartments. Gift shop and indoor pool open year-round. Children welcome, infants free, pets allowed, no designated nonsmoking. The miles of sandy beach invite you to beachcomb to your heart's content. The shallow creek running through to the ocean is especially appealing to small children. Swimming, piper boarding, and surfing provide fun for all. **Rates:** *6/30 to Labor Day: minimum 3 night stay.* Cottages - 2 people $62-$94, 4 people $72-$120; studio apts. - 2 people $62-$68, 4 people $72-$78; pets $10; over 4 people $10 per adult and $6 per child. Major credit cards. **Directions:** on coast Hwy 101 three miles north of Copalis Beach.

$38-$78 **SHADES BY THE SEA** , Box 67, **Copalis Beach, WA 98535, phone 360-289-3358.** Eight one and 2 bedroom units with queen beds and TV, sleep 2-6 people. Two units with full kitchens, 4 with kitchenettes. No nonsmoking units. Located on 8 acres of park-like setting. Within walking distance to the ocean, Copalis River, miniature golf, grocery store, and restaurants. Children welcome, infants free, small pets by arrangement. **Rates:** double occupancy $38-$78; extra person $8-$10; pets $8-$10. Visa & MasterCard. **Directions:** on Hwy 109 two blocks north of the Copalis River Bridge.

COSMOPOLIS (pop. 1, 370) is located in the central Grays Harbor area, one mile east of Aberdeen.

In Cosmopolis, the "Treaty Mural" commemorates the signing of the treaties between the US Government and the Chehalis Indian Nation. This site is the focal point of a river front park.
Located in Grays Harbor County the sales/use/lodging taxes are 10.9%. Also see Aberdeen and Hoquiam for lodging.

$65-$130 **COONEY MANSION BED & BREAKFAST**, 1705 5th, P. O. Box 54, Cosmopolis, WA 98537, phone 360-533-0602. There are 8 nonsmoking rooms in this turn-of-the-century home built by a lumber baron in 1908. Five guest rooms with private baths, and an additional 3 bedrooms with shared bath on the former "servant's floor". Sauna, workout room, jacuzzi, sundeck overlooking the golf course and rose garden. Full breakfast is provided. Shuttle by arrangement.

Children 10 and older - week days only, no pets. **Rates:** double occupancy $65-$85; suite $130. Major credit cards accepted. **Directions:** drive into Aberdeen to "H" St., go left following the signs for Cosmopolis and Raymond. Entering Cosmopolis you will be on 1st St., turn right at "C" St. and go to 5th St., then left to the top of the hill. The house is on a dead-end street.

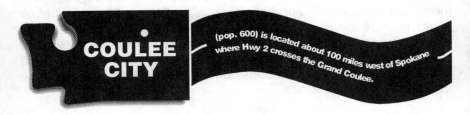

COULEE CITY

(pop. 600) is located about 100 miles west of Spokane where Hwy 2 crosses the Grand Coulee.

(KOO-lee) City is surrounded by numerous fishing lakes and offers many outdoor activities year-round.

Located in Grant County the sales/use taxes are 7.5%.

$35-$45 **ALA COZY MOTEL**, 9988 Hwy 2 E., Coulee City, WA 99115, phone 509-632-5703, fax 509-632-5383. A total of 10 units, 5 nonsmoking. Phones, TV, coffee/tea making facilities, and one unit has a kitchenette equipped with basic cookware. Outdoor pool, barbecue area, and 21 hole mini golf. Restaurant next door. Children welcome, infants free, pets allowed. 30 miles to Coulee Dam; view of Banks Lake; great fishing and hunting. **Rates:** single room (1 bed) $35-$40; suite (2 beds) $45; extra person $5; no charge for local phone calls. Master Card, Discover, & Visa. **Directions:** 1/2 mile east of Coulee City.

$29-$49 **BLUE LAKE RESORT**, 31199 Hwy 17 No., Coulee City, WA 99115, phone 509-632-5364. *Open April 1 to October 7.* Housekeeping cabins. Two small cabins - 1 double bed, 2 people, no bathroom; 7 large cabins sleep 4 and have bathrooms with shower. No designated nonsmoking units. Pets allowed on a leash. Camp store, bath house, lake swimming, water skiing, boat rentals, and fishing. **Rates:** small cabins $29; large cabins $49; extra person $5; pets $2; rowboats $12 per day. No credit cards. **Directions:** located 11 miles north of Soap Lake on Highway 17.

$27-$38 **BLUE TOP MOTEL**, 109 N. 6th, Coulee City, WA 99115, phone 509-632-5596. A total of 14 units, 6 nonsmoking. No coffee/tea making facilities in the rooms, but 9 units have equipped kitchenettes, and coffee is available in the office. Refrigerators in some units. Within walking distance of restaurants. Children welcome, 5 and under free, pets allowed. **Rates:** single room (1 bed) $27-$35; kitchen units $38; pets $5; extra person $5. Amex, MasterCard, & Visa. **Directions:** from Hwy 2 take 4th St., go 2 blocks, turn right on Walnut, and go 2 blocks.

$43-$53 **COULEE LODGE RESORT,** 33017 Park Lake Rd. NE, Coulee City, WA 99115, phone 509-632-5565. *Open from April 1st to October 1st.* Located on Blue Lake, the resort has 15 individual housekeeping units, no smoking restrictions. 8 units are cabins in a variety of sizes and 7 are housekeeping trailers. 14 units have private facilities and one small cabin uses the bathhouse shared with the RV park. All units have equipped kitchens. Children three and under free, pets allowed in cabins only. Fishing boats and jet skis for rent, grocery store, and laundry facilities. Two miles to golf course and horseback riding. **Rates:** $43-$53; extra person $5; pets $5. Master Card & Visa. **Directions:** from Hwy 2 turn south on Hwy 17 and travel 6 1/2 miles.

$30-$35 **LAKE VIEW II MOTEL,** 9811 Fordair Rd. NE, Coulee City, WA 99115, phone 509-632-5792. A total of 10 units, no nonsmoking, 6 units have equipped kitchenettes. TV, coffee/tea making facilities in the rooms. Indoor spa and sauna. Children welcome, infants free, pets allowed. **Rates:** single $30; double $35; extra person $5; pets free. Master Card & Visa. **Directions:** from Hwy 2 turn north on I-8 NE, go past 37th NE to Fordair Rd., motel is on the right.

$35-$40 **MAIN STAY BED & BREAKFAST,** 110 W. Main, Coulee City, WA 99115, phone 509-632-5687. Two nonsmoking rooms with private facilities in this modern home located in a quiet residential area. Continental breakfast and evening tea provided. Children welcome, 12 and under free, no pets. Sun Lakes Park 15 minutes away. **Rates:** single $35; double $40; extra person $10. No credit cards. **Directions:** from Hwy 2 turn south on 4th, go four blocks to Main St., turn left and go 2 1/2 blocks.

$57-$90 **SUN LAKES PARK RESORT, INC.,** 34228 Park Lake Rd. NE, Coulee City, WA 99115, phone 509-632-5291. *Open from April 15 to October 15.* A total of 49 cabins and 10 mobile homes. Cabins have kitchenettes (no dishes, cookware, or utensils), A/C, picnic tables, towels, and bedding. The mobile home sleeps 6, maximum allowed is 7. Heated pool, 9 hole golf course, snack bar, gift shop, rowboat and pedalboat rentals, mini golf, and lake sports. 112 RV sites. Children welcome, pets allowed. **Rates:** cabins, 1-4 people $57-$65; mobile homes $90; extra person charge $5; pets $5. Amex, Discover, Master Card, & Visa. **Directions:** located in Sun Lakes State Park on Hwy 17; 17 miles north of Soap Lake and 7 miles south of Coulee City.

COULEE DAM

(pop. 1,123) is located above Grand Coulee Dam, approximately 82 miles west of Spokane.

(KOO-lee) Dam, not to be confused with Grand Coulee, is located above the dam. The primary attraction here, of course, is Grand Coulee Dam. It has the world's largest laser light show, nightly Memorial Day through September 30.

Located in Grant County the sales/use taxes are 7.5%.

$62-$79 **FOUR WINDS GUEST HOUSE BED & BREAK-FAST**, 301 Lincoln St., Coulee Dam, WA 99116, **phone 509-633-3146 or 1-800-786-3146.** This B & B was built during the construction period of the dam and is the last of the government built homes still open to the public. It was originally the north dormitory for engineers during construction. Eleven nonsmoking rooms, 1 with private facilities; 2 rooms have adjoining shared bath; all others use separate men's and women's baths; all rooms have lavatories. Wake-up coffee/tea is available and a deluxe full gourmet breakfast is served at 8:30 a.m. The outdoor area provides BBQ grills and tables. Children over 8 welcome, no pets. **Rates:** $62-$79, taxes of 7.5% included. Discover, Amex, MasterCard, & Visa. **Directions:** 2 blocks from the visitor arrival center at the dam on Lincoln St. in Coulee Dam.

$49-$87 **PONDEROSA MOTEL**, 10 Lincoln St., Coulee Dam, WA 99116, phone 509-633-2100 or 1-800-633-6421, **fax 509-633-2633.** A total of 35 units, 95% nonsmoking, 2 equipped kitchenettes, and 2 jacuzzi suites. In-room amenities include phones, cable TV, coffee/tea making facilities, 11 rooms have refrigerators and micro-waves. Other amenities include outdoor heated pool, gift shop, espresso bar, and fax service. Children welcome, small pets allowed. Directly across the street from the dam and visitor arrival center. Within walking distance of restaurants, and 7 minutes to a 9 hole golf course. Close to water sports, fishing, movie theater, miniature golf, health club, etc. **Rates:** single room $49; double room $65; jacuzzi rooms $87; pets $10; local phone calls free. **Directions:** located on Hwy 155 directly across the street from Grand Coulee Dam and the visitor center.

COUPEVILLE see Whidbey Island for lodging.

CRYSTAL MOUNTAIN is located on the northeast side of Mt. Ranier. From Enumclaw follow Hwy 410.

At 7,000 feet, Crystal Mountain is Washington's highest destination ski resort. "Rainier Express," a high-speed quad chairlift takes you to the summit in 13 minutes. In the summer, ride the chairlift to the highest restaurant in the state, enjoy dinner and a breathtaking view of the sunset on Mt. Rainier. Also see Greenwater for lodging.

Located in Pierce County the sales/use/lodging taxes are 9.6%.

$40-$72   **ALPINE INN**, One Crystal Mt. Blvd., Crystal Mountain, WA 98022, phone 360-663-2262. *Open from November to April only, for the ski season.* 36 nonsmoking rooms, 8 units with private facilities, 28 with shared facilities. No coffee/tea making facilities, but there is a restaurant, bar, and deli on the grounds. Children welcome, no pets. Ski down from the lifts; fireplace in the lobby and bar. **Rates:** from $40 to $72; extra person $6. MasterCard & Visa. **Directions:** from Seattle take I-5 south, Exit 142A to Auburn. Follow 164 to Enumclaw and US 410 East for 33 miles. Left up the C.M. access road for 6 miles.

$58-$165 **CRYSTAL MOUNTAIN RESORT**, One Crystal Mt. Blvd., Crystal Mountain, WA 98022, phone 360-663-2265, fax 360-663-0145. *Open for summer.* 144 rooms in the summer. 25 hotel rooms and 30 condos are nonsmoking. All have private facilities and TV, no phones in the rooms. 100 units are family rooms. Two outdoor swimming pools, 1 sauna, 1 hot tub, tennis courts, horseshoe pits, mt. bike rentals, grocery store, post office, chair lift rides, Mt. Rainier viewing, sunset dinners from 7,000 feet, poolside cafe, two restaurants, 40 miles from transit. Children welcome, no pets.

Village Inn: offers inexpensive country style rooms for one or two with queen size or twin beds, a full bath, TV, VCR, and a refrigerator in each room. **Summer Rates:** $58, extra person $8. **Winter Rates:** $77.

Quicksilver Lodge: features queen size beds and private baths, designer fabric and custom furniture, TV, VCR, snack refrigerators and coffee makers. This savvy no-smoking hotel also offers double rooms or sleeping loft units which are ideal for the family. **Summer Rates:** 1-2 persons queen room $75, 1-4 person loft room $95. **Winter Rates:** queen room $95; loft room $110.

Silver Skis Chalet & Crystal Chalet Condos: completely equipped with kitchens and many with fireplaces. These condos are perfect for groups of 4 to 8. Silver Ski Chalet guests enjoy the exclusive use of a heated swimming pool. Crystal Chalet Condos - **Summer Rates**: 1 to 4 persons, 1 bedroom/$95, fireplace/$105; extra person $8. **Winter Rates:** $110-$143. Silver Skis Chalet Condos - **Summer Rates:** 1 to 4 persons, 1 bedroom/$105, fireplace/$115; 2 bedrooms/$135, fireplace/$145; extra person $8. **Winter Rates:** $115-$165. Amex, Visa, & MasterCard. **Directions:** from Enumclaw go through town, turn left on Roosevelt, which is also Hwy 410, stay on 410 for 35 miles to the Crystal Mt. access road, just before entering Mt. Rainier Natl. Park. Drive 6 miles up Crystal Mt. Blvd. to the resort.

CUSICK *(pop. 200) is located in the northeast corner of the state.*

(KYOO-sik) hosts the Pend Oreille County Fair with exhibits, horse shows, and a Blue Grass Festival.

Located in Pend Oreille County the sales/use taxes are 7.5%.

$32-$58 **BLUESLIDE RESORT & CAMPGROUND**, 400041 Hwy 20, Cusick, WA 99119, phone 509-445-1327. This scenic resort sits on the shore of the Pend Oreille River and offers year-round recreational activities. There are a total of 4 motel style units and 5 cabins. All the units have private facilities, the motel units also have a hot pot with coffee and tea. Cabins have fully equipped kitchens, 4 one bedroom cabins, 1 two bedroom cabin. Heated outdoor pool, playground for kids and adults, on 7.5 acres. The resort has a full service marina, country store, 50 R.V. sites, public restrooms, and showers. Children 3 and under free, pets allowed in RV park. **Rates:** motel room $32-$34; 1 bedroom cabin $43; 2 bedroom cabin $58; extra person $5. MasterCard, Visa, & Discover. **Directions:** from Spokane follow the Newport Hwy to Hwy 211, proceed on Hwy 211 for 19 miles, turn left at Hwy 20 junction, go to mile marker 400.

$40-$60 **The OUTPOST RESORT & RV PARK**, 405351 Hwy 20, Cusick, WA 99119, phone 509-445-1317. This small resort offers 3 small cabins, RV, and tent sites. The cabins sleep from 2 to 6 people. All with private facilities, fully equipped kitchens. Cabins are small, medium, and large. Restaurant on the premises is open from 6 a.m. to 8 p.m., 7 days a week. Children welcome, pets allowed on a leash. **Rates:** $40, $50, & $60; pets free. MasterCard & Visa. **Directions:** 12 miles north of Cusick, between Cusick and Ione on Hwy 20.

DARRINGTON (pop. 1,000) is located in the northwest corner of the state, about 30 miles east of I-5 on Hwy 530.

Darrington is the gateway to the North Cascades and Glacier Peak Wilderness. The major product of the community is the "green gold" of the forests, also outdoor recreational pursuits of all kinds. Hunting, fishing, whitewater rafting, archery, snowmobile grass drags, and rodeo are all big on the list. 30 miles southeast of Darrington is Kennedy Hot Springs. It is a 5 mile hike into the hot springs from the trailhead.

Located in Snohomish (snoh-HOH-mish) County the sales/use/lodging taxes are 10.2%.

$50 **HEMLOCK HILLS BED & BREAKFAST**, 612 Stillaguamish, P. O. Box 491, Darrington, WA 98241, phone 360-436-1274, or 1-800-520-1584. Two nonsmoking rooms with shared facilities on the main floor. Full country breakfast provided. This country home offers charm and hospitality from the hosts. There is a game room with TV, VCR, stereo, pool table, and a parlor with books. Children welcome, no pets. Within walking distance of restaurants and bus service. Family rates available. **Rates:** double $50. No credit cards. **Directions:** in Darrington take a right on Madison, go to stop sign and turn right. Go two blocks, then turn left on Stillaquamish, blue house on the left.

$50-$58 **SAUK RIVER FARM BED & BREAKFAST,** 32629 SR 530 NE, Darrington, WA 98241, phone 360-436-1794. Two nonsmoking rooms with shared facilities. This 19 acre farm reflects a gentle life-style with a touch of the past and present combined. Full

breakfast provided, TV in lounge, and a wood-fired outdoor hot tub. Children over 12 welcome, no pets. **Rates:** double $50; loft with sitting room $58; extra person $5; no charge for local phone calls. No credit cards. **Directions:** coming into town on route 530 from Arlington, turn left at stop sign and go 3.5 miles, first lane past Estes Rd.

Sauk River Farm Bed & Breakfast

DAVENPORT (pop. 1,495) is located on Hwy 2 between Spokane and Coulee Dam.

Davenport is a popular stopover spot for cross country bicyclers traveling on the rolling hills of Hwy 2. Many fishing lakes in the area and just 24 miles from Roosevelt Lake where houseboat rentals are available. Stop at the museum and get visitor information.

Located in Lincoln County the sales/use taxes are 7.6%. Also see Harrington for lodging.

$29-$44 **The BLACK BEAR,** 30 Logan, P. O. Box 106, Davenport, WA 99122, phone 509-725-7700. A total of 11 units, with 3 nonsmoking rooms. All units have refrigerators, coffee/tea making facilities, and cable TV with HBO. Children welcome, infants free, pets allowed. Within walking distance of restaurants, municipal pool, and park. **Rates**: single $29; double $34; family room $44; extra person $3; taxes included. Visa & MasterCard. **Directions**: on Hwy 2, east end of Davenport.

$37-$46 **DAVENPORT MOTEL**, 1205 Morgan, Davenport, WA 99122, phone 509-725-7071. This motel is a smoke free environment with 9 units. Rooms are wheelchair accessible, with paved parking by the door. Each room is attractively decorated. Coffee/tea making facilities in the rooms, phone, clock radios, AC, and cable TV with remote control. Children welcome, but capacity is limited, pets allowed by individual agreement. Restaurants, municipal pool, park, and museum within walking distance. **Rates**: single (1 bed) $37-$40; double $46; extra person $4; infants free; taxes included. No credit cards, personal checks okay. **Directions**: at the intersection of Hwy 2 and Hwy 28, west end of town.

DAYTON (pop. 2,600) is located in the southeast corner of the state, about 20 miles from the Oregon border on Hwy 12.

Dayton is rich in historical homes with 83 on the National Historic Register. The ornate courthouse and the Dayton Depot are also on the National Historic Register. Numerous recreational activities include skiing at Ski Bluewood, golfing, fishing, and hunting.
Located in Columbia County the sales/use taxes are 7.5%.

$36-$80 **BLUE MOUNTAIN MOTEL**, 414 Main, Dayton, WA 99328, phone 509-382-3040. A total of 23 units with 14 nonsmoking rooms. Phones and TV. No coffee/tea making facilities in the rooms, but available at the restaurant next door (opens at 6 a.m.). Children welcome, age 13 and under free with parents, pets allowed in smoking rooms. Within walking distance of restaurants and downtown shops. **Rates**: single (1 bed) $36-$40; double (2 beds) $42; suite $60-$80; extra person $4; rollaways $10; pets free. MasterCard & Visa. **Directions**: on Hwy 12, west end of Dayton.

$65-$110   The **WEINHARD HOTEL**, 235 E. Main St., Dayton, WA 99328, phone 509-382-4032, fax 509-382-2640. Orginally built by Jacob Weinhard (cousin to Henry) in 1889 to house the Weinhard Saloon and Lodge Hall, the hotel is a showcase of the era. This two story hotel has a Victorian roof garden for lounging. The 15 spacious rooms have high ceilings, overhead fans, and antique furnishings. Added modern conveniences include: queen beds, TV, phones, modem jack, tubs, and showers. One jacuzzi suite, and room 15 has French doors to the balcony. No coffee/tea making facilities in the rooms, but the Espresso Cafe opens at 7 a.m. for breakfast and lunch. Children welcome, pets allowed. "Romantic Getaway Package" available. **Rates**: single (1 bed) $65-$85; double (2 beds) $90; suite $110; youth bed $10; pets free. Amex, MasterCard, & Visa. **Directions:** downtown Dayton.

DEER HARBOR   see the San Juan Islands for lodging.

DEER PARK   see Spokane for lodging.

DEMING is located near the Canadian border, 8 miles east of Bellingham and I-5.

   The town's one tavern and one service station have been joined by the Nooksack Indian Tribe's new casino that opened in April, 1993. The Nooksack River Casino offers blackjack, craps, roulette, and poker games.
   Located in Whatcom (WHAHT-kuhm) County the sales/use taxes are 7.8%.

$60   The **GUEST HOUSE BED & BREAKFAST**, 5723 Schornbush Rd., Deming, WA 98244, phone 360-592-2343. This cottage type studio has a private entrance and offers quiet accommodations for two. The studio has a day bed trundle (makes into a king bed or twin beds), bathroom, TV, VCR, and equipped kitchenette. On your arrival a sparkling beverage awaits you and fixings for a country breakfast will be set up in your refrigerator. Relax on the swing next to a small stream or soak in the hot tub. Children are allowed, but space is tight, well-behaved pets allowed. **Rates**: double occupancy $60. MasterCard & Visa. **Directions:** from Bellingham, Exit 255 off I-5, follow the Mt. Baker Hwy for 14.5 miles, turn right on Hwy 9 south to Sedro Woolley, proceed 2 miles, turn left on Potter Rd, then left on Linnell Rd., right onto Schornbush.

$68-$78 **The LOGS RESORT**, 9002 Mt. Baker Hwy, Deming, WA 98244, phone 360-599-2711. Situated on Canyon Creek and the north fork of the Nooksack River, this resort offers 5 modern log cabins widely spaced along the creek among the trees. Each cabin features a natural rock fireplace, living room, fully equipped kitchen, bath, two bedrooms, each containing four twin size beds built bunk style. A double size hide-a-bed is in the living room. Outdoor solar heated pool, badminton, fishing, and hiking in the summer. In the winter, downhill and cross country skiing at Mt. Baker. Children welcome, pets allowed. **Winter Rates**: *minimum 2 nights, 3 on holiday weekends* - double occupancy $78; extra person (adults) $10, children $6; pets $3. **Summer Rates:** *4/01 to 10/31* - double occupancy $68. Weekly rates in summer only. **Directions:** from Bellingham take Hwy 542 east for 30.5 miles; 18 miles from Nooksack Casino, between Maple Falls and Glacier.

EASTSOUND

is on Orcas Island, the largest island in the San Juans. This thriving community has much to offer in the individual shops and gourmet restaurants. For lodging see the San Juan Islands.

EAST WENATCHEE

is in Douglas County, across the Columbia River from Wenatchee. For lodging see Wenatchee.

EATONVILLE (pop. 1,435) is located 30 miles southeast of Tacoma, 25 miles from Mount Rainier Park.

The community of Eatonville values its logging and lumbering past, but today boasts a diverse economy. An abundance of lakes and streams makes the Eatonville area a fishing paradise.

Located in Pierce County the sales/use/lodging taxes are 9.6%.

$49-$59 **MALCOM'S MILL VILLAGE MOTEL**, P. O. Box 609, Eatonville, WA 98328, phone 360-832-3200, fax 360-832-3203, reservations 1-800-832-3248. This modern two story motel offers 32 rooms, 26 nonsmoking. Rooms have phones and TV with

HBO. 11 units each have a wet bar with sink, refrigerator, and microwave (no cookware or dishes). No coffee/tea making facilities in the rooms, but available in the lobby. Three restaurants within walking distance. Conference and meeting room with a capacity of 50 people. Children 12 and under free, no pets. **Summer Rates:** *6/01 to 9/30* - single room (1 bed) $53-$55; one queen bed with wet bar $59; double room (2 queen beds) $59; extra person $5; local phone calls free. **Winter Rates:** $49-$55. Major credit cards accepted. **Directions:** from the north on Hwy 161 coming into Eatonville turn left at the stoplight, on Center St.

EDMONDS (pop. 31, 500) is located north of Seattle, from I-5 take Exit 177 for approximately 10 miles.

This residential waterfront community is located on Puget Sound. The Kingston/Edmonds ferry dock is at the foot of Dayton Street. The pier is the first public salt water pier constructed in the state, specifically designed for fishing.

Located in Snohomish (snoh-HOH-mish) County the sales/use/lodging taxes are 10.2%.

$85

DAYTON BED & BREAKFAST, 522 Dayton, Edmonds, WA 98020, phone 206-778-3611. One upstairs apartment overlooking the water, nonsmoking. Private entrance, living room, fully equipped kitchen, washer/dryer, TV, one queen bed, and 2 twins in a separate bedroom. Breakfast tray at the door. **Rates:** double occupancy $85; extra person $10. No credit cards. **Directions:** take Exit 177 from I-5 to Edmonds, turn right on Dayton.

$52-$89

EDMONDS HARBOR INN, 130 W. Dayton, Edmonds, WA 98020, phone 206-771-5021 or 1-800-441-8033. Located in the heart of Edmonds. The waterfront, marina, ferry terminal, and public pier are all within one block. This two story modern facility has 61 rooms, 40 nonsmoking and 9 have equipped kitchens. Phones and TV with HBO. No coffee/tea making facilities in the rooms, but a continental breakfast is available in the lobby. Free parking. Children 12 and under free, no pets. **Summer Rates:** *4/15 to 10/15* - single room (1 bed) $57-$67; double (2 beds); kitchen units $67-$89; extra person $5; rollaway $10; local phone calls free. **Winter Rates:** prices reduced 10%. Most major credit cards. **Directions:** take Exit 177 from I-5, west on 205th St. N. to the harbor.

$55-$65 **HARRISON HOUSE BED & BREAKFAST**, 210 Sunset Ave., Edmonds, WA 98020, phone 206-776-4748. Two rooms with private facilities are available in this new, informal, waterfront home. The spacious rooms have phones, TV, and coffee/tea making facilities. The room on the lower level has a private entrance and queen bed. The second floor room has a king bed and private deck overlooking the water. Full breakfast provided. Adults only, no pets, and no smoking. **Rates:** $55 & $65; $10 less for second night. No credit cards. **Directions:** take Exit 177 from I-5 to Edmonds ferry dock, Harrison House is one block north of the ferry dock.

TRAVELODGE, 23825 Highway 99, Edmonds, WA 98026, phone 206-771-8008 or 1-800-771-8009.

$45-$50 **HUDGENS HAVEN BED & BREAKFAST,** 9313 190th SW, Edmonds, WA 98020, phone 206-776-2202. One nonsmoking guest room with private facilities, furnished in colonial style antiques with a queen size bed. Continental breakfast provided. Children and pets by arrangement. Located in a quiet neighborhood with a striking view of the Olympic Mountains. Ample parking at the back of the house. **Rates:** single $45; double $50. No credit cards. **Directions:** take Exit 177 from I-5, follow Hwy 104 into Edmonds, turn left on Main St., right on 3rd Ave., follow Hwy 524 East signs 1 mile, turn left on Olympic View Dr., proceed 1/4 mile and turn right on 190th.

$39-$54 **K & E MOTOR INN,** 23921 Highway 99, Edmonds, WA 98020, phone 206-778-2181, fax 206-778-1516. A total of 32 rooms, 10 nonsmoking, 4 with kitchenettes, and 4 with kitchens. Basic cookware and dishes available at the office. Phones and TV. No coffee/tea making facilities in the rooms, but a continental breakfast is provided and restaurants are within walking distance. Children welcome, pets allowed. **Rates:** single $39; double $44; family room $54; extra person $5; local phone calls free; pets $5. Major credit cards accepted. **Directions:** take Exit 177 from I-5; follow Edmonds - Kingston Ferry (104W) and then take Hwy 99 north. Right turn at stop sign; first motel on your right.

$45-$50 **MAPLE TREE BED & BREAKFAST**, 18313 Olympic View Dr., Edmonds, WA 98020, phone 206-774-8420. One guest room with private facilities. Sitting room, queen bed, and balcony overlooking the sound and Olympic Mts. Choice of continental or full breakfast. Children okay, no pets, smoking permitted on the balcony. **Rates:** single $45; double $50; extra person $10; full breakfast $5 extra. No credit cards. **Directions:** take Exit 181 from I-5, turn west on 196th, proceed 3 miles to Olympic View, turn right, go 1 mile to High St., make right U-turn into driveway. SE corner of High and Olympic View Dr.

• ELBE is located 43 miles from Tacoma on the road to Mount Rainier National Park.

(EL-bee) is home of The Cascadian Dinner Train, a joint venture of the Mt. Rainier Scenic Railroad and the Mt. Rainier Dining Co. The ride is a 40 mile, 4 hour railroad excursion through breathtaking scenery. It is available from April through November. Or enjoy the one and one half hour trip from Elbe to Mineral Lake, weekends, Memorial Day through September.

Located in Pierce County the sales/use/lodging taxes are 9.6%.

$48   **EAGLES NEST MOTEL**, 52120 Mountain Hwy E., Eatonville, WA 98328, phone 360-569-2533. Ten cozy motel units overlook Alder Lake and have views of the mountains. TV, coffee/tea making facilities, queen beds, and 5 equipped kitchen units. Children under 18 free with parents, small pets okay. RV park with hookups. **Rates:** $48. MasterCard, Visa, & Discover. **Directions:** on Hwy 7, seven miles east of Eatonville, three miles before Elbe.

$70-$85   **HOBO INN**, 54106 Mountain Hwy E., P. O. Box 20, Elbe, WA 98330, phone 360-569-2500. Eight renovated cabooses offer unique lodging. The vintage cabooses date from 1916 to 1954. Each unit is air-conditioned and has been carefully outfitted with bed and bathroom, retaining many of the original features. One caboose has a full size bed and hot tub, one with a jacuzzi tub, two have 2 full size beds, and the others each have one full size bed. Two brightly painted dining cars are open 365 days a year for breakfast, lunch, and dinner. **Summer Rates:** two to four people $70-$85. MasterCard, Visa, & Discover. **Directions:** on Hwy 7, about 12 miles east of Eatonville.

see photo, next page

The Hobo Inn - Elbe

ELECTRIC CITY

(pop. 915) is 84 miles west of Spokane and is within three miles of Grand Coulee Dam.

One of three towns that cluster around Grand Coulee Dam. Also see Coulee Dam for lodgings.

Located in Grant County the sales/use/lodging taxes are 7.5%.

$47-$80   **SKY DECK MOTEL**, P. O. Box 325, Electric City, WA 99123, phone 509-633-0290.   Located on Banks Lake, you can fish from the yard. 21 units, 6 nonsmoking, and 5 kitchenettes. Phones, TV, outdoor pool, and hot tub. No coffee/tea making facilities in the rooms, but there is a restaurant within walking distance. Boat rentals and launch facilities located adjacent to the motel; seasonal rates; 5 minutes from Dam Tours and Laser Light Show. Children welcome, small pets allowed. **Rates:** single $47; double $60; suite $70-$80; extra person $5; pets $5; local phone calls free. Major credit cards. **Directions:** on Hwy 155, 3 miles southwest of Grand Coulee Dam on Banks Lake.

ELLENSBURG

(pop. 12,570) is located in the center of the state along Interstate 90.

This community offers arts, antiques, and agriculture. Ellensburg is the home of Central Washington University and the county seat of Kittitas County. Prior to its historic fire in 1889, that destroyed most of the business district, Ellensburg planned to petition Congress to be the state capital. A mansion was even built to house the governor on East 3rd Street. Although it did not become the capital, it was given the "Normal School" which is now Central Washington University. Some of the motels raise their rates during Rodeo Weekend.

Located in Kittitas (KIT-i-tas) County the sales/use taxes are 7.5%.

$49-$74 **ELLENSBURG INN Best Western**, 1700 Canyon Rd., Ellensburg, WA 98926, phone 509-925-9801, reservations 1-800-321-8791. 105 rooms, 58 nonsmoking. In-room amenities include phones, TV, and coffee/tea making facilities. Other amenities are the indoor pool, jacuzzi, fitness center, restaurant, lounge, and meeting rooms. Children 12 and under free, pets allowed. **Summer Rates:** single rooms $59; double $64; suites $74; extra person $5; local phone calls free. **Winter Rates:** $49-$64. Major credit cards. **Directions:** from I-90 Exit 109 to Canyon Road.

$34-$54 **I-90 INN MOTEL**, 1390 Dollarway No., Ellensburg, WA 98926, phone 509-925-9844. Two story motel close to restaurants and mini-mart. 73 rooms, 45 nonsmoking. Rooms have phones and cable TV. No coffee/tea making facilities in the rooms, but available in the lobby. Children 12 and under free, small pets allowed. Large parking lot for truck parking. **Summer Rates:** *5/15 to 10/15* - $40-$54; extra person $6; pets $5. **Winter Rates:** $34-$42. Major credit cards. **Directions:** just off I-90 at Exit 106.

$55-$60 **MURPHY'S COUNTRY BED & BREAKFAST**, 2830 Thorp Hwy So., Ellensburg, WA 98926, phone 509-925-7986. A turn-of-the-century frontier home has been carefully maintained in its original style. Two nonsmoking guest rooms have been refurbished to provide the visitor with turn-of-the-century style and twentieth century comfort. Shared facilities, queen beds, and a full breakfast. Located across the road from the Ellensburg Golf Course. Cross country ski on the golf course during the winter months. Children - some restrictions, no pets. **Rates:** single $55; double $60; extra person $15. Amex, MasterCard, & Visa. **Directions:** Exit 106 off I-90, turn at the KOA onto Thorp Hwy, continue on past Robinson Canyon Rd., second house on the left.

$40-$47 **NITES INN MOTEL,** 1200 S. Ruby, Ellensburg, WA 98926, phone 509-962-9600. 32 units, 13 nonsmoking. In-room amenities include phones and TV. Some rooms have refrigerators and microwaves. Morning coffee and tea are available in the lobby. Park-like grounds with barbecues. Restaurants within walking distance. Children 10 and under free, pets allowed. **Rates:** single room $40; double room $47; extra person $5; children 10 and over $2; pets $6; rollaways $8; refrigerators $3. Major credit cards. **Directions:** take Exit 109 off I-90, turn right, go a fourth of a mile, turn right at McDonalds.

$28-$51 **RAINBOW MOTEL,** 1025 Cascade Way, Ellensburg, WA 98926, phone 509-925-3544. Nine rooms, 7 non-smoking, all on one level. In-room amenities include phones and TV. No coffee/tea making facilities in the rooms. Guest laundry, picnic tables, and barbecue. Children welcome, no pets. **Summer Rates:** *5/01 to 9/30* -single room $38; double room $51. **Winter Rates:** single $28; double $41. MasterCard & Visa. **Directions:** Exit 106 off I-90, proceed east, motel on the left.

$35-$85 **THUNDERBIRD MOTEL & RESTAURANT,** 403 W. 8th Ave., Ellensburg, WA 98926, phone 509-925-5700 or 509-962-9856, reservations 1-800-843-3492. 72 units, 40 nonsmoking. In-room amenities include phones and TV. Morning coffee is available in the restaurant on the premises. Seasonal outdoor pool. Lounge on the premises features live entertainment on Friday and Saturday nights. Children 12 and under free, pets allowed. **Rates:** single room $35-$45; double room $44-$56; family room $55-$85; pets free; local phone calls free. Major credit cards. **Directions:** Exit 106 off I-90, come to 4-way stop, go straight for 2-3 miles, on the left side of the road.

$34-$120 **TRAVELER'S REGAL LODGE,** 300 W. 6th Ave., Ellensburg, WA 98926, phone 509-925-2547 or 1-800-523-4972. This two story motel has 30 rooms, 24 nonsmoking. In-room amenities include phones, cable TV, and coffee making facilities. Two units have equipped kitchenettes with refrigerators and microwaves. Other amenities include indoor pool open year-round. Children 6 and under free, outdoor kennel for pets. **Rates:** single (1 person) $34; double (2 people) $40; suite $60; extra person $10. **Rodeo Weekend Rates:** single $50; double $56; suite $69-$120. Major credit cards. **Directions:** Exit 106 off I-90, east to Water St., then right 2 blocks.

ELMA (pop. 3,000) is 27 miles west of Olympia on Hwy 8.

The most impressive structure in the area is the Satsop Powerplant. It is located 5 miles southwest of Hwy 12. Tours are conducted on Fridays and Saturdays.

Located in Grays Harbor County the sales/use/lodging taxes are 10.9%.

$10 **GRAYS HARBOR HOSTEL**, 6 Ginny Lane, Elma, WA 98541, phone 360-482-3119. Situated on 8 acres between Olympia and Grays Harbor the hostel is 42 miles from the ocean beaches. Hostel facilities include small dormitory and family rooms, large common room, 3 bathrooms, kitchen, self-service bicycle repair shop, storage area, outdoor hot tub, and picnic area. There are two sets of beds per room, the bottom bunk is a large double. Linen is provided if necessary. Well-behaved children okay, no pets. Check-in time 5 p.m. to 9 p.m., closed during the day. From Olympia take the Grays Harbor Transit #40. **Rates:** $10 per person; groups of 4 or more $8 per person. No credit cards. **Directions:** west of Olympia, turn right off Hwy 8 onto Fairgrounds Rd., first house on the right.

ENUMCLAW (pop. 7,450) is located approximately 25 miles east of Tacoma on Hwy 410.

(EE-nuhm-klaw) is known as the gateway to Mt. Rainier. This small, friendly community is located only 45 minutes from Sea Tac Airport and 33 miles from the foothills of Mt. Rainier. The pastoral land is noted for horse breeding.

Located in King County the sales/use taxes are 8.2%, lodgings with 60 or more units add another 2.8% for a total of 11%.

$40-$50 **KING'S MOTEL,** 1334 Roosevelt Ave. E., Enumclaw, WA 98022, phone 360-825-1626. This two story, well-kept motel has 44 rooms, 50% nonsmoking. Phones, basic cable TV, laundry room, AC, and balcony or patios. Queen, double, or twin beds. No coffee/tea making facilities in the rooms. There are 15 units available with kitchens, but cookware and dishes are not furnished. Seasonal outdoor pool and a fenced lawn area for pets. Children 16 and under free with parents, pets allowed. Within walking distance of two restaurants. **Rates:** single room (1 bed) $40; double (2 beds) $50; extra person $5; pets $5; local phone calls 50¢. Most major credit cards. **Directions:** north of King County Fairgrounds on Hwy 410. One mile east of town center.

$63-$75 **PARK CENTER MOTEL Best Western,** 1000 Griffin, Enumclaw, WA 98022, phone 360-825-4490, fax 360-825-3686. Two story motel with 40 rooms, 30 nonsmoking. All rooms have two queen beds and access to a landscaped, lighted courtyard with a fountain. Indoor spa and exercise facility. No coffee/tea making facilities in the rooms, but room service is available and the restaurant opens at 7:00 a.m. Each room has cable TV, telephone, and individual temperature control. Children 12 and under free, pets allowed. **Rates:** single room (1 bed) $63; double room (2 beds) $66-$75; extra person $5; pets $25 per night; local phone calls free. Major credit cards. **Directions:** centrally located downtown on the main street.

$85-$95 **The WHITE ROSE INN BED & BREAKFAST,** 1610 Griffin Ave., Enumclaw, WA 98022, phone 360-825-7194 or 1-800-404-7194. Classic elegance in this 1922 colonial mansion. A sweeping staircase in the spacious foyer leads to four guest rooms on the second floor, all with private facilities, all are nonsmoking. Enjoy two fireplaces in the winter or large deck and rose garden in summer. A full gourmet breakfast is provided. Children 12 and older, no pets. The White Rose Inn specializes in wedding receptions and special occasions. **Rates:** double occupancy $85-$95; extra person - child $10, adult $20; local phone calls free. MasterCard & Visa. **Directions:** from the north follow Hwy 164 into Enumclaw, this becomes Griffin Ave.; from the south follow Hwy 410 into Enumclaw, go left at sign to Renton/Auburn, follow Cole St. to Initial Ave., go left 3 blocks to Franklin, on the corner of Franklin and Griffin.

EPHRATA (pop. 5,470) is located in the center of the state in the Columbia Basin.

(e-FRAY-tuh) is five minutes away from Soap Lake at the junction of SR 282 and SR 283. This farming community offers the Grant County Museum and Pioneer Village. A small airfield has become home to a considerable number of glider pilots. The thermals in this area are some of the best in the U.S.

Located in Grant County the sales/use taxes are 7.5%.

$32-$52 **COLUMBIA MOTEL**, 1257 Basin SW, Ephrata, WA 98823, phone 509-754-5226. 15 rooms, 8 nonsmoking. All units have equipped kitchens, TV, phones, and AC. Within walking distance of restaurants. Shuttle provided for fly-ins to Ephrata Airport. Picnic and barbecue area. Children welcome, pets allowed. Six blocks to city park and public pool. **Summer Rates:** single room (1 bed) $42.50; double room (2 to 4 people) $52.50; pets $8; local phone calls free; taxes included. **Winter Rates:** *10/01 to 5/31* - $10 less. MasterCard & Visa. **Directions:** centrally located on the main street of Ephrata.

Ivy Chapel Inn Bed & Breakfast

$55-$100 **IVY CHAPEL INN BED & BREAKFAST**, 164 "D" St. SW, Ephrata, WA 98823, phone 509-754-0629. A 1940's Presbyterian Church has been converted to a bed and breakfast. The three story brick building has six unique theme rooms, including a Victorian bridal suite, all have private facilities. Guest rooms are located on the second and third floors. The chapel is used for reunions, weddings, conferences, etc. Full breakfast is served in the sunny morning room located on the second floor. Open-air deck with a large hot tub is provided. Within 25 miles of the Gorge amphitheater. Children by arrangement, no pets, no smoking. **Rates:** single $55; double occupancy $70; suite $100; extra person $10; local phone calls free. MasterCard & Visa. **Directions:** in Ephrata turn off 2nd Ave. SW and go two blocks.

$35-$50 **SHARLYN MOTEL**, 848 Basin SW, Ephrata, WA 98823, phone 509-754-3575 or 1-800-292-2965. 17 rooms, 6 nonsmoking. All units have TV, phones, king or queen beds, AC, and coffee/tea making facilities. 13 units have refrigerators. Within walking distance of a restaurant. Shuttle provided to the airport. Children welcome, infants free, no pets. **Rates:** single (1 person) $35; double room (2 people) $50; extra person $8; local phone calls free. Major credit cards. **Directions:** on Ephrata's main street, south end of town.

•EVERETT (pop. 70,000) is located 27 miles north of Seattle and 115 mils south of Vancouver, B.C.

(EV-er-it) Things to see and do: Everett Symphony, Animal Farm petting zoo, beachcombing, Jetty Island interpretive walks, Kayak Point State Park, boat tours to Deception Pass, and dinner cruise to Langley. Snohomish River Queen paddlewheel boat offers dinner, lunch, and Sunday brunch cruises. For many years, Everett was a lumber port and mill town, now it has turned to more high tech industries such as Boeing.

Located in Snohomish (snoh-HOH-mish) County the sales/use/lodging taxes are 9.9%.

$69-$87 **CASCADIA INN Best Western,** 2800 Pacific Ave., Everett, WA 98201, phone 206-258-4141, reservations 1-800-448-5544-2-2, fax 206-258-4755. A total of 134 rooms, 83 nonsmoking. All units have remote control TV with AM/FM radios, phones, and in-room coffee makers. The hotel features a free continental breakfast, heated pool, whirlpool spa, guest laundry, fax machine, and safe deposit boxes. Children welcome, ages 12 and under free, pets allowed. **Rates:** single (1 person) $69-$79; double (2 people) $77-$87; extra person $8; local phone calls free. Major credit cards. **Directions:** from the south Exit 193 from I-5 to Pacific Ave., go west two blocks; from the north, Exit 194 from I-5 to Hewitt Ave, go west two blocks to Cedar St., turn left to Pacific.

$30-$45 **CHERRY MOTEL,** 8421 Evergreen Way, Everett, WA 98208, phone 206-347-1100. 65 rooms, 33 non-smoking. All units have TV and phones. No coffee/tea making facilities in the rooms, but available in the lobby. Children welcome, ages 12 and under free, small pets allowed. **Winter Rates:** single room $30-$33; double room $38; family room (up to 4 people) $40; pets $5; local phone calls free. **Summer Rates:** add $3 to $5 more. Major credit cards. **Directions:** from I-5, Exit 189 west, Mukilteo 529 to Evergreen Way, turn left and go through 2 lights, behind Denny's.

COMFORT INN, 1602 S.E. Everett Mall Way, Everett, WA 98208, phone 206-355-1570, fax 206-347-3381, 1-800-221-2222.

CYPRESS INN, 12619 4th Ave. W., Everett, WA 98208, phone 206-347-9099, fax 206-348-3048, or 1-800-752-9991.

DAYS INN, 1122 N. Broadway, Everett, WA 98201, phone 206-252-8000, reservations 1-800-845-9490.

$33-$47 **FAR WEST MOTEL,** 6030 Evergreen Way, South Everett, WA 98203, phone 206-355-3007. 20 rooms, 8 nonsmoking, and 13 non-equipped kitchen units. All units have TV with HBO and phones. No coffee/tea making facilities in the rooms. Children welcome, ages 11 and under free, no pets. **Rates:** single room $33-$40; double room $40-$47; extra person $5; local phone calls free. MasterCard, Visa, & Amex. **Directions:** from I-5, Exit 189 west to Evergreen Way, turn right and go north to the Far West.

$30-$42 **TOPPERS MOTEL,** 1030 N. Broadway, Everett, WA 98201, phone 206-259-3151. 32 rooms, 2 nonsmoking, and 15 equipped kitchen units. All units have TV and phones. No coffee/tea making facilities in the rooms, but available in the lobby. Three rooms available for children, infants free, no pets. **Rates:** single room $30-$35;

double room $39-$42; extra person $3; local phone calls free. Major credit cards. **Directions:** from the south on I-5, take Exit 192 left to Broadway; from the north, take Exit 198 to Hwy 529, which is Broadway.

TRAVELODGE, 3030 Broadway, Everett, WA 98201, phone 206-259-6141 or 1-800-578-7878.

WELCOME MOTOR INN, 1205 N. Broadway, Everett, WA 98201, phone 206-252-8828, reservations 1-800-252-5512, fax 206-252-8880.

EVERSON (pop. 1,575) is 8 miles south of the Canadian border and 19 miles northeast of Bellingham. (EE-ver-suhn)

$35   **WILKIN'S FARM BED & BREAKFAST,** 4165 S. Pass Rd., Everson, WA 98247, phone 360-966-7616. Twenty acre country farm with three guest rooms that share two bathrooms, one with a shower and one with a tub. TV in the parlor, coffee available in the kitchen. Full Sicilian breakfast with wine or fruit juice provided. Wood stove in the kitchen. Children welcome, no pets. Fifteen minutes from Silver Lake, 50 minutes from Mt. Baker. **Rates:** double occupancy $35; children 12 and under $5; extra person $10. No credit cards. **Directions:** from Everson continue northeast towards the mountains for 3 miles, look for address on the mail box.

FERNDALE (pop. 6,000) is located in the northwest corner of the state between Bellingham and the U.S./Canadian border, just off I-5.

Ferndale is close to Birch Bay for swimming and clamming or skiing at Mt. Baker in the winter. Pioneer Park has the largest collection of log structures in Washington. Hovander Homestead Park features a restored turn-of-the-century farmhouse, big red barn, and one mile of river beach. In and around the barn are animals and antique farm implements. Major industries include BP Oil, Arco, and Intalco Aluminum.

Located in Whatcom (WHAHT-kuhm) County the sales/use taxes are 7.8%.

$27-$40 **ALICE & PAUL LARSON DAIRY BED & BREAK-FAST** 2780 Aldergrove Rd., Ferndale, WA 98248, phone 360-384-4835. This is a working dairy farm with 3 guest rooms available. One with private facilities, 2 with shared. Smoking is okay, but not in the bedrooms. Local phone calls free, but no phones in the rooms. There is TV in one room and in the parlor. Full farm breakfast served. Family atmosphere, children welcome, and pets allowed. Get a hands-on experience of life on a dairy farm. Help feed the baby calves, gather eggs, and watch the milking. **Rates:** single room $27; double $40; children $7. Credit cards accepted. **Directions:** call from Ferndale, someone will meet you.

$45 **MOUNTAIN VIEW BED & BREAKFAST**, 5659 Olson Rd., Ferndale, WA 98248, phone 360-384-3693. Enjoy a quiet country setting on this 200 acre cattle ranch. There are two guest rooms with shared facilities. TV in the parlor, country walking areas, and fish ponds. View of Mt. Baker, close to Canada, historic park, lakes, and the Alaska Ferry. Full country breakfast provided. Children welcome, infants free, no pets. **Rates:** double room $45; extra person $10. No credit cards accepted. **Directions:** from I-5 take Exit 262 into Ferndale, continue west on Mt. View Rd., 2 miles out of town. When you reach Olson Rd. turn left, first house.

$35-$46 **SCOTTISH LODGE MOTEL**, 5671 Riverside Dr., Ferndale, WA 98248, phone 360-384-4040, fax 360-380-1111. Located on the golf course, this motel has 97 rooms, 75 nonsmoking. Queen beds, cable TV, and phones in every room. No coffee/tea making facilities in the rooms, but available in the lobby. Outdoor pool. Children 12 and under free, pets by arrangement. **Rates:** single $35-$38; double $43-$46; pets $5; extra person $5; no charge for local phone calls. Major credit cards accepted. **Directions:** from I-5 take Exit 262.

$65-$85 **SLATER HERITAGE HOUSE BED & BREAK-FAST**, 1371 W. Axton Rd., Ferndale, WA 98248, phone 360-384-4273. There are four nonsmoking guest rooms with private facilities in this completely restored Victorian home. TV in parlor, house phone available. Family atmosphere, children welcome, no pets. Five and a half miles from Bellis Fair Mall, easy driving distance to Mt. Baker for skiing or hiking, day trips to Canada, on the Bellingham bus route. **Rates:** double occupancy $65-$85; extra person $10. MasterCard & Visa. **Directions:** from I-5 take Exit 262 east 1 mile, down Axton Rd. on the right side of road.

FIFE (pop. 3,870) is located between Tacoma and south Seattle.

Located in King County the sales/use taxes are 8.2%. Lodging tax of 2.8% applies to lodgings with 60 or more units for a total of 11% taxes.

COMFORT INN, 5601 Pacific Hwy E., Fife, WA 98424, phone 206-926-2301 or 1-800-221-2222.

DAYS INN, 3021 Pacific Hwy E., Fife, WA 98424, phone 206-922-3500 or 1-800-DAYS-INN.

EXECUTIVE INN Best Western, 5700 Pacific Hwy E., Fife, WA 98424, phone 206-922-0080 or 1-800-938-8500.

$30-$50 **HOMETEL INN,** 3520 Pacific Hwy E., Fife, WA 98424, phone 206-922-0555, 1-800-258-3520, fax 206-922-0690. Two story motel with 108 spacious rooms, 45% nonsmoking. Phones, TV with HBO (some remote controls). No coffee/tea making facilities in the rooms, but available in the lobby. Seasonal outdoor pool, laundry facilities, restaurant and lounge on the premises. Children 5 and under free, pets allowed. **Rates:** single room (1 bed) $30-$36; double room (2 beds) $40-$50; extra person $5; pets, one time charge $10; no charge for local phone calls. Major credit cards accepted. **Directions:** from the south take Exit 136B off I-5; from the north take Exit 136; use same entrance as Econo Lodge.

$30-$46 **KINGS MOTOR INN,** 5115 Pacific Hwy E., Fife, WA 98424, phone 206-922-3636 or 1-800-929-3509. Two story motel with 43 rooms, 20 nonsmoking. Phones and TV with HBO. No coffee/tea making facilities in the rooms, but available in the lobby. Laundry facilities and five equipped kitchen units. Children 12 and under free, pets allowed. Across from shopping center, sits back from the highway, large parking area. The motel was remodeled in early 1994. **Rates:** single room (1 bed) $30-$37; double room (2 beds) $46; extra person $5; pets, one time charge $5; no charge for local phone calls; taxes included. Most major credit cards accepted. **Directions:** from I-5 Exit 137, turn left on Pacific Hwy and proceed two blocks.

$56-$79 **ROYAL COACHMAN INN,** 5805 Pacific Hwy E., Fife, WA 98424, phone 206-922-2500 or 1-800-422-3051, fax 206-922-6443. This Tudor style motel has 94 rooms, 55 nonsmoking. Rooms have phones, instant coffee maker, TV with remote control and Showtime. 30 rooms have microwaves and refrigerators. One family style apartment with a small kitchen is available. Guest laundry. Access to an athletic club is 1 mile away. Full service restaurant is open from 6:00 a.m. to 7:30 p.m. during the week, 6:00 a.m. to 9:30 p.m. on weekends. Children 12 and under free, pets allowed. **Rates:** single room $56-$62; double room $62; family room $79; extra person $6; pets refundable deposit of $25; no charge for local phone calls. Major credit cards accepted. **Directions:** from I-5 take Exit 137 west to Pacific Hwy.

TRAVELERS INN, 4221 Pacific Hwy E., Fife, WA 98424, phone 206-922-9520 or 1-800-633-8300.

FORKS (pop. 3,310) is located in the northwest corner of the state on Hwy 101, nestled between the Olympic Mts. and the Pacific Ocean.

Forks is the ideal "base camp" for exploring the natural wonders on the Olympic Peninsula's north end. In addition to its proximity to the spectacular rain forests, beaches, lakes, rivers and mountains, the community offers a full range of services. Guided adventures include: river rafting, salmon & steelhead fishing, deer, elk & bear hunting, horseback rides, mountain biking, mushroom hunting, and scenic flight tours.

Located in Clallam County the sales/use taxes are 7.9%.

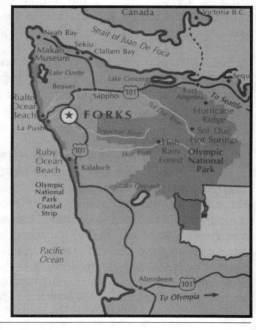

$50-$60 **FISHERMAN'S WIDOW BED & BREAKFAST**, 31 Huckleberry Lane, Forks, WA 98331, phone 360-374-5693. Two guest rooms on the main floor share facilities. The rooms are decorated with the outdoorsman in mind yet accented with a touch of lace. Breakfast features continental gourmet treats. Children ten and older, no pets, smoking allowed outside. **Rates:** double occupancy $50-$60; extra person $10. No credit cards; cash, personal checks, and traveler's checks. **Directions:** north end of town, turn west on Olympic Dr., which turns into Huckleberry Lane, second house on the left.

$44-$69 **FORKS MOTEL**, 351 Forks Ave. So., Forks, WA 98331, phone 360-374-6243, reservations 1-800-544-3416, fax 360-374-6760. This motel has 73 rooms, 40 nonsmoking, and 8 equipped kitchen units with 2 bedrooms. King, queen, and double beds, remote control cable TV, and phones in the rooms. No coffee/tea making facilities in the rooms, but available in the lobby. Outdoor pool, laundromat, and 12 mini-suites with microwaves and refrigerators. Children 12 and under free, no pets. **Rates:** single (1 bed) $44-$47; double (2 beds) $53-$56; mini-suite $66-$69; extra person $3; no charge for local phone calls. Major credit cards accepted. **Directions:** center of town on Hwy 101.

$35-$40 **FOSSIL CREEK RANCH LODGING**, 9772 Oil City Rd., Forks, WA 98331, phone 360-374-2553. One lodge, sleeps up to 6 people. Two bedrooms, two baths, fully equipped kitchen, and a hide-a-bed in the living room. Wood stove, plus electric heat. No phones or TV to interrupt your serenity. Listen to the peaceful sounds of the Hoh River contrasting with the roar of the Pacific Ocean. Within walking distance is the mouth of the river where it empties into the sea. Hiking, beachcombing, and fishing are favorite pastimes. Children under 5 free, no pets. **Summer Rates:** *July & August* - double occupancy $40; extra person $5. **Winter Rates:** *open January & February weather permitting, call ahead* - $35. No credit cards. **Directions:** 13.5 miles south of Forks, turn right on Oil City Rd., between mileposts 178 and 177, proceed for 9.8 miles, check in at the big white house on the right.

$30-$60 **HOH HUMM RANCH**, 171763 Hwy 101, Box 780, Forks, WA 98331, phone 360-374-5337. A working ranch with 5 lodgings, from single rooms to family size. All lodgings are nonsmoking with shared facilities. No phones, TV, or coffee/tea making facilities in the rooms, but a full breakfast is provided. The ranch is home to llamas, Sika deer, antelope, cattle, sheep, and goats. Located on the Hoh River, you can fish from the banks. Nearest restaurant is 13 miles south for meals other than breakfast. Children 16 and under free with parents, one room will accommodate pets. **Rates:** double occupancy $30-$60; extra person $10. No credit cards. **Directions:** 20 miles south of Forks on Hwy 101, milepost 172, west side of Hwy.

$52-$150 **KALALOCH LODGE, 157151 Hwy 101, Forks, WA 98331, phone 360-962-2271.** Perched on a bluff overlooking the Pacific Ocean, the lodge has a total of 57 accommodations; 39 individual cottages, 8 lodge rooms, and 10 suites. The lodge has 8 rooms, 4 with ocean views, a gift shop, dining room, lounge, coffee shop, and reading room. All the cabins have private facilities and non-equipped kitchenettes. The bluff cabins are ideal for families and groups, all have ocean views. Most of the cabins have Franklin-style fireplaces. Firewood is provided, bring utensils for cooking and eating. The suites offer quiet, roomy units with decks facing the ocean, 3 have fireplaces. Children under 5 free, pets allowed only in the cabins. A path leads down to the beach. **High Season Rates:** lodge rooms, double occupancy $80; cottages $99-$150; extra person $10; pets $10 per night. **Off Season:** *10/29 to 4/27* - $52-$62; ocean view cottages same price year-round. Major credit cards. **Directions:** on coast Hwy 101, 35 miles south of Forks, 70 miles north of Hoquiam.

Kalaloch Lodge

$55-$70 **MANITOU LODGE BED & BREAKFAST**, P. O. Box 600, Forks, WA 98331, phone 360-374-6295. The lodge has 5 nonsmoking rooms available, all with private facilities, queen, double, or two double beds. Also, one cabin with two units has private entrance, microwaves and refrigerators. The lodge amenities include covered outdoor barbecue, large stone fireplace, comfortable nooks for reading, and the Manitou Indian Gift Shop. Guest phone in the office or lodge, no TV. Full breakfast provided. Ten miles to the nearest restaurant. Activities: fishing, hiking, beachcombing, bird watching, and relaxing. Shuttle provided to local airfields and the Forks bus station. Children 12 and older, no pets. **High Season Rates:** *5/30 to 10/31* - double occupancy $60-$70; extra person $15. **Off Season:** $55-$65; fishermen $35 each. Discover, MasterCard, & Visa. **Directions:** just north of Forks go west on Hwy 110, right on Spur 110, right on Kilmer Rd. (first road past the single lane bridge over the Sol Duc River).

$55-$70 **MILLER TREE INN BED & BREAKFAST**, 654 E. Division St., P. O. Box 953, Forks, WA 98331, phone 360-374-6806. This is a "great old farmhouse" on three park-like acres. Six guest rooms on the second floor, 2 with private facilities and 4 share three full baths. There is a large hot tub on the back deck, lemonade on the lawn, kitchen privileges on request, TV, books, a piano, and board games. Hearty breakfast provided. Children 8 and over, leashed pets allowed. Smokers are invited to do so on the porch. Cater to fishermen in the winter season. Facilities to clean and freeze fish and game. Ample parking. **Rates:** double occupancy $55-$70; extra person $15; pets $5. MasterCard & Visa. **Directions:** 1/3 mile east of Hwy 101, turn east on Division.

$45-$75 **OLYMPIC SUITES**, 800 Olympic Dr., Forks, WA 98331, phone 360-374-5400, reservations 1-800-262-3433. 32 one and two bedroom condo units, all with fully equipped kitchens. No designated nonsmoking units. Located off the main highway in the trees by the Calawah River, trail leading to the river for fishing. TV in the rooms and ample parking. Two minutes from the Smokehouse Seafood Restaurant. Children 12 and under free, pets allowed only in two of the units. **Summer Rates:** *6/01 to 9/30* - double occupancy $55-$75; extra person $5; pets $5 per night. **Off Season:** $45-$65. Major credit cards accepted. **Directions:** 1 1/2 miles north of Forks by the Calawah River.

$38-$52 **PACIFIC INN MOTEL**, P. O. Box 1997, Forks, WA 98331, phone 360-374-9400, reservations 1-800-235-7344, fax 360-374-9402. 34 rooms, 20 nonsmoking. Phones, cable TV, and AC. No coffee/tea making facilities in the rooms, but available in the lobby. Restaurant within walking distance. Children welcome, ages 12 and under free, no pets. **Summer Rates:** *5/15 to 9/30* - single (1 bed) $48; double (2 beds) $52; extra person $5; local phone calls free. **Winter Rates:** $38-$47. Major credit cards. **Directions:** center of town on Hwy 101.

$10 **RAIN FOREST HOSTEL**, 169312 Hwy 101, Forks, WA 98331, phone 360-374-2270. All travelers are welcome to this country home with 4 nonsmoking rooms. Dorm style accommodations with 2 to 8 bunk beds. Private room or family room is possible with reservations. Blankets, pillows, and cases are provided. Guests have access to complete kitchen for cooking. There is a comfortable common room with library and fireplace. Outdoors there is a sundeck, badminton, and horseshoes. Nearby is fishing and over 800 miles of hiking trails within the Olympic National Park. Children welcome, pets must sleep in your car. **Rates:** per person $10; laundry $2; taxes included. No credit cards; cash or traveler's checks only. **Directions:** 23 miles south of Forks on Hwy 101 between milepost markers 169 and 170, at 169.3.

$50-$60 **RIVER INN BED & BREAKFAST**, 2596 Bogachiel Way, Rt. 3 Box 3858D, Forks, WA 98331, phone 360-374-6526. Classic northwest hideaway on the banks of the Bogachiel River. Accommodations feature two nonsmoking rooms with private facilities, king or single beds, cable TV, full breakfast. Spacious riverside decks and hot tub overlooking the river. For fishermen there is secure boat parking, pre-dawn breakfast, and a freezer for your catch. Not set up for children or pets. **Rates:** single $50; double $60; extra person $12; taxes included. No credit cards. **Directions:** from downtown Forks, turn southwest at the hospital sign onto (B St.) Bogachiel Way, and continue 2.5 miles.

$65-$75 **SHADYNOOK INN & COTTAGE**, P. O. Box 483, 81 Ash Ave., Forks, WA 98331, phone 360-374-5497. Three units available in this smoke free environment. Two rooms are in the main house and share one bathroom. There is one cottage that sleeps 4 with private facilities and kitchen. Phones on request, TV and fireplace in the living room of the main house. Centrally located, two blocks from town and 11 miles to the ocean. Large continental breakfast is provided. Adults preferred, well-behaved children over 12, no pets. **Rates:** entire house -

double occupancy $75; 4 people in same party $95; cottage $65; extra person $20. No credit cards. **Directions:** north end of main street, turn west at the BP Station and go for 2 blocks to the stop sign, house is on the left.

$30-$42 **TOWN MOTEL**, 1080 S. Forks Ave., Forks, WA 98331, phone 360-374-6231 or 1-800-742-2429. 20 rooms, 5 nonsmoking, and 8 equipped kitchen units. Remote control cable TV. No coffee/tea making facilities in the rooms, but available in the coffee room. Very quiet, next door to large one-stop shopping, 1/2 mile from city center, cozy atmosphere, walk through gardens, outdoor barbecue, and picnic table. Children welcome, infants free, pets allowed. **Rates:** single $30; double $36; family room (2 people) $42; extra person $6; pets $6. Major credit cards accepted. **Directions:** Hwy 101 south, by airport.

FOX ISLAND see Gig Harbor for lodging.

FREELAND see Whidbey Island for lodging.

FRIDAY HARBOR see San Juan Islands for lodging.

GEORGE see Quincy, Moses Lake, and Vantage for lodging.

GIG HARBOR (pop. 3,310) is 5 miles northwest of Tacoma over the Narrows Bridge.

There are two motels in Gig Harbor, both are just off Highway 16, one on the south end and one on the north end. All other lodgings are Bed & Breakfasts. Gig Harbor offers excellent anchorage and 24 hour moorage at the public dock. Waterfront restaurants provide tie-ups for boats. Unique shops dot the harbor to browse for that perfect one-of-a-kind gift.

Located in Pierce County the sales/use/lodging taxes are 9.9%.

$85-$95 **BEACHSIDE BED & BREAKFAST**, 679 Kamas Dr., Fox Island, WA 98333, phone 206-549-2524. This individual studio has an English decor and is only 15 feet from the beach. Amenities include private entrance, queen bed and sofa sleeper, cozy sitting area with fireplace, small equipped kitchen, large walk-in shower, cable TV, and VCR. Hot tub, private patio, buoy for boat, and deep moorage available.

Deluxe continental breakfast is provided. Children - infants okay, no pets, and no smoking. **Summer Rates:** *6/01 to 9/31* - double occupancy $95; extra person $25; taxes included. **Winter Rates:** double occupancy $85. Cash or personal check, no credit cards. **Directions:** from the Tacoma Narrows Bridge take the Gig Harbor City Center Exit, follow signs to Fox Island, cross the bridge, Fox Island Blvd. to 9th Ave., turn right, proceed to Kamas Dr., turn right, follow to the water.

$95   **The FOUNTAIN'S BED & BREAKFAST**, 926 120th St. NW, Gig Harbor, WA 98332, phone 206-851-6262. Overlooking Puget Sound's Colvos Passage and Vashon Island, this B & B is nestled in the woods just three miles north of downtown Gig Harbor. One suite is available with a private sitting room, TV, bedroom with queen bed, and private bath. A gourmet breakfast menu is provided to choose from five full breakfasts, including Eggs Benedict. Adults only, no pets, and no smoking. **Rates:** double $95. MasterCard & Visa. **Directions:** from the Tacoma Narrows Bridge take the Gig Harbor City Center Exit, follow Pioneer to Harborview Dr., turn left, turn right at Borgens Building Supply, follow to 96th St., turn right, proceed to Crescent Valley, turn left, go to Drummond and turn right, follow to Moller, turn left, follow to Hallstrom, proceed for 1.1 miles to 120th.

$52-$60   **GIG HARBOR MOTOR INN**, 4709 Pt. Fosdick Dr. NW, Gig Harbor, WA 98335, phone 206-858-8161. There are 21 units, 15 nonsmoking, in this "log cabin style" motel surrounded by tall evergreens. All units are on one level. Phones, TV, and instant coffee makers in each room. There are 4 equipped kitchen units available. Restaurants and shopping within walking distance. Children 18 and under free with parents, no pets. **Rates:** single room $52; with kitchen $56; double room $60; extra person $5. MasterCard, Visa, & Amex. **Directions:** from the Tacoma Narrows Bridge take the Olympic Dr. Exit, at the end of the ramp take a left at the light.

$95   **ISLAND ESCAPE BED & BREAKFAST**, 210 Island Blvd., Fox Island, WA 98333, phone 206-549-2044. This one bedroom executive suite is decorated with an international flare. The bedroom has a king size bed, spacious living room area, jacuzzi bath, private deck, and private entrance. This is a contemporary, waterfront home overlooking Puget Sound with views of the Olympic Mountains. Identify area birds that frequent the flower garden just outside your window, listen for the local sea lions barking, and learn about Fox Island's "clay babies". A relaxing adult getaway, no pets or smoking. Three course breakfast provided. **Rates:** double $95. MasterCard & Visa. **Directions:** from the Tacoma Narrows Bridge take the Gig Harbor City Center Exit, follow signs to Fox Island, cross the bridge and drive 0.4 mile, turn right on Cove Rd., turn right again on Island Blvd., drive 0.2 miles, turn left on Griffin Ln. (gravel road) to the end of the drive.

Island Escape Bed & Breakfast

$50-$75 **NO CABBAGES BED & BREAKFAST**, 7712 Goodman Dr., Gig Harbor, WA 98335, phone 206-858-7797. This old, well-loved beach house is on the east side of Gig Harbor. There are 3 guest rooms, 1 with private facilities and 2 with shared. Quiet surroundings with views of the water from your bed. A good place to relax, eat an incredible breakfast, or share in exciting conversations. Shuttle provided to airport or train station. Children welcome, pets allowed. **Rates:** double $50; suite $75; extra person $7. No credit cards. **Directions:** over the Narrows Bridge from Tacoma - east side of the Bay.

$60-$75 **The PARSONAGE BED & BREAKFAST**, 4107 Burnham Dr., Gig Harbor, WA 98335, phone 206-851-8654. This Victorian, older home was built and used for a parsonage for nineteen years. There are two rooms available, one with a double bed and one with a king bed. Shared bath and sitting room, full breakfast in the dining room, muffins are the specialty. Children and pets by arrangement. **Rates:** double occupancy $60 for shared facilities, $75 for private. No credit cards. **Directions:** over the Narrows Bridge from Tacoma take the Soundview Dr. Exit, follow to Burnham Dr.; from Bremerton take the Burnham Dr. Exit off Hwy 16, follow for 1.7 mile.

$95 **ROSEDALE BED & BREAKFAST**, 7714 Ray Nash Dr. NW, Gig Harbor, WA 98335, phone 206-851-5420. Traditional waterfront home located on Lay Inlet, 3 miles west of Gig Harbor. One suite is available with many amenities. Private entrance, spacious bedroom, bath, living room with fireplace, big screen TV, stereo, CD player, VCR, refrigerator, microwave, and coffee pot. Full breakfast is provided on the weekends. Children welcome, no pets, smoking outside. Enjoy boating, swimming, beach combing for treasures, clamming, or gathering oysters. **Rates:** double occupancy $95. MasterCard & Visa. **Directions:** from the Narrows Bridge take the second exit, proceed to Rosedale St., turn left (west) and proceed 3 miles to Ray Nash Dr., turn left, look for the Oar.

$55-$65 **STILL WATERS BED & BREAKFAST & DAY SPA**, 13202 Olympic Rd. S.E., Olalla, WA 98359, phone 360-876-8608. Located 8 miles north of Gig Harbor, this split level home, built in 1963, is surrounded by over two acres of gardens. The upstairs is dedicated to the bed and breakfast with 3 guest rooms. The queen bed room has a private bath, deck and Olympic view, the double bed rooms share a bath. Outdoor hot tub and day spa featuring Swedish or therapeutic massage, facials, herbal body wraps, seaweed body mask or body polish. Full breakfast with seasonal produce served around 8:30 a.m., coffee earlier. Adults only, no pets, smoking outside. **Rates:** double occupancy $55 & $65; massage (1 hour) $45. MasterCard & Visa. **Directions:** follow Hwy 16 from Tacoma or Bremerton, turn east on Burley/Olalla Rd., right at Olympic Rd., right at Still Water sign.

$44-$72 **WESTWYND MOTEL & APARTMENTS**, 6703 144th St. NW, Gig Harbor, WA 98332, phone 206-857-4047 or 1-800-468-9963. There are 24 units, 12 nonsmoking, in this two story motel decorated in a Northwest nautical motif. Satellite TV with HBO, some remote controls, phones, coffee/tea making facilities, and coin-operated laundry. 16 units have kitchens with dish packages available at the office. Within walking distance of a restaurant and tavern. Children 18 and under free with parents, pets allowed. **Rates:** single room $44-$48; 1 bedroom with kitchen $54-$59; 2 bedrooms with kitchen $65-$72; no charge for local phone calls or pets. Major credit cards. **Directions:** just off Hwy 16 on the north end of Gig Harbor, 9 miles from the Tacoma Narrows Bridge.

GLACIER is in the northwest corner of the state on the road to Mt. Baker.

The entrance to the Mt. Baker National Forest is located at Glacier, 33 miles east of Bellingham and less than two and one-half hours from either Vancouver, B.C. or Seattle. Within minutes of Glacier there are abundant hiking trails, views, and waterfalls. Fishing, hunting, alpine skiing, and cross country skiing are the main attractions in this area.

Located in Whatcom County the sales/use taxes are 7.5%.

$42-$135 **GLACIER CREEK MOTEL & CABINS**, P. O. Box 5008, Glacier, WA 98244, phone 360-599-2991. There are 21 units, no nonsmoking. Choice of motel-style rooms or rustic cabins. The motel rooms are small, primarily sleeping rooms. The cabins come in small, medium, and large, most have equipped kitchens. There is also a 2 bedroom house with kitchen and fireplace. The motel is located between Glacier and Gallup Creeks. The sound of rushing water provides an enchanting background for the rustic setting of the cabins. Barbecues, picnic tables, hot tub, gift shop, and espresso bar with hot pastries. Children 12 and under free, pets allowed in cabins only. Restaurant across the street. **Winter Rates:** *11/16 to 4/16* - motel room, 2 people $54; small cabin $50-$66; 2 bedroom cabin (4 people) $95-$115; 2 bedroom house (4 people) $115-$135; extra person $10; pets free. **Summer Rates:** $42-$130. Master Card, Visa, & Discover. **Directions:** from I-5 take the Mt. Baker Exit 255 and proceed for 33.5 miles on Hwy 542.

$55-$85 **SNOWLINE INN**, 10433 Mt. Baker Hwy, Glacier, WA 98244, phone 360-599-2788, fax 360-599-2772. A condominium complex with 45 units, 30 nonsmoking. This Bavarian chalet inn is located off the highway in the woods. All units have equipped kitchens and satellite TV, no phones in the rooms. The loft units are the larger units. Ski lockers are provided in the basement, copy machine, laundry facilities, game room, and some microwaves. Restaurant across the street. Children 10 and under free, no pets. **Winter Rates:** *ski season* - small units, 2 people $65; loft units (2 to 4 people) $85; extra person $5. **Summer Rates:** $55-$75. Most major credit cards. **Directions:** from I-5 take the Mt. Baker Exit 255 and proceed past Glacier, on the road to Mt. Baker ski area.

GLENWOOD is located at the base of Mt. Adams, 31 miles north of the Columbia River Gorge and approximately 85 miles east of Vancouver.

Glenwood provides a gateway to Mt. Adams recreational activities. Hiking, fishing, climbing, mountain biking, and relaxing are just a few of the things to do.

Located in Klickitat (KLIK-i-tat) County the sales/use taxes are 7%.

$55-$110 **FLYING L RANCH COUNTRY INN,** 25 Flying L Lane, Glenwood, WA 98619, phone 509-364-3488. This 160 acre retreat offers 13 nonsmoking accommodations, 10 with private facilities and 3 with shared. No phones or TV to disturb you, but available if necessary. Full breakfast is provided, as is use of the common kitchens, spa, lodge, bikes, ranch trails, and other facilities. Choose from the 6 rooms in the lodge, 5 rooms in the guest house, or two individual cabins. Children welcome, infants free, no pets. Beginning in July the Flying L offers guided Mt. Adams hiking packages. **Rates:** single (1 person) $55-$75; double (2 people) $65-$85; suite $90; cabins $100-$110; extra person $20. MasterCard, Visa, & Amex. **Directions:** take Hwy 141 north from White Salmon to BZ Corners (12 miles), turn right and continue for 19 miles to Glenwood, go east through town about 1/2 mile, turn left and proceed 1/2 mile to driveway.

GOLDENDALE (pop. 3,340) is 120 miles from Portland, 70 miles south of Yakima and 12 miles north of the Columbia River.

Hwy 97, the "Caribou Trail" from British Columbia to California, is the main route for those traveling to or from Goldendale. The Klickitat County Historical Museum is the most impressive building in town. The Goldendale Observatory State Park houses one of the nation's largest public telescopes on a hilltop just north of town. The park offers views of Mt. Hood and the Klickitat Valley . At night, clear skies enhance views of the moon, planets, stars, and galaxies.

Located in Klickitat (KLIK-i-tat) County the sales/luse taxes are 7%.

$38-$56 **BARCHRIS MOTEL**, 128 N. Academy, Goldendale, WA 98620, phone 509-773-4325. There are 10 kitchenette rooms in this comfortable, older, one story motel with 1 nonsmoking room. Air- conditioned, cable TV with HBO, and phones. Dishes and coffee pots are available on request. Children welcome, infants free, no pets. Lighted, covered parking. **Rates:** single (1 bed) $38; double (2 beds) $42; family room, sleeps 3-6 people $46-$56; extra person $5. MasterCard & Visa. **Directions:** from Hwy 97 turn into Goldendale on Hwy 142, go three blocks, turn left on Academy, motel is on the corner.

$37-$99 **FARVUE MOTEL**, 808 E. Simcoe Dr., Goldendale, WA 98620, phone 509-773-5881, reservations only 1-800-358-5881. 47 rooms, 31 nonsmoking. Two kitchen apartments with basic cookware, all units have mini refrigerators. No coffee/tea making facilities in the rooms, but available in the lobby. Restaurant and lounge on the premises. One suite with king bed and heart-shaped jacuzzi tub comes with champagne. **Rates:** single $37-$47; double $47; apartments $72-$76; jacuzzi suite $99; extra person $5. MasterCard, Visa, & Amex. **Directions:** parallel with Hwy 97.

$34-$45 **PONDEROSA MOTEL**, 775 E. Broadway, Goldendale, WA 98620, phone 509-773-5842. Two story motel with 28 rooms, half nonsmoking. Phones, cable TV, and four kitchen units with basic cookware. No coffee/tea making facilities in the rooms, but available in the coffee room. Children welcome, 7 years and under free, pets allowed, no extra charge. **Rates:** single (1 bed) $34-$40; double (2 beds) $45; kitchen units $5 more; extra person $5. Major credit cards. **Directions:** just off Hwy 97 on SR 142, first exit coming from the north, 3rd exit from the south.

$46-$175 **HIGHLAND CREEKS RESORT**, 2120 Hwy 97 Satus Pass, Goldendale, WA 98620 phone 509-773-4026. Nestled in the woods of the Simcoe Mountains this getaway offers 4 individual chalets, 18 units in duplex and four-plex chalets with hot tubs. Scattered throughout the trees along the creeks, all units have vaulted ceilings, queen beds under skylights, full baths, phones, outdoor decks or patios, and are nonsmoking. The lodge has two fireplaces and creeks flow past two sides of the dining room area. The restaurant, open 7 days a week from 7:30 a.m. to 9:00 p.m., offers a Sunday brunch. Children under 12 years old free, no pets. **Rates:** chalet (no hot tub) $46-$56; spa rooms $105-

$115; deluxe chalet $149-$175; rates are based on double occupancy - extra person charge $10. Major credit cards. **Directions:** just off Hwy 97 north of Goldendale.

GRAND COULEE see Coulee City, Coulee Dam, and Electric City for lodging.

GRANDVIEW

(pop. 7,350) is located in the Yakima Valley 40 miles southeast of Yakima.

Washington's oldest winery, Chateau Ste. Michelle, is located here and is open for tours daily. Agriculture supplies the backbone of Grandview's economy. The fertile soils of the valley produce such crops as apples, asparagus, corn, peaches, grapes, hops, and cherries.

Located in Yakima ((YAK-i-maw) County the sales/use taxes are 7.6%.

$30-$45 **APPLE VALLEY MOTEL**, 903 W. Wine Country Rd., Grandview, WA 98930, phone 509-882-3003. 16 units, 5 nonsmoking. Phones, TV, coffee/tea making facilities in the rooms, seasonal outdoor pool, some units have a stove and refrigerator. Restaurant located across the street. Children welcome, small pets allowed at no extra charge. Truck and RV parking. **Rates:** single $30; double $38; family room $45; extra person $5; no charge for local phone calls. Major credit cards. **Directions:** take Exit 73 off I-82, turn left and go 2 blocks.

$22-$45 **GRANDVIEW MOTEL**, 522 E. Wine Country Rd., Grandview, WA 98930 phone 509-882-1323. 20 units, 5 nonsmoking. Phones, TV, seasonal outdoor pool, storage space available. Children welcome, small pets allowed. Truck and RV parking. **Rates:** single $22-$35; double $38; family room $45; extra person $5; pets $2; no charge for local phone calls. Major credit cards. **Directions:** take Exit 75 off I-82, 3 blocks from City Center.

GRANGER

(pop. 2,065) is located in the Yakima Valley 22 miles southeast of Yakima. On the wine tour of this area you will find Eaton Hill Winery and Stewart Vineyards. See Sunnyside, Toppenish, and Yakima for lodging.

GRANITE FALLS see Marysville or Arlington for lodging.

• GRAYLAND is located on the Pacific Ocean along Hwy 105, just 8 miles south of Westport.

This area has good surf fishing and clam digging in season; also crabbing and bottom fishing off the docks at Tokeland or the jetty at Westport. Visit the four cranberry bogs and canneries, or fly a kite. Located between two of the most pristine bays on Washington's Pacific coast - Willapa Bay to the south (famous for its oysters) and Grays Harbor to the north, with miles of sandy ocean beach separating the two.

Located in Grays Harbor County the sales/use/lodging taxes are 10.9%.

$40-$60 **GRAYLAND MOTEL & COTTAGES**, 2013 State Rt. 105, Grayland, WA 98547, phone 360-267-2395 or 1-800-292-0845. Nine motel units, 4 cabins sleep 2-4, and 2 cottages sleep 5-9. No nonsmoking units or phones. Cable TV. Fourteen units have kitchens with basic cookware. The cabins are located on the dunes with views of the ocean. Crab nets are available for guests and there is an outside propane cooking area. Children 1 and under free, pets allowed in some rooms. **Rates:** motel units (double) $40; cabins $40; cottages $60; extra person $5; pets $5 one time charge. MasterCard, Amex, & Visa. **Directions:** on the main road in the center of Grayland.

$45-$65 **OCEAN SPRAY MOTEL**, Hwy 105, P. O. Box 86, Grayland, WA 98547, phone 360-267-2205. 10 individual cabins with private facilities, kitchenettes, and TV. Within walking distance of the beach, restaurant, grocery store, post office, and gift shops. Two blocks to cranberry fields. Shuttle provided to Westport Air Field. Children welcome, pets allowed. **Rates:** single $45; double $60; 3 beds (2 bedrooms) $65; extra person $5; pets $5. MasterCard & Visa. **Directions:** on the main road in Grayland, 4 1/2 miles south of Westport.

$35-$60 **SURF MOTEL & COTTAGES**, 2029 Hwy 105, Grayland, WA 98547, phone 360-267-2244. 3 individual cottages, one duplex, and two motel style rooms. The cottages and duplex have fully equipped kitchens, no phones. The motel rooms do not have coffee/tea making facilities, but there is a restaurant within walking distance.

Horseshoe pit, clam shack, and small playground. Children welcome, pets allowed. **Rates:** cottages sleep four $50; duplex (sleeps 6) $60; motel units (two people) $35; pets $5. MasterCard, Visa, & Discover. **Directions:** on Hwy 105 in Grayland.

$32-$98 **WALSH MOTEL**, 1593 Hwy 105, P. O. Box 64, Grayland, WA 98547, phone 360-267-2191. 24 units available in this ocean front lodging, 6 nonsmoking units. 12 modern motel-style units are right on the beach; the upstairs units have the best view, but all have decks overlooking the ocean. These units have an ice machine, coin-operated washer/dryer, phones available, no pets allowed. Rates vary depending on location. There are 12 fully equipped kitchen units, 9 fireplaces, 6 rooms with jacuzzi tubs, TV, coffee/tea facilities, and refrigerators. Twelve rooms can accommodate children, pets allowed in some rooms. **Summer Rates:** *Memorial Day to Labor Day* - single (1 bed) $36-$78; double room (2 beds) $68-$78; jacuzzi suites $98; family unit (2 bedrooms) $54-$60; extra person $6; no charge for local phone calls. **Winter Rates:** single $32-$55; double $56-$66; suite $58-$65; family unit $38-$54. Major credit cards. **Directions:** on Hwy 105 north side of Grayland.

$35-$50 **WESTERN SHORES MOTEL & R.V. PARK**, 2193 Hwy 105, Grayland, WA 98547, phone 360-267-6115. 7 motel units with TV, and fully equipped kitchens. No nonsmoking units or phones. Small, medium, and large units sleep from 4 to 12 people. The large units are mobile homes and no pets are allowed in these. Two fish cleaning houses. Within walking distance of restaurants, public transportation, and the beach. Children welcome, infants free, pets allowed. **Rates:** double occupancy - small units $35; medium units $40; large units $50; extra person $6; pets $5 one time charge. MasterCard & Visa. **Directions:** on Hwy 105 south end of Grayland, on the beach approach road.

GREENBANK see Whidbey Island.

GREENWATER is located on Hwy 410, at the northeast entrance to Mount Rainier National Park, 8 miles from the Crystal Mountain ski area.

$79-$159 **ALTA CRYSTAL RESORT at MT. RAINIER,** 68317 SR 410 E., Greenwater, WA 98022, phone 360- 663-2500. Located two miles from the NE entrance to Mt. Rainier National Park. 24 completely furnished chalets offer all the comforts of home in a spectacular mountain setting, plus one large log home. No designated nonsmoking units. Each unit has a fireplace, television (limited reception), fully equipped kitchen, and plenty of living space. The one bedroom chalets sleep up to four people, loft chalets sleep up to eight people with 2 baths, honeymoon cabin, and the log home sleeps 6 comfortably. Conference and retreat center available. The location makes this a resort for all seasons. Children 12 and under free, no pets. **Summer Rates:** *6/15 to 9/01* - one bedroom chalet $79-$89; loft chalet & log house (1-4 people) $109-$129; honeymoon cabin $89; extra person $8; taxes 11%. **Winter Rates:** loft chalet & log house (4 people) $109-$159; 1 bedroom chalet $79-$110; honeymoon cabin $89-$125. **Spring & Fall Specials offered.** MasterCard, Amex, & Visa. **Directions:** on Hwy 410 between mile markers 55 & 56.

HARRINGTON (pop. 474) is located on Hwy 28, approximately 35 miles west of Spokane.

$55 **THE HARRINGTON Bed & Breakfast,** So. 403 First, P. O. Box 185, Harrington, WA 99134, phone 509-253-4728. Two guest rooms on the second floor share facilities. Choose from a king or queen bed. The house was built in 1905 and has an indoor pool and sauna. Full breakfast provided, dinner can be arranged. Adults only, small pets, smoking outside. Close to golf course and a 5 minute walk to the nearest restaurant. **Rates:** double occupancy $55; pets $10 deposit; taxes 7.6%. No credit cards. **Directions:** turn off I-90 at Sprague and follow Hwy 23 northwest for 22 miles, centrally located.

HAZEL DELL see Vancouver for lodging.

HOLDEN see Lake Chelan for lodging.

HOME see Gig Harbor for lodging.

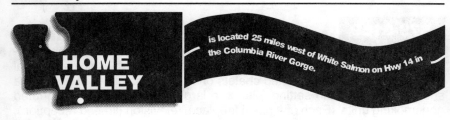

HOME VALLEY is located 25 miles west of White Salmon on Hwy 14 in the Columbia River Gorge.

$40-$115   **SOJOURNER INN Bed & Breakfast**, 142 Lyons Rd., Home Valley, WA 98648, phone 509-427-7070. There are 5 nonsmoking rooms available, all have private facilities. The Sojourner is nestled on a wooded ridge overlooking the confluence of the Columbia and Wind Rivers. A full breakfast for all overnight guests; public may reserve for breakfast. Dinner by reservations Thurs.-Sat. Hosts - Judy Yeckel & Bob Davis. Bob is a professional chef trained at the Cordon Bleu. The locals in Stevenson say this is the best place in the area to eat. Children 5 and up, no pets. **Summer Rates:** *6/01 to 9/30* - double occupancy $50-$115; taxes 7%. **Winter Rates:** $40-$90. MasterCard & Visa. **Directions:** from Hwy 14 enter Home Valley, turn on to Berge Rd., proceed for 4/10 of a mile, bear left onto Lyons Rd., continue for a block.

HOODSPORT is located on the western side of Hood Canal, about 30 miles north of Olympia.

This area is great for boating, saltwater or freshwater fishing, clamming or picking oysters, diving, and beachcombing.

Located in Mason County the sales/use taxes are 7.8%.

$50-$85   **GLEN-AYR CANAL RESORT**, N. 25381 Hwy 101, Hoodsport, WA 98548, phone 360-877-9522, reservations 1-800-367-9522. A modern, two story, wood motel with 16 units, 14 nonsmoking. Amenities include cable TV, marina, clubhouse, swim spa, and laundry. Two suites have equipped kitchens. 10 units have coffee/tea making facilities and coffee is also available in the lobby. Children in ground floor units only and must be supervised on grounds, marina, and in the lodge. No pets in the motel rooms. RV park, moorage by reservation. **Summer Rates:** *4/01 to 9/30* - single room (1 bed) $55-$58; double (2 beds) $62-$68; suite $85; third person $10; fourth person $5; rollaways $10;

moorage $8. **Winter Rates:** single room $50-$55; double room $57-$63; suite $85. Discover, MasterCard, & Visa. **Directions:** 1 mile north of Hoodsport on Hwy 101.

$50-$85 **SUNRISE MOTEL**, N. 24520 Hwy 101, P. O. Box 554, Hoodsport, WA 98548, phone 360-877-5301. There is nothing ornate about the Sunrise Motel, it is kept basic to meet the needs of the clientele, primarily divers. Located on the water with an underwater park, classes from Washington and Oregon universities come here to dive. There are 19 rooms and a dorm for large groups. All rooms have cable TV, most with remote control, and 11 have equipped kitchen units. The 8 upstairs rooms have balconies overlooking the water. Large dock, air, and boat moorage. Children 10 and under free, pets allowed at no extra charge. **Rates:** sleeping units, 2 people $50; 3 and more people $60; kitchen unit $60-$70; apartment (4 people) $85; dorm $50 per weekend (minimum 10 people),10% discount weekdays. Amex, MasterCard, Discover, & Visa. **Directions:** centrally located at Hoodsport.

•HOQUIAM (pop. 8,870) is located in central Grays Harbor County next door to Aberdeen on coast Hwy 101.

(HOH-kweeuhm) was built during the boom days of logging. Some of the finest cedar shingle artistry can be seen on numerous homes, and the Hoquiam Castle displays a wealth of interior furnishings of a bygone era. The Port of Grays Harbor's viewing tower lies midpoint between Aberdeen and Hoquiam on the waterfront. It provides a commanding view of shipping traffic and harbor birdlife.

Located in Grays Harbor County the sales/use/lodging taxes are 10.9%.

$75-$120 **LYTLE HOUSE BED & BREAKFAST**, 509 Chenault, Hoquiam, WA 98550, phone 360-533-2320 or 1-800-677-2320. There are 8 nonsmoking rooms available in this Queen Anne Victorian mansion on a hill overlooking Grays Harbor. Six have private facilities and 2 share one bathroom. Some rooms have phones, one has TV. Each room is uniquely furnished with classic antiques and queen size beds. Four parlors offer a wide selection of books and parlor games. In the morning, coffee is available near your room, and a full breakfast selected from a menu awaits guests in the dining room. Dessert is available from 4:00-8:00 p.m. The Lytle House is more than an inn, it is also a gallery, museum, and workshop. The furniture, collectibles, gifts, and antiques are available for purchase. Please call regarding children, no pets. **Rates:** double occupancy $75-$120; extra person $15. MasterCard & Visa. **Directions:** 2 blocks from Hwy 101 & 109; take Garfield to top of hill then left on Chenault.

Lytle House Bed & Breakfast

$40-$85 **WESTWOOD INN**, 910 Simpson, Hoquiam, WA 98550, phone 360-532-8161 or 1-800-562-0994, fax 360-533-6067. A large two story motel with 65 spacious rooms, 50% nonsmoking. Two phones per room, cable TV with HBO, and 15 equipped kitchen units. No coffee/tea making facilities in the rooms, but available in the lobby with a complimentary continental breakfast. Children 5 and under free, pets allowed. **Summer Rates:** *5/15 to 9/16* - single (1 bed) $53-$65; double (2 beds) $65-$75; kitchen units $10 more; extra person $7; pets $10. **Winter Rates:** single $40; double $55; kitchen units $65. Major credit cards. **Directions:** on the west side of the Hoquiam River.

HUMPTULIPS see Lake Quinault, Copalis Beach, or Hoquiam for lodging.

ILWACO see Long Beach Peninsula.

• INDEX (pop. 140) is located on the west side of Stevens Pass one mile north of Hwy 2.

Mt. Index towers over this small community. The popular whitewater Skykomish River runs through the heart of town. The town has seen many changes from its copper and silver mining days and busy railroad activity. Today driving into Index is like stepping back in time.

$60-$80 **The BUSH HOUSE COUNTRY INN**, 300 5th St., P. O. Box 359, Index, WA 98256, phone 360-793-2312, 1-800-428-2874, fax 360-793-3673. There are 11 elegant guest rooms in this quiet hideaway in the mountains. 10 rooms share two bathrooms, one has half a bath (sink and toilet). The entire establishment is nonsmoking, including the bar. The original Bush House closed in the 1930's and reopened 40 years later in 1975. After renovations in 1992-1993, the Bush House again welcomes visitors to its comfortable rooms, fine gourmet restaurant with a large stone fireplace, and rose garden. All the rooms are decorated in refined country style. There is a cozy sitting room for guests. The bar has a large screen TV. Children acceptable, 12 and under free, no pets. Continental breakfast. **Rates:** double occupancy $60-$80; extra person $15; taxes 10.2%. MasterCard & Visa. **Directions:** one mile off Hwy 2, cross the bridge, proceed for two blocks, on the left.

IONE see Metaline Falls for lodging.

ISSAQUAH (pop. 7,860) is located about 14 miles east of Seattle off I-90 at the south end of Lake Sammamish.

(IS-uh-kwah) is a small town that continues to grow rapidly. Gilman Village has numerous upscale speciality shops and restaurants. Boehm's Chocolate Factory is on the east end of town. The Washington Zoological Park is home to 300 animals representing 30 threatened and endangered species.

Located in King County the sales/use taxes are 8.2%. Lodging tax of 2.8% applies to lodgings with 60 or more units for a total of 11% taxes.

$65 **COUNTRY INN BED & BREAKFAST,** 685 NW Juniper St., Issaquah, WA 98027, phone 206-392-1010. Two guest rooms with private facilities in a quiet private setting with formal gardens and exotic bird aviary. The king room has a fireplace, private entrance, covered deck, cable TV, and VCR. Continental or gourmet breakfast provided. Adults only, pets by arrangement, smoking outside. Two blocks from Gilman Village. **Rates:** double occupancy $65; extra person $20. MasterCard, & Visa. **Directions:** take Exit 17 off I-90, turn right, in 1/2 block turn right on Gilman Blvd., go 1 block, turn left immediately after railroad tracks, proceed 5 blocks on the left before 7th, gold mailbox.

HOLIDAY INN, 1801 12th NW, Issaquah, WA 98027, phone 206-392-6421, 1-800-465-4329, fax 206-391-4650.

$49-$70 **MOUNTAINS & PLANES BED & BREAKFAST,** 100 Big Bear Pl. NW, P. O. Box 796, Issaquah, WA 98027, **phone 206-392-8068 or 1-800-231-8068.** This traditional Northwest cedar home has 3 guest rooms available. The suite is on the main floor and consists of two rooms with a shared bath between them. The upstairs bedroom has a private shower and feather bed. The "airplane room" is a common room with TV, wood stove, airplane pictures, books, and videos. Family style breakfast provided. The grounds include old growth cedar, flowers, herbs, and fruit trees. Within walking distance of downtown. School age children only, not equipped for toddlers or infants, pets only in cages. **Rates:** single room (1 bed) double occupancy $49-$55; suite (4 people) $70; extra person $5. Amex, MasterCard, & Visa. **Directions:** go east on I-90 to Exit 13, go east (left) on Newport Way to 2nd traffic light, turn right, proceed uphill to the T junction, turn left on W. Sunset and then right on Big Bear Pl.

KALALOCH see Forks or Lake Quinault for lodging.

•KALAMA (pop. 1,210) is located 28 miles north of Vancouver just off I-5.

(kuh-LAM-uh) runs parallel to Interstate 5 and has numerous antique stores for collectors. Located in Cowlitz (KOW-litz) County the sales/use/lodging taxes are 9.5%.

$32-$55   **COLUMBIA INN MOTEL,** P. O. Box 1069, Kalama, WA 98625, phone 360-673-2855. This basic motel has 44 units, 50% nonsmoking. Phones, TV, and AC. No coffee/tea making facilities in the rooms, but available in the lobby. Two units have equipped kitchens and there is an adjacent restaurant. Children under 18 free with parents, pets allowed. **Rates:** single room, 1 person $32-$35, 2 people $40-$45; double room $48-$55; no charge for local phone calls. MasterCard & Visa. **Directions:** Exit 30 into Kalama, turn left onto Frontage St., proceed for two blocks. The motel is parallel with I-5.

•KELSO (pop. 11,800) is located just west of I-5, 44 miles north of Vancouver.

In January and February the "smelt runs" up the Cowlitz River are so plentiful that Kelso is called the "Smelt Capitol of the World".

Located in Cowlitz (KOW-litz) County the sales/use/lodging taxes are 9.6%.

$42-$59   **ALADDIN MOTOR INN,** 310 Long Ave., Kelso, WA 98626, phone 360-425-9660 or 1-800-764-7378. 78 rooms, 38 nonsmoking. Phones, TV, and AC. No coffee/tea making facilities in the rooms, but provided in the lobby. There are 20 equipped kitchen units and a restaurant/bar on the premises. Indoor swimming pool, jacuzzi, and 24 hour desk. Children under 12 free, pets allowed. **Rates:** single room $42-$50; double room $54; kitchen units $59; family room $54; extra person $5; pets $5; no charge for local phone calls. Major credit cards. **Directions:** from the south, take Exit 39, go left at light, cross the drawbridge to 5th St., turn right. From the north Exit 40, go to stop sign, turn right, go to stoplight, turn right, go over the bridge.

COMFORT INN, 440 Three Rivers Dr., Kelso, WA 98626, phone 360-425-4600 or 1-800-228-5150.

$36-$49 **BUDGET INN IN KELSO,** 505 N. Pacific, Kelso, WA 98626, phone 360-636-4610. 51 rooms, 20 non-smoking. Phones, cable TV, AC, and queen size beds. No coffee/tea making facilities in the rooms, but available in the lobby. Two equipped kitchenette units. Children 12 and under free, pets allowed. **Rates:** single room $36-$40; double room $42-$44; kitchen units $5 extra; extra person $5; no charge for local phone calls; pets $5. MasterCard, Amex, & Visa. **Directions:** west of I-5, Exit 39, go towards town.

RED LION INN, 510 Kelso Dr., Kelso, WA 98626, phone 360-636-4400 or 1-800-547-8010.

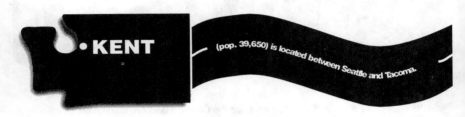

•KENT (pop. 39,650) is located between Seattle and Tacoma.

Kent is in the heart of the Puget Sound basin. It offers a range of recreational opportunities. Gems in the area include over 40 acres along the Green River Recreational Corridor, Mill Creek Canyon, and the Earthworks Park.

Located in King County the sales/use taxes are 8.2%. Lodging tax of 2.8% applies to lodgings with 60 or more units for a total of 11% taxes.

$35-$65 **The BEST INN,** 23408 30th Ave. So., Kent, WA 98032, phone 206-870-1280. 27 rooms, 13 nonsmoking. Phones and remote control cable TV with HBO. No coffee/tea making facilities in the rooms, but available in the lobby. Four equipped kitchenette units. Children 14 and under free, no pets. Two story, clean motel. **Rates:** single room $35-$52; double room $45-$65; kitchen unit $45; extra person $5-$10; local phone calls free. Major credit cards. **Directions:** from I-5 take Exit 149B.

CYPRESS INN, 22218 84th Ave. S., Kent, WA 98032, phone 206-395-0219 or 1-800-752-9991.

DAYS INN, 1711 W. Meeker, Kent, WA 98032, phone 206-854-1950 or 1-800-DAYS-INN.

KENNEWICK see Tri Cities.

KETTLE FALLS (pop. 1,305) is located on the upper Columbia River in the northeast corner of the state, 38 miles from the Canadian border.

The primary industry in this area is lumber. Kettle Falls once had the second largest waterfall on the Columbia. Grand Coulee Dam changed the landscape by backing up the river to create Lake Roosevelt. Also see Colville for accommodations.

Located in Stevens County the sales/use taxes are 7.5%.

$28-$48 **BARNEY'S,** Hwy 395 & Hwy 20 E., Kettle Falls, WA 99141, phone 509-738-6546. Barney's Cafe, Motel, Mini Store, & Gas Station. At present there are 8 rooms, no nonsmoking. Basic sleeping rooms with phones and TV. No coffee/tea making facilities. The restaurant and lounge are the only formal dining in the area, specializing in steaks and select ground beef. Children welcome, infants free, small pets allowed. **Rates:** single room $28; double room $35; family unit with 3 double beds $48; extra person $3; pets $3. MasterCard & Visa. **Directions:** at the junction of Hwy 395 and Hwy 20.

$34-$48 **GRANDVIEW INN MOTEL & RV PARK,** 978 Hwy 395 N, Kettle Falls, WA 99141, phone 509-738-6733. 13 motel units, 4 nonsmoking rooms. Phones, TV, microwaves, refrigerators, and coffee/tea making facilities. Four units have equipped kitchens. In a park-like setting, family oriented. View of Lake Roosevelt, gazebo, chairs, picnic tables, volleyball, badminton, and horseshoes. Children welcome, pets allowed free. Enjoy lake activities, hunting, fishing, skiing, or biking. **Rates:** single (1 bed) $34-$36; double (2 beds) $38; suite $48; local phone calls free. Major credit cards. **Directions:** located at the intersection of Hwys 395 and 25.

$36-$49 **KETTLE FALLS INN,** Box 598, Kettle Falls, WA 99141, phone 509-738-6514. 26 units, 9 nonsmoking. All rooms have phones, TV, microwaves, refrigerators, and coffee/tea making facilities. Three units have non-equipped kitchenettes. Restaurant and bar next door. Children welcome, infants free, pets allowed. **Summer Rates:** *5/01 to 9/30* - single (1 bed) $39-$44; double (2 beds) $49; kitchen units $10 extra; local phone calls free; extra person $5; taxes included. **Winter Rates:** single $36-$39; double $46. Major credit cards. **Directions:** Hwy 395 in the middle of town, next to the only stoplight.

KEYPORT see Poulsbo.

KIRKLAND (pop. 40,590) is located just off I-405, 15 miles east of Seattle, 7 miles north of Bellevue, and 22 miles northeast of Sea Tac Airport.

Kirkland is a picturesque city along the shores of beautiful Lake Washington, offering fine dining, unique shops, and an abundance of recreational activities.

Located in King County the sales/use taxes are 8.2%. Lodging tax of 2.8% applies to lodgings with 60 or more units for a total of 11% taxes.

CLARION INN, 12233 NE Totem Lake Way, Kirkland, WA 98034, phone 206-821-2202 or 1-800-221-2222.

$78-$125 **KIRKLAND INN Best Western**, 12223 NE 116th, Kirkland, WA 98034, phone 206-822-2300 or 1-800-332-4200. 110 units with 60% nonsmoking. The rooms have king beds or two queens, satellite TV with HBO, and VCR/movie rentals. Some units have sofas or large desks, jacuzzi jetted tubs, microwave, and refrigerator. A family suite is available with washer/dryer, dishwasher, and microwave, sleeps 5. No coffee/tea making facilities, but a continental breakfast is provided in the lobby. Children 17 and under free with parents, small pets allowed with a deposit. Shuttle provided within a 7 mile radius. **Rates:** $78-$90; extra person $6; family suite $125; local phone calls free. Major credit cards. **Directions:** from Hwy 405 north take Exit 20A; from Hwy 405 south take Exit 20, left on 124th, right on NE 124th, right on NE 116th, 1 block.

$65-$95 **SHUMWAY MANSION,** 11410 99th Place NE, Kirkland, WA 98033, phone 206-823-2303, fax 206-822-0421. This historic mansion has 8 guest rooms, all with private facilities. The rooms are decorated with European accents, queen beds, antiques, and easy chairs. One room is on the lower level close to the ballroom, other rooms are on the second floor. Full buffet breakfast is provided. Free use of the Columbia athletic club across the street. Three blocks away from the beach and 10 minutes to two major wineries. Homemade evening snacks. Many fine restaurants close by. Children 12 and older, no pets. **Rates:** double room $65-$85; suite $95; extra person $10; local phone calls free. MasterCard, Amex, & Visa. **Directions:** Hwy 405 north to Exit 20A, west on 116th to 99th Pl., turn left onto 99th, go 1.5 blocks to the Mansion.

Shumway Mansion

SILVER CLOUD INN, 12202 NE 124th St., Kirkland, WA 98034, phone 206-821-8300 or 1-800-551-7207.

LA CONNER

(pop. 720) is located 8 miles west of I-5 and Mt. Vernon.

This port town on the Swinomish Channel has docks, bait shops, and charters. In April, thousands of tourists flock to the area to admire the tulip fields in full bloom. Although La Conner is a small town, it offers a variety of unique shops and art galleries.

Located in Skagit (SKA-jit) County the sales/use taxes are 7.8%.

$69-$101   **The HERON**, 117 Maple Ave., La Conner, WA 98257, phone 360-466-4626. This Victorian style country inn has 12 nonsmoking guest rooms with private facilities. Phone and TV in each room, fireplaces in some rooms. Hot tub in the backyard or relax by the stone fireplace in the parlor. View rooms and a jacuzzi suite. Continental breakfast provided. Children 12 and over welcome, no pets. **Rates:** double occupancy, single (1 bed) $69; double room $83; suite $101. MasterCard & Visa. **Directions:** located at the entrance to town. Take the first left when you pass the Shell gas station.

$70-$110   **HOTEL PLANTER**, 715 First St., P. O. Box 702, La Conner, WA 98257, phone 360-466-4710 or 1-800-488-5409. This historic hotel was built in 1907; it has been completely renovated and reopened in 1989. The 12 beautifully decorated rooms all have private facilities, phones, and TV. No coffee/tea making facilities in the rooms, but available in the lobby. This is a nonsmoking inn with a bricked garden courtyard complete with a gazebo-covered hot tub. All the rooms are located on the second floor. Children acceptable week days, no pets. **Rates:** double occupancy, single room $70-$90; jacuzzi suite $110. Major credit cards. **Directions:** located in the center of town on the main street.

$65-$85   **KATY'S INN BED & BREAKFAST**, 503 S. Third, La Conner, WA 98257, phone 360-466-3366 or 1-800-914-7767. Captain John Peck built this house overlooking the Swinomish Channel in 1876. This country Victorian home has 4 nonsmoking guest rooms, 2 with private facilities and 2 with shared. All guest rooms on the second floor have access to the wrap-around porch. The double/queen beds are covered with feather duvets and lots of fluffy pillows. A hearty gourmet breakfast can be brought to your door on request or served on the porch. Relax in the parlor library, rock on the porch, play croquet, or soak in the hot tub under the gazebo. Parking is available on site, bicycles may be stored in the basement. Children by arrangement, no pets. **Summer Rates:** *4/01 to 9/30* - shared facilities $69-$80; private facilities $85; extra person $15. **Winter Rates:** $65-$80. MasterCard & Visa. **Directions:** on Third St. in downtown La Conner.

$60 **LIGHTHOUSE INN**, 512 S. 1st St., La Conner, WA 98257, phone 360-466-3147. One guest room overlooking the Swinomish Channel. Outside deck, queen bed, phone, AC, TV, private bath, and parking spot. Located on the main street of town above the Lighthouse Inn Restaurant. No coffee/tea making facilities in the room. Restaurant/lounge and deli downstairs, the deli section opens at 11:00 a.m. Children are welcome, but there is only one bed, no pets. **Rates:** double occupancy $60. Amex, MasterCard, Discover, & Visa. **Directions:** centrally located on the main street of town.

$75-$125 **RIDGEWAY BED & BREAKFAST**, 1292 McLean Rd., P. O. Box 475, La Conner, WA 98257, phone 360-428-8068 or 1-800-428-8068 (US & Canada). This country estate is surrounded by tulip fields. There are 5 nonsmoking guest rooms in the main house and a cottage with two guest rooms. Two rooms in the main house have private facilities and three share two baths. Four rooms are on the second floor and one on the main floor. A sixth room is available on the third floor for groups that want the entire house. Each bedroom has a pedestal sink and a king or queen bed. The cottage has two guest rooms with private facilities, shared kitchen and living room. A hearty farm breakfast is prepared for guests in the main house and there is homemade dessert in the evenings. The cottage is supplied with a buffet breakfast for guests to have at their leisure. Not equipped for small children or pets. **Rates:** double occupancy $75-$125; extra person $25. MasterCard, Amex, Discover, & Visa. **Directions:** located halfway between La Conner & Mt. Vernon.

$65-$125 **WHITE SWAN GUEST HOUSE BED & BREAK-FAST**, 1388 Moore Rd., Mount Vernon, WA 98257, phone 360-445-6805. A storybook Victorian farmhouse with 3 guest rooms that share two full baths. The Garden Cottage has its own bath, kitchen, private sun deck, and sleeps four comfortably. No phones or TV. Bring your bike and ride through the surrounding farmland and country roads. A filling, country continental breakfast is served every morning. Children welcome in the cottage, no pets. **Rates:** single room $65; double room $75; cottage $125; extra person $20. MasterCard & Visa. **Directions:** from I-5 take Exit 221, follow Conway/La Conner signs, turn right on Fir Island Rd. for 5 miles to Moore Rd. at the yellow light. One mile down Moore Rd.

LA PUSH is located on the Pacific Ocean, west of Forks.

(luh-POOSH) is the home of the Quileute Indian Tribe. This is a good place to watch the whale migration during March, April, and May.

$36-$125 **OCEAN PARK RESORT**, P. O. Box 67, La Push, WA 98350, phone 360-374-5267 or 1-800-487-1267. Open year-round with a total of 55 units. The variety of lodging includes motel units, cabins, deluxe camper cabins, and campers' cabins. The 20 motel units have an ocean view and equipped kitchenettes. Cabins are 1-3 bedrooms, 8 have oceanfront decks, 7 have fireplaces, 4 have woodstoves, and 3 have balconies overlooking the ocean. Two deluxe campers' cabins are set among the trees. Eight A-frame campers' cabins sleep up to 6 people, no hot water or showers, sleeping bags required. Brochures are available with more detailed description of each lodging. Children 6 and under free, pets allowed only in the A-frame campers' cabins. No daily maid service provided. RV and tent sites. **Rates:** motel units $50-$65; cabins, 1-3 bedrooms $65-$125; glass front cabins $78; deluxe campers' cabins $50; campers' cabins $36; extra person $10; pets $10 per night; tent site $10; RV hookup $12; taxes 7.9%. MasterCard, Discover, & Visa. **Directions:** 13 miles west of Forks at Pacific First Beach.

LACEY see Olympia.

LAKE CHELAN is located 37 miles north of Wenatchee in Central Washington.

Chelan, Manson, and Stehekin have lodgings on the lake. Lake (she-LAN) is 55 miles long and approximately 1500 feet deep. The top 20 feet is dammed to control snowmelt run-off and generate electricity. The lake level is lowered during winter and restored to full capacity by July. Fish for salmon, kokanee, rainbow, cutthroat, mackinaw trout, and a cod called burbot cod.

CHELAN

(pop. 3,020) is a sunny oasis nestled in the Eastern Cascades. Chelan is a premier year-round resort area located on beautiful Lake Chelan. Daily boat service is available from May 1 to October 31st to the remote community of Stehekin 55 miles up-lake. Stehekin is accessible only by boat or plane. Winter activities include snowmobiling, ice fishing, alpine skiing at Echo Valley, and xc skiing at Echo Ridge.

Located in Chelan County the sales/use taxes are 8%.

$30-$59   **APPLE INN MOTEL,** 1002 E. Woodin Ave., P. O. Box 1450, Chelan, WA 98816, phone 509-682-4044. 41 units, 19 nonsmoking. Phones, cable TV, A/C, heated outdoor swimming pool, indoor hot tub, complimentary coffee in the lobby. No coffee/tea making facilities in the rooms, but 4 units have fully equipped kitchenettes. Children welcome, infants free, no pets. Within walking distance of a restaurant. One mile to public transportation; shuttle provided to the Lady of the Lake boat dock and Chelan Airport. **Summer Rates:** *Memorial Day to Labor Day* - standard room $49; kitchen units $55; deluxe rooms $59; extra person $5. **Winter Rates:** standard room $30; kitchen and deluxe rooms $34. Major credit cards. **Directions:** located on Chelan's main street, Woodin Ave., on the east end of town 8 blocks from the city center.

$63-$80   **BRICK HOUSE INN BED & BREAKFAST,** P. O. Box 1976, Chelan, WA 98816, phone 509-682-2233 or 1-800-799-2332. Built in 1904, this modernized Victorian is just one block to the city center. Five clean, cozy, nonsmoking guest rooms share two baths, plus a suite with private facilities, equipped kitchenette, and TV. There is a TV lounge area, guest kitchen, and large covered wrap-around porch. A "no-host" continental breakfast is available daily in the guest kitchen. Children welcome, pets allowed, smoking permitted outside. **Summer Rates:** *Memorial Day to Labor Day; minimum 2 night stay on* *weekends* - guest rooms $63; suite $80; extra person $8. **Winter Rates:** check with management. MasterCard, Visa, & Discover. **Directions:** coming into town from the west, turn right on Sanders; from the east turn left on Sanders, go one block to the corner of Wapato St.

$63-$112 **CABANA MOTEL**, 420 Manson Rd., P. O. Box 596, Chelan, WA 98816, phone 509-682-2233 or 1-800-799-2332. This "family motel" has 12 units, 7 nonsmoking. TV, heated outdoor pool, A/C, BBQ, and 10 units have kitchenettes equipped with dishes and cooking utensils. Directly across from city park, lake, and bumper boats. Children welcome, pets allowed at no charge. **Summer Rates:** *Memorial Day to Labor Day* - double occupancy standard room, no kitchen $63; pool side/kitchen $78; upstairs lake view with balconies - 4 people $98; large suites - 4 people $112; extra person $8. **Winter Rates:** check with management. MasterCard, Visa, & Discover. **Directions:** coming into Chelan follow directions to Manson, across from City Park.

$48-$288 **CAMPBELL'S RESORT & CONFERENCE CENTER**, 104 W. Woodin Ave., P. O. Box 278, Chelan, WA 98816, phone 509-682-2561 or 1-800-553-8225, fax 509-682-2177. The historic Campbell's Hotel has been in continuous operation since 1901. The original hotel is now the restaurant and bar, catering to the conference center and the 150 rooms available at the resort. Spanning 8 acres on the shore of Lake Chelan all rooms have spectacular up-lake views. There are 94 nonsmoking rooms and two handicapped accessible. Deluxe rooms feature microwaves, wet bars, and refrigerators. All rooms have private patios or lanais. Some cottages offer full kitchens with basic cookware. Children 18 and under free with parents, no pets. **Summer Rates:** *6/16 to 9/04*- double occupancy $100-$288; extra person $10; cribs and rollaways $5; boat moorage $10; local phone calls free. **Winter Rates:** standard room $48; cottage $84. Major credit cards and personal checks. **Directions:** centrally located, downtown Chelan.

$35-$89 **CHELAN COUNTRY LODGE**, 531 E. Woodin Ave., P. O. Box 1961, Chelan, WA 98816, phone 509-682-8474 or 1-800-373-8474. This brand new motel caters to couples. All six nonsmoking rooms are on one level with one handicapped accessible room. The rooms are decorated in turn-of-the-century style and feature a microwave, fridge, and remote cable TV. One room will accommodate well-behaved children, no pets. Receive bonus coupons year-round for Mill Bay Casino worth $60 per couple. **Summer Rates:** *Memorial Day to 9/14* -

double occupancy $75-$89. **Winter Rates:** $35-$40. MasterCard & Visa. **Directions:** on Chelan's main street east of the traffic light at Robinson and Woodin. Look for the antique street clock.

$50-$220 **DARNELL'S RESORT MOTEL,** 901 Spader Bay Rd., P. O. Box 506, Chelan, WA 98816, phone 509-682-2015 or 1-800-967-8149. Right on the lake, every room has a view. 38 units, all nonsmoking. Phones, TV, indoor sauna, outdoor hot tub, and pool. This resort has numerous amenities - boat moorage, launching, tennis courts, bicycles, BBQ, putting green, canoes, etc., all free of charge. 34 units have equipped kitchens. Children welcome, no pets. Shuttle provided to Chelan Airport. **Summer Rates:** *6/18 thru Labor Day* - double occupancy sleeping loft, no kitchen $80; 1 bedroom 4 people $140-$155; 2 bedroom units 6 people $180-$220; extra person charge for over 4 people $10. **Winter Rates:** sleeping loft 2 people $50-$60; 1 bedroom 4 people $65-$92; 2 bedrooms, 6 people $90-$100. Weekly rates. Major credit cards. **Directions:** Darnells is in the city of Chelan, a few blocks southwest of city center on the Manson Highway (SR150).

$55-$95 **HIGHLAND GUEST HOUSE BED & BREAKFAST,** 121 E. Highland Ave., P. O. Box 2089, Chelan, WA 98816, phone 509-682-2892 or 1-800-681-2892. This 1902 two story home has been restored to capture its original charm and atmosphere. Three guest rooms are located on the second floor. The spacious Rose &

Highland House Bed & Breakfast

Wicker room has a private bath and its own balcony. The other two guest rooms share one bath. All rooms are tastefully decorated with antiques and memorabilia. A full gourmet breakfast is available starting at 7:30, coffee earlier, special diets are observed. Special occasion, private breakfasts can be arranged on the porch of the Rose & Wicker room. Children 6 years or older by arrangement, no pets, and no smoking on the premises. *Two night minimum stay on holiday weekends.* **Summer Rates:** *5/16 to 10/14* - double occupancy $75-$95; extra person $10; group discount 5-10%; weekly discount 10%. **Winter Rates:** $55-$65. MasterCard & Visa. **Directions:** in Chelan follow Hwy 150 toward Manson, turn right on Highland (last street leaving town across from the City Park), continue on Highland for 4 blocks. Parking on the street.

$17-$56 **HOLDEN VILLAGE BED & BREAKFAST**, Rt 1 Box 147-B, Chelan, WA 98816, phone 509-687-9695. Six nonsmoking rooms share two bathrooms. This B & B is primarily a stopover for guests traveling up-lake to Holden Village, but other guests are more than welcome. Beautiful, peaceful setting. Enjoy a hearty breakfast; the closest restaurant is 20 miles away in Chelan for other meals. Plan on changing your own bed linens. **Summer Rates:** *6/01 to 9/30* - single room $33; double $45; 3 bed dorm $19 per person; two room family rate $56. **Winter Rates:** single $28; double $39; 3 bed dorm $17 per person; family $50. No credit cards, personal checks okay. **Directions:** 3 miles up-lake from Fields Point ferry landing and just beyond 25 Mile Creek, South Shore Rd. ends shortly after Holden Village property.

$54-$120 **KELLY'S RESORT**, Rt 1 Box 119, Chelan, WA 98816, phone 509-687-3220. Ten individual cottages in the woods across the road from the lake. Pine-panelled cottages have living room, bedroom, bath, full kitchen, and Franklin fireplaces - they sleep 5 people maximum. The larger cottages have screened sleeping porches and sleep 8 people maximum. The main building at the water's edge has a store, fireplace room, spacious deck, and ping-pong porch. There is a sandy sunbathing area, lake swimming area with diving board, docks, and boat moorage for the guests. The upper cottage area has a grassy play yard. Two lakeside duplexes are also available. Children welcome, pets allowed. **Summer Rates:** *Memorial Day to mid September* - standard cottage 2 adults $80; large cottage 4 adults $105; extra person $7; lakeside duplex $110-$120; pets $10 weekly. **Winter Rates:** standard cottage $54; large cottage $71; duplex $75-$80 Weekly rates available. MasterCard, Amex, & Visa. **Directions:** 14 miles up-lake from Chelan on the South Shore Rd.

$75-$125 **MARY KAY'S WHALEY MANSION BED & BREAK-FAST**, 415 Third, Chelan, WA 98816, phone 509-682-5735 or 1-800-729-2408, fax 509-682-5385. Big emphasis on "breakfast", a decadent 4 course affair featuring hand dipped chocolates and gourmet entrees. All six rooms have private facilities with TV, VCR, refrigerator, AC, and overhead fans. The whole house and guest rooms are decorated with collectable antiques. An unusual decorating touch is the walls finished with upholstery material instead of wall paper. There are 3 guest rooms on the second floor and 3 on the third floor. Wear your goodsocks and observe the shoes off policy at the door, then snuggle your toes into the soft textured carpets. No children, no pets, and smoking outside. **Summer Rates:** *5/16 to 9/15, 2 night minimum on weekends, 3 nights on holidays* - double occupancy $105-$125. **Winter Rates:** *excluding holidays* - $75-$95. MasterCard & Visa, no personal checks. **Directions:** follow Hwy 97ALT to 3rd St., turn towards the lake, half a block on the right.

Mary Kay's Whaley Mansion

$35-$110 **MIDTOWNER MOTEL**, 721 Woodin Ave., P. O. Box 1722, Chelan, WA 98816, phone 509-682-4051. 46 units, 20 nonsmoking. No coffee/tea making facilities, but 6 units have fully equipped kitchens. All units have refrigerators, microwaves, AC, phones, and cable TV. Enjoy the indoor jacuzzi and heated, year-round outdoor pool. There is also a coin-op laundry and truck parking. Children 18 and under free with parents, pets allowed in the smoking units. Restaurant across the street; shuttle provided to the Lady of the Lake boat dock and local airport. **Summer Rates:** *5/20 to 9/15* - $57-$110; extra person $10; pets $5 per night. **Fall Rates:** *9/16 to 10/31* - $45-$60. **Winter Rates:** *11/01 to 5/19* - $35-$60. Major credit cards, no checks. **Directions:** from city center go east, 4 blocks from the traffic light.

$29-$60 **MOM'S MONTLAKE MOTEL**, 823 Wapato S.E., Chelan, WA 98816, phone 509-682-5715. 10 very tidy, nonsmoking units with flowers in the window boxes. Coffee/tea making facilities and TV. Four units have fully equipped kitchens. There are picnic tables, shade trees, and lawn in a quiet setting. Located within walking distance of restaurants, 8 blocks to the lake. Shuttle provided to the Lady of the Lake boat dock. Well-behaved children welcome, no pets, and no parties. **Summer Rates:** *7/01 thru Labor Day* - double occupancy $50; kitchen units $10 extra; extra person $10. **Winter Rates:** single $29; double $36; kitchen units $10 extra. MasterCard & Visa. **Directions:** 6 blocks from the city center and 1 block off the main street, Woodin Ave.

$30-$65 **PARKWAY MOTEL**, 402 No. Manson Hwy, P. O. Box 1237, Chelan, WA 98816, phone 509-682-2822. 15 units, 4 nonsmoking. The units are small, with knotty pine interior. Eight kitchen units are connected to small basic rooms and make into larger family units. TV and AC. A large front lawn faces the lake and is equipped with swings and picnic tables. Children welcome, pets allowed in the off-season. Centrally located, within walking distance of city center, across the street from the lake, bumper boats, and Lake Shore Park. **Summer Rates:** *Memorial Day thru Labor Day* - basic room $35; kitchen units $65; honeymoon suite $60; extra person $5. **Winter Rates:** basic room $30; kitchen units $45; honeymoon suite $55. No credit cards, checks okay. **Directions:** in Chelan follow the road to Manson, across from City Park.

$70-$130 **WATSON'S HARVERENE RESORT**, Rt 1 Box 95, Chelan, WA 98816, phone 509-687-3720 or 1-800-697-3720. Cabins and units sleep from 4 to 10 people, one cabin with a fireplace. This family resort offers quiet, low-keyed relaxation in cozy, beachside housekeeping cottages nestled in the tall pines. No phones, no TV. Enjoy sandy beaches, heated pool, hot tub, and even a complimentary ride aboard the 40 foot "Executive Suite" yacht. **Summer Rates:** *4 person minimum* $130 per night; extra person $10. **May, June, & September Rates:** 2 people $70; 3 people $75; 4 people $80; moorage stall $8 per day. No credit cards. **Directions:** from Wenatchee take Hwy 97ALT north going to Chelan. Follow signs to Lake Chelan State Park. At intersection on So. Lake Shore Rd. go straight across the intersection to Watson's Resort.

$48-$155 **WESTVIEW RESORT MOTEL,**2312 W.Woodin Ave., Rt. 1 Box 14, Chelan, WA 98816, phone 509-682-4396, reservations 1-800-468-2781. 25 units, 13 nonsmoking. Coffee making facilities in every room, TV, phones, private decks - each with a view of the lake. Five units have fully equipped kitchens, 20 units have small refrigerators and microwaves. Heated swimming pool, spa, laundry, private dock, and beach access. Adjoining Lakeside Park with playground and picnic area. Children welcome, no pets. **Summer Rates:** *Memorial Day thru Labor Day* - based on double occupancy $98; larger units with full kitchens $135-$155; extra person $10, maximum 4 people to a room. **Winter Rates:** double $48; larger units $78 and up. Major credit cards. **Directions:** next to Lakeside Park on the south shore of Lake Chelan, first motel coming into Chelan from the west on Hwy 97ALT.

MANSON

is 9 miles up-lake on the north shore. This small community is located in the heart of the fruit growing region, primarily apples. Many visitors enjoy the rural atmosphere and tree-lined streets that lead to Manson Bay Park.

$60-$65 **APPLE COUNTRY BED & BREAKFAST**, 5220 Manson Blvd., Manson, WA 98831, phone 509-687-3982. *Open May 1st- September 30th.* Located in the middle of orchards this is the place to get away from the crowds, but if you miss them the Mill Bay Casino is only four miles away. This 1930 ranch house has two guest rooms that share one bathroom. One guest room features a queen bed and the other room has two twin beds. A full breakfast is available at 8:30 a.m. and coffee earlier. Shuttle is provided by arrangement to the Lady of the Lake dock in Manson. Cannot accommodate children or pets. **Rates:** $60 & $65. No credit cards, personal checks okay. **Directions:** coming into Manson turn right at the sign to Mill Bay Casino, continue past the casino 4 miles on Wapato Lake Rd., turn left on Manson Blvd. for .3 mile, turn left on dirt road into orchard, sign reads Margaret and Don Janicke.

$75-$95 **HUBBARD HOUSE BED & BREAKFAST**, P. O. Box 348, Manson, WA 98831, phone 509-687-3058. *Open May - September.* There are three rooms on the second floor in this 1920's French Normandy home. Two rooms have a view of the lake. One room has private facilities; two rooms share a bath; all rooms have sinks, overhead fans, feather mattresses, and are decorated with antiques. There is private lake access for swimming and a lush English rose garden. On weekends a full breakfast is provided, 8:30 a.m. to 10 a.m., featuring special apple dishes, coffee is available earlier. Breakfast is served on the deck overlooking Lake Chelan, weather permitting. During the week a generous continental breakfast is available. Children and pets by arrangement. Within walking distance of restaurants and bus service. **Rates:** *two night minimum on weekends in July and August* - guest rooms $75-$85; family room $95; extra person $10. Inquire about golf packages. MasterCard & Visa. **Directions:** in Manson continue 3/4 mile beyond entrance to Wapato Point, through town along lake and watch for "Hubbard House" sign, on the left.

Hubbard House Bed & Breakfast

$36-$105 **MOUNTAIN VIEW LODGE**, 25 Wapato Point Parkway., P. O. Box 337, Manson, WA 98831, phone 509-687-9505 or 1-800-967-8105. 30 units, 19 nonsmoking. One unit available with equipped kitchenette, gas barbecue, and private balcony. No coffee/tea making facilities in the rooms, but provided in the lobby. In-room phones, TV, small refrigerators, and AC. Outdoor features are pool, hot tub, large lawn, volleyball, picnic tables, BBQs, and a beautiful view. Within walking distance of 6 restaurants, free public transportation, and the lake. Shuttle provided to the local airport. Children welcome, no pets. The lodge's prices vary depending on the day and season (they have 5 seasons), be sure and check on rates when booking. **Summer Rates:** king bed (midweek) $69 (Fri/Sat) $75; double queen (midweek) $83 (Fri/Sat) $89; family suite (midweek) $99 (Fri/Sat) $105; kitchen suite $105; holidays $5 extra per night. **Off-Season Rates:** king bed $36-$65; double queen $42-$69; family suite $53-$84; kitchen suite $73-$84; holidays $5 extra per night. Major credit cards. **Directions:** from Chelan, 7 miles up the north shore on Wapato Way, one mile past the Mill Bay Casino.

STEHEKIN

(pop. 70) is an isolated community at the head of Lake Chelan and is only accessible by boat or airplane. (steh-HEE-kin) is an Indian word meaning "the way through".

$69-$95 **NORTH CASCADES LODGE**, Stehekin, WA, P. O. Box 186, Stehekin, WA 98816, phone 509-682-4584. This remote lodge is located 55 miles up-lake and is only accessible by boat or plane, making it one of the most pristine environments available. 28 rooms available, 4 nonsmoking, and 2 handicapped accessible. Seven housekeeping units with equipped kitchens sleep 2 to 8 people. Deluxe rooms have a view of the lake, standard rooms have a view of the forest. Activities include fishing, hiking, boating, horseback riding, river rafting, interpretive tours, and bicycling. No phones, TV, or radios. The restaurant is open year-round. Children welcome, infants free, no pets. **Rates:** deluxe rooms $75; standard rooms $69; family rooms $80; housekeeping units $80-$95; children ages 2 to 11 $5; ages 12 and over $10. **Directions:** call the business office for boat schedule.

$65-$135 **SILVER BAY LODGING BED & BREAKFAST** & Guest Cabins, P. O. Box 85, Stehekin, WA 98852, phone 509-682-2212 Monday - Friday 8 a.m. to 5 p.m., reservations 1-800-555-7781. Nestled in the heart of the Cascades at the headwaters of Lake Chelan, these waterfront accommodations have spectacular views. Enjoy the comforts of home in a true wilderness area. Transportation provided to and from the Stehekin landing. Two night minimum stay, 5 nights for cabins (July thru Sept.). Three rooms in the B & B. The master suite has a bath with soaking tub, lake and river view decks, queen bed, and sitting room. The cabins on the lake's edge have fully equipped kitchens. Generous continental breakfast. Adults only in the B & B, children over 8 years old in the cabins, no pets. Open year-round. **Rates:** B & B mt. view $65; river view $85; suite $120; cabins $135; extra person $20.

$55 **STEHEKIN VALLEY RANCH**, P. O. Box 36, Stehekin, WA 98852, phone 509-682-4677 9 a.m. to 5 p.m. *Open from 6/09 to 9/30.* The Courtney's ranch is another unique one-of-a-kind place to experience. It may be best described as a fancy campground or a rustic resort. It has an outdoor flavor with some soft touches, such as hot showers. There are 12 sleeping cabins that house 1 to 5 guests, with shared facilities in a separate bathhouse. Maximum capacity of 30 people. Three hearty meals a day are provided for guests.

Horseback riding available. Children welcome, no pets. **Rates:** adults $55 per person; children 7-12 years old $45; 6 and under $30; rates are $5 less if you provide your own sleeping bag; horseback riding $32 for 3 hours. No credit cards. **Directions:** from Chelan or Fields Point take the Lady of the Lake up-lake to Stehekin, the Courtney's will provide transportation to the ranch 9 miles up the valley.

LAKE CLE ELUM for lodging, see Cle Elum - The Last Resort.

LAKE QUINAULT is just off coastal Hwy 101, 67 miles south of Forks.

(Lake kwin-AWLT) is in the Quinault rain forest located in the Olympic National Park and Olympic National Forest (32 miles east of Kalaloch). Glacier-carved Lake Quinault has deep clear waters and a forest-ringed shore. This is a popular fishing site; you can obtain a fishing permit from the Quinault Indian Reservation at local stores. Hiking and mushroom hunting are other popular activities. There is lodging on the south shore in Quinault and on the north shore in Amanda Park.
Located in Grays Harbor County the sales/use/lodging taxes are 10.9%.

AMANDA PARK is on the west end of Lake Quinault and is the address of the north shore resorts.

$40-$45 **AMANDA PARK MOTEL,** 8 River Dr., P. O. Box 624, Amanda Park, WA 98526, phone 360-288-2237, reservations 1-800-410-2237. Eight units with 4 nonsmoking rooms available. All units have TV and 5 units have refrigerators. Morning coffee is available at the store down the street. All rooms have a view of the Quinault River and are within easy walking distance of store, cafe, and post office. Children 9 and under free, no pets. **Summer Rates:** *7/01 to 9/30* - single $40; double $45; extra person $5. Amex, Visa, & MasterCard. **Directions:** in Amanda Park, behind Amanda Park Mercantile.

$50-$65 **LOCHAERIE RESORT,** 638 North Shore Rd., Amanda Park, WA 98526, phone 360-288-2215. Five rustic cabins, all have fireplaces, complete kitchens, and bathrooms with showers. Guests are provided with linens, all kitchen utensils, and firewood. This quiet retreat is minutes from the hiking trails of the Quinault rain forest and the park interior. Fish the streams, rivers, and lakes; mushrooming in spring and autumn; the Pacific Ocean is a short drive away. Four cabins have a view of Lake Quinault. Children under 2 free, no pets. **Rates:** based on double occupancy $50-$65; extra person $8. No credit cards. **Directions:** take Hwy 101 to Lake Quinault. On North Shore Rd., Lochaerie is 4 miles on the right.

QUINAULT

(kwin-AWLT) is on the south shore road. The Olympic National Park Ranger Station is a great place to stop for literature on hiking trails and current activities in the area.

$52-$125 **LAKE QUINAULT LODGE**, P. O. Box 7, Quinault, WA 98575, phone 360-288-9200, for reservations 1-800-562-6672. 92 rooms, some nonsmoking, in either the quaint original lodge built in 1926, the fireplace wing, or the newer lakeside building. In keeping with the tranquility of the region, there are no phones or TVs in the rooms. Coffee/tea making facilities in the lakeside and fireplace rooms, also available in the lobby. Restaurant is open year-round. Indoor pool/spa, sauna, game room, cocktails, TV sports and news in the Forest Room, summer rental boats. Children 5 and under are free, pets allowed only in the Annex rooms. **Summer Rates:** *6/16 to 10/07* - $92-$125; extra person $10; pet charge $10 per night. **Winter Rates:** midweek, based on double occupancy $52; Fri/Sat rates $65-$99; (*summer rates apply 12/20 to 1/02).* Visa, MasterCard, & Amex. **Directions:** from Hwy 101 go north from Aberdeen to the Lake Quinault south shore exit and proceed for two miles.

$39-$150 **RAIN FOREST RESORT VILLAGE**, 516 South Shore Rd., Quinault, WA 98575, phone 360-288-2535, reservations 1-800-255-6936. Surrounded by natural beauty, the resort has 16 motel style rooms and 18 cabins. Eight cabins are available only in the summer. Coffee/tea making facilities in the 16 motel rooms at the inn. There are fireplaces in 10 cabins, five have jacuzzi tubs, and five have non-equipped kitchens. Restaurant/lounge on the premises, open year-round for dinner. Gift shop, general store, laundromat, boat launch, and RV facilities. Situated on the lake, 10 cabins and 12 motel units have views of the lake. Children welcome, infants/ toddlers free, no pets. **Summer Rates:** *7/01 to 9/30 - double occupancy*, cabins $105-$150; motel units $77-$82; extra person $10. **Winter Rates:** (midweek) cabins $50-$95; motel $39-$44; (Fri/Sat) cabins $75-$135; motel $55-$60. Discover, Amex, Visa, & MasterCard. **Directions:** from Hwy 101 take the Lake Quinault Exit and proceed for 3 1/2 miles on the South Shore Rd.

LAKE WENATCHEE is located 20 miles northwest of Leavenworth, off Stevens Pass Hwy 2.

Lake (wuh-NACH-ee) is glacier fed by the White River. Activities include golf, hiking, canoeing, kayaking, swimming, boardsailing, fishing, cross country skiing and snowmobiling. Also see Leavenworth for lodging.

Located in Chelan County the sales/use taxes are 8%.

$45-$115 **COUGAR INN RESORT,** 23379 SR 207, **Lake Wenatchee, Leavenworth, WA 98826, phone 509-763-3354.** Located at the head of Lake Wenatchee, there are 9 units available, 5 with private facilities and 4 with shared. There are 5 rooms upstairs above the restaurant/lounge. The cabins and suite have TV and 2 cabins have equipped kitchens. Tennis courts and, of course, the lake. The resort is noted for its outstanding Sunday brunch and all you can eat seafood/prime rib buffet on Friday nights. Dining on the deck when weather permits. Children welcome, no pets. **Rates:** single rooms $45; cabins $80; suite $115. Amex, Visa, & MasterCard. **Directions:** turn off Hwy 2 onto Hwy 207 at Coles Corner, proceed for 10 miles to the head of the lake.

$95-$135 **LAKE WENATCHEE HIDE-A-WAYS,** 2511 **Kinnikinick Dr., Leavenworth, WA 98826, phone 509-763-2611 or 1-800-883-2611.** Ten individual vacation cabins set in the woods or on the lake, some with views of the lake. The least expensive ones are in the woods. Nine cabins are nonsmoking, four have TV and VCR, all have equipped kitchens. Moorage and hot tub at select cabins. The cabins sleep 4 to 8 people comfortably. Children welcome, infants free. Pets allowed in only one cabin. **Rates:** *minimum of 2 nights on Leavenworth's festival weekends* - double occupancy $95-$135; extra person $10. Amex. **Directions:** directions will be given to individual cabins at time of booking.

$69-$125 **PINE RIVER RANCH BED & BREAKFAST,** 19668 **Hwy 207, Leavenworth, WA 98826, phone & fax 509-763-3959 or 1-800-669-3877.** This 32 acre ranch is home to horses, chickens, and one resident llama. There are 4 guest rooms in the main house and two suites in a separate cottage. The two upstairs rooms share a bath, all the other rooms have private facilities. All rooms are supplied with robes, slippers, extra pillows, and hot tub towels. Select rooms have overhead fans, fireplaces, espresso makers, and CD players. There is a beverage center well stocked with ice, coffee, tea, cocoa, and cookies. In the winter there is a tracked xc ski area covering 200 acres. The river is a short stroll away. Full breakfast provided. Close to golf course, the St. Park, and 20 minutes from Stevens Pass ski area. Children by arrangement, no pets, and no smoking indoors. **Rates:** *two night minimum stay on Leavenworth's festivals weekends and holidays* - double occupancy $69-$125; suites $95 midweek, 2 night minimum. **Winter Rates:** $5 extra per room. MasterCard & Visa. **Directions:** from Hwy 2 turn north on Hwy 207 and proceed 1.8 miles, the entrance is on the left.

Pine River Ranch Bed & Breakfast

$50 **SQUIRREL TREE INN**, 15251 Hwy 2, Leavenworth, WA 98826, phone 509-763-3157. Six basic motel units, no nonsmoking, adjacent to the Squirrel Tree Restaurant. No coffee/tea making facilities in the rooms, but the restaurant opens at 6:00 a.m., lounge closes at 10:00 p.m. during the week and 1:00 a.m. weekends. Mini-mart, pay phone, and gas. Children welcome, pets by arrangement. **Rates:** double occupancy $50; extra person $5; pets $10 per night. Most major credit cards. **Directions:** at the junction of Hwy 2 and Hwy 207.

LEAVENWORTH (pop. 1, 705) is located 22 miles northwest of Wenatchee on Hwy 2.

In the 1960's the town decided to take advantage of its natural beauty and similarity to the European Alps and is now one of the prime tourists' spots in the Cascades. A major face lift turned the community into a Bavarian style town. Almost everything is centered around that theme, and people come from all over to enjoy the alpine scenery as well as the Bavarian facade and cross country skiing.

Located in Chelan County the sales/use taxes are 8%.

$70-$145 **ABENDBLUME INN,** 12570 Ranger Rd., Leavenworth, WA 98826, phone 509-548-4059 or 1-800-669-7634. Five spacious guest rooms with an accent on comfort and privacy. All rooms have private facilities and fine European bedding. Most have private balconies. Breakfast is served in the traditional Austrian breakfast room. The common areas include old world archways, limestone foyer, hand-forged curved stairway, carved walls and ceilings. Children by arrangement, no pets. Smoke free environment. **Rates:** *two night minimum stay on weekends, festivals, and holidays* - double occupancy $70-$90; suites $125-$145. Amex, MasterCard, & Visa. **Directions:** from Seattle turn left on Ski Hill Dr.; from Wenatchee turn right on Ski Hill Dr., then continue 1 mile to Ranger Rd.

$85-$125 **ALL SEASONS RIVER INN BED & BREAKFAST,** 8751 Icicle Rd., P. O. Box 788, Leavenworth, WA 98826, phone 509-548-1425 or 1-800-254-0555. Six spacious riverfront rooms, furnished with antiques. Each room has a seating area with river and mountain views, private bath, riverfront deck or patio. Some rooms have jacuzzi tubs and fireplaces. TV viewing in the upstairs library. The living room has a bay window seating area overlooking the river and wood burning stove. Bicycles are available for guests to use. Gourmet breakfast in the dining room or on the deck, weather permitting. Children 16 and older, no pets. Smoking is not permitted on the premises. **Rates:** *two night minimum stay on weekends, festivals, and holidays* - double occupancy $95-$125; seasonal weekday rates $85-$115. MasterCard, Visa, & personal checks.

Directions: from Seattle turn right on Icicle Rd.; from Wenatchee turn left on Icicle Rd., cross the bridge, 2nd house on the left.

$75-$150 **ALPENROSE INN,** 500 Alpine Pl., Leavenworth, WA 98826, phone 509-548-3000 or 1-800-582-2474. 15 rooms, all with private facilities. Phones and basic cable TV. Most rooms have fireplaces and private balconies. Complimentary breakfast buffet. There is a leisure room for visiting, bridge, or reading. Year-round spa, seasonal outdoor pool, and large deck for picnicking or sunning. Each room is different and individualized. Children by arrangement, no pets, and no smoking. 13 rooms are under $100 a night, double occupancy, 3 of these rooms do not have fireplaces. **Rates:** *two night minimum stay during festivals and holidays;* double occupancy $75-$98; double jacuzzi suites $135 and $150; local phone calls free. Major credit cards. **Directions:** from Seattle turn right on Icicle Rd. (first street coming into town), go one block, turn left on Alpine Place, proceed 1/2 block.

$65 **AUTUMN POND BED & BREAKFAST,** 10388 Titus Rd., Leavenworth, WA 98826, phone 509-548-4482 or 1-800-222-9661. Five guest rooms, all with private baths. This home was built to be a bed and breakfast. Located on 3 acres with good views and a pond. Full breakfast is provided. Half a mile to town. Children by arrangement, no pets, and no smoking. **Rates:** double occupancy $65; extra adult $10. MasterCard & Visa. **Directions:** turn north off Hwy 2 onto Ski Hill Dr., go 1/2 mile, turn right on Pine St., then left on Titus Rd., proceed for 1/2 mile.

$69-$85 **BAYERN on the RIVER,** 1505 Alpensee Strausse, Leavenworth, WA 98826, phone 509-548-5875 or 1-800-873-3960 (USA) 1-800-255-3151 (Canada). 27 guest rooms, 25 nonsmoking. All rooms have balconies or patios overlooking the Wenatchee River. Phones and basic cable TV. No coffee/tea making facilities in the rooms, but available in the lobby, and there are 4 equipped kitchen units. Outdoor pool and hot tub. Six blocks to town. Children welcome, infants free, pets allowed. **Rates:** *minimum 2 night stay on festival weekends -* single room (1 bed) $69; double room (2 beds) $77; kitchen unit $79; family room with kitchen, 4 people $85; extra person $8; pets $10; local phone calls free. Most major credit cards. **Directions:** on Hwy 2 going east, at the east end of town, turn left just before the bridge.

See the photo on the next page.

Bayern on the River

$50-$60   **BINDLESTIFF'S RIVERSIDE CABINS**, 1600 Hwy 2, Leavenworth, WA 98826, phone 509-548-5015. 8 modern cabins, 2 nonsmoking. All have private facilities, country decor, and basic cable TV. No coffee/tea making facilities in the cabins, but available in the office with a continental breakfast. Located in a wooded setting, the cabins have a sliding glass door opening onto a patio overlooking the Wenatchee River. Children welcome, pets allowed at no charge. **Rates:** *2 day minimum on festival weekends and holidays* - double occupancy, single room $50; double room (2 beds, 2-4 people) $60. MasterCard, Amex, & Visa. **Directions:** on Hwy 2 going east, at the east end of town, turn left immediately after crossing the bridge.

$69-$98   **BLACKBIRD LODGE**, 305 8th St., Leavenworth, WA 98826, phone 509-548-5800 or 1-800-446-0240. Downtown location, overlooking Blackbird Island. Three floors, 15 rooms, and one adjacent cottage. The 9 river-view rooms have fireplaces and balconies, these are adult only rooms. All rooms have TV, phones, and hand-hewn wood furniture. An extended continental breakfast is served to your door through a private two-way cabinet. Year-round outdoor spa. Cross country ski trail just steps away from the door. Children welcome, no pets, smoke free environment. **Rates:** *2 night minimum on festival weekends and holidays* - standard room mid-week $69, Friday & Saturday $79; deluxe room mid-week $74, Friday & Saturday $88; fireplace rooms mid-week $84, Friday & Saturday $98; extra person, 12 and older $10, under 12 $2.50; local phone calls free. All major credit cards. **Directions:** turn into town at stoplight, go 2 blocks to Commercial, turn right, 1 block to Lodge.

$61-$120   **BUDGET HOST CANYON'S INN**, 185 Hwy 2, Leavenworth, WA 98826, phone 509-548-7992 or 1-800-693-1225. 32 rooms, 70% nonsmoking. All rooms have phones and cable TV. Coffee is available in the suites and also in the lobby. Indoor pool, outdoor hot tub. 1.5 blocks from downtown. Children 6 and under free, pets allowed. **Rates:** *2 day minimum on festival weekends and holidays* - single room (1 bed) $61; double room (2 beds) $70; family room $110; jacuzzi suite $120; extra person $10; pets $10 per night; local phone calls free. All major credit cards. **Directions:** on Hwy 2 west of town 1.5 blocks.

$66-$134   **DER RITTERHOF MOTOR INN**, 190 Highway 2, Leavenworth, WA 98826, phone 509-548-5845 or 1-800-255-5845 (WA). 54 units, 40 nonsmoking. Phones and TV, most with remote control. No coffee/tea making facilities in the rooms, but available in the lobby. Six equipped kitchen units available. Heated outdoor pool, 2 hot tubs, putting green, barbecue pit, volleyball, badminton, horseshoes, and children's play area. Children 5 and under free, pets allowed. **Rates:** *2 night minimum on festival weekends and holidays* - single room (1 bed) $66; double room (2 beds) $72; kitchen unit $72; family room $87-$90; suite $134; extra person $8; pets free; local phone calls free. MasterCard, Amex, & Visa. **Directions:** 2 blocks west of town.

$78-$167   **ENZIAN MOTOR INN**, 590 Hwy 2, Leavenworth, WA 98826, phone 509-548-5269 or 1-800-223-8511 (WA). With authentic German design and furnishings, the Enzian is a blend of old world atmosphere and contemporary comfort. There are 104 rooms, 60% nonsmoking. No coffee/tea making facilities in the rooms, but a complimentary European breakfast buffet is provided upstairs in the solarium room and coffee is available in the lobby. Amenities include: outdoor and indoor pools, hot tubs, racquetball court, ping-pong room, exercise equipment, use of cross country ski equipment, comfortable lobby with fireplace and grand piano. Convention facilities. Children 5 and under free, pets allowed in some rooms on the main floor. **Rates:** *2 night minimum during Autumn Leaf Festival and Christmas Lighting (festival card required)* - single room (1 bed) $78-$88; double room (2 beds) $92; family room $98; suites $132-$167; extra person $10; pets $10 per night; local phone calls free. Major credit cards. **Directions:** on Hwy 2, west end of town.

$60-$125   **EVERGREEN INN**, 1117 Front St., Leavenworth, WA 98826, phone 509-548-5515 or 1-800-327-7212 (US & Canada), fax 509-548-6556. This is an older, well-kept motel in a quiet homey setting with 39 rooms, 36 nonsmoking. All rooms have phones, coffee/tea making facilities, and TV. Some rooms have fireplaces and there are 12 equipped kitchen units available. Complimentary continental breakfast on weekends. Hot tub, private park, and ample parking. Children 18 and under free with parents, pets allowed. One block stroll to the village center. **Rates:** *2 night minimum on festival weekends* - single room (1 bed) $60; double room (2 beds) $72-$80; suites $90-$125; rollaway $10; pets $10 per night; local phone calls free. Major credit cards. **Directions:** from the west, go through town, turn right onto Front St. (just past the Food Giant) proceed for two blocks, on the left. From the east, cross the bridge going into town and take the first left.

$79-$89 **HAUS LORELEI BED & BREAKFAST**, 347 Division St., Leavenworth, WA 98826, phone 509-548-5726. The architecture of this 1903 lodge is awesome. The foundation is river rock and there is a large river rock fireplace in the main parlor. The ten spacious guest rooms are exquisitely furnished with lace and antiques. All rooms have private facilities, robes, and feather mattresses. There are 5 rooms on the main floor, two with private entrances, and five on the second floor. Each room is unique and lavish. The setting is above the Wenatchee River surrounded by tall evergreens. Amenities include the outdoor hot tub overlooking the river, tennis courts, basketball, trampoline, and bicycles. Cross country ski trails are adjacent to the property. Children welcome, no pets, and no smoking. Full breakfast served from 8 to 10 a.m., coffee available at 7 a.m. **Rates:** *two night minimum stay on weekends* - double occupancy $79-$89; children 4 and older $10; adults $20. No credit cards. **Directions:** from Hwy 2 turn into town at the stoplight, go to Commercial, turn left, go 2 blocks to Division, turn right and follow road to the end.

Haus Lorelei Bed & Breakfast

$40 **INGALL'S CREEK LODGE**, 3003 Highway 97, Leavenworth, WA 98826, phone 509-548-6281. Located on the northern approach to Swauk/Blewett Pass, this modern log lodge has 4 lodge rooms, 3 nonsmoking. All rooms have private facilities, cable TV, AC, and a queen bed. No coffee/tea making facilities in the rooms, but the Hofbrau Cafe is open from 8 a.m. to 5 p.m. every day except Tuesday and Wednesday. Ingalls Creek hiking trail is just across the street. Fish in Ingalls Creek or Peshastin Creek. Adults only, no pets. **Rates:** single (1 bed) $40; pay phone 25¢. MasterCard & Visa. **Directions:** 7 miles south of the junction of Hwy 2 and Hwy 97, at milepost 178 on Hwy 97.

$70-$165 **LEAVENWORTH VILLAGE INN**, 1016 Commercial, Leavenworth, WA 98826, phone 509-548-6620 or 1-800-343-8198 (USA). This nonsmoking Inn offers 11 standard rooms under $100 and 7 luxury suites. The rooms are handsomely decorated, all have phones and basic cable TV. No coffee/tea making facilities in the rooms, but a continental breakfast is available in the sunny morning room. Children 18 and under free with parents, no pets. Convenient downtown location and off-street parking. The morning room is well-suited for small group functions, group rates are available. **Rates:** *two night minimum on holidays and festival weekends* - single queen room $70; double queen room $85; extra person in standard room $10; suites $125-$165; extra person $15; local phone calls free. MasterCard, Amex, & Visa. **Directions:** on Hwy 2 at stoplight turn towards town, go 2 blocks, turn left, go one block.

$75-$105 **LINDERHOF MOTOR INN**, 690 Hwy 2, Leavenworth, WA 98826, phone 509-548-5283 or 1-800-828-5680 (US & Canada). 26 units, 22 nonsmoking. All rooms have phones and remote control TV with HBO. No coffee/tea making facilities in the rooms, but a continental breakfast is provided in the lobby. There are 10 family townhouse suites with equipped kitchens that sleep 6-8 people. Outdoor pool and hot tub. Children 6 and under free, no pets. **Rates:** *2 night minimum on festival weekends* - standard room $75; family townhouse suites (2 people) $105; extra person $10; local phone calls free. Major credit cards. **Directions:** on the highway coming into town from the west.

$50-$100 **LORRAINE'S EDEL HOUSE INN**, 320 9th Street, Leavenworth, WA 98826, phone 509-548-4412 or 1-800-487-3335. "Thee" place to dine in Leavenworth and lodging, too. There are 3 rooms available in the main house and one cottage. The rooms have private baths, queen beds with comforters, cable TV, and terry robes to wear to the hot tub. A cottage suite features double jacuzzi tub, coffee maker, fireplace, stereo, and a private entrance. Off-street parking. No smoking and no pets. A short walk to park or shopping. **Rates:** *2 night minimum on* *festival weekends* - Friday & Saturday, guest rooms $70, cottage $100; Sunday through Thursday guest rooms $50, cottage $80; extra person $5. Guests receive a 50% discount on a lunch or dinner at the Edel House restaurant. MasterCard, Discover, & Visa. **Directions:** from Hwy 2 turn toward town at the stoplight, go to the end of the street.

$90-$305° **MOUNTAIN HOME LODGE**, P. O. Box 687, Leavenworth, WA 98826, phone 509-548-7077. Located high on a hill overlooking the Cascade Mountains, this nonsmoking lodge has 9 guest rooms all with private facilities. Decorated in cozy country, price varies by view. Outdoor pool, hot tub, tennis court, mountain bike trails, volleyball, croquet, 1700 foot sled run, and cross country ski trails. Free use of xc ski equipment and snowshoes. Guided snowmobile tours priced separately. In the winter this is a true destination lodge. Park at the end of the road and a snow cat picks up guests and transports them to the lodge. All meals are furnished in the winter months from 11/15 to 3/31, including dinner on the night of arrival. Breakfast in the summer is included in the price and other meals charged separately. Adults only, no pets. Reservations are recommended one year in advance for winter weekends. **Summer Rates:** double occupancy $90-$175. **Winter Rates:** *two night minimum stay* - double occupancy $225-$305 weekends; midweek $185-$265. Major credit cards. **Directions:** from the west go through town on Hwy 2, cross the Wenatchee River Bridge, turn right on E. Leavenworth Rd., go to Mt. Home Rd., turn left and proceed 2.5 miles to the end.

$47-$73 **MRS. ANDERSON'S LODGING HOUSE**, 917 Commercial, Leavenworth, WA 98826, phone 509-548-6173 or 1-800-253-8990 (US & Canada). Located in the heart of downtown, the lodge is the oldest frame house in town. Nine guest rooms available, 7 with private facilities and 2 with shared. All rooms have remote control TV and views of Leavenworth, 2 rooms have private balconies. Four rooms are located on the main floor and 6 on the second. Cozy rooms with queen beds, tapestry throws, and antiques. Complimentary breakfast buffet. Children 6 and under free, no pets, and no smoking. Quilt Shoppe on the main floor. **Rates:** *2 night minimum on festival weekends* - standard room, shared bath $47-$51; private bath $58-$73. Major credit cards. **Directions:** from Hwy 2 turn south on 9th, left on Commercial.

$61-$75 **OBERTAL MOTOR INN**, 922 Commercial, Leavenworth, WA 98826, phone 509-548-5204 or 1-800-537-9382 (US & Canada). 25 units, 70% nonsmoking. All rooms have phones and basic cable TV. Coffee available in certain rooms, and also in the lobby. Outdoor hot tub. Children 6 and under free, pets allowed in certain rooms.

Rates: *2 night minimum on festival weekends* - single room (1 bed /2 people) $61-$70; double (2 beds 2-4 people) $75; extra person $10; pets $10; local phone calls free. All major credit cards. **Directions:** go to stoplight on Hwy 2, turn toward town, go 2 blocks, turn left, 1 block.

$75-$165 **PENSION ANNA**, 926 Commercial, Leavenworth, WA 98826, phone 509-548-6273 or 1-800-509-ANNA, fax 509-548-4656. This Austrian style chalet has 15 rooms furnished with authentic Austrian and German furniture. All rooms have private baths, phones, and TV. Suites have double jacuzzi tubs and fireplaces. A traditional European breakfast is included. Children welcome, unable to accommodate pets, all rooms are nonsmoking. **Rates:** *2 night minimum on festival weekends and some holidays* - double occupancy $75; suites $140-$165; extra person $10; rollaway $15; local phone calls free. Major credit cards. **Directions:** on Hwy 2 coming into town from the west, turn right at light, go 2 blocks on 9th, turn left on Commercial.

Pension Anna

$65-$90 **PHIPPEN'S BED & BREAKFAST**, 10285 Ski Hill Dr., Leavenworth, WA 98826, phone 509-548-7755 or 1-800-666-9806 (USA). Two guest rooms and a studio apartment are available, all with private facilities. The studio also has an equipped kitchen and deck with barbecue. Seasonal outdoor pool and year-round hot tub. Full breakfast provided. Adults only, pets by arrangement, no smoking on the premises. **Rates:** *2 night minimum on festival weekends* - standard rooms $65-$75; studio $90; extra person $10. MasterCard, Discover, & Visa. **Directions:** coming into town from the west turn left on Ski Hill Dr. (next to Kristall's Restaurant) and proceed for 1/2 mile.

$55-$70 **The RIVER'S EDGE LODGE**, 8401 Hwy 2, Leavenworth, WA 98826, phone 509-548-7612 or 1-800-451-5285. Located on the Wenatchee River, this is a great spot to watch river rafters and kayakers. A two story lodge with 23 rooms, 12 nonsmoking. All rooms have phones, cable TV, balcony or patio with outdoor furniture. No coffee/tea making facilities in the rooms, but available in the lobby, and there are 7 equipped kitchen units. Outdoor pool, hot tub, and river access. The best whitewater is in May and June. Children welcome, pets allowed in specific rooms at no charge. **Rates:** *two night minimum on festival and holiday weekends* - single room (1 bed) $55-$70; double room (2 beds, 2-4 people) $63-$68; extra person $6; local phone calls free. MasterCard, Discover, & Visa. **Directions:** 3.5 miles east of Leavenworth.

$90-$140 **RUN OF THE RIVER BED & BREAKFAST**, 9308 E. Leavenworth Rd., P. O. Box 285, Leavenworth, WA 98826, phone 509-548-7171 or 1-800-288-6491. A very special retreat. This natural log lodge has large picture windows exposing a spectacular Icicle River and Cascade panorama. There are 6 guest rooms that have hand-hewn log furniture, private baths, spacious decks, cable TV, and easy access to the hot tub overlooking the river. One suite features a jacuzzi, two wood stoves, loft and private deck. The lodge is surrounded by a bird refuge, flowers, foliage, mountains, and the river. Complimentary use of mountain bikes and trail maps. A low fat, healthy, full breakfast is served each morning. Adults only, no pets, and no smoking on the premises. **Rates:** *two night minimum stay on all weekends and holidays* - double occupancy $90-$140. MasterCard, Amex, & Visa. **Directions:** located east of town, from Hwy 2 turn onto E. Leavenworth Rd., drive 1 mile, turn down gravel driveway.

$85 **SAIMONS HIDE-A-WAYS**, 16408 River Rd., Leavenworth, WA 98826, phone 509-763-3213 or 1-800-845-8638. Two A-Frame cabins tucked away in the woods across the road from the Wenatchee River, 10 minutes from Lake Wenatchee. Cabin #2 is 1,000 square feet with 2 bedrooms with queen beds, whirlpool tub, and sleeps up to 8 guests. Cabin #3 is 1,200 square feet, 2 bedrooms with queen beds, loft, and living room, sleeps up to 8 guests. Barbecues, firepit, and picnic tables. One block from river access. Smoking restricted to outside. Children welcome, infants free, pets allowed. Larger cabins also available. **Rates:** *two night minimum weekends* - cabins 2 & 3 double occupancy $85; each additional guest $15. Major credit cards. **Directions:** 17.5 miles northwest of Leavenworth, 9 miles east of Lake Wenatchee in the Plain Valley, along the Wenatchee River; call for directions.

$55-$115 **SLEEPING LADY RETREAT & CONFERENCE CENTER**, P. O. Box 1060, Leavenworth, WA 98826, phone 509-548-6344 or 1-800-742-4253. Friends of the earth will give applause to the thoughtful construction of the Sleeping Lady Retreat. Like a butterfly transformed - originally a CCC camp in the '30s, then a church camp until 1992. The complex covers 70 forested acres and includes 49 sleeping units, 2 conference houses, kitchen, dining lodge, organic gardens, Chapel Theater and Salmon Gallery, library, dance studio, sauna house, rock pool, and art shop . There are four clusters of cabins, each cluster surrounds a courtyard and contains 10 units that sleep 2; the Forest Cabins have 6 units that sleep 4; the Eyrie is a seclusion for two on Woodpecker Hill; the Rookery is an open cabin with 2 showers and 8 bunk beds. Conference rates include lodging, 3 meals, and meeting room. Special rates vary by number in group and length of stay. **Rates:** *per person, per day; two night minimum* - single $115; double $80; triple $75; quad $70; bunk $55. Major credit cards. **Directions:** from Hwy 2 turn on Icicle Rd. and continue to just past the cemetery before the road curves.

$65-$125 **TYROLEAN RITZ HOTEL**, 633 Front St., Leavenworth, WA 98826, phone 509-548-5455 or 1-800-854-6365. This small, European style hotel has 16 nonsmoking rooms. Phones, refrigerators, coffee/tea making facilities, and basic cable TV. All rooms are on the second floor. Continental breakfast provided in the lobby. Private parking lot for guests. Children welcome, pets allowed with deposit. **Rates:** single room (2 people) $65; double room (2-4 people) $75-$100; family room (3 beds, 6 people) $100; suites (2-4 people) $110-$125; extra person $10; crib $10; pet deposit $30, refundable $20; local phone calls free. Major credit cards. **Directions:** on the main street of town across from the brewery and Gustov's.

$58-$68 **WEDGE MOUNTAIN INN,** 7335 Hwy 2, Cashmere, WA 98815, phone 509-548-6694 or 1-800-666-9664. Located halfway between Cashmere and Leavenworth, this motel has 28 rooms, 50% nonsmoking. Phones, cable TV, private decks, and mountain views from every room. No coffee/tea making facilities in the rooms, but available in the lobby. The Y Cafe next door opens at 6 a.m. Ample parking for large trucks. Children 18 and under free with parents (limit of 2), no pets. **Rates:** *2 night minimum during Autumn Leaf Festival and Christmas Lighting* - midweek - single room (1 bed) $58; double room (2 beds) $62; Fri/Sat. - single room $63; double room $68; extra person $5; local phone calls 25¢. MasterCard, Discover, & Visa. **Directions:** 1/4 mile east of Hwy 2 and Hwy 97 (Blewett Pass) junction, turn into the entrance of the Y Cafe.

LONG BEACH PENINSULA is on the Pacific Ocean in the extreme southwest corner of the state.

The Long Beach Peninsula includes the towns of Chinook, Ilwaco, Long Beach, Nahcotta, Ocean Park, and Nahcotta, Seaview. The peninsula is two miles wide and surrounded on the west by the Pacific Ocean and on the east by Willapa Bay. The ocean beach is 28 miles of hard packed sand for horseback riding, kite flying, mountain bike riding, clam digging in season, beachcombing, and storm watching.

Located in Pacific County the sales/use taxes are 7.8%.

CHINOOK

(shi-NOOK) took its name from a local Indian tribe. From the very beginning the fishing industry dominated the economy of Chinook and still does today. The Port of Chinook is one of three major fishing centers on the Long Beach Peninsula.

$10-$13   **FORT COLUMBIA HOSTEL**, P. O. Box 224, Chinook, WA 98614, phone 360-777-8755. One curtained-off family room, 2 dorm style rooms with 12 men's beds and 5 women's beds, all with shared facilities. Family atmosphere, children welcome, no pets and no smoking. All you can eat pancake breakfast, coffee and tea for 50¢. Fully equipped kitchen, fireplace, games and music in the lounge. Surroundings include secluded river coves, private hiking on forest trails, and 28 miles of pristine beaches near-by. **Rates:** members $10, children $5; non-members $13, children $8; surcharge on family room $6; pay phone 25¢; breakfast 50¢; taxes included. Visa & MasterCard. **Directions:** 3 miles north of Astoria/Megler Bridge on Hwy 101, 1 mile south of Chinook.

ILWACO

(pop. 856) (il-WAH-koh) - Highlights: Lewis & Clark Interpretive Center, centennial murals, port docks, charter offices, fresh fish market, bait & tackle shops, Cape Disappointment Lighthouse, Fort Canby State Park, Waikiki Beach, North Jetty, and North Head Lighthouse. Fishing is still the main industry.

$35-$69   **HARBOR LIGHTS MOTEL**, Restaurant, Lounge, & Charters, P. O. Box 866, Ilwaco, WA 98624, phone 360-642-3196. The only motel in the harbor of Ilwaco has 23 rooms, no designated nonsmoking. TVs in the rooms, indoor hot tub, and harbor views. Morning coffee is available at the restaurant at 7 a.m. Bar and beauty shop on the premises. Children okay, pets by arrangement. **Summer Rates:** *5/26 to 9/30* - double occupancy, standard room $59; room with a view $69. **Winter Rates:** $35-$45. Major credit cards accepted. **Directions:** west end of Ilwaco Port docks.

$60-$150 **CHICKADEE INN AT ILWACO**, 122 Williams St. NE, P. O. Box 922, Ilwaco, WA 98624, phone 360-642-8686. Once the Ilwaco Presbyterian Church, the Inn has 12 nonsmoking guest rooms. Ten rooms have private facilities and two share one bath. The Inn stands proudly on a wooded knoll overlooking the fishing port. No phones or TV to interrupt the solitude of the guests. A full breakfast is served family style in the light-filled parlor. Children 13 and older, no pets. **Rates:** double occupancy, shared bath $60; private facilities $75-$86; suite $150. **Winter Special:** *after Labor Day to Memorial Day* - midweek dinner is included free. Visa & MasterCard. **Directions:** one block east of the stoplight in downtown Ilwaco.

LONG BEACH

(pop. 1,230) The boardwalk along the beach has informational plaques, picnic benches, and lights for nighttime strolls. In the summer, the city sometimes holds dances on the boardwalk. The gateway to 28 miles of sandy beach starts here.

$32-$81 **ARCADIA COURT**, P. O. Box 426, Long Beach, WA 98631, phone 360-642-2613. Eight one and two bedroom units all with color TV. There are 5 units with kitchens, cookware, and linens. The suite is a 2 bedroom unit and sleeps 6. Picnic area and barbecues. No nonsmoking units. Free beverages available in the office. Local phone calls free. Located on the dunes, it is a 5 minute walk to the beach, restaurants, and stores. **Summer Rates:** single room (1 bed) $39-$61; suite $81; extra person $5; pets $3. **Winter Rates:** single $32-$47; suite $75. Major credit cards accepted. **Directions:** one block west of the highway, 3 blocks north of the second traffic light at N. 4th and Boulevard.

$45-$73 **BOARDWALK COTTAGES**, 800 Ocean Beach Blvd., Long Beach, WA 98631, phone 360-642-2305. 10 units (4 rooms & 6 cottages) all nonsmoking. All units have equipped kitchenettes or kitchens, cable TV, and decks. Homemade cinnamon rolls in the morning from 9-9:30. Children welcome, infants free, no pets. **Summer Rates:** *7/01 to 9/09* - kitchen unit $63; one bedroom cottage $68; 2 bedroom cottage $73; extra person $5. **Winter Rates:** *9/10 to 2/28* - $45-$55. **Spring Rates:** *3/01 to 6/30* - $53-$63. Discover, MasterCard, & Visa.

Directions: turn on 10th St. (south end of town) on beach access road, turn right on Blvd. So., one block on right-hand side.

$55-$105 **BOREAS BED & BREAKFAST**, 6th St. No., P. O. Box 1344, Long Beach, WA 98631, phone 360-642-8069. This 1920's beach home has 4 nonsmoking rooms available, three upstairs and a garden suite downstairs. Two with private facilities and 2 with shared. All rooms have views of either the ocean or the coastal mountains. There is also a large hot tub located in an enclosed sundeck. Full breakfasts include homemade breads, fresh fruit, and delicious egg dishes, often with local seafood. Within walking distance of the boardwalk, shopping, and restaurants. Children are welcome by arrangement, no pets. **Summer Rates:** $65-$105; extra person $10. **Winter Rates:** $10 less. MasterCard & Visa. **Directions:** 5 blocks north of the stoplight, turn left on 6th St. No., proceed one block and turn right, second building on the left, parking lot across the street.

Boreas Bed & Breakfast

$35-$75 **BOULEVARD MOTEL**, 301 Ocean Blvd. No., P. O. Box 1008, Long Beach, WA 98631, phone 360-642-2434. 22 units, no nonsmoking. All units have TV, some have fireplaces, and the indoor pool is open year-round. No coffee/tea making facilities in the rooms, but 18 units have kitchens with basic cookware and dishes. Four duplex cottages sleep 6 and face the ocean. The upstairs motel units have

views of the ocean and sand dunes. Children under 2 free, pets allowed.
Summer Rates: *05/15 to 9/15* - double occupancy, cottage - $75; 2nd floor motel units $75; 1st floor $55; streetside $50; extra person $5; pets $5 first night. **Winter Rates:** $35-$60. MasterCard & Visa. **Directions:** turn west at the 2nd traffic light, then right on Ocean Blvd., at the end of the block.

$37-$145 **CHAUTAUGUA LODGE,**14th St. No., P. O. Box 757, Long Beach, WA 98631, phone 360-642-4401 or 1-800-869-8401. 180 units, 20 nonsmoking. All units have TV, phones, coffee/tea making facilities, and oceanside units have gas fireplaces. There are 60 equipped kitchenettes. Hot tub, sauna, and indoor heated pool. Restaurant across from the lobby. Children welcome, pets allowed on the ground floor. Suites available. During summer, some rooms have a two night minimum stay on weekends. **Summer Rates:** *6/01 to 9/30* - double occupancy, basic room $55, oceanside $70-$85; kitchen units, oceanside $85-$100; suites sleep 4 to 7 people $115-$145; extra person $5-$10; pets $8. **Winter Rates:** basic room $37; oceanside $50-$60; kitchen $65-$75; suites $85-$95. Major credit cards. **Directions:** 14 blocks north of the city center, turn west on 14th St. to the ocean.

$47-$59 **The LIGHTHOUSE MOTEL**, Rt. 1 Box 527, Long Beach, WA 98631, phone 360-642-3622. 9 units, no nonsmoking. All units have TV, fireplaces, kitchens with basic cookware, decks, and views of the ocean. There are 2 one bedrooms units and 7 two bedrooms units. Children welcome, pets allowed. **Summer Rates:** one bedroom $47; 2 bedrooms $59; extra person $5; pets $5. Ask about winter rates. Amex, MasterCard, & Visa. **Directions:** 2 1/2 miles north of town.

$35-$99 **LONG BEACH MOTEL**, 1200 Pacific Hwy So., Long Beach, WA 98631, phone 360-642-3500. 4 cottages and 4 motel units, one nonsmoking. TV and coffee/tea making facilities in all the units. There are four fully equipped kitchen units with microwaves. In the summer there is a picnic table with lawn chairs and umbrella. Area in the back for self-contained RVs. Children welcome, pets allowed. **Summer Rates:** *6/16 to 9/15* - motel units $49-$55; cottages with kitchens $69-$99; pets $5. **Winter Rates:** $35-$79. MasterCard, Discover, & Visa. **Directions:** on the main street coming into town from the south.

NENDELS INN, 409 10th St. SW, P. O. Box 793, Long Beach, WA 98631, phone 360-642-2311 or 1-800-547-0106.

$38-$75   **OCEAN LODGE**, 101 Boulevard St. No., P. O. Box 337, Long Beach, WA 98631, phone 360-642-2777. 23 units, 20 are motel style and 3 are cabins, no nonsmoking. All units have TV, some have gas or wood burning fireplaces and fully equipped kitchens. Outdoor pool, sauna, workout room, and spa. Children welcome, infants free, pets allowed. **Summer Rates:** *5/20 to 10/01* - based on the individual room and the number of beds $45-$75; extra person $3. **Winter Rates:** $38-$70. MasterCard & Visa. **Directions:** centrally located, turn toward the beach at the second stoplight, one block, on the right.

$45-$75   **OUR PLACE at the Beach**, 1309 South Blvd., P. O. Box 266, Long Beach, WA 98631, phone 1-800-538-5107 or 360-642-3793. Well maintained, two story motel with 25 units, including 4 housekeeping units with fully equipped kitchens, no nonsmoking. Two of the apartment units have fireplaces. The top floor rooms have a nice view of the ocean. All units have cable TV, phones, refrigerators, and coffee/tea making facilities. The fitness center has 2 jacuzzi pools, tiled steam room, sauna, and exercise room. Fish and clam cleaning sink area. Children welcome, pets allowed. **Spring Rates:** *5/15 to 6/30* - $50-$70. **Summer Rates:** *7/01 to 9/04* - single (1 bed) $54; double (2 beds) $59; kitchen units $64-$75; extra person $5; pets $5; local phone calls free. **Winter Rates:** *10/01 to 5/14* - $45-$70. Major credit cards. **Directions:** coming into town, turn towards the beach on 14th St. So. and proceed for 2 blocks.

$42-$88   **PACIFIC VIEW MOTEL**, 203 Bolstad Ave., P. O. Box 302, Long Beach, WA 98631, phone 360-642-2415. 8 cabins and two rooms, 5 nonsmoking units. The cabins have fully equipped kitchens and cabin #9, #6, and #3 have fireplaces. All have TVs, no phones. Units #10 and #11 have small refrigerators and second floor views, no pets allowed in these two rooms, and no coffee/tea making facilities. Located on the Long Beach approach overlooking the Boardwalk. Children welcome, pets allowed in some cabins. **Summer Rates:** $56-$88. **Winter Rates:** $42-$78. MasterCard & Visa. **Directions:** at the second stoplight turn towards the beach.

$30-$70   **RIDGE COURT MOTEL**, P. O. Box 483, Long Beach, WA 98631, phone 360-642-2412. 13 individual cabins, no nonsmoking, 9 with fully equipped kitchens. Coffee/tea making facilities in the rooms and TV. Heated indoor pool, clam and fish cleaning room.

Children 2 and under free, pets allowed in some rooms. **Summer Rates:** single room, no kitchen $40; single, with kitchen $48; double (2 beds) no kitchen $60; with kitchen $70; extra person $5; pets $5. **Winter Rates:** $30-$65. Most major credit cards. **Directions:** at second stoplight turn towards the beach one block, then turn right.

$27-$33 **The SANDS MOTEL,** Rt. 1 Box 531, Long Beach, WA 98631, phone 360-642-2100, fax 360-642-8837. Small, quiet motel with 4 basic rooms, no nonsmoking. In-room amenities include 1 double bed, 1 twin bed, cable TV, chest of drawers, writing desk, and chairs. No coffee/tea making facilities in the rooms. Children 12 and under free, pets allowed. **Summer Rates:** $33 daily; $161 weekly; extra person $3; pets $5, charged once. **Winter Rates:** $27 daily; $133 weekly. MasterCard, Visa, & Discover. **Directions:** north of Long Beach on Hwy 103, just pass milepost 4, "on the beach".

$70-$125 **SCANDINAVIAN GARDENS INN BED & BREAKFAST,** 1610 California Ave. S., Rt. 1 Box 36, Long Beach, WA 98631, phone 360-642-8877 or 1-800-988-9277. There are 5 nonsmoking guest rooms in this quiet hideaway. Each room is decorated with the theme of a different Scandinavian country. All rooms have private bathrooms with instant hot water and imported Swedish queen beds. Relax in the cozy living room with its fireplace and library. There is also another large fireplace in the social room. Indoor spa, sauna, and exercise equipment are available in the recreation room. A full breakfast buffet featuring Scandinavian dishes is served by the hosts in their traditional costumes. Rooms are limited to 3 people, no infants and no pets. **Summer Rates:** double occupancy $75-$90; honeymoon suite $125; extra person $15. **Winter Rates:** 15% discount ($70-$106) Monday to Thursday. Discover, MasterCard, & Visa. **Directions:** coming into town, turn left on 16th So., one block to California.

$49-$84 **SHAMAN MOTEL,** 115 3rd St. SW, P. O. Box 235, Long Beach, WA 98631, phone 360-642-3714 or 1-800-753-3750. 42 large rooms with queen beds, phones, and TV. 12 nonsmoking units. Some rooms have ocean views and fireplaces. There are 20 kitchen units, but guests must furnish their own cookware and dishes. Coffee/tea making facilities in the rooms and some have refrigerators. Heated swimming pool in the summer. Children 3 and under free, pets allowed. **Summer Rates:** *7/01 to 8/30* - single room (1 bed) $74-$84; double room (2 beds) $79; extra person $5; pets $5 charged once; no charge for local phone calls. **Spring/Fall/Winter Rates:** $49-$69. Major credit cards. **Directions:** centrally located on main street.

$28-$65 **The WHALE'S TALE**, 620 So. Pacific Hwy., P. O. Box 418, Long Beach, WA 98631, phone 360-642-3455. 8 suites, one nonsmoking. One and two bedrooms, all with TV and kitchens. Dishes and basic cookware are available on request. A metal detector and a rubber life raft with fresh water fishing gear are also available to guests. The recreation hall has a pool table, ping-pong, workout room, sauna, and spa. Bookstore on the premises is open from 10:00 a.m. to 5:00 p.m. seven days a week. One or 2 children under 12 free, extra charge for 3 or more, dogs allowed. **Summer Rates:** weekends $65, weekdays $55 for two; extra person $5 (8 max.); weekly rates. **Winter Rates:** $28-$38. MasterCard & Visa. **Directions:** centrally located on main street of downtown.

NAHCOTTA

(NAH-KAH-tuh) The piles of discarded oyster shells from Nahcotta to Oysterville are evidence of the prime industry here.

$60-$85 **MOBY DICK HOTEL BED & BREAKFAST**, Long Beach Peninsula, Sandridge Rd., P. O. Box 82, Nahcotta, WA 98631, phone 360-665-4543, fax 360-665-6887. This landmark, 1929 Willapa Bay hotel is now a bed and breakfast. All the rooms have been restored and refurbished with period decor of the '30s. 10 nonsmoking rooms are available, 9 second floor rooms share facilities. Six rooms share 3 baths between adjoining rooms and 3 rooms share one bath down the hall. The cottage room on the main floor has a private entrance, deck, and facilities. This is a funky, relaxed place with its own working oyster farm and organic gardens. A full country breakfast is served. Children welcome, infants free, well-behaved dogs allowed with owner's guarantee of responsibility. **Summer Rates:** upstairs rooms $65-$80; cottage room $85; extra person $10; dogs $10 per night. **Winter Rates:** $60-$85. MasterCard & Visa. **Directions:** in Ocean Park follow Bay Ave. east, then turn right on Sandridge Rd., go 1/2 block.

OCEAN PARK

(pop. 1,400) is the commercial hub of the north Long Beach Peninsula. In the summer, an estimated 10,000 seasonal residents enjoy the area.

$50-$66 **OCEAN PARK RESORT**, 259th & R St., P. O. Box 339, Ocean Park, WA 98640, phone 360-665-4585 or 1-800-835-4634. 12 motel units, RV hookups, and tent area. The motel units sleep from 1 to 4 people, all have phones, TV, and some have equipped kitchens. Outdoor swimming pool, indoor jacuzzi, recreation hall, free pancake breakfast, clam digging equipment rentals (in season), horseshoe pits, and more. All on ten wooded acres. Children welcome. Pets welcome if: on a leash, not left unattended, and cleaned up after. **Rates:** single room $50-$55; double room $58-$66; extra person $5; pets $5. Major credit cards. **Directions:** from Hwy 103, turn right on 259th, 2 blocks.

$54-$64 **SHAKTI COVE COTTAGES**, P. O. Box 385, Ocean Park, WA 98640, phone 360-665-4000. Eclectic get-away with 10 cabins on three secluded, wooded acres. No nonsmoking. All have private facilities and TV. Equipped kitchens with basic cookware, nothing fancy. Five minute walk to the beach, no views and no fireplaces, just peace and quiet. Children welcome, pets allowed free. **Rates:** single room $54; double room $64. **Directions:** turn towards the ocean on 253rd, go 2 blocks and you come into Shakti Cove.

$59-$119 **SUNSET VIEW RESORT**, P. O. Box 399, Ocean Park, WA 98640, phone 360-665-4494 or 1-800-272-9199. 52 beach units on seven acres, 27 nonsmoking rooms. Phones, TV, large family rooms, some with equipped kitchens and fireplaces. Tennis court, sauna, hot tubs, volleyball, horseshoes, and barbecues. Children under 10 free, small pets only. **Rates:** sleeping rooms, no view, 2-4 people $59-$69; view rooms with kitchen & fireplace (2 people) $84-$104; suites (4 people) $94-$119; extra person $5; pets $10 per stay. Off-season discounts available. Major credit cards. **Directions:** 9 miles north of Long Beach in Ocean Park.

SEAVIEW

Tourists used to flock to Seaview by way of steamship, rail, and stage from Astoria and points south. In 1966, with the construction of the Astoria-Megler bridge, access became much easier. The toll was the same for 25 years, $1.50 for a car or pickup; this toll was stopped on 12/31/93. The 4.4 mile long bridge is in the Guinness Book of World Records as the longest continuous-truss bridge in North America.

$65-$100 **GUMM'S BED & BREAKFAST**, 3310 Hwy 101 & 33rd, P. O. Box 447, Seaview, WA 98644, phone 360-642-8887. Built in 1900, this home has 4 nonsmoking rooms, 2 with private facilities and 2 with shared. The rooms are large with queen beds and decorated for the comfort of the guests. All rooms are on the second floor. Full breakfast provided. Year-round hot tub. Tennis courts 3 blocks away, one mile to beach entrance. Children one month and older welcome, no pets, smoking outside. **Rates:** shared facilities $65; private facilities $80;

family (2 rooms) $100; extra person $5. MasterCard & Visa. **Directions:** Hwy 101 ends in Seaview. Turn left and proceed 6 blocks towards Ilwaco. Large yellow house with white picket fence.

$35-$99 **SOU'WESTER LODGE**, P. O. Box 102, Seaview, WA 98644, phone 360-642-2542. This historic lodge is a B&(MYOD)B (bed & make your own damn breakfast). It was originally the Westborough House, built in 1892 as the summer estate of a U.S. Senator from Oregon. The 3 story lodge offers 3 rooms on the ground floor that share the large cozy kitchen, bathroom, and a living room filled with collectibles. There are six complete apartment style units on the upper two floors, each with unique character. Cedar-shingled, fully equipped cabins face the dunes in front of the lodge. For a true experience there is a collection of classic house trailers, each with a different theme, i.e. the African Queen. These are fondly referred to as TCH! TCH!, Trailer Classics Hodgepodge. The clientele of the Sou'wester tend to be artists, writers, musicians, and other creative people who find inspiration in the setting and fellow guests. Children welcome, pets not allowed in the lodge. **Rates:** lodge rooms (ground floor) $54-$59; lodge apts. $63-$99; cabins $75 (off-season $50); TCH! TCH! $35-$87; extra person $3-$5. Discover, MasterCard, & Visa. **Directions:** Beach Access Rd. (38th Place) 1 1/2 blocks southwest of the flashing traffic light at the intersection of 101 & 103.

LONGVIEW
(pop. 31,730) is located 5 miles west of I-5 and 50 miles north of Vancouver.

Longview is an industrial city at the confluence of the Cowlitz and Columbia Rivers. Port Longview is 66 miles inland from the Pacific Ocean and offers a full service marine terminal. It is one of the top three deep-water ports in the state. If you are in the vicinity of the Civic Center and wonder what the "Nutty Narrows Bridge" is, it is a 60 foot skybridge specially designed for squirrels to cross over Olympia Way safely.

Located in Cowlitz County the sales/use/lodging taxes are 9.6%.

$26-$36   **HUDSON MANOR MOTEL**, 1616 Hudson St., Longview, WA 98632, phone 360-425-1100, fax 360-578-1057. This two story basic motel has 25 rooms, 14 nonsmoking. Phones, TV, refrigerators, and AC. No coffee/tea making facilities in the rooms, but hot pots are available and there is coffee in the lobby. There are 4 equipped kitchen units. Children welcome, infants free, pets by arrangement. **Rates:** single room (1 bed) $26-$34; double room (2 beds) $34-$36; kitchen units $4-$5 extra; extra person $5; pets $20 refundable deposit; no charge for local phone calls. Major credit cards. **Directions:** from I-5 take Longview Exit to Washington St., turn left, go past the Civic Center, turn left on Hudson and go one block.

$35-$40   **LEWIS & CLARK MOTOR INN,** 838 15th Ave., Longview, WA 98632, phone 360-423-6460, fax 360-425-6878. This two story motel has 32 rooms, 2 nonsmoking. Phones and TV in every room, 2 non-equipped kitchen units. No coffee/tea making facilities in the rooms, but there is a restaurant and coffee shop within walking distance. Children 12 and under free, pets allowed. **Rates:** single room $35; double room $40; extra person charge $5; pets $5 per night; no charge for local phone calls. Most major credit cards. **Directions:** across from St. Johns Hospital on 15th.

$34-$110   **MONTICELLO HOTEL/MOTEL**, 1405 17th Ave., Longview, WA 98632, phone 360-425-9900, fax 360-425-3424. This 6 story hotel, built in 1923, has 4 one and two bedroom suites available on the second floor. Suites have kitchenettes with microwaves, refrigerators, and coffee pot - no cookware or dishes. The adjacent motel units have cable TV, phones, and refrigerators. Children 12 and under free, no pets. Restaurant and lounge in the hotel. **Rates:** suites $85-$110; motel units, single room $34-$36; double room $40; extra person $4; no charge for local phone calls. Major credit cards. **Directions:** from the north, Exit 40 off I-5, turn right at the stop sign, take Kelso Ave. to the traffic signal, turn right onto Cowlitz Way, this becomes Washington Way soon after you cross the bridge. You will come to a circle, go 1/4 way around the circle. From the south, take Exit 36 and go over the freeway, take Hwy 432 west to 15th and turn right, go north 7 stoplights to Broadway and turn left, go halfway around the circle.

$26-$42 **TOWN CHALET MOTOR HOTEL**, 1822 Washington Way, Longview, WA 98632, phone 360-423-2020. 24 rooms, 7 nonsmoking. Phones and TV. No coffee/tea making facilities in the rooms, but there is a coffee shop on the premises and there are 16 equipped kitchen units. Children 12 and under free, pets allowed. **Rates:** single room (1 bed) $26-$32; double room (2 beds) $36-$42; pets $5 per day; local phone calls free. Major credit cards. **Directions:** take the Longview/Kelso Exit off I-5, go west across the bridge into Longview, turn right onto Washington Way, past the Civic Center.

$34-$38 **TOWN HOUSE MOTEL**, 744 Washington Way, Longview, WA 98632, phone 360-423-7200. 28 rooms, 10 nonsmoking. Phones and TV in every room, three units have AC. No coffee/tea making facilities in the rooms, but available in the lobby. Outdoor pool. Children welcome, pets allowed. **Rates:** single room (1 bed) $34; double room (2 beds) $36-$38; extra person (includes children of all ages) $5; pets $5 per night; local phone calls free. Major credit cards. **Directions:** take the Longview/Kelso Exit off I-5, go west across the bridge into Longview, to Washington Way.

LOOMIS is located approximately 13 miles from the Canadian border and 18 miles west of Oroville.

$40-$45 **CHOPAKA LODGE**, 1913 Loomis Hwy, Loomis, WA 98827, phone 509-223-3131. *Open from April 1st to October 31st.* Three individual cabins on Palmer Lake. All cabins have private facilities, equipped kitchens, and fireplaces. Lake fishing, nut orchards, wildlife, and water sports. Nearest restaurant 9 miles. RV parking. Children welcome, pets allowed. **Rates:** cabins, double occupancy $40-$45; taxes 7.6%. No credit cards. **Directions:** 9 miles north of Loomis on Palmer Lake, 27 miles northwest of Tonasket.

LOON LAKE is located 26 miles north of Spokane.

Loon Lake is one of the area's largest lakes. The crystal clear water is surrounded by towering pines, firs, and cedars at an elevation of 2400 feet. An ideal lake for fishing and vacationing for a day, week, or entire summer with complete facilities. It is twenty minutes to the golf course.

Located in Stevens County the sale/use taxes are 7.5%.

$55-$175 **GRANITE POINT PARK**, 41000 Granite Point Rd., Loon Lake, WA 99148, phone 509-233-2100. *Open May through September*. This "vacation paradise" is a family oriented resort that offers 25 individual cottages with lake views, sleep 2 to 12 people, no designated nonsmoking. The modern lakefront cottages have fully equipped kitchens. The resort has acres of lawn and 3/4 mile of beach with swimming areas. Pedal boats, canoes, and rowboats are for rent. Gas, dock, store, snack bar, playground, game room, and boat launch. Children welcome, no pets. **Rates:** nightly $55-$175; weekly $300-$700. No credit cards. **Directions:** turn off Hwy 395 onto Granite Point Rd., 26 miles north of Spokane.

$40-$45 **LOON LAKE MOTEL**, P. O. Box 310, Loon Lake, WA 99148, phone 509-233-2916. 8 rooms, no non-smoking. Phones, TV, and refrigerators in every room. No coffee/tea making facilities in the rooms, but there is a 24 hour restaurant across the street. Seasonal outdoor pool. Children welcome, no pets. **Rates:** single room $40; double room $45; extra person $5; local phone calls free. MasterCard & Visa. **Directions:** just off Hwy 395 on Hwy 2.

LUMMI ISLAND is west of Bellingham and the Lummi Indian casino. A six minute ferry ride, across Hale Passage, leaves at ten minutes past the hour.

Lummi (LUHM-ee) Island has 18 miles of roads ideal for bicycling. The Beach Store Cafe is open from spring through fall. Island artists and craftspeople include Good Thunder Arts Pottery, Blue Earth Signs, and Arkworks Woodcarving.

Located in Whatcom County the sale/use taxes are 7.5%.

$90 **WEST SHORE FARM BED & BREAKFAST**, 2781 West Shore Dr., Lummi Island, WA 98262, phone 360-758-2600. Two guest rooms are available in this unique octagonal home. The upper level has a sweeping seascape view and a 12 sided fireplace. The lower level is devoted to the guest rooms. Each room has a view of the offshore seal colony. The Eagle Room features a reading corner with a leather recliner. The Blue Heron Room has a built-in sink vanity. Both rooms have a table, two chairs, king bed, and private cedar paneled bathroom across the hall. The reading room is well stocked, and there are two bicycles available for touring the island. Full breakfast at 9:00 a.m. and other meals by reservation. Closest restaurant is 3 miles away. Children by arrangement, no pets, and no smoking indoors. **Rates:** double occupancy $90; extra person $10; local phone calls free. Amex, MasterCard, & Visa. **Directions:** from I-5 take Exit 260, turn west and follow Slater Rd. 3.7 miles to Haxtow Way, turn left and proceed 6.7 miles to the ferry. Departing ferry, turn right and follow N. Nugent Rd. to West Shore Dr. to the west side of the island.

LYLE is 32 miles southwest of Goldendale and 63 miles east of Vancouver on the Gorge Hwy 14.

Lyle is a popular boardsailing area. In fact, in September of 1991 a windsurfer, skimming the waves at Doug's Beach near Lyle, gained national notoriety for the fastest speed surfing record in America. Traveling at 47.4 mph, the boardsailor affirmed what area boardsailors have said for years: the Columbia Gorge is a premium place to sail.

$38-$48 **LYLE HOTEL & RESTAURANT**, P. O. Box 838, 7th St., Lyle, WA 98635, phone 509-365-5953. *Open Wednesday to Monday from May 1st to October 1st, and Thursday to Sunday in the off-season.* This is one of Washington's oldest existing hotels in the Columbia Gorge, offering 9 nonsmoking rooms that share 3 bathrooms. The hotel was built in 1911 to house railroad workers, so the rooms are small, but cozy, and individually decorated. Nearly all the rooms have views of the river. No coffee/tea making facilities in the rooms, but available in the lobby with fresh baked goodies. The full service restaurant specializes in fresh seafood and pasta with outdoor dining in the courtyard during the summer. Smoking allowed in the cocktail lounge and courtyard. No pets. **Rates:** single $38; double $48; extra person $10; taxes 7%. Visa & MasterCard. **Directions:** from Hwy 14 turn south on 7th Street, located at the end of the street.

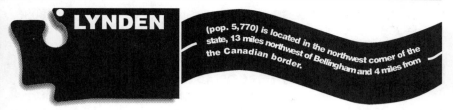

LYNDEN (pop. 5,770) is located in the northwest corner of the state, 13 miles northwest of Bellingham and 4 miles from the Canadian border.

The terrain of Lynden consists of level to gently sloped agricultural land with Mt. Baker in the distance. The primary industries are food processing and dairy products.

Located in Whatcom County the sales/use taxes are 7.8%.

$60-$85   **CENTURY HOUSE BED & BREAKFAST**, 401 South B.C. Ave., Lynden, WA 98264, phone 360-354-2439. This century old Victorian homestead has 3 nonsmoking guest rooms, one with private facilities and 2 with shared. Full breakfast is included and early morning coffee is available. The tower suite has a TV and there is also one in the formal living room. Children welcome, no pets. **Rates:** double occupancy $60-$65; suite $85. MasterCard & Visa. **Directions:** 15 miles north of Bellingham on Hwy 539 to Lynden, go 1 1/2 miles east on Front St. to So. B.C. Ave., turn right on So. B.C., go 3 blocks.

$32-$50   **WINDMILL INN**, 8022 Guide Meridian Rd., Lynden, WA 98264, phone 360-354-3424. This cozy motel, decorated in a Dutch theme, has 15 rooms and 2 mobile homes. Majority of rooms are nonsmoking. The rooms all have phones, cable TV, and refrigerators. Coffee is available in the lobby, also coffee/tea in rooms on request. There are 2 units with equipped kitchens. Picnic tables available, RV trailer park, and playground. Children welcome, pets by arrangement. **Rates:** single room $32-$39; double room $43-$45; kitchen units $45-$50; extra person (all ages) $4; local phone calls free. MasterCard, Amex, Discover, & Visa. **Directions:** from I-5 take Exit 256 to Lynden.

LYNNWOOD (pop. 29,110) is located about 15 miles north of downtown Seattle.

Shop at Lynnwood's 77 acre Alderwood Mall or play golf at the 18 hole golf course. Located in Snohomish County the sales/use/lodging taxes are 10.2%.

HOLIDAY INN EXPRESS, 4117 196th St. SW, Lynnwood, WA 98036, phone 206-775-8030 or 1-800-HOLIDAY.

$58-$72 **HOTEL INTERNATIONAL**, 5621 196th St. SW, Lynnwood, WA 98036, phone 206-771-1777, for reservations 1-800-626-5750, fax 206-776-8520. The lobby of this hotel has an elegant, comfortable decor. There are 53 tastefully decorated guest rooms, 25 nonsmoking. Ten rooms have coffee/tea making facilities. Four have microwaves, refrigerators, and sinks. Coffee is also provided in the lobby. Shuttle provided to the airport free with advance reservations. Children under 5 free, no pets. The staff here is very cordial and helpful. **Rates:** single room $58-$68; double room $72; extra person $8; local phone calls 40¢. Major credit cards. **Directions:** from I-5 southbound: Exit 181, turn right at traffic light, 196th and proceed for 1 1/2 miles; northbound: Exit 181, turn left at traffic light, 44th Ave., and left at 196th, proceed to hotel.

$49-$69 **LANDMARK HOTEL Best Western** , 4300 200th St. SW, Lynnwood, WA 98036, phone 206-775-7447 or 1-800-528-1234, fax 206-775-8063. 103 rooms available, 75% non-smoking. Phones and TV in every room. No coffee/tea making facilities in the rooms, but available in the lobby with a continental breakfast from 6:30 a.m. to 10 a.m. Restaurant and lounge with entertainment on the premises. Close to Alderwood Shopping Mall. Independent shuttle service to the airport for a fee. Children 12 and under free, small pets allowed. **Rates:** single room $49-$59; double room $59-$69; extra person $4; pets $10 per night; local phone calls free; shuttle to airport $17. Major credit cards. **Directions:** coming from the south on I-5 take the 44th St. Exit, turn right on 200th; from the north, Exit 181, turn left at 37th and proceed west.

$37-$55 **LYNNWOOD MOTOR INN** , 18109 Hwy 99, Lynnwood, WA 98036, phone 206-778-2808. This 4 year old motel offers 36 rooms, 6 nonsmoking. Phones and TV are in every room. No coffee/tea making facilities in the rooms, but available in the lobby, and 15 units have kitchens. Some cookware and dishes are available in the office. Two blocks north of Costco, close to Alderwood Mall and Lynnwood Mall. Adults only, no pets. **Rates:** single room $37; double room $50; kitchen units $42-$55; rollaway $5; local phone calls 25¢. MasterCard, Visa, & Amex. **Directions:** from I-5 take Exit 181, go west to Hwy 99, turn right.

LYNNWOOD SILVER CLOUD INN , 19332 36th Ave. W., Lynnwood, WA 98036, phone 206-775-7600 or 1-800-551-7207.

MANSON see Lake Chelan for lodging.

• MAPLE VALLEY is located 25 miles east of Sea Tac Airport.

Recreation includes fishing in lakes and rivers for trout and bass, mushroom hunting in spring and fall, rafting on the Green River, antique shops, bird watching, and berry picking.

$45-$65   **MAPLE VALLEY BED & BREAKFAST**, 20020 SE 228th, Maple Valley, WA 98038, phone 206-432-1409, fax 206-432-1409. The warmth of natural wood permeates every corner of this large home with cedar walls, open-beamed ceilings, peeled-pole railings, and detailed trim. Two guest rooms with shared facilities are available. One room has an enormous hand-hewn 4 poster log bed. Guest rooms are on the second floor with wide French doors leading to decks overlooking the family orchard and native trees. The upstairs sitting room is complete with binoculars and a field guide for identifying wildlife and birds. On cool evenings a "hot baby", sand-filled, heated bed warmers, are available. Full breakfast, the house specialty is plate-sized Hootenanny oven pancakes. Children welcome, no pets. **Rates:** single room $45-$60; double $50-$65; extra person, all ages $15; taxes 8.2%. No credit cards. **Directions:** sent with confirmation.

MARYSVILLE (pop.10,970) is located just off I-5, 35 miles north of Seattle.

Marysville has Puget Sound to the west and Mt. Pilchuck and the Cascade Range as a backdrop to the east. A Class III casino was opened in 1992 by the Tulalip Tribes and is already too small to meet demands.

$53-$60　**VILLAGE MOTOR INN**, 235 Beach Ave., Marysville, WA 98270, phone 360-659-0005. This three story motor inn has 45 rooms, 18 nonsmoking. All rooms have coffee/tea making facilities, remote controlled cable TV, phones, and AC. Adjacent to Village Restaurant, famous for its homemade pies. Children 17 and under free with parents, pets allowed with deposit. **Rates:** single room (1 bed) $53-$58; double (2 beds) $60; extra person $5; pet fee $10; local phone calls free; taxes 10.2%. Major credit cards. **Directions:** just east of I-5, Marysville Exit.

MATTAWA is located on Hwy 243 about 47 miles north of Richland.

$38-$48　**DESERT AIRE MOTEL**, 5 Desert Aire Dr., Box 1248, Mattawa, WA 99344, phone 509-932-4300. This destination getaway has 24 rooms, 3 nonsmoking. There are phones and cable TV with HBO in the rooms. Morning coffee may be obtained at the mini-mart on the premises. Twelve units have kitchens and cookware/dishes can be obtained by arrangement. Restaurant and lounge adjacent. Laundromat and tavern close by. Children 12 and under free, no pets. Next to 18 hole golf course and the Columbia River. Boat ramp, fishing, and water sports. **Rates:** single room $38-$43; double (2 beds) $48; extra person $5; local phone calls free; taxes 7.5%. Most credit cards. **Directions:** 4 miles south of Mattawa on SR 243.

MAZAMA is located in the North Cascades just east of Washington Pass. Mazama is 114 miles from Sedro Woolley and Winthrop is 13 miles to the east.

(muh-ZAH-muh) Also see Winthrop for lodging. The North Cascade Highway is closed in the winter due to heavy snow; driving time from Sea Tac is about 5 hours, from Wenatchee 2.5 hours. Mazama is a world-class cross country ski area with 150 kilometers of groomed ski trails. When there is no snow there are numerous other activities, such as fishing, hiking, and mountain biking. Mazama in Spanish means "mountain goat".

Located in Okanogan County the sales/use taxes are 7.6%.

$68 **CHOKECHERRY INN BED & BREAKFAST**, P. O. Box 249, Mazama, WA 98833, phone 509-996-2049.
This small B & B has two guest rooms with private facilities. The rooms have knotty pine wainscoting, table and chairs. Just 35 feet from the Methow riverbank. Both rooms look out at the river. Deck with hot tub, sitting areas, panoramic river and mountain views. No phones or TV in the rooms. Full breakfast provided, refrigerator available for guests. Adults only, no pets. **Rates:** double occupancy $68; extra person $15. No credit cards, cash or checks only. **Directions:** 14 miles west of Winthrop on Hwy 20 at Early Winters area.

$80-$140 **EARLY WINTERS CABINS**, St. Rt. Box 50, Mazama, WA 98833, phone 509-996-2355, evenings 509-996-2843. Six rustic housekeeping cabins (you keep house) in the woods. Fully equipped kitchens and two cabins have dishwashers. Recently remodeled interiors, thermo pane windows, decks, gas fireplaces, electric heat, and barbecues. Three cabins sleep 2 people, 2 sleep 6, and one sleeps 4. Each cabin is on the Early Winters Creek. Fish out the back door or walk to a beautiful alpine lake with a 65 foot waterfall. Children welcome, no pets. **High Season Rates:** *6/30 to 9/03 & 12/16 to 3/11* - $95-$140. **Off-Season Rates:** $80-$120. MasterCard & Visa. **Directions:** 15 miles west of Winthrop on Hwy 20.

$50-$65 **LOST RIVER RESORT**, 672 Lost River Rd., Mazama, WA 98833, phone 509-996-2537 or 1-800-996-2537.
Close to the Pasayten Wilderness, this getaway resort has six cabins with wood stoves and electric heat. Each cabin has a fully furnished kitchen. The chalet sleeps 4-10 people; duplex units sleep 2-4; one bedroom cabin with hide-a-bed in living room. Hiking, skiing, fishing, mountain biking, etc. Children 6 and under free, pets allowed. **Rates:** double occupancy, duplex $50; cabin $55; chalet $65; extra person $10. MasterCard & Visa. **Directions:** leave Hwy 20 at Mazama turn off, Lost River Rd. comes to a T, turn left, go 6.4 miles.

$65-$170 **MAZAMA COUNTRY INN**, HCR 74 Box B9, Mazama, WA 98833, phone 509-996-2681 or 1-800-843-7951 (WA). This mountain lodge has an upscale "pseudo rustic", western decor. A massive stone fireplace dominates the sitting room with its vaulted ceilings and floor-to-ceiling windows. There are 14 rooms and 4 cabins available. No phone or TV to distract from the beauty of the surroundings. Three meals are supplied in the winter to lodge guests and consist of a hearty country breakfast, a pack-your-own lunch, a country gourmet dinner, and hors d'oeuvres in the lounge prior to dinner. In the summer, meals are optional, chosen from a menu. The 4 cabins have equipped kitchens. Ski rental shop, instructors, hot tub, and sauna. In the winter, ski from your doorstep on miles of groomed trails. In the summer there are mountain bike rentals and horseback riding. Children 14 and over welcome during the winter, all ages in the summer, no pets, and no smoking. **Winter Rates:** in the lodge, double occupancy plus 3 meals $155-$170; cabins *2 night minimum* (no meals), double occupancy $95-$120; extra person in cabins $20-$25. **Summer Rates:** lodge rooms, 2 people $65-$80; cabins $95-$120. MasterCard & Visa. **Directions:** 14 miles west of Winthrop on Hwy 20.

$70-$150 **NORTH CASCADES BASECAMP**, 255 Lost River Rd., Mazama, WA 98833, phone 509-996-2334. *Closed during April & November.* A family-style lodge in a secluded setting at the upper end of the Methow Valley. Facilities in the lodge include 6 guest rooms with shared facilities and 1 cabin with private facilities and equipped kitchen. The lodge offers Bed & Breakfast in spring, summer, and fall, or Full Board (3 meals) all seasons. Cabin guests may arrange for meals if space is available. Baby-sitting can be arranged with prior notification. Hot tub, ice skating or swimming pond, and ski or biking trails. Children 3 and under free, no pets, and no smoking in the buildings. **Spring/Summer/Fall Rates:** lodge, double occupancy, B&B $70, Full Board $110; extra person $12-$35; cabin (maximum 6 adults) $125 first and second night, 3rd night $75. **Winter Rates:** *December through March* - double occupancy, full board $135; cabin $150 first night. No credit cards. **Directions:** turn onto Lost River Rd. to Mazama, make a left at next junction, go 2.2 miles, on the left.

•McCLEARY is on Hwy 8 going west from Olympia.

$40 **OLD McCLEARY HOTEL**, P. O. Box 1127, McCleary, WA 98557, phone 360-495-3678. This 1912 three story wooden structure provides a historic setting for dinners, weddings, receptions, and other memorable occasions. There are 2 rooms with private facilities for overnight guests. Guests may enjoy meals served in the original dining room, reservations required. These budget priced rooms tend to be very popular with touring bicyclists. The owners are in the process of restoring this historic old hotel. Children welcome, no pets. **Rates:** single room (1 bed) $40; taxes included. No credit cards. **Directions:** on Hwy 108 in McCleary, 42 Summit Road.

MEAD see Spokane for lodging.

MERCER ISLAND (pop. 21,190) is just east of Seattle in Lake Washington, accessed by the I-90 bridge.

$55-$70 **MOLE HOUSE BED & BREAKFAST**, 3308 W. Mercer Way, Mercer Island, WA 98040, phone 206-232-1611. A rambling contemporary home with views of Lake Washington, the Olympic Mountains, and Seattle. Two guest rooms and a "mother-in-law" apartment, all have private facilities. The suite has a private entrance, living room with hide-a-bed, double bedroom, and deck with a 270° view. The two guest rooms are furnished with antiques and have a "peek-a-boo" view of the lake. A gourmet breakfast is served each morning. Well-behaved children welcome, no pets, and no smoking. 10 minutes to Seattle and 20 minutes to Sea Tac Airport. **Rates:** single room $55; double room $65; apt. $70; extra person $5; taxes 11%. No credit cards. **Directions:** from I-5 take I-90 east, first exit west of Mercer Way, go south 3/4 mile, then turn left on 33rd, it is the first house on the right.

METALINE FALLS (pop. 210) is located in the northeast corner of the state 97 miles north of Spokane,

$28-$32 **CIRCLE MOTEL**, HC #2 Box 616, Metaline Falls, WA 99153, phone 509-446-4343. A country setting with a lot to offer. The motel has 8 rooms, no designated nonsmoking. Phones, TV, refrigerators, and coffee/tea making facilities in every room.

Outdoor hot tub, microwave in the office with complimentary coffee and quick bread. Spectacular view of the mountains and mountain goats. Excellent hiking, cycling, golf course 1 mile away. Children welcome, pets allowed. **Rates:** single room $28; double room $32; extra person $4; taxes 7.5%. MasterCard, Amex, & Visa. **Directions:** 2 miles north of Metaline Falls on Hwy 31, 10 miles from the Canadian border.

MINERAL is approximately 50 miles south of Tacoma and 17 miles from the entrance to Mount Rainier National Park.

$45-$55 **MINERAL LAKE RESORT**, P. O. Box 22, Mineral, WA 98355, phone 360-492-5367. Located on a pristine fishing lake with unobstructed views of Mt. Rainier. The resort has 4 sleeping cabins with equipped kitchenettes. All cabins share portable fiberglass toilets. There are cable hookups in the cabins, but no TV; bring your own TV and bedding. Dock fishing and swimming area. Fishing boats and pontoon available to rent. RV spaces with full hookups. Restaurant 4 miles away. Children welcome, no pets. **Rates:** cabins $45-$55; RV space $16; taxes 7.6%. No credit cards. **Directions:** 1 hour southeast of Tacoma off Hwy 7 between Elbe and Morton.

MOCLIPS is located on the Pacific Ocean, approximately 20 miles north of Ocean Shores on Hwy 109.

(MOH-klips) has a beautiful sandy beach for long beach walks, clamming in season, kite flying, or storm watching. Coming from the south, this is the last town with lodging before turning inland away from the ocean.

Located in Grays Harbor County the sales/use/lodging taxes are 10.9%.

$74-$94 **HI TIDE OCEAN BEACH RESORT**, P. O. Box 308, Moclips, WA 98562, phone 360-276-4142 or 1-800-662-5477. This resort has 24 condo-style units, 13 nonsmoking. All units have equipped kitchens, fireplaces, decks or lanais, and TV. Some have covered parking. Located on the ocean at the confluence of the Moclips River. Children under 5 free, dogs allowed in some units with restrictions.

Closest restaurant is 2 miles away. Minimum stays are required at certain times of the year. **Summer Rates:** *03/16 to 10/01* - double occupancy, one bedroom condo units $84-$94; extra person $10; pets $10. **Winter Rates:** $74-$84. Amex, Discover, MasterCard, & Visa. **Directions:** from Hwy 109 turn west into town, cross the bridge, turn right and proceed to the end of the road.

$45-$64 **MOONSTONE BEACH MOTEL,** P. O. Box 156, Moclips, WA 98562, phone 360-276-4346. Ocean front location with 7 rooms and one cabin. One nonsmoking unit. All units have ocean views, decks, cable TV, and equipped kitchens. Just 40 feet to the beach. Children under 2 free, pets allowed. Rooms sleep from 2 to 5, cabin sleeps up to 6. **Summer Rates:** *4/01 to 9/30* - double occupancy, rooms $59; cabin $64; extra person $5; pets $5. **Winter Rates:** $45-$50. MasterCard & Visa. **Directions:** from Hwy 109 turn left to ocean, cross the bridge to Pacific street, and turn right.

$75 **O'BRIEN'S,** P. O. Box 276, Moclips, WA 98562, phone 360-276-4676. This 2 bedroom house sleeps up to 6 and is completely furnished. It has a wood stove, cable TV, living room, equipped kitchen, washer and dryer. Located on a bluff that overlooks the ocean. Children welcome, no pets. Daily and weekly rates. **Rates:** double occupancy $75. No credit cards. **Directions:** Hwy 109, directly across from the post office.

$42-$125 **OCEAN CREST,** Sunset Beach, Moclips, WA 98562, phone 360-276-4465 or 1-800-684-8439. This resort has a total of 45 units, no designated nonsmoking. One room studios to one and two bedroom apartments, most have ocean views and fireplaces. Phones, TV, and coffee/tea making facilities in all the rooms. Cooking is restricted to the fully equipped kitchen units. Fireplace units are provided with 3 logs per day. The resort sits on a bluff overlooking the ocean. Beach access is a wooden staircase that traverses through a fern grotto in the cliff side. The restaurant is a very popular place, reservations are recommended. Be sure to visit their gift shop. Recreation center with indoor pool, spa, sauna, exercise room, tanning bed, and an on-site massage therapist. Children under 3 free, no pets. **Summer Rates:** *3/15 to 9/17* - double occupancy $56-$125; extra person $11; children under 15 - $6; rollaway $6; crib $3. **Spring/Fall:** *2/17 to 3/14 & 9/18 to 10/29* - $48-$106. **Winter Rates:** *10/30 to 2/16* - $42-$94. Most major credit cards. **Directions:** on Hwy 109, 18 miles north of Ocean Shores.

MONROE (pop. 4, 780) is located northeast of Seattle and east of Everett on the Stevens Pass Highway (Hwy 2).

Monroe has recently experienced a period of rapid growth from Seattle commuters who find the small town atmosphere and agriculture area a bit more restful.

Located in Snohomish County the sales/use/lodging taxes are 10.2%.

$48-$61 **FAIRGROUND INN MOTEL**, 18950 Hwy 2, Monroe, WA 98272, phone 360-794-5401. Two story motel with 60 rooms, 20 nonsmoking. Phones and TV in every room. No coffee/tea making facilities, but there is a restaurant next door. Four kitchen units, cookware available at the office with a deposit. Indoor hot tub. Large parking area for trucks; close to shopping center and fairgrounds. Children welcome, free with parents, pets allowed. **Rates:** single room (1 bed) $48; double room (2 beds) $61; rollaway $5; pets $5; no charge for local calls. MasterCard, Amex, & Visa. **Directions:** on Hwy 2, west end of town.

$30-$48 **MONROE MOTEL**, 20310 Old Owen Rd., Monroe, WA 98272, phone 360-794-6751. Two blocks off the main highway, this older motel has 22 rooms, 2 nonsmoking. Rooms have phones and TV, no coffee/tea making facilities. There are 9 kitchen units that are not furnished with cookware or dishes. Located on Woods Creek. The motel has a large grassy area. Children welcome, no pets. **Rates:** single room (1 bed) $30; double room (2 beds) $42-$48; kitchen units $3-$4 extra; no charge for local phone calls. Most major credit cards. **Directions:** at the east end of town, turn north on Old Owen Rd. and proceed for 2 blocks.

$45-$75 **NORA & ED'S BED & BREAKFAST** , 215 S. Blakely, Monroe, WA 98272, phone 360-794-8875. Two nonsmoking guest rooms, with shared facilities, are available in this Dutch colonial house. One room has twin beds, the other has a double bed. Phone and TV are accessible in the living room. A continental breakfast is served in the kitchen. Adults only, no pets. **Rates:** single (1 person/twin bed) $45; double bed room (2 people) $55; 2 people/twin beds $75. No credit cards. **Directions:** from Hwy 2 turn south onto Lewis St., proceed to Main St., turn right at light, turn left on S. Blakely.

MONTESANO (pop. 3,060) is located on Hwy 12, 37 miles west of Olympia.

Montesano was derived from two Spanish words: "Monte" (mountain) and "Sano" (health)...healthy mountain. Noted for Lake Sylvia State Park, where visitors have access to two miles of a self-guided forest trail with 15 learning stations.

Located in Grays Harbor County the sales/use/lodging taxes are 10.9%.

$35-$55   **MONTE SQUARE,** 518 1/2 S. 1st St., Montesano, WA 98563, phone 360-249-4424. 10 units, all non-smoking. Nine units are upstairs above the Food Mart, and one is next door. Phones and cable TV with remote control and Showtime. No coffee/tea making facilities in the rooms, but available at the office. One unit has an equipped kitchen. Smoking is restricted to the balcony. Children welcome, pets allowed. **Rates:** *Sunday - Thursday -* double room $35; kitchen unit $45. *Friday & Saturday -* double room $45; kitchen unit $55; extra person (all ages) $5; pets free; no charge for local calls. Major credit cards. **Directions:** from the east take the Montesano Exit and follow the exit ramp across 1st St.; from the west take the Montesano Exit, on the north side of freeway.

$60-$80   **ABEL HOUSE BED & BREAKFAST**, 117 Fleet St. S., Montesano, WA 98563, phone 360-249-6002 or 1-800-235-ABEL. This 1908 Colonial Dutch stone house has 5 guest rooms, 2 with private facilities and 3 with shared. All rooms are on the second floor, the third floor has a game room and lounge for guests to use. The house occupies 5 lots with landscaped gardens. Full breakfast provided. Close to Lake Sylvia, museum, and historical court house. Two blocks to the nearest restaurant. Well-behave children welcome, pets by arrangement, smoking allowed in the garden and on the front porch. **Rates:** double occupancy $60-$80. Amex, MasterCard, & Visa. **Directions:** from Hwy 12 take the cut off to Montesano, right turn on Main St., 4 blocks to the court house, left turn, two blocks, left on Fleet.

MORTON (pop. 1,125) is located on the north side of Mt. St. Helens, 45 miles east of I-5.

Highway 12 goes past Morton and is the main road from I-5 leading to the White Pass Ski Area and Yakima.

Located in Lewis County the sales/use taxes are 7.6%.

$27-$50 **EVERGREEN MOTEL**, P. O. Box 205, Morton, WA 98356, phone 360-496-5407. Centrally located off the highway. 12 rooms, all on one level, no nonsmoking. TV in the rooms, parking outside your door. No coffee/tea making facilities in the rooms, but 6 units have equipped kitchens. Restaurant and bar within walking distance. Children welcome, pets allowed. **Rates:** single room (1 bed) $27; double room (2 beds) $35-$40; family room (3 beds) $50; pets free. MasterCard & Visa. **Directions:** from Hwy 7 one block east of the stoplight.

$39-$85 **ROY'S MOTEL & RV PARK**, 161 2nd St., Morton, WA 98356, phone 360-496-5000. Centrally located on Hwy 7. Seven rooms, 3 nonsmoking. Phones, TV, AC, queen beds, and refrigerators. No coffee/tea making facilities in the rooms, but available in the lobby. Children 12 and under free, pets by arrangement. **Summer Rates:** *6/01 to 10/01* - single room (1 bed) $39-$48; double room (2 beds) $48-$58; jacuzzi suite $75-$85; extra person $6; local phone calls free. **Winter Rates:** $39-$69. MasterCard, Amex, & Visa. **Directions:** Hwy 7 center of town.

$59-$69 **ST. HELENS MANORHOUSE BED & BREAKFAST**, 7476 Hwy 12, Morton, WA 98356, phone 360-498-5243 or 1-800-551-3290. A 1910 manor house with 4 guest rooms, 2 with private facilities, 2 with shared. All rooms are on the second floor. The spacious rooms are decorated with antiques. Phone available, TV in the parlor, and numerous book collections throughout the house. Within walking distance of the lake for great fishing. Full breakfast served at 8 or 9 a.m., coffee earlier, evening dessert in the summer. Children 12 and older welcome, no pets, and no smoking. Located on 20 mile Riffe Lake with boat launch. **Rates:** single or double room $59-$69; extra person $20. No credit cards. **Directions:** Exit 68 from I-5 onto Hwy 12, proceed 37 miles, just beyond milepost 103, to driveway on south side.

$50-$60 **The SEASONS MOTEL,** 200 Westlake, Morton, WA 98356, phone 360-496-6835. The largest motel in this area with 50 rooms, 31 nonsmoking. Phones and TV. No coffee/tea making facilities, but a continental breakfast is provided in the lobby. On site restaurant opens at 5 a.m. to 10 p.m. Two story motel with ample parking for large trucks and easy freeway access. Children 12 and under free, small pets allowed. **Rates:** single room $50; double room $60; extra person $5; pets $5; no charge for local phone calls. Most major credit cards. **Directions:** at junction of Hwy 12 and Hwy 7.

$30-$35 **STILTNER MOTEL,** P. O. Box 474, Morton, WA 98356, phone 360-496-5103. This older motel has 7 individual cabins. All cabins have TV and equipped kitchens with microwaves. Children welcome, pets allowed, both free. **Rates:** single room $30; double room $35; rollaway $5. No credit cards. **Directions:** on the north side of town, a little row of green cabins.

MOSES LAKE (pop. 11,420) is in the center of the state 107 miles west of Spokane and 179 miles east of Seattle.

Moses Lake is the commercial hub of the Columbia Basin. The lake is made up of three main arms which are over 18 miles long and up to one mile wide. The lake has 120 miles of shoreline and covers 6,500 acres. Sullivan Dam, the Potholes Reservoir, and Winchester Wasteway make this area popular for all types of water activities.

Located in Grant County the sales/use taxes are 7.5%.

HALLMARK INN Best Western, 3000 Marina Dr., Moses Lake, WA 98837, phone 1-800-235-4255.

$30-$45 **IMA EL RANCHO MOTEL,** 1214 S. Pioneer Way, Moses Lake, WA 98837, phone 509-765-9173, reservations 1-800-341-8000, fax 509-765-1137. 21 rooms, 9 nonsmoking, and 9 kitchen units with basic cookware. Phones, cable TV, AC, queen beds, and a seasonal outdoor pool. No coffee/tea making facilities in the rooms, but available in the lobby. 24 hour wake-up service, easy freeway access. Children 11 and under free, pets allowed no charge. Picnic area and barbecue. Clean, quiet, and comfortable. **Rates:** single $30-$36; double $34-$42; kitchen unit $42; suite $42-$45; extra person $3; no charge for local phone calls. Major credit cards. **Directions:** from I-90 Exit 179, proceed for 1 1/2 miles north on business route 90.

$39-$59   **INTERSTATE INN,** 2801 W. Broadway, Moses Lake, WA 98837, phone 509-765-1777, reservations 1-800-777-5889. 30 rooms, 14 nonsmoking. Phones and TV with HBO. Some rooms have microwaves and refrigerators. Indoor pool, sauna, and spa. No coffee/tea making facilities in the rooms, but available in the lobby. Restaurant, bar, and coffee shop are next door. Children welcome, infants free, pets allowed. Close to the lake and Washington State Park. Convenient to fishing and hunting. **Rates:** single room $39-$46; double room $46-$59; family room $59; extra person $3-$6; pets $5; local phone calls 25¢. Major credit cards. **Directions:** from I-90 Exit 176, next to Perkins Restaurant.

$35-$85   **LAKESIDE MOTEL,** 802 W. Broadway, Moses Lake, WA 98837, phone 509-765-8651. This motel overlooks the lake. There are 22 rooms, 10 nonsmoking, and 7 have non-equipped kitchens. Cable TV with HBO, phones, and AC. Coffee makers in kitchen units and instant coffee in others. Family atmosphere, children welcome, no pets. **Summer Rates:** *5/01 to 10/30* - single room (1 bed) $42-$65; double room (2 beds) $75-$85; local phone calls free. **Winter Rates:** $35-$55. MasterCard, Visa, & Discover. **Directions:** from I-90 Exit 176, go east on Broadway approximately 2 miles, on your left.

$35-$45   **MAPLES MOTEL,** 1006 W. 3rd, Moses Lake, WA 98837, phone 509-765-5665. 44 units, 4 nonsmoking, and 2 non-equipped kitchen units. Phones, TV, outdoor pool, and sauna. No coffee/tea making facilities in the rooms, but available in the lobby. Children and pets free. Within walking distance of parks, restaurants, mini-mart, and lake. **Rates:** single room $35; double room $45; no cost for local phone calls. Major credit cards. **Directions:** from the west, Exit 176, follow Broadway to the center of town, from the east Exit 179 from I-90, turn right onto Pioneer Way, this becomes Broadway, proceed to the center of town.

$36-$46   **OASIS MOTEL,** 466 Melva Ln., Moses Lake, WA 98837, phone 509-765-8636 or 1-800-456-2747. 35 units, 15 nonsmoking, and 7 equipped kitchens. Phones and cable TV with HBO. No coffee/tea making facilities in the rooms, but a continental breakfast is served in the lobby. There is also an espresso cart for the serious coffee drinkers. Facilities include the pool, hot tub, barbecue grills, picnic tables, and volleyball. Children welcome, infants free, pets allowed with a refundable deposit. **Summer Rates:** *5/01 to 10/30* - single room (1 bed) $38-$42; double room (2 beds) $42; kitchen units $46; extra person $4; pet deposit $25; local phone calls free. **Winter Rates:** $2 less per room. Amex, Discover, MasterCard, & Visa. **Directions:** from I-90 take Exit 176.

$32-$45 **SAGE "N" SAND MOTEL**, 1011 S. Pioneer Way, Moses Lake, WA 98837, phone 509-765-1755 or 1-800-336-0454. 37 units, 4 nonsmoking, and 9 non-equipped kitchens. Phones, cable TV with HBO, mini refrigerators, and some units have microwaves. Seasonal outdoor pool. No coffee/tea making facilities, but donuts and coffee are available in the lobby. Children free with parents, pets allowed. **Summer Rates:** single (1 bed) $37; double (2 beds) $45; kitchen unit $45; extra person $5; pets $5; local phone calls free. **Winter Rates:** $5 less per room. Major credit cards. **Directions:** from I-90 take Exit 179, on to Pioneer Way, proceed for 2.2 miles.

SHILO INN, 1819 E. Kittleson, Moses Lake, WA 98837, phone 509-765-9317 or 1-800-222-2244.

$30-$50 **SUNLAND MOTOR INN**, 309 E. Third Ave., Moses Lake, WA 98837, phone 509-765-1170. 22 units, 6 nonsmoking. Seven units have recently been remodeled and have non-equipped kitchenettes. Phones, TV, refrigerators, and microwaves. No coffee/tea making facilities in the rooms, but available in the office. Children 2 and under free, pets free. Within walking distance of restaurant, lake, and shopping. **Summer Rates:** single room (1 bed) $35; double room (2 beds) $43; 3 beds/3 people $50; extra person $5; local phone calls free. **Winter Rates:** single $30; double $38. Amex, MasterCard, & Visa. **Directions:** Exit 179 off I-90, located downtown.

MOSSYROCK (pop. 450) is located 20 miles east of I-5, just off Hwy 12 going to Mt. St. Helens.

$45-$55 **BOTZER HOUSE BED & BREAKFAST**, 323 Court St., P. O. Box 374, Mossyrock, WA 98564, phone 360-983-3792. Dr. William Botzer had this home built in 1923; his office was located in the basement which is now a guest apartment that sleeps up to 8 people. Private outside entrance into the living room decorated with a variety of memorabilia. There is a fully equipped kitchen, bedroom, and bath. A full breakfast is provided. The hosts are collectors of garage sale treasures you are sure to appreciate. Children welcome, no pets. **Rates:** double occupancy $45-$55; extra person $5; taxes 7.6%. MasterCard & Visa. **Directions:** Exit 68 off I-5, 20 miles west on Hwy 12, turn right into Mossyrock, go 3 blocks, turn left 2 blocks.

$35-$60 **LAKE MAYFIELD RESORT**, 350A Hadaller Rd., Mossyrock, WA 98564, phone 360-985-2357. The new owners plan to keep the resort open year-round. There are 4 sleeping rooms and 2 cabins available. The sleeping rooms are above the bathhouse and are very basic. Cabins have fully equipped kitchens and private facilities. Located on the lake, good fishing, store, boat launch, and moorage. Children 12 and under free, pets allowed on a leash. **Rates:** sleeping rooms $35; cabins $50-$60; parking $2; extra person $2; pets free; taxes 7.6%. MasterCard & Visa. **Directions:** Exit 68 off I-5, 16 miles west on Hwy 12, after crossing Lake Mayfield Bridge take the 1st right, Wilson Creek Rd., go 1.5 miles to Hadaller Rd., make a right 1.1 miles to the resort.

•MOUNT VERNON (pop. 18,700) is located in the northwest corner of the state just off I-5.

Mt. Vernon is a busy, thriving community that becomes busier in the spring when the surrounding iris, daffodil, and tulip fields burst into color. Maps of various flower fields and a calendar of events can be obtained at the Chamber of Commerce. Mt. Vernon's downtown district is a vibrant focal point of speciality shopping and local culture.

Located in Skagit (SKA-jit) County the sales/use taxes are 7.8%.

Also see La Conner for lodging.

$45-$65 **COLLEGE WAY INN Best Western**, 300 W. College Way, Mt. Vernon, WA 98273, phone 360-424-4287 or 1-800-528-1234, fax 360-424-6036. 66 units, 51 nonsmoking. Phones, cable TV with HBO, coffee/tea making facilities in the rooms, and 9 equipped kitchen units. Continental breakfast. Hot tub and seasonal outdoor pool. Restaurant next door. Children under 12 free, pets allowed. Large vehicle parking. **Summer Rates:** single room $59; double room $62; kitchen units $65; extra person $5; local phone calls free; pets $5 for the first night. **Winter Rates:** $45-$55. Major credit cards. **Directions:** take Exit 227 from I-5, go 1 1/2 blocks from exit.

$59-$120 **COTTONTREE INN Best Western**, 2300 Market, Mt. Vernon, WA 98273, phone 360-428-5678 or 1-800-662-6886, fax 360-428-1844. 120 units, 85 nonsmoking. Phones, remote control cable TV with HBO, and AC. Coffee/tea making facilities in some rooms, continental breakfast in the lobby. VCR and movie rentals. Seasonal pool and adjacent health club. Restaurant/lounge on the premises. Children under 18 free with parents, pets allowed. **Seasonal Rates:** single room or double room $59-$69; suite $120; local phone calls free; no charge for pets. Major credit cards. **Directions:** from the south take Exit 229 east to Burlington Blvd. (stoplight), turn right, hotel is 1/2 mile from light.

DAYS INN, 2009 Riverside Dr., Mt. Vernon, WA 98273, phone 360-424-4141 or 1-800-882-4141.

$65-$85 **FULTON HOUSE BED & BREAKFAST,** 420 Fulton St., Mt. Vernon, WA 98273, phone 360-336-2952. There are 3 guest rooms on the second floor of this 1908 Victorian. All rooms have private facilities. Choose a queen, king, or sleigh bed. The room with the sleigh bed also has a day bed and view of the Olympic Mountains. Full breakfast is served in the dining room. Dietary restrictions can be accommodated with advance notice. Children welcome, no pets, smoking outside. Off-street parking. **Rates:** *Sunday -Thursday:* double occupancy $65 & $75; *Friday & Saturday* - $75 & $85; third night free. Major credit cards. **Directions:** from I-5 take Kincaid St. Exit, turn west, go to 2nd, turn right, follow to the east side of freeway to Fulton.

Fulton House Bed & Breakfast

$75 **The INN at THIRTEEN FIRS BED & BREAK-FAST,** 2329B Hwy 9 Lake McMurray, Mt. Vernon, WA 98273, phone 360-445-3571. This cottage type studio has a private entrance and offers quiet accommodations for two by the lake. The kitchen is completely equipped with microwave and dishes, cable TV, queen bed, and large deck. The trail to the lake is less than 200 feet, where there is a fishing/swimming dock. The lake has a 5 mile per hour speed limit, perfect place to bring a canoe or kayak. A continental breakfast of juice, fresh fruit, and homemade muffins is provided the evening before, breakfast is optional. Children by arrangement, no pets, and no smoking indoors. Five miles to the nearest restaurant, 14 miles to LaConner, 12 miles to Mt. Vernon. **Rates**: double occupancy $75. No credit cards, personal check or cash preferred. **Directions:** from I-5 take Exit 221(5 miles south of Mt. Vernon) head east on Hwy 534 to the first stop sign, turn right onto Hwy 9, follow curves to the Lake McMurray general store and proceed for another .7 mile to the white sign.

$42-$55   **TULIP VALLEY INN,** 2200 Freeway Dr., Mt. Vernon, WA 98273, phone 360-428-5969 or 1-800-599-5969. This tidy motel has 40 rooms, 26 nonsmoking. In-room amenities include cable TV with HBO, phones, and AC. There are 7 units with kitchens, basic cookware available on request. Morning coffee is available in the lobby. Children 5 and under free, no pets. **Summer Rates:** single room (1 bed) $42-$45; double room $55; kitchen units (1 bed/2 people) $49; extra person $7; local phone calls free. Check on winter rates. Major credit cards. **Directions:** from I-5 take Exit 227, turn west one block, turn north 500 yards, on the right.

$30-$45   **WEST WINDS MOTEL,** 2020 Riverside Dr., Mt. Vernon, WA 98273, phone 360-424-4224. This one story motel has 40 rooms, 20 nonsmoking. Phones, TV with HBO, and coffee/tea making facilities in the rooms. With lodgings of three days or more, there are microwaves and refrigerators available. Children under 12 free, pets allowed. **Summer Rates:** *4/01 to 9/30* - single room (1bed) $35-$40; double room $45; extra person $5; pets $5; local phone calls free. **Winter Rates:** $30-$40. Major credit cards. **Directions:** from I-5 take Exit 227, turn east to the first major intersection, then turn left, go half a block.

$65-$95   **WHISPERING FIRS BED & BREAKFAST,** 1957 Kanako Lane, Mt. Vernon, WA 98273, phone 360-428-1990 or 1-800-428-1992. There are 3 guest rooms in this modern brick rambler, all with private facilities. The suite has a king waterbed, changing room, and sliding glass doors that open onto a deck with a hot tub. A family room is available with two queen beds, hide-a-bed, and picture window with views of the San Juans. The third room has a regular king bed with private bath across the hall. Full breakfast provided. Ten minutes to the nearest restaurant. Children welcome, pets by arrangement, smoking outside. Off-street parking. **Rates:** double occupancy $65, $85, & $95. No credit cards. **Directions:** from I-5 take Exit 221, make a quick left on Cedardale, proceed for 2.5 miles parallel to the freeway. Turn right at Stackpole Rd., 1 mile to Kanako Ln., going off the bridge make a hard right and follow gravel drive for almost a mile.

NACHES (pop. 605) is located on Hwy 12, 15 miles northwest of Yakima.

(NA-CHEEZ) conjures up visions of an Indian village complete with tepees and woven baskets. In reality this small community is the P. O. Box for many residents and resorts located on Chinook Pass and White Pass. Stop at the local espresso stand before heading west, take a right to Chinook Pass or go left to White Pass.

Located in Yakima (YAK-i-maw) County the sales/use taxes are 7.6%.

CHINOOK PASS

(shi-NOOK) This area's activities include fishing on the Naches River, hunting, bicycling, 4-wheeling in the hills, and snowmobiling.

$65-$80 **COZY CAT BED & BREAKFAST**, 12604 SR 410, Naches, WA 98937, phone 509-658-2953. Two non-smoking rooms with private facilities in this country home on scenic Chinook Pass. One room has a queen brass bed. The "mini suite" has a queen bed and adjoining TV room with knotty pine walls and a day bed. The living room has a fireplace in the winter and small coffee room for early birds. Breakfast is continental and varies day to day - "cooks whim". Children welcome, pets allowed on an individual basis, horse accommodations. Within walking distance of the river, situated among tall pines. **Rates**: double occupancy $65; suite $80; extra person $10. Visa & MasterCard. **Directions:** 32 miles from Yakima on SR 410 between milepost 104 and 105.

$48 **ELKRIDGE LODGE**, 13880 SR 410, Naches, WA 98937, phone 509-658-2258. Three cabins share a central bathhouse and sleep 4 people. Fully equipped kitchens, double beds, living rooms with hide-a-beds, and air-tight wood stoves. 14 RV sites. Children 12 and under free, pets on a leash. **Rates**: double occupancy $48; extra person $7; pets free. No credit cards. **Directions:** 18 miles north of Naches on State Route 410.

$49-$69 **SQUAW ROCK RESORT**, 15070 SR 410, Naches, WA 98937-9406, phone 509-658-2926. Four motel units, 5 cabins, no nonsmoking. All have private facilities and TV, no phones. Coffee/tea making facilities in the motel units; full kitchens with basic cooking utensils in the cabins. Three cabins have fireplaces. Seasonal outdoor pool, hot tub, gift shop, meeting hall, grocery store, gas, restaurant, and cocktails. Children 6 and under free, small pets allowed.

Open year-round. **Rates**: motel units, double occupancy $49-$54; extra person $10; cabins, double occupancy $59-$69; extra person $10; pets $10. MasterCard & Visa. **Directions:** 20 miles north of Naches on SR 410.

$59-$189 **WHISTLIN' JACK LODGE**, 20800 SR 410, Naches, WA 98937, phone 509-658-2433 or 1-800-827-2299. Eight motel units with bay windows overlooking the Naches River. There is a hot tub at the end of the complex. Eight cottages, 6 with individual hot tubs, and 2 bungalows. All the cottages have kitchens with basic cooking utensils, 7 have fireplaces. No phones or TV. Grocery store, restaurant, and lounge featuring live entertainment Thursday thru Saturday. Open year-round. Children 12 and under free, no pets. This upscale resort offers "Smile Package" rates and "Ski Packages". **High Season Rates**: *6/01 to 11/25* - motel units, double occupancy $89; extra person $10; cottages, 4 people $129-$189; bungalows, 2 people $139. **Off-Season Rates:** motel units mid-week $59; cottages $15-$20 less. MasterCard, Visa, & Discover. **Directions:** 25 miles north of Naches, 35 miles to Yakima, on SR 410.

WHITE PASS

is in the Wenatchee National Forest and forks to the left out of Naches on Hwy 12 leading to the White Pass Ski Area.

$35-$160 **GAME RIDGE MOTEL & LODGE**, 27350 Hwy 12, Naches, WA 98937, phone 509-672-2212. 16 motel units, 5 nonsmoking. All have private facilities. Five fully equipped kitchen units, 12 of the motel units have coffee/tea making facilities. One small cabin, with private hot tub. One house, sleeps 9, with private hot tub. No phones or TV. Children welcome, pets allowed. Located on the river, large BBQ area, riverside hot tub, seasonal heated pool, recreation room, and fish cleaning area. Closest restaurant just down the street at the Trout Lodge. **Rates**: motel units: single $35-$45; double $46-$54; family room $70-$79; cabin, double occupancy $95; house, *minimum 2 night stay*, 4-6 people $160. Most major credit cards. **Directions:** on Hwy 12, 30 miles west of Yakima, 22 miles east of White Pass Ski Area.

$28-$40 **TROUT LODGE**, 27090 Hwy 12, Naches, WA 98937, phone 509-672-2211. 4 motel units, no nonsmoking. No phones, TV in the lodge. No coffee/tea making facilities in the rooms, but the lodge and restaurant across the street opens at 8 a.m. Children welcome, pets allowed. Quiet location. The lodge/restaurant is on the river side of the highway, motel units across the street. **Rates**: single $28; double $40; extra person $4. MasterCard & Visa. **Directions:** on Hwy 12, 30 miles west of Yakima, 22 miles east of White Pass Ski Lodge.

NAHCOTTA see Long Beach Peninsula.

NEAH BAY is located on the upper westward tip of the Olympic Peninsula on the Makah Indian Reservation.

(NEE-uh Bay) The narrow, winding road into Neah Bay threatens to slip into the Strait of Juan de Fuca. Neah Bay is primarily a fishing village, but many people come here to visit the Makah Cultural and Research Center that exhibits artifacts from the 2,000 year old buried ruins of Ozette Village.

Located in Clallam County the sales/use taxes are 7.9%.

$15-$55 **CAPE FLATTERY RESORT & HOSTEL**, P. O. Box 117, Neah Bay, WA 98357, phone 360-645-2251 or 1-800-377-9439. Once an air force facility, the barracks have been remodeled into 48 motel style rooms. GI issue double and twin beds, private facilities. The 12 hostel rooms have not been remodeled and have 2-4 beds per room. Bedding furnished. Two rooms share one bathroom. There is a common kitchen and lounge area. On site 24 hour deli serves soup and chowder. Located on the ocean side one mile from the beach. Children free with parents, pets allowed, no smoking in the rooms. Three miles to the nearest restaurant. **Rates:** motel rooms - single $45; double $55; extra person $5. Hostel beds $15. MasterCard, Amex, & Visa. **Directions:** follow Hwy 112 into Neah Bay, go through town and follow signs.

$18-$60 **CAPE MOTEL & RV PARK**, P. O. Box 136, Neah Bay, WA 98357, phone 360-645-2250. A total of 10 units and 2 shanties (hard top tents with bunks), no designated nonsmoking. The shanties are available in the summer only, no bedding. Five equipped kitchen units and 5 sleeping units sleep 5-6 people. All rooms have a TV with four channels. Large RV park with hot showers and laundry. Morning coffee in the lobby. Restaurant/store/deli across the street. Children welcome, infants free, pets by arrangement. **Summer Rates:** sleeping rooms $40-$50; kitchen units $55-$60; shanty - single $18; double $25; extra person $7. **Winter Rates:** standard room $35-$45; kitchen units $45-$50. MasterCard, Discover, & Visa. **Directions:** first motel in town on Main St.

$45-$60 **HILDEN'S MOTEL**, P. O. Box 181, Neah Bay, WA 98357, phone 360-645-2306. A total of 5 housekeeping units right on the beach. No nonsmoking units. All units have equipped kitchens and phones are available. TV reception is poor - you may want to bring a VCR. Two of the rooms have views of the water. Children free under 5, no pets. Rates are higher in the winter because of the extra electricity. **Summer Rates:** single (1 person) $45; double $55; extra person $10; children $5. **Winter Rates:** single $50; double $60. No credit cards. **Directions:** 2 miles east of Neah Bay.

$44 **SILVER SALMON RESORT**, P. O. Box 156, Neah Bay, WA 98357, phone 360-645-2388. A total of 9 motel units, no nonsmoking. All rooms have 2 beds, TVs, and kitchens available. Across from boat launch and charter service. Freezer space available, propane, and gift shop. Children 2 and under free, pets by arrangement. **Rates:** per room $44; extra person $8; rollaway $5. MasterCard, Discover, & Visa. **Directions:** on Hwy 112, city center.

$39-$50 **TYEE MOTEL**, P. O. Box 193, Neah Bay, WA 98357, phone 360-645-2223. A total of 41 motel units, no nonsmoking. TV and kitchens available. Close to the Makah Museum, beaches, hiking trails, and excellent fishing. Children 9 and under free, pets free. **Rates:** single room (1 bed) $39; double (2 beds) $50; extra person $7. MasterCard & Visa. **Directions:** in downtown Neah Bay.

NEWPORT. (pop. 1, 600) is located on the Idaho-Washington border at the intersection of Hwy 2 and Hwy 20, approximately 50 miles northeast of Spokane.

Newport is surrounded by forested hillsides and mountains at the end of the Pend Oreille River Valley (pronounced Pond-er-ray). Recreational sports are pursued on numerous lakes and rivers in the area.

Located in Pend Oreille County the sales/use taxes are 7.5%.

$10-$12 **BEAR PAW CAMP**, 581 Bear Paw Dr., Newport, WA 99156, phone 509-447-3900 or 1-800-277-6113. *Open May 1st to October 31st.* Group lodging only, minimum of 35 people, maximum of 150. This retreat center is ideal for church groups and family reunions. Located on the Pend Oreille River, there are numerous outdoor activities: tennis, volleyball, baseball, canoeing, swimming in the large outdoor pool, archery, fishing, and hiking. The indoor game room features ping-pong, a pool table, and foosball. There are 12 small cabins, 4 dormitories, and a duplex. Each person should bring a sleeping bag and pillow. Groups are responsible for their own food and food preparation in the large community kitchen. **Rates:** 35 to 50 people $12 each; 51 to 75 people $11 each; 75 and over $10 each. **Directions:** on Hwy 2 cross the bridge into Idaho and take the first left, LeClerc Rd., and proceed for 11 miles along the river, turn left onto dirt road that leads to the camp.

$36-$48 **GOLDEN SPUR MOTEL**, 924 West Hwy 2, Newport, WA 99156, phone 509-447-3823. A total of 24 units, 12 nonsmoking. In-room amenities include phones and TV. Morning coffee is available in the lobby and there are 3 fully equipped kitchen units. Restaurant and lounge on the premises. Children welcome, infants free, pets allowed. **Summer Rates:** single (1 bed) $38; double (2 beds) $48; local phone calls free; extra person $5; pets $5 per night. **Winter Rates:** $36-$46. Major credit cards. **Directions:** on Hwy 2 just south of town.

$30-$70 **KNOTTY PINES MOTEL & COTTAGES**, 324051 N. Hwy 2, Diamond Lake, Newport, WA 99156, phone 509-447-5427, fax 509-447-2455. Two modern cottages, one jacuzzi suite, and 4 motel units. The cottages have living room, fully equipped kitchen, bath, bedroom, phone, TV, and VCR. The suite has a double wide jacuzzi, small refrigerator, and TV/VCR. All units have coffee/tea making facilities, 4 nonsmoking units available. Children welcome, infants free, no pets. Large grassy area. **Rates:** cottages, 1 person $50; 2 people $65-$70; motel units $30-$45; extra person $5; local phone calls free. Visa, MasterCard, & Amex. **Directions:** on Hwy 2 10 miles west of Newport, 32 miles north of Spokane.

$34-$46 **NEWPORT CITY INN**, 220 N. Washington, P. O. Box 9, Newport, WA 99156, phone 509-447-3463. 13 units, 6 nonsmoking. Phones, TV with remote control. No coffee/tea making facilities, but a restaurant, coffee shop, and bar are right across the street. Children 6 and under free, pets with prior arrangement. Picnic area. **Summer Rates:** single (1 person) $40; double $44; 3 people $46; extra person $6; local phone calls free. **Winter Rates:** $34-$40. Most major credit cards. **Directions:** at junction of Hwy 2 and 20, north end of Newport.

NORTH BEND (pop. 2,010) is located off I-90, Exit 31, 29 miles east of Seattle and 30 minutes from the Snoqualmie Pass Ski Areas.

North Bend was founded in 1889. It was originally a railroad town with trains going to eastern Washington from Seattle. The area offers numerous recreational activities - fishing, hunting, hiking, mountain climbing, camping, golf, and shopping - just to name a few. The new factory outlet stores along I-90 attract a lot of shoppers.

Located in King County the sales/use taxes are 8.2%.

$50-$95 **EDGEWICK INN**, 14600 468th Ave. SE, North Bend, WA 98045, phone 206-888-9000, fax 206-888-9400. 44 units, 18 nonsmoking. Phones and satellite TV. No coffee/tea making facilities in the rooms, but available in the lobby. Adjacent to a 24 hour restaurant. Two jacuzzi suites, large parking spaces, and indoor hot tub. Children 10 and under free, no pets. **Rates:** single room $50; double room $58; suite $95; extra person $6; local phone calls free. MasterCard, Amex, & Visa. **Directions:** at Exit 34 off I-90, across from truck stop.

$49-$59 **NOR'WEST MOTEL & RV PARK**, 45810 SE North Bend Way, North Bend, WA 98045, phone 206-888-1939. Quiet, country setting surrounds this newly renovated motel. Rooms

open onto a wide country-style verandah surrounded by lush flower gardens. 16 rooms, 9 nonsmoking. All rooms have phones, TV, microwave, refrigerator, or (2) fully equipped kitchens. Complimentary morning coffee. Children welcome, no pets. Five minute walk to Mt. Si Tavern, which specializes in local brews, 1/2 mile walk to a restaurant. Behind the motel is the RV park in a wooded setting. **Rates:** single room $49; double room or kitchen unit $59; extra bed $5; local phone calls free. MasterCard & Visa. **Directions:** from I-90 take Exit 34, go west 1/2 mile on SE North Bend Way.

OAK HARBOR see Whidbey Island.

OCEAN CITY is on the Pacific Ocean, "up the beach" from Ocean Shores. It has been called "the clam digging capital of the world."

$30-$55 **NORTH BEACH MOTEL**, 2601 St Rt 109, Ocean City, WA 98569, phone 360-289-4116 or 1-800-640-8053. The beach is within 3 blocks. There are 16 units, no nonsmoking, with phones and cable TV. Two 2 bedroom cabins, with equipped kitchens and microwaves, sleeps six. There are 9 units with equipped kitchens; the other units do not have coffee/tea making facilities. Children "always welcome", 5 and under free, pets free. **Rates:** based on double occupancy, single room $30; kitchen units $30-$55; cabin $55; extra person $4; local phone calls free; taxes 10.9%. Major credit cards. **Directions:** in downtown Ocean City.

$30-$56 **PACIFIC SANDS**, 2687 SR 109 , Ocean City, WA 98569, phone 360-289-3588. Conveniently located just north of Ocean Shores. This is the place to enjoy the fresh, clean ocean air, throw a log on the fire, put your feet up, relax and enjoy yourself. There are 9 units, no nonsmoking. Seven have fully equipped kitchens, and 3 have fireplaces. Children 2 and under free, pets allowed on a leash. Children's play area, seafood cleaning facility, picnic tables, cable TV, and seasonal pool. **Summer Rates:** units with no kitchens $40; kitchen units $50-$56; extra person $5; pets $6; taxes 10.9%. **Winter Rates:** $30-$46. MasterCard & Visa. **Directions:** one mile north of Ocean Shores.

$32-$100 **WEST WINDS RESORT MOTEL**, 2537 SR 109, Ocean City, WA 98569, phone 360-289-3448 or 1-800-867-3448. Playground, spacious lawns, and wooded area. Beach access is uniquely provided by a raft across a winding stream. There are 10 units available (no nonsmoking). Units include a rustic log cabin, a penthouse, and an A-frame. Eight have fully equipped kitchens and the other two have semi-kitchens. All have cable TV. The A-frame house has a woodstove, microwave, 2 bathrooms, and sleeps 8. There is a well equipped, seafood cleaning facility for your catch of the day. Children under 2 free, pets allowed. **Rates:** double occupancy $32-$60; penthouse $40; A-frame (6 people) $100; extra person $4; pets $3; taxes 10.9%. MasterCard, Amex, & Visa. **Directions:** 1 1/2 mile north of Ocean Shores turn off.

OCEAN PARK see Long Beach Peninsula.

OCEAN SHORES (pop. 2,400) is on the Pacific Ocean west of Aberdeen.

Ocean Shores is located on a five mile long peninsula with a 27 mile canal system connecting three fresh water lakes. The canals and lakes hold year-round fishing opportunities for bass, perch, and trout. The 6,000 acre peninsula is at the mouth of Grays Harbor, the only deep water port on the Pacific coast north of San Francisco. Originally developed in 1960, Ocean Shores is one of Washington's most popular retirement/resort destinations. In season, a passenger ferry shuttles visitors between the Ocean Shores Marina and Westport, just across the harbor. There are plenty of outdoor activities, including an 18 hole championship golf course.

Located in Grays Harbor County the sales/use/lodging taxes are 10.9%.

$42-$78 **DISCOVERY INN**, 1031 Discovery Ave. SE, Ocean Shores, WA 98569, phone 360-289-3371 or 1-800-882-8821. Seven minutes away from downtown, 3 minutes to the beach, and within walking distance of the ferry to Westport. 22 units, 2 nonsmoking. All units have phones, queen beds, coffee/tea making facilities, microwaves, and TV. Some units have fireplaces and there are 16 equipped kitchen units. Private fishing dock on the Grand Canal, outdoor pool, hot tub, row boats, and barbecues. Children 5 and under free, pets on the ground floor only. **Summer Rates:** *5/01 to 9/30* - double occupancy $52-$78; extra person $5; pets $10 per night. **Winter Rates:** $42-$62. Most major credit cards. **Directions:** from the Ocean Shores entrance, proceed 5 miles down Pt. Brown, take a left at the "Y" on Discovery Ave., go 1 block.

$45-$60 **EBB TIDE,** 839 Ocean Shores Blvd., Ocean Shores, WA 98569, phone 360-289-3700. Every room is a suite with a private bedroom, fireplace, living room, and view of the ocean. Eight units, no nonsmoking, cable TV, coffee/tea making facilities, and 7 units have equipped kitchens. Shuttle provided to all points in Ocean Shores. Children 12 and under free, pets by arrangement. **Summer Rates:** *6/01 to 9/15* - double occupancy $60; extra person $5; pets $5. **Winter Rates:** $45. MasterCard, Discover, & Visa. **Directions:** first right after Gateway into Ocean Shores, 1/4 mile.

$40-$75 **GITCHE GUMEE MOTEL,** 648 Ocean Shores Blvd. NW, Ocean Shores, WA 98569, phone 360-289-3323 or 1-800-448-2433. A total of 80 units, nonsmoking units can be provided, 45 kitchen units. Phones and TV in every room. No coffee/tea making facilities in units without kitchens, but available in the lobby. Indoor and outdoor pools, 2 saunas. Children 12 and under free, pets allowed in some rooms. Many families come here for family reunions. There is a large meeting room that holds up to 49 people with a kitchen and fireplace. There are also townhouses available for large groups. **Summer Rates:** *5/01 to 9/30* - double occupancy, sleeping unit $40-$50; kitchen units $60-$75; extra person $5; pets $10 per stay. **Winter Rates:** discounted up to 40% with a two night minimum stay. Major credit cards. **Directions:** come through the Gateway to Ocean Shores to first stop sign, turn right, go to next stop sign, turn left, 3 blocks on the left side of street.

$50-$125 **OCEAN SHORES MOTEL,** 681 Ocean Shores Blvd. NW, Ocean Shores, WA 98569, phone 360-289-3351, 1-800-464-2526. This motel has 40 rooms, 30% nonsmoking. Phones, TV, and 11 rooms have jacuzzi tubs. No coffee/tea making facilities in the rooms, but available in the lobby. Two kitchen units with basic cookware. Children 6 and under free, pets allowed. **Summer Rates:** *5/04 to 10/31* - double occupancy, single room (1 bed) $58; double $70; jacuzzi suites $90-$125; kitchen units $85-$120; extra person $5; pets $10 per night. **Winter Rates:** $50-$125. Amex, MasterCard, & Visa. **Directions:** coming into town, go right at the 1st stop sign, proceed to Ocean Shores Blvd., turn left.

$30-$50   **OCEAN SIDE MOTEL**, P. O. Box 699, Ocean Shores, WA 98569, phone 360-289-2040. This complex has 37 guest rooms, no nonsmoking. No phones or coffee/tea making facilities, but coffee is available in the lobby. All rooms have TV. There is a mini golf course in the courtyard, hot tub outside on an enclosed deck, and paths going to the ocean. The lobby has a microwave, pool table, video games, and a large fireplace. Children welcome, no pets. **Rates:** single (1 bed) $30-$45; double (2 beds) $50. MasterCard & Visa. **Directions:** turn right onto Ocean Shores Blvd.

$45-$119   **POLYNESIAN CONDOMINIUM RESORT**, 615 Ocean Shores Blvd., P. O. Box 998, Ocean Shores, WA 98569, phone 360-289-3361 or 1-800-562-4836. This oceanfront complex offers a variety of accommodations from motel units to 3 bedroom penthouses. There are 71 units total, 30% nonsmoking. Three floors - all upper floors have balconies, lower floors facing the ocean have patios. Units on the south side are basic motel rooms, no patios. All rooms have phones and TV. Coffee/tea making facilities in all but the 5 basic motel units. Children 12 and under free, no pets. Indoor pool, spa, and sauna. Private park with barbecues, picnic tables, basketball, volleyball, horseshoes, slide, and swings. 200 yards from the ocean. Polynesian restaurant and lounge on the premises. **Summer Rates:** *4/01 to 10/01* - double occupancy, motel units $69; studio $69-$92; one bedroom suite $104-$119; extra person $10; local phones calls 25¢. **Winter Rates:** midweek rates are 25-30% less, lowest price is $45. MasterCard, Discover, Amex, & Visa. **Directions:** from the main gates follow Pt. Brown Ave. to Chance-Ala-Mer, turn west to Ocean Shores Blvd., turn south.

$35-$110   **ROYAL PACIFIC MOTEL**, 781 Ocean Shores Blvd., Ocean Shores, WA 98569, phone 360-289-3306 or 1-800-562-9748. 46 rooms available, no nonsmoking. Phones, TV, and coffee/tea making facilities in every room. 44 units have equipped kitchens and 43 have fireplaces. Outdoor pool and guests may use the indoor pool, sauna, and spa at the Sands. Children under 2 free, pets on ground floor only. **High Season Rates:** *3/15 to 9/30* - double occupancy, studio $49; studio w/kitchen $59; one bedroom suite $79-$89; 2 bedroom suite (4 people) $89-$110; local phones calls 25¢; children under 12 - $2; extra person $6; pets $10 per day. **Low Season Rates:** $35-$85. Major credit cards. **Directions:** take the first right coming into Ocean Shores, then proceed for 1/2 mile, on the right.

$59-$95 **The SANDS RESORT**, 801 Ocean Shores Blvd. NW, Ocean Shores, WA 98569, phone 360-289-2444 or 1-800-841-4001. One of the best things about this resort is the indoor pool, sauna, spa, and jacuzzi. There is also a large, wind-protected patio and sundeck. Only a 5 minute walk to the beach. A total of 106 spacious rooms, 26 nonsmoking. All rooms have TV, 79 have phones, most have coffee/tea making facilities, and 35 units have equipped kitchenettes. Donuts and coffee are provided in the morning. Guests may use the outdoor pool at the Royal Pacific. Shuttle to town, marina, and ferry dock. Children free, pets on the first floor. **High Season Rates:** econo studio, $59-$69; one & two bedroom suites $75-$95; local phone calls free; pets $10. Major credit cards. **Directions:** take the first right coming into Ocean Shores, proceed to The Sands.

$35-$90 **SILVER KING**, 1070 Discovery Ave. SE, Ocean Shores, WA 98569, phone 360-289-3386 or 1-800-562-6001. Located on the bay close to the marina and passenger ferry to Westport, this two story condominium motel has 50 units, 6 nonsmoking. Cable TV in all the rooms and 27 units have equipped kitchenettes. No coffee/tea making facilities in the rooms, but available in the lobby. Closest restaurant is 4 miles away. Outdoor fireplace, barbecue, volleyball, and horseshoes. Children 5 and under free, pets by approval on the first floor. **Summer Rates:** *5/15 to 9/30* - double occupancy $40-$50; kitchen units $45-$55; family room $75-$90; extra person $5; pets $10 per night. **Winter Rates:** $35-$80 weekdays. MasterCard, Amex, Discover, & Visa. **Directions:** go through gates and follow signs to the Marina, 4.8 miles.

$30-$150 **The WEATHERLY**, 675 Ocean Shores Blvd. NW, Ocean Shores, WA 98569, phone 360-289-2430 or 1-800-562-8612. Within walking distance of the ocean, The Weatherly has 15 rooms, no nonsmoking. All rooms have TV, equipped kitchens, and 14 units have fireplaces. Indoor pool, sauna, and workout room. Children free with parents, no pets. **Summer Rates:** studio $60; 1 bedroom units $110; jacuzzi suite $150. **Winter Rates:** specials Sunday -Thursday 50% discount $30-$75. MasterCard, Amex, & Visa. **Directions:** beach access road (Chance-Ala-Mer) in middle of town.

OKANOGAN (pop. 2,375) is just off Hwy 97, 50 miles south of the Canadian border.

(oh-kuh-NAH-guhn) The plants and animals around Okanogan seem more common to Mexico than northern Washington. This is due to low rainfall and 300 days of sunshine a year. Both factors contribute to making this area a vacation destination for sun lovers.

The Colville Indian Tribe recently opened a new casino here featuring bingo and slot machines, open 16 hours a day.

Located in Okanogan County the sales/use taxes are 7.6%.

$44-$54 **CEDARS INN,** Hwy 97, One Apple Way , Okanogan, WA 98840, phone 509-422-6431, fax 509-422-4214. This three story motel has 78 units, 50 nonsmoking. Phones, TV, and 4 kitchenette units with basic cookware. No coffee making facilities in the rooms, but available in the lobby. Seasonal outdoor pool, restaurant, bar, and coffee shop on the premises. Children 12 and under free, pets allowed. 200 yards away from the casino. **Rates:** single $44, double $51; suite $54; extra person $5; pets $5; local phone calls free. Major credit cards. **Directions:** at the junction of Hwy 97 and Hwy 20.

$37-$42 **PONDEROSA MOTOR LODGE,** 1034 S. Second Ave., Okanogan, WA 98840, phone 509-422-0400 or 1-800-732-6702. This newly remodeled motel has 25 units, 9 nonsmoking. Phones, cable TV with HBO, and coffee/tea making facilities in the rooms. Seven kitchen units with basic cookware. Units offer queen beds, 2 double beds, or twin beds. Microwaves and refrigerators available at no extra charge. Outdoor pool and restaurant on the grounds. Children free with parents, pets by arrangement. Coin-op laundry and RV hookups. **Rates:** single $37, double $42. Major credit cards. **Directions:** first motel on 2nd Avenue coming into town.

$26-$35 **U & I MOTEL,** 838 Second N., Okanogan, WA 98840, phone 509-422-2920. 9 units, 5 nonsmoking. TV, coffee/tea making facilities in the rooms, one equipped kitchen unit. Restaurant and bar within walking distance. Children welcome, pets allowed. Rustic setting on the Okanogan River next door to park and County Historical Museum. Eight parking bays, backyard with barbecue. **Rates:** single (1 person) $26, double $33; family room $35; extra person $2. MasterCard & Visa. **Directions:** off Hwy 97, on 2nd Ave. North.

Olalla see Gig Harbor.

OLYMPIA

(pop. 34, 850) is located at the south end of Puget Sound along I-5.

Washington's capitol city is home to the tallest, domed, masonry state capitol building in the US. Evergreen State College is located in western Olympia and is the site for many cultural events. The newest attraction is Yashiro Japanese Garden. Olympia's sister city in Japan, Yashiro, helped with funds and labor. Olympia Brewery gives guided tours daily.

Located in Thurston County the sales/use taxes are 7.9%.

$55-$70 **ALADDIN MOTOR INN Best Western**, 900 Capitol Way, Olympia, WA 98501, phone 360-352-7200, reservations 1-800-367-7771, fax 360-352-0846. 100 units, 78 nonsmoking. Phones, cable TV with remote control, VCR & movie rentals; guest laundry, king and queen beds. Two-thirds of the rooms have microwaves and refrigerators. No coffee/tea making facilities in the rooms, but available in the lobby. Restaurant and lounge on the premises. Outdoor pool. Children 12 and under free, pets allowed. **Rates:** single room $55-$65; double room $65-$70; extra person $5; pets $5; local phone calls free. Major credit cards. **Directions:** from I-5 take Exit 105 and follow signs to the State Capitol, corner of Capitol Blvd. and 9th.

$35-$42 **BAILEY MOTOR INN**, 333 Martin Way, Olympia, WA 98502, phone 360-491-7515. 48 units, 6 nonsmoking. Phones, equipped kitchenettes, and TV. No coffee/tea making facilities in the rooms, but provided in the lobby. Restaurant, bar, cardroom, and coffee shop on the premises. Children 5 and under free, pets allowed. **Rates:** single room (1 bed) $35; double room $42; extra person $6; pets $6 per night; local phone calls 50¢. Major credit cards. **Directions:** from I-5 take Exit 109, travel west one mile on Martin Way.

$51-$60 **CAPITOL INN MOTEL**, 120 College St. SE, Lacey, WA, 98503 phone 360-493-1991 or 1-800-282-7028. 83 units, 15 nonsmoking. Phones, refrigerators, microwaves, and TVs with remote control and Showtime. There are 4 kitchen units, cookware and dishes may be obtained at the office. No coffee/tea making facilities in the rooms, but a continental breakfast is provided in the lobby. Sauna and exercise room. Children 16 and under free with parents, pets allowed in first floor rooms. **Rates:** single room $51-$55; double room $59-$60; extra person $3; pets $5 per night; local phone calls free. Most major credit cards. **Directions:** from I-5 take Exit 109 one block west, turn west onto College.

$42-$54 **CARRIAGE INN MOTEL,** 1211 S. Quince, Olympia, WA 98501, phone 360-943-4710, fax 360-943-0804. 62 units, 41 nonsmoking. Phones, refrigerators, microwaves, VCR/TV, and radios. No coffee/tea making facilities in the rooms, but a continental breakfast is provided from 6:00 a.m. to 9:30 a.m. Quiet area off the freeway on a small knoll. Five minute drive to inlet, lake, shops, and restaurants. Children 15 and under free with parents, pets by arrangement. **Rates:** single room $42; double room $54; extra person $3; pets $3; local phone calls free. Major credit cards. **Directions:** from I-5 take Exit 105, follow "Port of Olympia" signs to Plum St., turn first right, proceed to motel.

$52-$57 **CINNAMON RABBIT BED, BREAKFAST & BAK ERY,** 1304 7th Ave. SW, Olympia, WA 98502, phone 360-357-5520. Quiet neighborhood close to downtown and waterfront. One guest room with private facilities. Hot tub, bookshelves, and piano. Full breakfast. Children welcome, no dogs, and no smoking. **Rates:** single $52; double $57; extra person $10. MasterCard & Visa. **Directions:** from I-5 take SR 101 west, turn off at Black Lake Exit, head north through 2 lights, turn left on Decature, go 2 blocks to 7th, turn right.

COMFORT INN, 4700 Park Center Ave. NE, Lacey, WA 98516, phone 360-456-6300 or 1-800-221-2222, fax 360-456-7423.

$31-$54 **GOLDEN GAVEL MOTOR HOTEL,** 909 Capitol Way, Olympia, WA 98501, phone 360-352-8533. Two story motel with 27 rooms, 10 nonsmoking. Phones, queen or double beds, and basic cable TV. No coffee/tea making facilities in the rooms, but available in the lobby. Restaurants within walking distance. Children welcome, infants free, no pets. **Summer Rates:** *6/01 to 9/30* - single room $32-$45; double room $49; suite $54; extra person $3; local phone calls free. **Winter Rates:** single $31-$35; double $41; suite $47. Most major credit cards. **Directions:** from I-5 take Exit 105, follow the signs to the Capitol Building, turn right on Capitol Way.

$60-$125 **HARBINER INN BED &BREAKFAST**, 1136 E. Bay Dr., Olympia, WA 98506, phone 360-754-0389.
This 1910 mansion has white columns and wide balconies that overlook Budd Inlet and the marina. There is a hillside waterfall fed by an artesian well viewed from 2 of the 4 guest rooms. All rooms have private facilities. House phone available, TV in the library, and books to borrow. Breakfast is continental, plus. Children 10 and older welcome, no pets, and no smoking. **Rates:** double $60-$125. MasterCard, Amex, & Visa. **Directions:** from I-5 take Exit 105B, follow "Port of Olympia" signs, Plum turns into East Bay Dr., on the right.

$35-$48 **LEE STREET SUITES**, 348 Lee SW, Tumwater, WA 98501, phone 360-943-8391. *Four day minimum stay.*
Two story townhouse with 8 suites, 1 nonsmoking. Cable TV, fully equipped kitchens, fireplaces, covered carports, and laundry room. Phone service is available through U.S. West. Children 18 and under free with parents, pets allowed. Weekly housekeeping services. **Rates:** two bedroom suites $35-$48. Most major credit cards. **Directions:** from I-5 Exit 102, turn left to stoplight, turn right to the office at 5895 Capitol Blvd. So.

$79-$89 **PUGET VIEW GUESTHOUSE**, 7924 61st Ave. NE, Olympia, WA 98516, phone 360-459-1676. One cedar shake cottage overlooking the water. The cottage has one queen bed and 1 full sleeper sofa. Continental breakfast. A microwave, mini fridge, and hotplate with teapot are provided. Deck and barbecue. Scuba dive in the underwater park offshore, go canoeing in the protected waters, or explore downtown Olympia. Ask about the "romantic retreat package". Children welcome, small pets by arrangement, smoking allowed. **Summer Rates:** double occupancy $89; extra adult $15. **Off-season rates:** $79. MasterCard & Visa. **Directions:** from I-5 Exit 111, follow Marvin Rd. north 3.5 miles to 56th NE, turn right, go 1 mile, turn left at 61st NE, third driveway on the right.

QUALITY INN Westwater, 2300 Evergreen Park Dr., Olympia, WA 98502, phone 360-943-4000 or 1-800-551-8500.

RAMADA INN Governor House, 621 S. Capitol Way, Olympia, WA 98501, phone 360-352-7700 or 1-800-2RAMADA.

$26-$41 **SHALIMAR SUITES**, 5895 Capitol Blvd. South, Tumwater, WA 98501, phone 360-943-8391. *Four day minimum stay.* Two story townhouse with 17 suites, 2 nonsmoking. Cable TV, fully equipped kitchens, off street parking, and laundry room. Phone service is available through U.S. West. Children free with parents, pets allowed. Weekly housekeeping services. **Rates:** studio suites $26-$36; one bedroom suites $27-$38; two bedroom suites $30-$41. Most major credit cards. **Directions:** from I-5 Exit 102, turn left to next stoplight, turn right to the office at 5895 Capitol Blvd. So.

$52-$79 **TUMWATER INN MOTEL Best Western** , 5188 Capitol Blvd., Tumwater, WA 98501, phone 360-956-1235 or 1-800-848-4992 (WA). This two story brick motel has 89 rooms, 75% nonsmoking. In-room amenities include phones, microwaves, refrigerators, and remote control TV with Showtime. No coffee/tea making facilities in the rooms, but a continental breakfast is provided in the lobby. Hot tub, sauna, exercise room, and guest laundry. Children under 5 free, pets allowed. **Rates:** single room $52-$58; double room (2-4 people) $62-$79; extra person $5; pets $5; local phone calls 25¢. Major credit cards. **Directions:** from I-5 take Exit 102 east of freeway, turn left at light.

$49-$150 **WEST COAST TYEE HOTEL**, 500 Tyee Dr., Tumwater, WA 98512, phone 360-352-0511 or 1-800-386-8933, fax 360-943-6448. This large complex has 145 rooms, 56 nonsmoking. Phones and basic cable TV in the rooms. The nicely landscaped grounds have a swimming pool, tennis court, and a pickle ball court. No coffee/tea making facilities in the rooms, but room service is available. Restaurant/lounge on the premises. Children 18 and under free with parents, pets allowed. **Seasonal Rates:** single room $49-$79; double room $49-$72; suite $95-$150; extra person $6; pets $6; local phone calls 35¢. Major credit cards. **Directions:** from I-5 take Exit 102, west of freeway.

OMAK (pop. 4, 120) is 45 miles south of the Canadian border just off Hwy 97.

(OH-mak) The name comes from the Indian word "Omache" meaning "good medicine" or "plenty" which was given to nearby bodies of water. Omak is the retail hub of the county and is probably best known for its world famous Omak Stampede & Suicide Race held each year in August.

Located in Okanogan County the sales/use taxes are 7.6%.

$35-$100 **LEISURE VILLAGE MOTEL**, 630 Okoma Dr., Omak, WA 98841, phone 509-826-4442 or 1-800-427-4495 **(E. WA only).** 33 units, 15 nonsmoking, and 1 mobile home that sleeps 6. Phones, small refrigerators, queen beds, TV, and AC. There are 5 kitchen units with microwaves and basic cookware. No coffee/tea making facilities in the other rooms, but a continental breakfast is provided in the lobby. Heated indoor pool, sauna, and hot tub. Children free with parents, pets allowed. **Rates:** single (1 bed) $35-$40; double (2 beds) $46; suites, with kitchens $65; mobile home (6 people) $100; pets $5. Major credit cards. **Directions:** take the Omak Exit off Hwy 97 to downtown, proceed south.

$40-$47 **MOTEL NICHOLAS**, 527 E. Grape, Rt. 3 Box 353, Omak, WA 98841, phone 509-826-4611. 21 units, 16 nonsmoking. Queen beds, phones, small refrigerators, coffee/tea making facilities, TV, and AC in all the rooms. Children welcome, infants free, no pets. **Rates:** single (1 bed) $40; double (2 beds) $43; 3 beds (3-4 people) $47; extra person $4; no charge for local calls. Major credit cards. **Directions:** three blocks south of the shopping mall on Hwy 97.

$28-$31 **ROYAL MOTEL**, 514 E. Riverside, P. O. Box 3273, Omak, WA 98841, phone 509-826-5715. 10 units, 5 nonsmoking. In-room amenities include phones, TV, and AC. Morning coffee is available in the office with a continental breakfast, and 3 units have kitchens with basic cookware. Large grassy area with swing set, barbecue, and picnic tables. On site beauty salon and tanning parlor. Children welcome, infants free, dogs allowed with refundable deposit. **Rates:** single (1 bed/1 person) $28; double $31; extra person $5; pet deposit $20-$50; no charge for local calls. Visa & MasterCard. **Directions:** turn off Hwy 97 at stoplight, go down Riverside Dr., second motel on the left.

$30-$45 **STAMPEDE MOTEL**, 215 W. 4th, P. O. Box 955, Omak, WA 98841, phone 509-826-1161. 14 units, no nonsmoking. Phones, TV, coffee/tea making facilities in the rooms, and 11 units have kitchens with basic cookware. Children welcome, infants free, pets free. This older motel has a life-sized statue of a horse out front and flowers in every window box. **Rates:** single $30; double $36; three bed unit $45; no charge for local calls. Most major credit cards. **Directions:** approximately 4 blocks south of downtown.

Orcas see San Juan Islands.

OROVILLE (pop. 1,505) is just four miles south of the Canadian border on Hwy 97.

(OR-vil) The customs and immigration station is kept busy with an average of 1,500 vehicles passing through each day. Oroville is located just north of the confluence of the Similkameen (si-MIL-i-kih-MEEN) and the Okanogan Rivers and south of Lake Osoyoos (oh-SOY-yuhs), so water sports are in abundance. Oroville was originally noted for its mining and timber, but today over 52% of the land is devoted to agriculture - primarily apples.

Located in Okanogan County the sales/use taxes are 7.6%.

$28-$50 **CAMARAY MOTEL**, 1320 Main St., P. O. Box 923, Oroville, WA 98844, phone 509-476-3684, fax 509-476-3122. 38 units, 17 nonsmoking. Queen beds, phones, TV with HBO, and a seasonal outdoor pool. No coffee/tea making facilities in the rooms, but available in the lobby. Within walking distance of restaurants. Children welcome, pets allowed. **Rates:** single $28-$34; double $37; 4 people/2 beds $50; no charge for local calls; taxes included. Major credit cards. **Directions:** centrally located downtown.

$32-$54 **RED APPLE INN**, P. O. Box 598, Oroville, WA 98844, phone 509-476-3694. 37 units, 20 nonsmoking. Phones, TV, and a seasonal outdoor pool. No coffee/tea making facilities in the rooms, but available in the lobby from 7 a.m. to 10 a.m. Six units have kitchens with basic cookware. Quiet location, picnic area on the Okanogan River, and just three blocks to local restaurants. Children 6 and under free, pets allowed in smoking rooms only. **Rates:** single (1 bed) $32-$47; double (2 beds) $47; kitchen unit $47; family room $54; extra person $4; no charge for local calls; pets free. Major credit cards. **Directions:** on Hwy 97, 1/4 mile north of town center.

$53 **SUN COVE RESORT**, Rt. 2 Box 1294, Oroville, WA 98844, phone & fax 509-476-2223. *Open April (1st day of fishing season) to November 1st.* Located on the shores of Wannacut Lake, the resort offers lodging in 10 log constructed housekeeping units and 2 family cottages. The 10 housekeeping units face out to the lake and have fully equipped kitchens, double beds, a large window in the kitchens with a lake view, and double dutch doors to the porch. Two units share a barbecue. The "mama bear" and "papa bear" cottages rent by the week and sleep 6 to 8 people, no bedding or linen is supplied in the cottages. The resort has boat moorage, a country grocery store, laundry facilities, playground, basketball, and volleyball. There are also tent sites and RV spaces. Children 6 and under free, no pets. **Rates:** double occupancy $53; extra person charge $5; mama bear cottage (6 people) $425 per week; papa bear cottage (8 people) $550 per week. MasterCard & Visa. **Directions:** *best route for trailers and motor homes* - from the south 10 miles before Ellsford turn west and follow signs to the Loomis Hwy, 5 miles to Sun Cove sign, go north 5 miles to the resort road. From the north, in Oroville turn west on 12th St., over the Similkameen River bridge, south 1/4 mile, turn right at Golden Rd. (it turns south right away) follow through orchard to Sun Cove sign at Wannacut Lake, follow gravel road 6 miles around lake to resort.

OTHELLO (pop. 4,640) is located in central Washington, approximately 20 miles south of Moses Lake.

This area is known for waterfowl and pheasant hunting. Othello is only 15 miles from O'Sullivan Dam Reservoir and the Potholes fishing area.

Located in Adams County the sales/use taxes are 7.6%.

$35-$48 **ALADDIN MOTOR INN**, 1020 E. Cedar St., Othello, WA 99344, phone 509-488-5671. This basic two story motel has 52 units, 29 nonsmoking. Phones, TV, and a seasonal outdoor pool. No coffee/tea making facilities in the rooms, but available in the office. There is a restaurant, bar, and coffee shop on the premises. Eleven units have kitchens with basic cookware available at the office. Rooms fill up fast during the upland game hunting season, early reservations are recommended. Children welcome, infants free, pets allowed. **Rates:** single (1 bed) $35; double room $44; suite $48; kitchen units $39; extra person $4; pets $5 per night; no charge for local calls. Most major credit cards. **Directions:** one mile north off Hwy 26, then 10 blocks east; or 1 mile west off Hwy 17 on Cunningham Rd.

$26-$65 **CABANA MOTEL**, 655 E. Windsor, Othello, WA 99344, phone 509-488-2605, reservations 1-800-442-4581. This second generation, family owned and operated motel has 55 units, 20 nonsmoking. Phones and cable TV with HBO in the deluxe rooms. No coffee/tea making facilities in the rooms, but available in the office, and there is a restaurant 1 block away. Three units have equipped kitchens. Heated outdoor pool and indoor hot tub spa. Quiet, relaxing atmosphere. Three golf courses nearby. 15 full hookups for RVs. Children welcome, pets allowed with management's approval. **Rates:** single (1 bed) $26-$37; double (2 beds) $42-$48; kitchen units $37-$44; suite $65; family room $48-$56; extra person $5; no charge for local calls. Most major credit cards. **Directions:** located in downtown Othello.

$30-$45 **CIMARRON MOTEL & Restaurant**, 1450 Main St., P. O. Box 529, Othello, WA 99344, phone 509-488-6612. This two story motel has 45 units, 10 nonsmoking. Phones and TV in all the rooms. No coffee/tea making facilities in the rooms, but available at the restaurant from 6:00 a.m to 10:00 p.m. The lounge has live music on Friday and Saturday nights. Seasonal outdoor pool and indoor hot tub spa. Parking for large trucks and RVs. Children 11 and under free, pets allowed. **Rates:** single room $30-$35; double room $39-$45; suite $44; extra person $5; pets $10 one time charge; local calls 25¢. MasterCard, Visa, & Discover. **Directions:** 1/4 mile off Hwy 17, on Main Street in Othello.

$36-$72 **MAR DON RESORT**, 8198 Hwy 262 E., Othello, WA 99344, phone 509-346-2651 or 1-800-416-2736. Located on the Potholes Reservoir, this resort has 21 motel style rooms. No designated nonsmoking. No phones or TV, only the beach! The dock, two city blocks long, is used for fishing and boat moorage. There is a roped-off area for swimming. No coffee/tea making facilities in the rooms, but a restaurant is one block away, and there are 10 non-equipped kitchen units available. Children 8 and under free, pets allowed. **Rates:** single room (1 bed) $36-$38; family room $55-$72; extra person $3; pets $5 per night. MasterCard, Visa, & Discover. **Directions:** from I-90, Exit 179 south at Moses Lake, onto Hwy 17 for 1 mile, take "M" Road 7 miles to Hwy 262, then right for 7 miles.

PACIFIC BEACH is on the beach approximately 17 miles north of Ocean Shores.

$38-$100 **SAND DOLLAR MOTEL**, 56 Central Ave., P. O. Box 16, Pacific Beach, WA 98571, phone 360-276-4525. Seven motel style units and 3 cabins. All have equipped kitchens, cable TV, and views of the ocean. Children 5 and under free, pets allowed. Restaurant within walking distance. The motel units are 500 feet from the beach, cabins 150 feet. Guest laundry facilities. **High Season Rates:** *3/01 to 10/30* - double occupancy, single room (1 bed) $43; double (2 beds) $53; cabins $70-$100; extra person $5; pets $5 one time charge; taxes 10.9%. **Off-Season Rates:** $5 less. MasterCard & Visa. **Directions:** follow Hwy 109 to Pacific Beach, corner 2nd and Central.

$45-$85 **SHORELINE MOTEL**, 12 First St. So., P. O. Box 183, Pacific Beach, WA 98571, phone 360-276-4433 or 1-800-233-3365. This two story motel has 10 units, no nonsmoking. The 4 upstairs units all have views of the ocean, downstairs units have partial views. All rooms have queen beds, phones, TV, and equipped kitchens. Located in the center of town just 200 feet from the beach. Children welcome, no pets. **Rates:** $45-$85; pets $5 per night; taxes 10.9%. Discover, MasterCard, Amex, & Visa. **Directions:** on Hwy 109 at the 4 way stop, turn west, proceed for 4 blocks, turn left on 1st St.

PACKWOOD is on the south side of Mount Rainier on Hwy 12.

$20-$38 **HOTEL PACKWOOD**, 104 Main St., P. O. Box 130, Packwood, WA 98361, phone 360-494-5431. This recently renovated, two-story wooden hotel, built in 1912, is across the street from the park. It has 9 nonsmoking rooms, 2 with private facilities and

7 with shared. TV in the rooms. No coffee/tea making facilities, but coffee is available in the lobby 24 hours. Children free with parents, no pets. Within walking distance of cafes, bar, and shopping. **Rates:** single room (1 twin bed/shared bath) $20; bunk rooms $25; double room $38; extra person $5; taxes 7.6%. No credit cards. **Directions:** downtown on Main St.

$45-$75 **The INN OF PACKWOOD**, 13032 Hwy 12, P. O. Box 390, Packwood, WA 98361, phone 360-494-5500. This family owned and operated Inn has 33 rooms, 25 nonsmoking. Phones and TV. Handmade pine furnishings create the rustic warmth of a country home. Three equipped kitchenettes available. No coffee/tea making facilities in the rooms, but coffee and rolls are available at 8:00 a.m. Heated indoor pool and outdoor spa. Pizza parlor on the premises. White Pass Ski Area is only 19 miles to the east. Children welcome, infants free, no pets. **Seasonal Rates:** single room (1 bed/2 people) $45-$53; double room $49-$75; extra person $5; local phone calls free; taxes 7.6%. MasterCard, Discover, & Visa. **Directions:** downtown on Main St.

$42-$220 **TATOOSH MOTEL & CABINS**, 12880 Hwy 12, Packwood, WA 98361, phone 360-494-9226, fax 360-494-9239. 14 individually decorated units reflecting comfortable homestyle "elegance". All rooms have TV and there are 6 equipped kitchenettes. No coffee/tea making facilities in the rooms, but available at the office. Mountain cabins and chalets are also available that sleep from 2 to 8 people. Outdoor spa and small conference room. Within walking distance of restaurants. Children 6 and under free, no pets, and no smoking. **Rates:** single room $42-$65; double room $62-$75; suite $65-$140; cabins $85-$220; extra person $4; taxes 7.6%. MasterCard, Discover, & Visa. **Directions:** 1/4 mile west of Packwood on Hwy 12.

PASCO see Tri Cities.

PATEROS (pop. 570) is located in north central Washington on Hwy 97 at the confluence of the Methow River and the Columbia River.

(puh-TIAR-uhs) is the eastern gateway to the Methow Valley. This is cowboy country, and there are some first-rate dude ranches in the area. Alta Lake State Park sits in the shadow of 1,624 foot Goat Mountain. Alta Lake is a very popular fishing spot.
Located in Okanogan County the sales/use taxes are 7.6%.

$38-$78   **ALTA LAKE RESORT**, P. O. Box 85, Pateros, WA 98846, phone 509-923-2359 or 1-800-557-2359 (E. WA). Adjacent to the 18 hole golf course, this resort has 24 rooms and offers golf packages with lodging. There are 4 nonsmoking rooms available. Coffee/tea making facilities in the rooms, TV, and queen beds. 12 rooms have kitchenettes equipped with microwaves and dishes. Pro shop, snack bar, large community kitchen, barbecue, outdoor pool, and picnic area. Children welcome, no pets. **Summer Rates:** *Memorial Day to Labor Day* - single room (1 bed) $48-$50; double room (2 beds) $58; kitchen units $70-$78; extra person $5-$8. **Winter Rates:** 20% off midweek. MasterCard & Visa. **Directions:** 2 miles up the Methow Valley from Pateros, follow signs to Alta Lake State Park, 1 1/2 miles off Hwy 153.

$50-$60   **AMY'S MANOR BED & BREAKFAST**, P. O. Box 411, Pateros, WA 98846, phone 509-923-2334. This stately 1928 home has 2 nonsmoking guest rooms with shared facilities. High on a bluff overlooking the Methow River, the Manor is surrounded by 170 acres of gorgeous country. Home to goats, ducks, chickens, rabbits and cows. Wake up to the smell of fresh country air, or the coffee brewing for breakfast. Chef Pamela teaches cooking classes and features fresh fruit and vegies from the Manor's organic garden. After cross country skiing in the winter, curl up in front of the large stone fireplace and relax. Use the tennis court, go for a hike, or fish in nearby lakes and rivers. Children 12 and over, no pets. **Rates:** single $50; double $60. MasterCard & Visa. **Directions:** 5 miles north of Pateros on Hwy 153, sign by the driveway.

$54-$62 **LAKE PATEROS MOTOR INN**, P. O. Box 25, Pateros, WA 98846, phone 509-923-2203 or 1-800-444-1985. Centrally located on the Columbia River in downtown Pateros, this 2 story motor inn has 30 units, 15 nonsmoking. Phones, TV, seasonal outdoor pool, barbecues, boat dock, and picnic tables. No coffee/tea making facilities in the rooms, but available in the lobby. Children 10 and under free, small pets allowed. **Summer Rates:** *4/01 to 10/31* - single room (1 bed) $54-$58; double room (2 beds) $62; extra person $6; pets $5 per night. Check on winter rates. MasterCard & Visa. **Directions:** just off Hwy 97 in the center of town, by the river.

$35-$45 **WHISTLIN PINE RANCH**, P. O. Box 284, Pateros, WA 98846, phone 509-923-2548. *Open mid-April thru Labor Day.* Fully outfitted pack trips from 3 to 10 days; day trips and horseback riding are available. Accommodations are by reservation only. There are 2 small rustic cabins with one double bed and power. Six tent cabins, no power, have 4 wooden bunks, wood stove, and picnic table. Bring your own bedding and towels. Tent and RV sites available. Community bath house. On the south end of Alta Lake. Children welcome, pets on a leash. **Rates:** small cabin $30; tent cabins $40; tent site (up to 4 people) $13; RV site (up to 4 people) $18; extra person $5; booking fee per reservation $5. No credit cards. **Directions:** from Pateros, follow signs to Alta Lake State Park, 3 miles off Hwy 153 at the south end of lake.

PESHASTIN see Leavenworth for lodging.

POMEROY (pop. 1,414) is located in the southeast corner of the state approximately 28 miles west of Clarkston and the Snake River.

$35-$50 **PIONEER MOTEL**, 1201 Main St., Pomeroy, WA 99347, phone 509-843-1559. Centrally located in the middle of town, the Pioneer has 14 units, no nonsmoking. Phones, TV, and coffee/tea making facilities in the rooms. Two rooms have equipped kitchens. Use the hot tub after a day of hunting, cross country skiing, or snowmobiling. Children welcome, pets allowed free. **Rates:** single room $35-$40; double room $40-$45; kitchen units $50; local phone calls free; taxes 7.5%. MasterCard & Visa. **Directions:** in the center of town.

PORT ANGELES

(pop. 17,890) is located on the Olympic Peninsula along the coast, on the northern edge of the coast, on Hwy 101.

This fishing and logging port is the largest city on the northern Olympic Peninsula. It is the ferry terminal for year-round ferry service across the Strait of Juan de Fuca to Victoria, B.C. The waterfront park has an observation tower that provides 360° views of the city, harbor, and Olympic Mountains. The Arthur D. Feiro Marine Laboratory has hands-on displays and exhibits of the area's sea life, with volunteers available to answer questions.

Located in Clallam County the sales/use taxes are 7.9%.

$60 **CLARKS' HARBOR VIEW BED & BREAKFAST**, 1426 W. 4th St., Port Angeles, WA 98362, phone 360-457-9891. This new home, on a quiet street, has one guest room with private facilities and an unobstructed close-up view of the harbor, Strait, and island/mountain panorama. Rec room with pool table adjoins the guest room. Full breakfast provided. Shuttle provided to and from the ferry and airport. Adults only, no pets. **Rates:** double occupancy $60. No credit cards; personal checks okay. **Directions:** from the ferry go west on Front St., this becomes Marine Dr., proceed to Tumwater St., turn left, go uphill and curve to the right on 5th St., continue to G St., then right half a block to 4th St.,left again, 4th house on the left.

$25-$49 **EVERGREEN MOTEL & RV**, 3111 Hwy 101 E., Port Angeles, WA 98362, phone 360-457-3071. 10 rooms, no nonsmoking. Phones and TV. Three kitchen units have stove and refrigerator, no cookware or dishes. No coffee/tea making facilities in the rooms. Within walking distance of a restaurant. Ten RV spaces with full hookups. Children welcome, no pets. **Summer Rates:** *6/01 to 9/01* - single room $25-$35; double room $38-$49; local phone calls free. Check on winter rates. MasterCard & Visa. **Directions:** when traveling from the east on Hwy 101, it is the first motel on the right, 2.5 miles to town.

$38-$69 **FAIRMOUNT MOTEL**, 1137 Hwy 101 W., Port Angeles, WA 98362, phone 360-457-6113. 14 units, 4 nonsmoking. 10 one bed units, 2 two bedroom units, and 2 suites have 2 beds and a hide-a-bed, all have cable TV. No coffee/tea making facilities in the rooms. Adjacent to Deli-Grocery-Gas, restaurant, lounge, and RV park. Children welcome, infants free, no pets. **Rates:** single room $38; double room $49; suite $59-$69; extra person $5. MasterCard & Visa. **Directions:** 1/2 mile west of Port Angeles city limits on Hwy 101.

$34-$84 **FLAGSTONE MOTEL**, 415 E. First St., Port Angeles, WA 98362, phone 360-457-9494. 45 newly remodeled rooms in this older style motel, 12 nonsmoking. All rooms have cable TV and phones. No coffee/tea making facilities in the rooms, but a continental breakfast is provided in the lobby. Four blocks to the ferry terminal, three blocks to downtown. Children welcome, small pets allowed. **Summer Rates:** *5/28 to 9/15* - single room (1 bed) $42-$45; double room (2 beds) $54-$57; family room $58-$84; extra person $6; local phone calls free. **Winter Rates:** $34-$62. Major credit cards. **Directions:** west on Hwy 101 to Peabody, left 1 block, then left again 1/2 block. Traveling east, on Hwy 101 across from the post office.

$35-$105 **HILL HAUS MOTEL**, 111 E. Second St., Port Angeles, WA 98362, phone 360-452-9285 or 1-800-421-0706. Located on a bluff above downtown Port Angeles, this motel has major views of the harbor and mountains. A three story motel with 23 units, 14 nonsmoking. Remote cable TV, phones, and coffee/tea making facilities in the rooms. Children welcome for a fee, no pets. **Seasonal Rates:** single room, no view $35-$69, with view $45-$95; double room, no view $39-$72, with view $52-$105; extra person $12; local phone calls free. MasterCard, Discover, & Visa. **Directions:** 1 block off Hwy 101 on the bluff above town.

$60-$89 **HOUSE OF THE MERMAID BED & BREAKFAST**, 1128 E. 5th St., Port Angeles, WA 98362, phone 360-457-4890. In a quiet location, this older home has 4 guest rooms, 2 with private facilities and 2 with shared. The house is decorated with antiques. Full breakfast provided. Some mountain and water views. Children over 12 welcome, no pets. **High Season Rates:** *5/01 to 11/01* - double occupancy $65-$89; extra person $30. **Low Season:** $60-$80. MasterCard & Visa. **Directions:** from Hwy 101, east or west, go to Chambers St. (on the east side of town), turn south on Chambers, proceed to 5th St., turn left.

$67-$110 **LAKE CRESCENT LODGE**, 416 Lake Crescent Road, Port Angeles, WA 98362-9798, phone 360-928-3211. *Regular season April 23 - October 30.* 52 units available, no designated nonsmoking. 47 have private facilities and 5 have shared. Types of accommodations include historic lodge rooms, motor lodge, cottages, and four historic cottages with fireplaces. No phones, TV, or coffee/tea making facilities in most of the lodgings. The Roosevelt Fireplace Cottages are equipped with coffeemakers and refrigerators. A restaurant and lounge are on the premises. The lodge is nestled among giant fir and hemlock trees on the shore of Lake Crescent. Children welcome, pets allowed. **Rates:** double occupancy $67-$110; extra person (all ages) $10; pets $10. Major credit cards. **Directions:** 20 miles west of Port Angeles.

$27-$49 **The POND MOTEL**, 1425 W. Hwy 101, Port Angeles, WA 98362, phone 360-452-8422. This rural motel is situated on five acres, overlooking an acre-size pond. The spacious grounds offer wooded and grassy areas, perennial gardens, picnic tables, and a gas barbecue. 10 units, 7 nonsmoking. All units have cable TV and 6 units have views of the pond. No coffee/tea making facilities in the rooms, but there are 6 equipped kitchen units. Children welcome, infants free, pets allowed. **Summer Rates:** 6/15 to 9/15 - single room $42; double room (2 beds) $49; extra person $5; pay phone 25¢. **Winter Rates:** $27-$45. MasterCard & Visa. **Directions:** two miles west of Port Angeles.

$44-$85 **PORTSIDE INN**, 1510 E. Front St., Port Angeles, WA 98362, phone 360-452-4015 or 1-800-633-8300, fax 360-452-4364. This 3 story motel has 109 rooms, 68 nonsmoking. Phones and TV in every room. No coffee/tea making facilities in the rooms, but available in the lobby. Suites have refrigerators and wet bars. Outdoor swimming pool and spa. Conference room for 40 people. Children 11 and under free, no pets. **Summer Rates:** 5/15 to 9/30 - double occupancy $64; suites $85; extra person $4; local phone calls free. **Winter Rates:** $44-$65. Major credit cards. **Directions:** corner of Alder & Front St.(Hwy 101east).

$44-$76 **ROYAL VICTORIAN MOTEL**, 521 E. First St., Port Angles, WA 98362, phone 360-452-2316. This two story motel is centrally located downtown. 20 rooms, 9 nonsmoking. Remote control TV, phones, and air conditioning. No coffee/tea making facilities in the rooms, but available in the lobby. 15 rooms have refrigerators and microwaves. Shuttle provided to the ferry. Children 12 and under free, no pets. **Summer Rates:** single room (1 bed/2 people) $52-$70; double room $62-$76; extra person $4-$6; local phone calls free. **Winter Rates:** $44-$68. MasterCard, Amex, Discover, & Visa. **Directions:** centrally located downtown on 1st St.

$78-$88 **SOL DUC HOT SPRINGS**, P. O. Box 2169, Port Angeles, WA 98362, phone 360-327-3583. *Open mid-May through September.* The Indian name "Sol Duc" means "sparkling water". Since 1912, visitors have come to experience the mineral pools. 32 units - 26 single cabins and 6 kitchen cabins (cookware and dishes available at the office), RV sites, and campgrounds. Amenities include massage

therapy, swimming mineral pools, restaurant, bar, pool side deli, gift shop, and grocery store. Children under 4 free, pets allowed. Smoking requested on the porch, not in the rooms. **Rates:** *two night minimum stay for holidays;* single cabins, double occupancy $78; duplex cabins with kitchen $88; extra person $13; pets $2; pay phone 25¢. Amex, MasterCard, Visa, & Discover. **Directions:** 30 miles west of Port Angeles, then 12 miles off Hwy 101.

Sol Duc Hot Springs

$40-$60 **SPORTSMEN MOTEL**, 2909 E. Hwy 101, Port Angeles, WA 98362, phone 360-457-6196. 18 units, 6 nonsmoking. Most units are on one level. TV and coffee/tea making facilities in the rooms. 11 units have equipped kitchens, some have microwaves. Children 18 and under free with parents, no pets. **Rates:** single (1 bed) $40; double (2 beds) $55; suite $60; kitchen units $5 extra. MasterCard & Visa. **Directions:** on highway coming into town from the east.

$75-$120 **TUDOR INN BED & BREAKFAST**, 1108 S. Oak St., Port Angeles, WA 98362, phone 360-452-3138. The Inn is of English design, constructed in 1910. It has been tastefully restored to capture the charm and atmosphere of the era. There are 5 guest rooms, all with private facilities. The rooms are furnished with antiques and have views of the water or mountains. Full country breakfast is served in the formal dining room. Children 12 and older welcome, no pets, and no smoking. **Summer Rates:** *5/15 to 10/15* - double occupancy $85-$120. **Winter Rates:** $75-$120. MasterCard & Visa. **Directions:** continue on Hwy 101 south on Lincoln St., through downtown to 11th St., turn right and go 2 blocks to Oak.

$52-$115 **UPTOWN MOTEL**, Second & Laurel Streets, Port Angeles, WA 98362, phone 360-457-9434 or 1-800-858-3812. On the bluff overlooking the harbor and town. This motel has 51 units, 50% nonsmoking. All rooms have phones, cable TV, picture windows, king or queen beds, and coffee/tea making facilities. Seven equipped kitchen units, mini suites with microwave and small fridge. Indoor jacuzzi. Most rooms have an ever-changing panorama of marine or mountain views. Ample parking for car, boat, or trailer. Children welcome, small dogs allowed in smoking rooms on the ground floor. **Summer Rates:** *7/01 to 9/30* - View rooms $75-$115; economy rooms, no view $52-$65. Major credit cards. **Directions:** from the east follow Hwy 101 (Front St.) downtown, turn left on Lincoln, proceed to Second St., turn right; from the west, coming into town on Hwy 101 turn left onto Second St. and go to the end of the block.

PORT HADLOCK is located 9 miles south of Port Townsend.

$85-$125 **OAK BAY COTTAGES**, 3659 Oak Bay Rd., Port Hadlock, WA 98339, phone 360-437-0380 or 1-800-727-4706. *Two night minimum.* Enjoy 7 acres and 400 feet of water front. Roads for walks to the beach with picnic tables and glorious morning sunrise. Three homes, 2 and 3 bedrooms. Completely furnished, including all appliances, phone, and cable TV. Hot tub suite has a private 20' x 30' room with wicker furniture, and panoramic view of the water. Port Ludlow Golf Course and country stores are 5 miles away. 12 miles to Port Townsend. Children by arrangement, no pets. Smoking allowed outside on the sun porch. **High Season Rates:** *5/01to 10/30* - $92-$125; extra person $10-$15; taxes 7.9%. **Off-Season:** $85-$125. MasterCard & Visa. **Directions:** from the Hood Canal Bridge, take the first right, follow to the first stop sign, go right on Oak Bay Rd. for 5 miles.

$45-$115 **The OLD ALCOHOL PLANT LODGE**, 310 Alcohol Loop Rd., P. O. Box 1369, Port Hadlock, WA 98339, phone 360-385-7030 or 1-800-785-7030, fax 360-385-6955. The Old Alcohol Plant Lodge has an interesting history. From the time it closed in 1913, the buildings stood vacant until Ray Hansen bought the plant in 1978 and set about the 9 year task of turning it into a hotel and resort. There are 25 spacious rooms, 21 nonsmoking. All rooms have TV and phones. The standard rooms have either 1 queen or 2 double beds; deluxe, two level townhouse suites with fireplace and kitchenette; and a luxurious two level penthouse with rooftop decks. No coffee/tea making facilities in the rooms, but available in the lobby. Restaurant/lounge on the main floor. The lobby and exterior of the buildings have been accented with stucco and tile, projecting a Mediterranean style. Children 18 and under free with parents, no pets. The full service marina has 96 slips and on-shore facilities. Fishing and crabbing from the resort piers or digging for clams on the beach. **Summer Rates:** standard room $49-$79; townhouse suites $90-$115; taxes 7.9%. **Winter Rates:** standard room $45-$60; townhouse suites $85-$95. Major credit cards. **Directions:** from Port Angeles take Hwy 101 east to Discovery Bay, turn left on Rt. 20 and go north to Four Corners, turn right and go east to Hadlock intersection, turn left toward Indian Island. Coming over the Hood Canal Bridge take the first right toward Port Ludlow, continue north on Oak Bay Rd., turn right on the Alcohol Loop Rd.

PORT ORCHARD (pop. 5,000) is located 25 miles north of Tacoma and 12 air miles west of Seattle across Puget Sound.

Port Orchard's downtown has a quaint, historic flavor with covered sidewalks. The shops are filled with antiques, pre-owned treasures, and art quality crafts. The waterfront park has a stage for local concerts and plays.

Located in Kitsap County the sales/use taxes are 8.1%.

$45-$75 **NORTHWEST INTERLUDE BED & BREAKFAST**, 3377 Sarann Ave. E., Port Orchard, WA 98366, phone 360-871-4676. Great views of the traffic on Sinclair Inlet and the Olympic Mountains from the upper and lower decks. There are 3 guest rooms available, 1 with private facilities and 2 with shared. Lounge area with phone, cable TV, VCR, music, and reading material. TV is available in the rooms by request. The rooms are decorated with old-fashioned charm and whimsical touches. Breakfast - guests receive a wake-up coffee tray with scones or muffins, followed by a full gourmet breakfast. Children by arrangement, no pets, smoking on the deck. **Rates:** double occupancy $45-$75; extra person $5-$10. MasterCard & Visa. **Directions:** in Port Orchard take Bay St./Beach Dr. 3 miles to Hillcrest, take a hard right and go up hill 1 1/2 blocks to Sarann, turn left, 2nd driveway.

Northwest Interlude Bed & Breakfast

$55-$90 **REFLECTIONS A Bed & Breakfast Inn,** 3878 Reflection Lane E., Port Orchard, WA 98366, phone 360-871-5582. This spacious home has 4 guest rooms, 2 with private facilities and 2 with shared. There are views of Bainbridge Island and Port Orchard Passage from each of the guest rooms, the patio, deck, or hot tub. A full breakfast is served in the formal dining room. Children 15 and older, no pets. **Rates:** double occupancy $55-$90; extra person $20. MasterCard & Visa. **Directions:** from the BP Station in Port Orchard go left along Bay St./Beach Dr. 3.2 miles to Reflection Lane, turn right, up the private road, first house on the right.

$33-$50 **VISTA MOTEL,** 1090 Bethel Ave., Port Orchard, WA 98366, phone 360-876-8046. A quiet, two story motel with 28 units, 10 nonsmoking. Phones, basic cable TV, and coffee/tea making facilities in the rooms. Five equipped kitchen units. Children welcome, infants free, small dogs allowed with a deposit. **Rates:** single room $33-$37; double room $40; kitchen units $45-$50; extra person $3; local phone calls 25¢. Major credit cards. **Directions:** from Tacoma, take the first Port Orchard Exit, go right at the stop sign, go to the first traffic light, take a left, proceed 2 miles down the road.

PORT LUDLOW see Port Hadlock or Port Townsend for lodging.

PORT TOWNSEND (pop. 7,230) is located on the Olympic Peninsula across Admiralty Inlet from Whidbey Island.

The "City of Dreams", as it is called, is a picturesque community of grand old Victorian homes and is considered to be the Victorian bed and breakfast capital of Washington. In the 1890's lumber tycoons and ship captains built these stately homes with the dream of the railroad coming to town. Suddenly the "golden railroad" halted its tracks in Seattle and the flourishing business district all but deteriorated until the 1970's. Fort Worden is one of the many forts built at the turn-of-the-century to protect Puget Sound from a naval attack. The fort became a state park in 1973.

Located in Jefferson County the sales/use taxes are 7.9%.

$55-$99 **ALADDIN MOTOR INN**, 2333 Washington St., Port Townsend, WA 98368, phone 360-385-3747 or 1-800-281-3747, fax 360-385-5099. This 3 story waterfront motel has 30 rooms, 90% nonsmoking. In-room phones, remote control TV, microwaves, refrigerators, and king or queen beds. Most rooms have balconies overlooking the water. No coffee/tea making facilities in the rooms, but pastries and coffee are provided in the office. Children welcome, 10 and under free, small pets allowed. **High Season Rates:** *5/15 to 10/15* - single room (1 bed) $60-$90; double room $75-$99; extra person $5; pets $7 per night; local phone calls free. **Off-Season Rates:** single $55-$75; double $65-$80. Major credit cards. **Directions:** from Hwy 20 turn towards the water on Kearney, then right onto Washington.

$75-$165 **ANN STARRETT MANSION BED & BREAKFAST**, 7 Clay St., Port Townsend, WA 98368, phone 360-385-3205 or 1-800-321-0644. This grand Victorian mansion, built in 1889, may very well be the most spectacular of all the great Victorian estates in Port Townsend. A free-hanging, three tiered spiral staircase leads to a domed ceiling. The eight-sided dome is actually a solar calendar with frescos depicting the Four Seasons and Four Virtues. On the first days of each new season the sun shines through dormer windows on a ruby red glass causing a red beam to point toward the appropriate seasonal panel.

There are 11 guest rooms, all with private facilities on three floors, decorated with a plethora of antiques. A full decadent breakfast is served. Children 12 and older, no pets, no smoking. **Rates:** both single and double rooms $75; suite $145-$165; extra person $25. Most major credit cards. **Directions:** entering town on Hwy 20, take a left on Kearney, proceed to Lawrence and turn right, continue to Adams St., turn right, proceed one block to Clay St.

Ann Starrett Mansion

$50-$150 **ANNAPURNA INN BED & BREAKFAST,** 538 Adams, Port Townsend, WA 98368, phone 360-385-2909 or 1-800-868-2662. The Inn, circa 1881, is located in the heart of the Uptown National Historic District and is primarily a retreat center dedicated to health and well-being. There are 4 rooms, 3 with private facilities, and a 2 bedroom suite with one bath. Vegan gourmet breakfasts, sauna and steambath spa. Two licensed massage therapists offer foot reflexology, therapeutic deep tissue massage, cranio/sacral therapy, and Thai massage with the retreat packages. Retreat packages are for 3 days, 1 week, or 3 weeks. Children welcome, pets allowed by arrangement. **Rates:** *B & B* single room (1 bed) $65-$75; double room $75-$85; suite $100-$150; extra person $5-$15. Mid-week winter rates $50. Massage - 1 1/2 hours $50; reflexology $40. *Retreat packages:* 3 day package $225 per person; 1 week retreat $600. Visa & MasterCard, preferred payment cash or check. **Directions:** traveling northeast on Water St. turn left on Monroe, left on Clay to Adams. On the corner of Adams & Clay.

$55-$75   **BAKER HOUSE BED & BREAKFAST**, 905 Franklin, Port Townsend, WA 98368, phone 360-385-6673. Restored 1898 house located two blocks from downtown. 4 rooms, 2 with private facilities and 2 with shared. Rooms are on the second floor with private entrances from the verandah. Three rooms have views of the sound and garden. Full 3 course breakfast. Adults only, no pets, no smoking. **Rates:** double occupancy $55-$75. Personal checks, MasterCard, or Visa. **Directions:** from the Haller Fountain go to the top of the stairs and proceed one block to Franklin. If driving on Hwy 20 turn onto Kearney, proceed to Lawrence, turn right and proceed to Taylor, then turn right, proceed two blocks.

$75-$85   **BAY COTTAGE**, 4346 S. Discovery Rd., Port Townsend, WA 98368, phone 360-385-2035. Two small seaside cottages are on the bluff at Discovery Bay. Completely equipped kitchens, featherbeds, and fresh flowers. Fix breakfast at your leisure, sip morning coffee from the private deck, or barbecue clams freshly dug from the shore. Walk along the private, sandy swimming beach strewn with sand dollars. Children welcome, no pets, no smoking. **Summer Rates:** *4/01 to 10/15* - double occupancy $85; extra person $5. **Winter Rates:** mid-week $75. Personal checks or cash only. **Directions:** follow Hwy 20 west on S. Discovery Rd., 1/2 mile on the left.

$49-$89   **BELMONT INN RESTAURANT & SALOON**, 925 Water St., Port Townsend, WA 98368, phone 360-385-3007. Located on the water. 4 rooms, all with private facilities are on the second floor. Two rooms overlook the water and 2 have a view of Old Town. Victorian style with high ceilings and exposed brick. Coffee/tea making facilities in the rooms. Restaurant/bar on the premises. Centrally located downtown. **Summer Rates:** single room (1 bed) $69; double (2 beds) $89. **Winter Rates:** $49-$69. Most major credit cards. **Directions:** on the main street in the center of town.

$95   **The CABIN BED & BREAKFAST**, 839 N. Jacob Miller Rd., Port Townsend, WA 98368, phone 360-385-5571. One small cabin tucked in the woods on the Strait of Juan de Fuca. The beach, with private access, can be explored at low tide. The cabin has a fully equipped kitchen, skylight in the bathroom, double feather bed, deck, and a firepit for barbecuing. Awake in the morning to freshly baked delectables and make yourself breakfast with the farm fresh eggs, bacon, and bread you will find in your refrigerator. Choice of champagne or orange juice. Adults only, pets allowed, no smoking. **Rates:** double occupancy $95. No credit cards. **Directions:** follow Hwy 20 west to Jacob Miller Rd. (4 miles), go to the end of the road, turn left onto gravel drive. The Cabin is at the third and last driveway.

$80-$125 **CHANTICLEER INN BED & BREAKFAST,** 1208 Franklin, Port Townsend, WA 98368, phone 360-385-6239 or 1-800-858-9421. Restored 1876 Victorian home located high above the water. 4 rooms, all with private facilities. Each room has king or queen feather beds and is individually decorated. A creative breakfast is accompanied by the live sounds of the classic concert harp. Adults only, no pets, no smoking. **Rates:** double occupancy $80-$125. MasterCard & Visa. **Directions:** on Hwy 20 proceed to the 2nd traffic light, turn left on Washington, go up the hill 8 blocks, left on Fillmore and proceed 2 blocks to Franklin.

$65-$95 **The ENGLISH INN BED & BREAKFAST,** 718 F St., Port Townsend, WA 98368, phone 360-385-5302 or 1-800-254-5302. This 1885 home is on a hill overlooking the valley and Olympic mountain range. The style is Italianate Victorian, a simple box-like form, with two story bay windows and bracketed friezes. It is one of only a few examples of this type in Port Townsend. Five guest rooms, all have private facilities. One room on the main floor, 4 on the second floor. Garden, hot tub, and gazebo in a private patio setting. Big breakfast included. Children 14 and older, no pets, no smoking. **Summer Rates:** *5/01 to 9/30* - double occupancy $75-$95. **Winter Rates:** $65-$85. Amex, Discover, MasterCard, & Visa. **Directions:** in Port Townsend follow Hwy 20 west to Kearney, make a half-left uphill on Washington 2 blocks, left on Walker several blocks, right on "F" St. 2 blocks. Parking at corner of "F" and Willow.

$9-$14 **FORT FLAGGLER HI HOSTEL,** 272 Battery Way, Port Townsend, WA 98368, phone 360-385-0655. *Open year-round, hours 8 a.m. to 9:30 a.m. & 5 p.m. to 10 p.m.* A 1940's vintage barracks is an alternative to the opulent Victorian mansions of Port Townsend, and the price can't be beat. There are 2 men and women's dorm rooms, each with 6 beds and 5 couples/family rooms, 3 bathrooms, a common room, and kitchen. The rooms may be Spartan, but the surrounding grounds are first class. 450 acres of State Park grounds with gardens, museums, restaurant, and of course the beach. **Rates:** members $11 each; non-members $14; cyclists $9-$12; couples room surcharge $8. MasterCard, & Visa. **Directions:** follow signs to Fort Warden. Hostel is located behind the Park office.

$64-$130 **HARBORSIDE INN**, 330 Benedict St., Port Townsend, WA 98368, phone 360-385-7909 or 1-800-942-5960 (US & Canada), fax 360-385-6984. 63 rooms, 60% nonsmoking. Two equipped kitchenette units, one executive unit. Phones, remote control cable TV, refrigerators, and drip coffee makers in every room. Microwaves available. Seasonal, heated swimming pool and year-round spa. Each room has a private patio. All third floor rooms have a water view. Meeting room, capacity 65 people. Children 12 and under free, small pets allowed only in smoking rooms. **Rates:** $64-$130; extra person charge $5; pets $5 per night; prices increase $10 per floor. *Call for off-season rates.* Major credit cards. **Directions:** from Hwy 20 turn on Benedict at the Shell Station.

$72-$142 **HERITAGE HOUSE BED & BREAKFAST INN**, 305 Pierce St., Port Townsend, WA 98368, phone 360-385-6800, fax 360-379-0498. This stately Italianate home, built in 1870, sits on a bluff overlooking the bay and Olympic Mountains. There are six guest rooms, 4 with private facilities and two with shared. Each room has a queen bed, down comforter, and is distinctly furnished with a variety of Victorian antiques. Full breakfast served in the dining room. Children over 12 welcome, no pets, no smoking. **Rates:** double occupancy $72-$97; suite $142. *Off-season specials.* MasterCard, Visa, & Amex. **Directions:** centrally located downtown at the corner of Washington and Pierce.

$72-$125 **HOLLY HILL HOUSE BED & BREAKFAST**, 611 Polk, Port Townsend, WA 98368, phone 360-385-5619. This 1872 Victorian has 3 guest rooms in the main house and 2 in the carriage house, all have private facilities. Two rooms have views of Admiralty Inlet, Mt. Baker, and the Cascades. Full breakfast served in the dining room. Children over 12 welcome, no pets, smoking limited to the porch. **Rates:** double occupancy $72-$125; extra person $15. MasterCard & Visa. **Directions:** from the ferry turn left, at stoplight turn right, go two blocks to Lawrence, proceed for 11 blocks to Polk, turn right one block.

$70 **HORSE HAVEN INN**, 2823 Hastings Ave., Port Townsend, WA 98368, phone 360-385-7784. One suite available at this unique country retreat. Therapeutic hot tub on a private deck, spacious private room, and sun-filled bath. Brass bed, TV, coffeemaker, and refrigerator. Mapped, wooded trails for walking or riding. One child okay, no pets, smoking outdoors. Horseback riding and massages available for a fee. Horse boarding available for those traveling with equine friends. Continental breakfast provided, also a wine, cheese, and fruit welcoming basket. **Rates:** double occupancy $70. MasterCard & Visa.

Directions: on Hwy 20, west of town, turn onto Sheridan, go to 2nd stop sign, turn left on Hastings and proceed for 1 mile.

$75 **HUNT MANOR GUEST HOUSE**, 1110 Jackman, Port Townsend, WA 98368, phone 360-379-9241. Two spacious rooms with king size beds, dressing room, and bath. One room on the main floor and one downstairs, handicap accessible with elevator. Large screen TV and VCR in adjacent living space. Buffet continental breakfast. Adults only, no pets, no smoking. **Rates:** double occupancy $75; taxes included. No credit cards. **Directions:** on Hwy 20, west of town, turn onto Sheridan, go to 10th, turn right, proceed to Jackman and make a left.

$65-$150 **JAMES HOUSE BED & BREAKFAST**, 1238 Washington, Port Townsend, WA 98368, phone 360-385-1238 or 1-800-385-1238. A grand Victorian mansion, built in 1889, sits on the bluff overlooking the water, mountains, and historic downtown. There are 11 guest rooms and one cottage. Ten have private facilities, 2 rooms on the 2nd floor share one bath. The 2nd and 3rd floor bedrooms are spacious with water and mountain views. The Master/Bridal suite, on the 2nd floor, has a private bathroom with clawfoot tub, wood burning fireplace, sitting room, and private balcony with a view. The Garden Suites are 2 bedroom suites located on the ground floor with a separate entry and private bath. One room has a fireplace and one has a wood stove. The Gardener's Cottage is located at the back of the property and offers quiet seclusion. Full breakfast. Children over 12, no pets, no smoking. **Rates:** double occupancy, there are 2 rooms for $65; 4 rooms for $95; 3 for $100; suites $110-$150. Amex, MasterCard, & Visa. **Directions:** in town go past Safeway and make an immediate left up the hill. Go 3 blocks.

$70-$135 **LIZZIE'S BED & BREAKFAST**, 731 Pierce, Port Townsend, WA 98368, phone 360-385-4168. 1888 Victorian mansion decorated with authentic antiques. Seven rooms, all with private facilities. Bay windows in some of the rooms and one room has a fireplace. Two parlors have fireplaces, leather sofas, and a collection of books. The grand piano is meant for use, not ornament. Full breakfast served in the grand old kitchen. Children over 10, no pets, no smoking. **Rates:** double occupancy $70-$135. MasterCard, Discover, & Visa. **Directions:** entering town on Hwy 20 turn left at the stoplight (Kearney), go 2 blocks, turn right at Lawrence, go uphill 7 blocks, turn left on Pierce.

$65-$175 **MANRESA CASTLE**, P. O. Box 564, 7th & Sheridan, Port Townsend, WA 98368, phone 360-385-5750 or 1-800-732-1281 (WA), fax 360-385-5883. This 40 room castle was built in 1892 by the first mayor of Port Townsend for his bride. It was at one time occupied by the Jesuit Order which named it Manręsa Hall after the town in Spain where the Order was founded. The rooms all have private baths, cable TV, and telephones; no designated nonsmoking rooms. Decorated with European antiques and hand-printed wall coverings. Located on top of a hill, the Castle has a commanding view. No coffee/tea making facilities in the rooms, but a continental breakfast is included. Restaurant and lounge on the premises. Children welcome, no pets. **Summer Rates:** *5/01 to 10/ 30* - standard room $70-$75; small suite $85-$100; suites $135-$175; extra person $10. **Winter Rates:** $65; $85; $100-$105. Discover, MasterCard, & Visa. **Directions:** entering town on Hwy 20, turn left on Sheridan.

Manresa Castle

$79-$175 **OLD CONSULATE INN BED & BREAKFAST**, 313 Walker at Washington, Port Townsend, WA 98368, phone 360-385-6753 or 1-800-300-6753. This perfect example of a Queen Anne Victorian sits high on the bluff commanding spectacular views of the bay, Mt. Rainier, and the Olympics. A total of 8 guest rooms all have private facilities, 4 on the second floor and 4 on the third floor. The main floor offers room to read or sit by two working fireplaces. The formal parlor has a grand piano and an antique organ. Breakfast is a multi-course affair served in the dining room with a view of the harbor. Evening tea, dessert, and cordial. A large gazebo with hot tub overlooks the water. Children over 12 welcome, no pets, no smoking. **High Season Rates:** *4/01 to 10/30* - double occupancy, 2nd floor rooms $110; suite $115-$175; 3rd floor rooms $79-$115; suite $140. **Winter Rates:** $79-$145. MasterCard, Amex,& Visa. **Directions:** entering town on Hwy 20, go to stoplight at Kearney, turn left up to the bluff, Washington St., first corner of Walker at Washington.

$55-$119 **PALACE HOTEL,** 1004 Water St., Port Townsend, WA 98368, phone 360-385-0773 or 1-800-962-0741. This 1889 hotel has been restored in grand Victorian style. There are 15 rooms, 11 nonsmoking. Accommodations range from multi-room suites with kitchens and private baths to continental bedrooms with shared bath. 12 rooms have private facilities and 3 share one bath. The hotel is 3 stories and has no elevator. The rooms start on the second floor; 60 steps to the third floor. All rooms have cable TV, microwaves, and coffee/tea making facilities. Three kitchenettes with fridge and toaster oven. In-house restaurant and off-street parking. Children 11 and under free, no pets. **Summer Rates:** *5/01 to 10/01* - double occupancy $65-$119; extra person $10. **Winter Rates:** $55-$99. Discover, MasterCard, Amex, & Visa. **Directions:** centrally located on the main street of town.

$45-$120 **POINT HUDSON MOTEL RESORT & MARINA,** Point Hudson, Port Townsend, WA 98368, phone 360-385-2828 or 1-800-826-3854. The Point Hudson Resort has an interesting history. It was built in 1934 as a customs office and quarantine hospital for immigrants. However, no immigrants were ever detained for treatment. From 1939 to 1953 the military occupied the property. Today the hospital is the event pavilion, the enlisted men's quarters the motel, and the officers' house provides more elegant accommodations. The mess hall is a restaurant and the post exchange the company store. The parade ground serves as an RV park and the nurses' quarters is the shower house. There are 25 rooms, 17 have private facilities and 8 have shared. Five rooms have TV, one is wheelchair friendly, 1 for pets, 6 for smokers. The view suites, with private baths receive a complimentary breakfast. Children and groups always welcome. Pay phone and free coffee in the lobby. Located on 2,000 feet of beach frontage; within walking distance of town. The marina has 60 slips, moorage is 50¢ per foot per day. **Summer Rates:** *5/01 to 9/30* - motel $55-$85; suites $95-$120. **Winter Rates:** $45-$75. MasterCard & Visa. **Directions:** from the ferry follow Water Street to the end, turn left 1 block, turn right, go to the wharf.

$44-$88 **PORT TOWNSEND MOTEL & SPA,** 2020 Washington St., Port Townsend, WA 98368, phone 360-385-2211 or 1-800-822-8696. This 2 story, modern colonial has 25 units, 8 nonsmoking. Phones, TV, and coffee/tea making facilities in the rooms.

Two equipped kitchen units available. Large central hot tub. Continental breakfast is included. Close to downtown, golf course 3 blocks away, and bowling next door. Children free with parents, pets allowed. **Summer Rates:** *6/01 to 10/30* - single room, double occupancy $68-$88; double room $78-$88; local phone calls free. **Winter Rates:** $44-$64. Major credit cards. **Directions:** on Hwy 20 coming into town, 50 yards past third traffic light, on the left.

$65-$165 **RAVENSCROFT INN BED & BREAKFAST,** 533 Quincy, Port Townsend, WA 98368, phone 360-385-2784 or 1-800-782-2691, fax 360-385-6724. This Charleston style single house was built in 1987. There are 8 rooms available and 2 suites, all with private facilities. Three rooms have fireplaces, three have French doors opening onto the verandah, and three are garden level. A multi-course breakfast is served to piano music by your host. Children over 12 welcome, no pets, and no smoking. **Summer Rates:** *5/15 to 9/15* - double occupancy $67-$135; suite $155-$165; extra person $30. **Winter Rates:** $65-$125; suites $135-$140. Most major credit cards, personal checks. **Directions:** entering town on Hwy 20, at stoplight take a left on Kearney, proceed to Lawrence, turn right, go past the blinking light 3 blocks to Quincy, turn right, on the next corner.

$58-$124 **The TIDES INN,** 1807 Water St., Port Townsend, WA 98368, phone 360-385-0595 or 1-800-822-8696. This waterfront motel has 21 rooms, 2 nonsmoking. Phones and TV in every room. No coffee/tea making facilities in the rooms, but a continental breakfast is provided in the lobby and there are 5 equipped kitchen units. 19 units have a private deck and 9 rooms have jacuzzis on their deck. Children free with parents, pets on approval. **Summer Rates:** *6/16 to 10/15* - single room $88; double room (2 beds) $98; jacuzzi suite $115-$124; pets free. **Mid Season:** *4/01 to 6/15* - $78-$115. **Winter Rates:** $58-$105. Major credit cards. **Directions:** on the main highway coming into Port Townsend, on the right side of the road before town.

$85-$135 **TRENHOLM HOUSE BED & BREAKFAST,** 2037 Haines St., Port Townsend, WA 98368, phone 360-385-6059 or 1-800-575-6059. This three story, 1890 Victorian farmhouse is close to the golf course. There are 4 rooms available, all with private facilities. One room on the main floor is handicap accessible, 2 rooms are on the 2nd floor, and the suite is on the 3rd floor. A separate cottage has a sitting room, bedroom, and bath. Full breakfast is provided, as is the shuttle to the ferry. Children welcome, no pets, and no smoking. **Rates:** $85-$135; cottage $95; extra person $25. MasterCard, Visa, and personal check. **Directions:** coming into town on Hwy 20 make a left on Kearney (at the stoplight), left on Blaine, and right on Haines.

$85-$125 **The VICTORIAN SUITE at the Club,** 229 Monroe St., Port Townsend, WA 98368, phone 360-385-6560. This is an unusual setting for an elegant, two bedroom Victorian suite overlooking the water. It is located in the corner of the Athletic Club. The lodging includes complete use of the club's sauna, spa, Nautilus equipment, free weights, and racquetball court. The suite has a wet bar, refrigerator, and TV. A complimentary $10 breakfast certificate is for guests to use at the Salal Cafe. Children 12 and older, no pets, and no smoking. **Summer Rates:** *6/01 to 9/30* - double occupancy $105; 4 people $125. **Winter Rates:** $85-$105. MasterCard & Visa. **Directions:** coming into town on Hwy 20 follow Water St. to the end, turn left and go one block, on the corner.

$45-$125 **WATER STREET HOTEL,** 635 Water St., Port Townsend, WA 98368, phone 360-385-5467 or 1-800-735-9810. This historic hotel was built in 1889 and was completely renovated in 1990. There are 16 guest rooms, 3 nonsmoking. 11 rooms have private facilities and 5 have shared. Some rooms have equipped kitchens, all have TV. No coffee/tea making facilities in the rooms, but there are 5 restaurants within 1/2 a block. Children 11 and under free, pets allowed. **Summer Rates:** *5/01 to 9/30* - double occupancy $50-$85; suite $95-$125; extra person $8; pets $10 per night, $20 deposit. **Winter Rates:** $45-$100. MasterCard, Amex, & Visa. **Directions:** centrally located on the main street of town at the foot of Quincy Street/Victoria Clipper Dock.

⍥POULSBO (pop. 5,140) is located on Kitsap Peninsula, 14 miles from Bremerton.

(PAWLZ-boh) is a Norwegian fishermen's village on the northern shore of Liberty Bay at the intersection of Hwy 3 and 305. The terrain consists of rolling hills with scenic views of the bay. Located in Kitsap County the sales/use taxes are 8.1%.

$75-$100 **AGATE PASS WATERFRONT BED & BREAKFAST,** 16045 Hwy 305, Poulsbo, WA 98370, phone 360-842-1632 or 1-800-869-1632. Once the Agate Pass Nursery, this bed and breakfast offers two very private guest rooms. Each room includes a Euro kitchenette with refrigerator stocked for breakfast, spacious bedroom, queen bed, sitting area, private bath, TV/VCR, and porch. Extensive gardens and spectacular views, just steps away from the beach. Children by arrangement, no pets, smoking outside. **Rates:** garden room $75; waterfront room $100. MasterCard & Visa. **Directions:** from the ferry follow Hwy 305, across the Agate Pass Bridge, take the first left after the bridge, drive down a lane to the B&B.

$39-$76 **CONTINENTAL INN**, P. O. Box 285, Keyport, WA 98345, phone 360-779-5575 or 1-800-537-5766, fax 360-779-5579. Located across the bay and south of Poulsbo at 1783 Highway 308. This two story, Spanish-style inn has 20 units, 10 nonsmoking. Phones and TV in all the rooms. No coffee/tea making facilities in the rooms, but a restaurant and coffee shop are on the premises. Eight units have equipped kitchenettes. Adjacent to the National Underwater Naval Museum. Children 6 and under free, no pets. **Rates:** single room $39-$44; double room $44; suite $49-$76; extra person $5; local phone calls free. Major credit cards. **Directions:** drive north from Bremerton on Hwy 3, turn east on Hwy 308, proceed to Keyport.

CYPRESS INN, 19801 NE 7th Ave., Poulsbo, WA 98370, phone 360-697-2119 or 1-800-752-9991, fax 360-697-2707.

$75 **FOXBRIDGE BED & BREAKFAST**, 30680 Hwy 3 NE, Poulsbo, WA 98370, phone 360-598-5599, fax 360-598-3588. Three spacious guest rooms, all with private facilities on the 2nd floor. The rooms are uniquely decorated and all have territorial views. A three course, full gourmet breakfast is available from 7:30 a.m. to 10 a.m. Other amenities include the library, fruit orchard, trout pond, spacious grounds, and native animals. Children 16 and older, no pets, smoking outside. Six miles to the nearest restuarant. **Rates:** double occupancy $75; extra person (with prior arrangements) $20. MasterCard & Visa. **Directions:** on Hwy 3 six miles north of Poulsbo, mile marker 59, one mile south of the Hood Canal Bridge.

$53-$105 **POULSBO'S INN**, 18680 Hwy 305, Poulsbo, WA 98370, phone 360-779-3921, reservations 1-800-597-5151, fax 360-779-9737. 73 rooms, 50% nonsmoking. All rooms are spacious with cable TV, phones, and queen size beds. No coffee/tea making facilities in the rooms, but available in the lobby, and there are 22 equipped kitchen units. Seasonal outdoor pool and spa. Children welcome, infants free, pets allowed. **Rates:** single room (1 bed) $53-$57; double (2 beds) $61-$65; kitchen units start at $59; suite $75-$105; extra person $4-$10; pets, one time charge $5-$35; local phone calls 25¢. Major credit cards. **Directions:** from the Bainbridge Island ferry follow Hwy 305 12 miles into Poulsbo, the Inn is on the right just before town.

PROSSER

(pop. 5,000) is located in the Yakima Valley wine country in south central Washington off I-82 between Yakima and Richland.

Area wineries include: Chinook Winery, Hinzerling Vineyards, Hogue Cellars, Pontin Del Roza Winery, and Yakima River Winery. The Great Prosser Balloon Rally takes place in late September.

Located in Benton County the sales/use taxes are 7.5%.

$38-$98 **The BARN MOTOR INN**, North 6th St., P. O. Box 818, Prosser, WA 99350, phone 509-786-2121, fax 509-786-4106. A total of 30 units, 16 nonsmoking. Phones, TV, AC, and small refrigerators available. No coffee/tea making facilities in the rooms, but room service is available. Two executive suites have a heart shaped jacuzzi tub, wet bar, and king bed. Seasonal outdoor pool, restaurant/lounge with piano bar, banquet facilities, and gift shop. Two children 11 and under free, no pets. RV parking sites, airport within walking distance. **Rates:** single (1 bed) $38-$44; double room $44; suite $98; extra person $6; local phone calls free. Major credit cards. **Directions:** Exit 80 off I-82.

$27-$36 **PROSSER MOTEL**, 1206 Wine Country Rd., Prosser, WA 99350, phone 509-786-2555. A total of 16 units, 6 nonsmoking. Phones, TV, coffee/tea making facilities in the rooms. Picnic area in shaded courtyard. Centrally located in downtown Prosser, within walking distance of restaurants. Children welcome, infants free, pets allowed. **Rates:** single (1 bed) $27; double room $36; extra person $4; pets $2; local phone calls free. Major credit cards. **Directions:** Exit 80 off I-82.

$75 **WINE COUNTRY INN**, 1106 Wine Country Rd., Prosser, WA 99350, phone 509-786-2855, fax 509-786-7414. A total of 4 nonsmoking rooms, 2 with private facilities, 2 with shared. Queen beds and coffee/tea making facilities in the rooms. Phone in the hall, sitting area, and access to the riverside verandah. Full breakfast is provided to guests, and the restaurant has a special luncheon menu, gourmet dinners, and weekend brunch. High Teas are a house specialty. Children welcome, infants free, no facilities for pets, but they may be boarded at a nearby kennel. **Rates:** double occupancy $75; extra person $20; local phone calls free. MasterCard, Amex, & Visa. **Directions:** Exit 80 off I-82, travel south 1.5 miles. As soon as you cross the bridge, the Inn is on the left.

PULLMAN •

(pop. 23,478) is located on the eastern edge of Washington State, seven miles from the Idaho/Washington border.

The terrain surrounding Pullman consists of rolling hills planted with wheat, peas, and lentils. It is located in the heart of the Palouse region and is home to Washington State University. Located in Whitman County the sales/use taxes are 7.5%.

$38-$59   **AMERICAN TRAVEL INN**, So. 515 Grand, Pullman, WA 99163, phone 509-334-3500. A total of 34 rooms, 9 nonsmoking, in this typical two story motel. Cable TV, phones, queen and longboy beds. No coffee/tea making facilities in the rooms, but available in the lobby. Heated outdoor pool. Children welcome, pets allowed in some rooms. **Rates:** single (1 bed) $38-$42; double room $48; suite $59; extra person $4; local phone calls free. Major credit cards. **Directions:** take the Pullman Exit off Hwy 195 to the stoplight, turn right on Grand Ave.

$34-$48   **COUGAR LAND MOTEL**, West 120 Main St., Pullman, WA 99163, phone 509-334-3535 or 1-800-334-3574. Three story motel, the 2nd floor rooms have recently been remodeled. A total of 42 rooms, 31 nonsmoking. Phones, TV, and outdoor pool. No coffee/tea making facilities in the rooms, but available in the lobby. There are 9 non-equipped kitchen units. Children 10 and under free, pets by arrangement. **Rates:** single room $34; double room $44; kitchen units $48; pets $5-$10 refundable deposit; local phone calls free. Most major credit cards. **Directions:** follow Grand Ave. to Main St., turn west and go up the hill 1/2 block.

$40-$100   **COUNTRY BED & BREAKFAST**, Rt 2 Box 666, Pullman, WA 99163, phone & fax 509-334-4453. This B & B has 6 guest rooms, 3 with private facilities and 3 with shared. One room on the main floor and 3 on the second. There is also a detached cottage (the playroom) that can accommodate 8-10 people and a 5th wheeler that sleeps up to 5 people. Guests enjoy patios, gardens, and a view of the rolling hills of the Palouse country side. Full, continental, buffet breakfast. Children welcome, pets by arrangement, no smoking. Six miles to the nearest restaurant. **Rates:** double occupancy $40-$100. MasterCard & Visa. **Directions:** going east on Hwy 195, from the last stoplight out of Pullman, go 5.8 miles, turn left on Staley Rd., 3rd house.

$31-$90 **HILLTOP MOTOR INN,** 928 Olson, P. O. Box 155, Pullman, WA 99163, phone 509-334-2555. 15 rooms, bungalow or rustic, and 1 private home available for special events, 8 nonsmoking. No coffee/tea making facilities in the rooms, but there is a landmark, fine dining restaurant/bar on the premises. The restaurant has a view of Pullman. Children 9 and under free, pets by arrangement. **Rates:** single (1 bed) $31-$37; double $43; suite $90; extra person $6; pets $10 per stay; local phone calls free. Major credit cards. **Directions:** from the north on Hwy 195, turn into Pullman - corner of Wawawai and Davis Way.

$35-$45 **MANOR LODGE MOTEL,** 455 SE Paradise, Pullman, WA 99163, phone 509-334-2511. Downtown location near the WSU campus. There are 31 rooms, 12 nonsmoking. Phones, TV, AC, and 5 equipped kitchen units. All rooms without kitchens have refrigerators and microwaves. No coffee/tea making facilities in the rooms, but available in the lobby. Children welcome, infants free, pets allowed. **Rates:** single room $35; double room $40-$45; extra person $5; pets $3; local phone calls free. MasterCard & Visa. **Directions:** downtown on one-way street going towards Moscow and WSU.

$35-$65 **NENDELS INN,** 915 SE Main St., Pullman, WA 99163, phone 509-332-2646, fax 509-332-2525. This privately owned, franchised motel is across from WSU. There are 59 rooms, 47 nonsmoking. All have phones and TV with HBO. Refrigerators and microwaves are available. Morning coffee is available in the lobby with donuts. Outdoor pool and airport service. Children 12 and under free, pets allowed. **Summer Rates:** *6/01 to 9/01-* single (1 bed) $35-$39; double $39-$44; extra person $5; local phone calls free. **Winter Rates:** single $45-$48; double $47-$65. Major credit cards. **Directions:** right at the base of WSU.

QUALITY INN, Paradise Creek, SE 1050 Bishop Blvd., Pullman, WA 99163, phone 509-332-0500 or 1-800-669-3212.

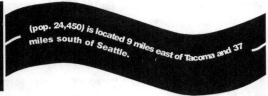

PUYALLUP

(pop. 24,450) is located 9 miles east of Tacoma and 37 miles south of Seattle.

(pyoo-AL-uhp) is an Indian word meaning "generous people". The Western Washington Fairgrounds is located here. There are 120 acres dedicated to buildings/arena and parking facilities that are being utilized for year-round activities. Lodging prices go up $10 a night per room at most motels during the three weeks of the fair.

Located in Pierce County the sales/use/lodging taxes are 9.9%.

$45-$65   **HART'S TAYBERRY HOUSE BED & BREAKFAST**, 7406 80th St. E., Puyallup, WA 98371, phone 206-848-4594. A Victorian house with stained glass, open stairway, elevator, and a tin ceiling in the kitchen. Three guest rooms available on the 2nd floor, 1 with private facilities, and 2 with shared. The rooms come in small, medium, and large. The queen bed room has a balcony overlooking the valley. A full breakfast is served on green depression glass china. Children 12 and older, no pets. Smoking is allowed outside on the covered porch with a gazebo. One mile to the nearest restaurant. **Rates:** $45, $55, & $65. **Directions:** in downtown Puyallup take Pioneer Way going west 1.8 miles, turn left on Fruitland Ave., go 1 block, turn right on 80th.

$45-$75   **MOTEL PUYALLUP**, 1412 S. Meridian St., Puyallup, WA 98371, phone 206-845-8825. 63 rooms, 50% nonsmoking. Every room has cable TV with HBO, phones, and AC. No coffee/tea making facilities in the rooms, but available in the lobby with a continental breakfast. 19 equipped kitchen units. Some rooms have mini refrigerators and microwaves. VCR/movie rentals. Children under 12 free, pets allowed. **Rates:** single (1 bed) $45-$70; double $54-$68; family room $67-$75; kitchen unit $4 extra; extra person $4; pets $5 per night; local phone calls free. Major credit cards, no personal checks. **Directions:** on Puyallup's main street, same side of the street as the fairgrounds.

$35-$75   **NORTHWEST MOTOR INN**, 1409 S. Meridian St., Puyallup, WA 98371, phone & fax 206-841-2600 or 1-800-845-9490. Across the street from the fairgrounds, this motel has 51 rooms, 18 nonsmoking. Every room has cable TV with HBO, phones, and AC. No coffee/tea making facilities in the rooms, but available in the lobby with a continental breakfast. 13 equipped kitchen units, guest laundry, and outdoor hot tub. 24 hour restaurant close by. Children under 12 free, pets allowed. **Rates:** single room $35-$57; double $43-$62; family room $65-$75; kitchen unit $3 extra; extra person $5; pets $5 per night; local phone calls free. Major credit cards. **Directions:** from I-5 take Puyallup Exit 127, on the main street 2 blocks south of the fairgrounds.

$28-$41   **TAMARAK MOTEL**, 403 W. Meeker, Puyallup, WA 98371, phone & fax 206-845-0466. This 30 year old motel is two stories and has 20 rooms, 2 nonsmoking. Phones, basic cable TV, guest laundry, and outdoor pool. No coffee/tea making facilities in the rooms. All units have kitchenettes, cookware and dishes available at the office. Children under 18 free with parents, pets by arrangement. **Rates:** single room $28-$33; double $37; suite $41; extra person $6; no charge for local phone calls. MasterCard & Visa. **Directions:** from Meridian take a right on Main St., corner of 4th and Main.

QUINAULT   see Lake Quinault.

QUINCY (pop. 5,470) is located in the center of the state in the Columbia Basin.

In the late 1800's, this arid land was used solely for cattle and horse ranges. Following the introduction of irrigation in 1951, Quincy has become the hub of the Columbia Basin's agriculture industry. The popular Gorge outdoor concert amphitheater is 10 miles to the south. Located in Grant County the sales/use taxes are 7.5%.

$43-$61   **TRADITIONAL INNS**, 500 "F" Street SW, Quincy, WA 98848, phone 509-787-3525, fax 509-787-3528. 24 units, 14 nonsmoking. All rooms have phones, TV, microwaves, hair dryers, refrigerators, and AC. No coffee/tea making facilities in the rooms, but available in the lobby. Children under 12 free, pets allowed free. Guest laundry, fax available, and shuttle provided to the Quincy airport. **Summer Rates:** *Memorial Day thru Labor Day* - $53-$61; extra person $8; local phone calls free. **Winter Rates:** $43-$51. Major credit cards. **Directions:** on Quincy's main street, two blocks west of the town center.

$48-$58   **VILLAGER INN MOTEL & RV PARK**, 711 2nd Ave. SW, Quincy, WA 98848, phone 509-787-3515, fax 509-787-9111. 21 units, 6 nonsmoking. All rooms have phones, TV with

HBO, microwaves, refrigerators, AC, and coffee making facilities. Seven non-equipped kitchen units. Outdoor pool and RV park. Children under 12 free, pets by arrangement. **Summer Rates:** *6/01 to 9/29* - $53-$61; extra person $8; local phone calls free. **Winter Rates:** 2 people $48; 4 people $58. Midweek discounts for truckers and construction workers. Major credit cards. **Directions:** at the stoplight in Quincy go north to 2nd St., turn left.

RANDLE is located at the junction of Hwy 12 and FSR 25, between Mt. Rainier and Mt. St. Helens.

This is mountain country, north of Mt. St. Helens and Mt. Adams, south of Mt. Rainier. If your interest is whitewater rafting, trail riding in the Gifford Pinchot National Forest, or hiking, there is a convenient information booth in Randle.

$45 **MEDICI MOTEL & GIFTS**, 471 Cispus Rd., Randle, WA 98377, phone 360-497-7700 or 1-800-697-7750. Four very clean rooms, 2 with private facilities, 2 with 1/2 baths (toilet and sink) share the shower room. Limited TV, equipped kitchenettes. This is a secluded rural setting with a small trout pond. Children definitely welcome, pets allowed on a leash. There are also limited use RV and tent sites with a sheltered picnic area. 36 miles from Mt. St. Helens. **Rates:** double occupancy $45, taxes included; rollaway $5. MasterCard & Visa. **Directions:** 3 miles south of Randle on the Cispus Rd.

$30-$45 **RANDLE MOTEL**, 9780 Hwy 12, P. O. Box 194, Randle, WA 98377, phone 360-497-5346. 10 rooms, 1 nonsmoking. All rooms have TV, some rooms have coffee/tea making facilities. Four units have kitchens, but no cookware or dishes. Within walking distance of restaurants. Closest motel to Mt. St. Helens, east face viewing facilities. 36 miles from Windy Ridge. Children free with parents, pets by arrangement. **Summer Rates:** single (1 bed) $35; double $45; pets free; taxes included. **Winter Rates:** $30 & $40. MasterCard & Visa. **Directions:** 17 miles east of Morton on Hwy 12, milepost 115.

$38-$48 **TALL TIMBER LODGE**, 10023 Hwy 12, Randle, WA 98377, phone 360-497-2991. One level motel with 6 basic sleeping rooms, no designated nonsmoking. All rooms have private facilities and cable TV. No coffee/tea making facilities in the rooms, but a restaurant on the premises opens at 6 a.m. Children free, pets allowed. **Rates:** single room $38; double room (2 beds) $43; family room $48; pets $10 per night; taxes included. MasterCard, Discover, & Visa. **Directions:** one mile east of Randle on Hwy 12.

•RAYMOND (pop. 2,890) is located in the southwest corner of Washington on coast Hwy 101, just inland from Willapa Bay.

Raymond and South Bend are lumber ports on the Willapa River. Raymond is the home of the largest area mural, an 85 foot-wide portrait of an old-time logger (5th & Raymond). Located in Pacific County the sales/use taxes are 7.8%.

$60 **BRACKETT'S LOG COTTAGE**, Rt 1 Box 140C, Raymond, WA 98577, phone 360-942-6111. One 2 bedroom cottage. One king bed, 2 queens, fully equipped kitchen, fireplace and electric heat. Full continental breakfast provided in the cottage. Located on 60 acres, herb gardens, catch and release fishing pond, and privacy. Children welcome, 1 small dog allowed. **Rates:** double occupancy $60; extra person $10, child $5. No credit cards. **Directions:** 5 minutes east of Raymond on Hunt Club Rd.

$36-$50 **MAUNU'S MOUNTCASTLE MOTEL**, 524 3rd St., Raymond, WA 98577, phone 360-942-5571 or 1-800-400-5571. 28 units, no nonsmoking. All rooms have phones, TV, and coffee/tea making facilities. Two rooms have equipped kitchens. Children 5 and under free, pets allowed. **Rates:** single (1 bed) $36-$44; double $50; extra person $4; pets $4; local phone calls free. Major credit cards. **Directions:** on Third Street downtown Raymond.

$69 **RIVERVIEW INN BED & BREAKFAST**, 544 Ballentine St., Raymond, WA 98577, phone 360-942-5271. Step back in time and enjoy the casual elegance of this 1908 home built by a lumber baron. Features include: a wrap-around porch, wainscotting in the elegant dining room, plate rails, leaded glass windows, antiques, and views of the Willapa River. Two nonsmoking rooms with shared facilities are available for adult guests. The spacious rooms feature queen beds and large picture windows with cozy window seats. A full gourmet breakfast is served in the formal dining room using china, crystal, and silver. Adults only, no pets. **Rates:** double occupancy $69. MasterCard & Visa. **Directions:** from Hwy 101 turn on Fowler St., go 1 block to Lincoln, turn right, go 1 block to Ballentine St., turn right again, at the crest of the hill.

REDMOND (pop. 38,500) is located 13 miles east of downtown Seattle.

Redmond is located at the northern end of Lake Sammamish. Often referred to as the "high tech capital of Washington" because of its computer software and peripheral equipment companies, Microsoft and Nintendo, plus bio-tech companies. Also known as the Bicycle Capital of the Northwest the community hosts major bike races throughout the year.

Located in King County the sales/use/ taxes are 8.2%. Lodging taxes of 2.8% apply to lodgings with 60 or more units for a total of 11%.

$65-$75 **COTTAGE CREEK MANOR BED & BREAKFAST**, 12525 Avondale Rd. NE, Redmond, WA 98052, phone 206-881-5606. An English Tudor manor surrounded by 3 1/2 acres that include wooded paths, wide lawns, flower garden, fish pond, and a creek where salmon spawn in the fall. There are two guest rooms on the 2nd floor with private facilities. One room has a view of the gardens, the other overlooks the creek. A generous continental breakfast is served on fine china. Children 12 and older, no pets, smoking outside in designated areas. **Rates:** double occupancy $65-$75 MasterCard & Visa, checks or cash preferred. **Directions:** go east on Hwy 520 until it ends in Redmond, where 520 becomes Avondale Rd., continue north for 3 miles, turn left into drive.

$70-$85 **REDMOND INN**, 17601 Redmond Way, Redmond, WA 98052, phone 206-883-4900 or 1-800-634-8080. This 3 story complex has 137 rooms, 75% nonsmoking. Choose either a room with a king bed or 2 queens. All rooms have phones, cable TV with Showtime, and AC. Four kitchenette suites are available. Outdoor pool, indoor spa. Children 18 and under free with parents, pets by arrangement. **Rates:** double occupancy (1bed) $75; double (2 beds) $70-$80; suites $75-$85; extra person $10. Major credit cards. **Directions:** from Sea Tac go north towards Seattle, take I-405 north towards Bellevue/Renton, 14 miles to Exit 14, Hwy 520, turn east, proceed 7 miles on 520 to the end, turn right.

SILVER CLOUD INN, 15304 NE 21st St., Redmond, WA 98052, phone 1-800-551-7207.

The *Spirit of Washington Dinner Train* , (1-800-876-7245), offers a 3 1/2 hour excursion that showcases the beauty of the Puget Sound region.

Located in King County the sales/use/ taxes are 8.2%. Lodging taxes of 2.8% apply to lodgings with 60 or more units for a total of 11%.

$90-$98 **HOLLY HEDGE HOUSE**, 908 Grant Ave. S., Renton, WA 98055, phone 206-226-2555. A private bed and breakfast with all the comforts of home in this one bedroom house meant for one or two people. A bountiful breakfast is provided for you to prepare in a well stocked kitchen. Whirlpool bathtub, 4 poster queen bed, videos, CDs, and a cozy fireplace. This quiet setting also offers a private hot tub and swimming pool in the back yard. Secured parking, adults only, no pets, and no smoking. Minutes away from Sea Tac airport or downtown Seattle. **Summer Rates:** *2 night minimum on weekends* - double occupancy $98; business rate, single $80; double $90. **Winter Rates:** $90. MasterCard, Amex, & Visa. **Directions:** southbound on I-405 take the Renton/Enumclaw Exit 4; north on I-405 take Exit 4B - follow Sunset Blvd. north, turn right on Bronson Way N., remain in left lane for 5 blocks, turn left onto Mill Ave. S., proceed 2 blocks, cross railroad tracks, turn left uphill, turn left on So. 7th, 1 block, turn right on Grant.

SILVER CLOUD INN, 1850 Maple Valley Hwy, Renton, WA 98055, phone 1-800-551-7207.

The TRAVELERS INN, 4710 Lake Washington Blvd. NE, Renton, WA 98056, phone 206-228-2858, fax 206-228-3055.

Surrounded by the Okanogan and Colville National Forests, Republic is nestled in a scenic valley between Sherman Pass and Wauconda Pass. The economy is based on agriculture, gold mining, and logging. The spectacular mountains ringing the town provide many opportunities for year-round outdoor recreation.

Located in Ferry County the sales/use taxes are 7.5%.

$35-$65 **COLLINS BLACK BEACH RESORT**, 848 Black Beach Rd., Republic, WA 99166, phone 509-775-3989. Located on Curlew Lake, this resort is *open from 4/01to 10/31,* motel units year-round. The 13 accommodations have fully equipped kitchens and TV. 6 cabins, 3 motel units, and 4 duplexes, no nonsmoking. Step out the front door to the lake and rent a rowboat, or bring your own. There is a small grocery store and gift shop on the premises. RV hookups, large grassy area, and boat launch. Children welcome, pets allowed. Rates based on unit. **Rates:** cabins (2-6 people) $35-$65; motel units $49-$59; extra person $5. MasterCard & Visa. **Directions:** 8 miles from Republic on W. Curlew Lake Rd.

$25-$65 **FISHERMAN'S COVE RESORT,** 1157 Fisherman's Cove Rd., Republic, WA 99166, phone & fax 509-775-3641. *Open year-round.* 37 waterfront acres on the northeast shore of Curlew Lake. This is one of the top fishing lakes in the state, featuring rainbow trout and large mouth bass. There are 16 cabins, 11 have private facilities and equipped kitchens. The other five have coffee/tea making facilities and share the community bathhouse. Restaurant, RV hookups, store, tackle, laundry, horseback rides, volleyball, boats, boat launch, free moorage, and swimming beach. Children free with parents, pets allowed if kept on a leash and cleaned up after. **Rates:** double occupancy $25-$65; extra person $5; pets $3. No credit cards. **Directions:** 11 miles north of Republic on the N.E. shore of Curlew Lake.

$36-$65 **FRONTIER INN,** 979 S. Clark, Republic, WA 99166, phone 509-775-3361. 33 rooms, 15 nonsmoking in this western style Inn with modern conveniences. TV, phones, sauna, suntan bed, AC, and jacuzzi. No coffee/tea making facilities in the rooms, but available in the lobby. The honeymoon suite has a heart-shaped jacuzzi for two. Children 10 and under free, pets allowed. **Rates:** single (1 bed) $36-$39; double room (2 beds) $45; suite $41-$65; extra person $4; pets $20 refundable deposit. Amex, MasterCard, & Visa. **Directions:** centrally located in downtown Republic on South Clark.

$36-$44 **KLONDIKE MOTEL,** 150 N. Clark, P. O. Box 614, Republic, WA 99166, phone 509-775-3555. 20 rooms, 11 nonsmoking, all on one level. Phones, TV, and 5 equipped kitchen units. No coffee/tea making facilities in the rooms, but available in the lobby.

Children 10 and under free, pets allowed with restrictions. **Rates:** single room $36-$42; double room $44. Amex, Discover, MasterCard, & Visa. **Directions:** in downtown Republic two blocks north of traffic light.

$50-$100 **PINE POINT RESORT**, 1060 Pine Point Rd., Republic, WA 99166, phone 509-775-3643. Located on Curlew Lake, this resort is *open from mid-April to October 31st*. There are 13 bungalows, no nonsmoking. All have equipped kitchens, electric heat, private facilities, picnic tables, spacious decks, and views of the lake. Two cottages sleep 4, five sleep 6, 4 cabins sleep 2, one large house sleeps 6, 2 three bedroom units sleep 12, and one mobile home sleeps 4. Country store, canoe, kayak, and paddleboat rentals. Roped-off swimming area, sandy beach, and the best fishing dock on the lake. Children welcome, pets allowed on a leash. **Rates:** cottages $55-$100; cabins $50; large house $100; mobile home $55; extra person $5. MasterCard & Visa. **Directions:** 10 miles north of Republic on Hwy 21, on the east shore of Curlew Lake.

$42-$112 **TIFFANYS RESORT**, 1026 Tiffany Rd., Republic, WA 99166, phone 509-775-3152. Located on Curlew Lake, this resort is *open from mid-April to October 31st*. There are 18 modern cabins with gas heat, gas ranges, fridge, private facilities, bedding, towels, dishes, and cooking utensils. Coin-operated laundry. The cabins vary in size and price, some have fireplaces and some have microwaves. Children 5 and under free; pets discouraged, but allowed if on a leash and cleaned up after. Store, sandy beach, swimming area, fishing and moorage docks. Boats and motors to rent, fishing tackle, propane, marine gas, and 14 RV hookups. **Rates:** 2 person cabins $42-$50; 4 person cabins $58-$71; 3 and 4 bedroom cabins (4 people) $107-$112; extra person $12; junior (5-15) $6. MasterCard & Visa. **Directions:** 12 miles north of Republic, on the west shore of Curlew Lake.

$10-$40 **TRIANGLE J RANCH HOSTEL**, 423 Old Kettle Falls Rd., Republic, WA 99166, phone 509-775-3933. Two bed and breakfast rooms are available in the main house, continental breakfast is provided. Hostel facilities include a four bed dormitory with cooking facilities, bathroom, and shower. Additional sleeping accommodations are available in the bunkhouse (no heat). Camping space is available next to the ranch gardens. Large outdoor pool, hot tub, and pool-side barbecue area. Library, VCR/TV, and pool table are in the recreation area in the main house. **Rates:** B&B single $30; double $40; hostel $10; camping $6, plus $2 for use of recreational facilities. No credit cards. **Directions:** from Republic take Hwy 20 east, turn left on Hwy 21 N., proceed 1/3 mile to Old Kettle Falls Rd. (Cooke Mt. Rd.), turn right, 1/3 mile on the left.

RICHLAND see Tri Cities.

RITZVILLE (pop. 1,725) is approximately 60 miles southwest of Spokane, just off I-90.

This friendly community has a rich pioneer heritage. The overall architecture of the historic district is essentially turn-of-the-century. The nine hole golf course is open from February through November.

Located in Adams County the sales/use taxes are 7.6%.

$38-$60 **COLWELL MOTOR INN**, 501 W. 1st, Ritzville, WA 99169, phone 509-659-1620, reservations 1-800-341-8000. 25 rooms, 12 nonsmoking, all on one level with parking at the door. Phones, TV, coffee/tea making facilities, exercise equipment, sauna, and guest laundry. Park-like area with outdoor barbecue. Children welcome, under 1 year old free, pets allowed. **Rates:** single room (1 bed) $38-$44; double room (2 beds) $46-$50; jacuzzi king suite $55; family suites $58-$60; extra person $4; pets $4 per night, $25 refundable deposit. Winter rates. Major credit cards. **Directions:** from I-90 take Exit 220 into town.

HERITAGE INN Best Western, 1405 Smitty Blvd., Ritzville,WA 99169 phone 509-659-1007 or 1-800-528-1234.

$59-$74 **The PORTICO VICTORIAN BED & BREAKFAST**, 502 S. Adams St., Ritzville, WA 99169, phone 509-659-0800. This stately, 1902 towered mansion has two premier guest rooms for discriminating bed and breakfast patrons. Amid rare and exquisite antiques, capture the richness and romance of the Victorian past. Includes sumptuous breakfast, private bath, parlor fireplace, and cable TV. Children must be well-behaved, no pets. **Rates:** double occupancy $59 & $74. MasterCard, Discover, & Visa. **Directions:** from I-90 take Ritzville Exit, follow Division St. to 5th, turn left, on the corner of 5th & Adams.

$31-$46 **WESTSIDE MOTEL**, 407 W. First, Ritzville, WA 99169, phone 509-659-1164 or 1-800-559-1164. 11 rooms, 5 nonsmoking. Phones, TV, and coffee/tea making facilities in the rooms. Walking distance to downtown. Quiet location, unique rooms. Children free with parents, pets allowed free. **Rates:** single (1 bed) $31-$36; double $38-$42; suite $46. MasterCard & Visa. **Directions:** from I-90 take Exit 220, proceed 3/4 mile to Westside Motel.

ROCKPORT is located on the North Cascades Highway (Hwy 20), between Concrete and Marblemount.

$43-$97 **CLARK'S SKAGIT RIVER CABINS,** 5675 Hwy 20, Rockport, WA 98283, phone 360-873-2250 or 1-800-273-2606, fax 360-873-4077. This family owned resort has 23 individual cabins, all with private facilities. Eight "theme cabins" have fireplaces, kitchens, decks, and mountain views. The "country cabins" have kitchens and 1-3 bedrooms. The "coffee bar" units have 1 bedroom, no kitchen. Restaurant, RV park, tent sites, and cabins are situated on 125 acres, 40 acres front the Skagit River. Trails lead to the river with bunnies everywhere. Children welcome, pets allowed, but must be on a leash. **Rates:** theme cabins $65-$97; country cabins $47-$59; coffee bar cabins $43-$49; children $6-$8; extra adult $9; pets $10 per night; taxes 7.6%. MasterCard, Discover, Amex, & Visa. **Directions:** on Hwy 20 - 2 1/2 miles west of Marblemount, between mile markers 103 & 104, 6 miles east of Rockport.

$54-$104 **ROSS LAKE RESORT,** Rockport, WA 98283, phone 206-386-4437. *Open June through October.* This secluded lodging is a floating resort accessible only by boat. The entire resort is situated in a line of 10 individual cabins and 3 bunkhouses built on log floats. There are 3 types of cabins, all have electricity and equipped kitchens, 11 have private facilities, and 2 have shared. The 8 modern cabins have large picture windows and spacious dining-living rooms. Two smaller cabins are more rustic and share a bathroom. Three bunkhouses are for parties of 6-10 people; private bathroom and bunk beds. The resort has a full service marina that rents boats, kayaks, and canoes. Bring provisions, there is no restaurant or store. Guests are transported to the resort by tugboat and truck. Children 3 and under free, pets discouraged. **Rates:** modern cabins, double occupancy $81, extra person $10; small cabins $54, extra person $6; bunkhouse 1-6 people $104, extra person $8; transport charges $10 per person round trip; taxes 7.5%. MasterCard & Visa. **Directions:** turn off I-5 at Burlington, drive 65 miles east to Diablo Dam, cross Diablo Dam, turn right, park at the Resort parking lot. Board the Seattle City Light tugboat at 8:30 a.m. or 3:00 p.m., it's a 25 minute boat ride.

Roslyn see Cle Elum for lodging.

Royal City see Othello for lodging.

SALKUM is located 12 miles east of I-5 on Hwy 12 en route to Mt. St. Helens and Mt. Rainier.

Two miles east of Salkum is Mayfield Lake, a destination for pleasure seekers enjoying all varieties of water sports and fishing.

Located in Lewis County the sales/use taxes are 7.6%.

$55-$70 **The SHEPHERD'S INN BED & BREAKFAST,** 168 Autumn Heights Dr., Salkum, WA 98582, phone 360-985-2434 or 1-800-985-2434. Located on the way to Mt. St. Helens and Mt. Rainier, this large country home overlooks the Cowlitz Valley and the rolling hills beyond. Five guest rooms, 3 with private facilities, and two with shared, feature king, queen, or twin beds. A two-person jacuzzi tub is available to the guests. Breakfast features house specialties like huckleberry crepes, homemade cinnamon rolls, and more. Children by arrangement, no pets, and no smoking. Horse and carriage rides to the Cowlitz River will soon be offered for a fee. **Rates:** $55-$70; extra person $15; rollaway $15. Off-season rates available. Amex, Discover, & personal checks. **Directions:** from I-5 take Exit 68, travel 13 miles east on Hwy 12, turn right on Fischer Rd., go 1/2 mile and turn left onto Autumn Hts. Dr., drive 1/2 mile into the woods, at the end of the road; from the west on Hwy 12 go 6 miles west of Mossyrock, turn left on Fischer Rd.

$26-$28 **WHITE SPOT MOTEL,** 2527 Hwy 12, P. O. Box 144, Salkum, WA 98582, phone 360-985-2737. This older motel and trailer camp is small and spotless. The 6 rooms have knotty pine accents and propane wall heaters. The TV reception is good, no phones or coffee/tea making facilities in the rooms. Four units have non-equipped kitchens. Well-behaved children welcome, pets with some restrictions. **Rates:** single room $26; double room $27; kitchen units $28. No credit cards. **Directions:** from I-5 take Exit 68, travel 13 miles east on Hwy 12.

SAN JUAN ISLANDS (pop. 11,300) are located in the northwest corner of the state. They are accessible by the state ferry system, boat, and plane.

Not to be confused with San Juan, Puerto Rico, this group of islands lies between Washington State and Vancouver Island. There are more than 170 islands total, named by Spanish explorers. Orcas, San Juan, Lopez, and Shaw are the largest islands. These four islands are accessible by the state ferry system from Anacortes. In the summer the popularity of the islands sometimes creates delays in boarding the ferry, so plan accordingly.

Bicycling has become a popular mode of touring the islands. By using this form of transportation, you are certain to get back on the ferry during the busy summer tourist season. Lopez is the flattest, most pastoral, and the easiest to ride for the whole family. Orcas Island is the hilliest; you need to be in pretty good shape to tour this island on a bicycle. Test your endurance on the climb up Mt. Constitution - what a trip down. San Juan Island is somewhere in between the extremes.

Lodging - There is a plethora of accommodation types: resorts, beach cabins, bed and breakfasts, lodges, hotels, villas, and inns. Reservations are necessary from May to September. During the "off-season" always inquire about the current rates, this is when to find the bargains (and less people!).

Directions from Seattle: drive north on I-5, Exit 230, follow Spur 20 west to Commercial Ave. in Anacortes, take a left on 12th St. at the San Juan Ferry sign, stay on this road about 3 miles until the next San Juan Ferry sign, turn right. Tell the ticket booth operator which island you are visiting.

Located in San Juan County the sales/use taxes are 7.5%.

LOPEZ

(pop. 1,486) in contrast to Orcas Island and San Juan, Lopez Island is more of a farming community. It does not have the deep sea harbors necessary to attract yachtsmen, but there are still sandy beaches to explore. This family-oriented island is a place to relax.

$79-$139 **ALECK BAY INN BED & BREAKFAST**, Rt. 1 Box 1920, Lopez, WA 98261, phone 360-468-3535, fax 360-468-3533. A romantic waterfront hideaway. There are 4 nonsmoking rooms, all with private facilities. Judging from the guest register, the hosts, May and Dave, make this more than just a bed and breakfast. Enjoy tea, espresso, and pastries on arrival. Indoor/outdoor jacuzzis, private beach, sun deck. The rooms contain small fireplaces, queen size beds, phones, and TV. Select among several entrees for your full breakfast - second helpings encouraged. Adults preferred, children by arrangement, no pets. **Rates:** double occupancy $79-$115; suite $139; extra person $20. Visa, Amex, Discover, & MasterCard. **Directions:** from the ferry landing, turn left, south on Ferry Rd., right on Center Rd. to the end, left on Mud Bay Rd., right to Alec Bay Rd., to Alec Lane.

$75-$140 **EDENWILD INN BED & BREAKFAST**, P. O. Box 271, Lopez, WA 98261, phone 360-468-3238. This nonsmoking Inn has 8 large guest rooms, all with private facilities. Some rooms have fireplaces; water and garden views. Full family style breakfast served in the summer, continental in the winter. Within walking distance of shops and restaurants. There is a restaurant at the Inn that serves dinner Tuesday - Sunday in the summer; Thursday, Friday, & Saturday in the winter. Shuttle provided to the ferry, seaplane, or airport. Children welcome, infants free, no pets. **Summer Rates:** double occupancy $100-$140; children 12 and under $15; extra person $25. **Winter Rates:** all rooms $75. Visa & MasterCard. **Directions:** from the ferry take Ferry Rd., this becomes Fisherman Bay Rd., make right on So. Lopez Rd. to Lopez Village.

$50-$75 **ISLAND FARMHOUSE**, Rt. 2 Box 3114, Lopez, WA 98261, phone 360-468-2864. This may be the "best deal" on the island. One guest room with a private entrance and 1 newly remodeled cabin. This active 12 acre farm is home to horses, cows, and chickens. A pond at the edge of the woods attracts wildlife. The guest room has a double bed and is decorated in cozy country. A coffee maker and refrigerator are provided. The cabin has a queen bed, TV, VCR, private bath, equipped kitchenette, and deck. Children welcome, no pets, and no smoking. **Rates:** guest room $50; cabin $75; extra person $5. No credit cards. **Directions:** from the ferry turn right on Ferry Rd., it turns into Fisherman Bay Rd., proceed to Hummel Lake Rd., go up a steep hill, first house on the right.

$55-$275 **ISLANDER LOPEZ MARINA RESORT**, P. O. Box 459, Lopez, WA 98261, phone 360-468-2233 or 1-800-736-3434, fax 360-468-3382. This two story lodge has 28 nonsmoking rooms, all with private facilities and cable TV. Coffee/tea making facilities are available in the "deluxe rooms". There is a restaurant and bar on the premises, plus a store, full marina, and gas. Outdoor pool and year-round jacuzzi. Children 16 and under free, no pets. **Summer Rates:** 5/25 to 9/30 - single room (1 queen bed) $80-$90; (1 king bed) $125; double (2 queen beds) $100; suite $220-$275; extra person $10. **Winter Rates:** single $55-$60; double queen $70; king $80; suites $170-$225. Major credit cards. **Directions:** from the ferry turn right on Ferry Rd., go to Fisherman Bay Rd., 5 miles from the ferry landing.

$49-$99 **LOPEZ LODGE**, P. O. Box 117, Lopez, WA 98261, phone 360-468-2500. Located in the heart of Lopez Village, the lodge is within easy walking distance of grocery store, restaurants, and shops. All three rooms are on the second floor and have water views. One unit has a fully equipped kitchen, two queen beds, and a private bath. The double room has 2 queen beds, and the other room has one queen bed. These two rooms share facilities. TV and coffee makers in all the rooms. Children welcome, no pets, and no smoking. **Summer Rates:** *4/01 to 10/14 first & second nights* - double occupancy, single room $69; double room/4 people $79; kitchen unit/4 people $99; all 3 rooms $229; extra person $10. **Winter Rates:** $49, $59, & $79. MasterCard & Visa. **Directions:** from the ferry take Ferry Rd., this turns into Fisherman Bay Rd., turn right on Weeks Rd., curve left at stop sign onto Lopez Road. The lodge is the back part of Lopez Plaza.

$69-$139 **MACKAYE HARBOR INN BED & BREAKFAST**, Rt. 1 Box 1940, Lopez, WA 98261, phone 360-468-2253. Originally built in 1904, the Inn was given a make-over in 1985 to restore it to its earlier charm. The Inn now offers five guest rooms with furnishings reminiscent of the past. Two suites with private facilities and three rooms share two and a half baths. The "harbor suite" has a fireplace, sunroom, and French doors leading to a deck. Mountain bike and kayak rentals are available with instruction. There is a view of the harbor from the parlor and 1/4 mile of sandy beach right out front. Full breakfast is served as well as snacks. Children over 9 years old welcome, no pets, no smoking. **Summer Rates:** *5/01 to 9/30* - double occupancy $89-$139; extra person $18. **Winter Rates:** $69-$119. MasterCard & Visa. **Directions:** from the ferry go south, turn left on Center Rd., Center Rd. becomes Mud Bay Rd., go 8 miles, turn right on MacKaye Harbor Rd., proceed to the water and Inn, at the end of the beach.

ORCAS ISLAND

(pop. 3,216) Shaped like a horseshoe, Orcas is the largest of the islands. It has the most shoreline and protected water. The major communities are Deer Harbor, Doe Bay, Eastsound, Olga, and Orcas. The most popular tourist attraction is probably Mt. Constitution in Moran State Park. The summit is 2,400 feet above the surrounding sea, and you can climb the rock tower for spectacular views of the other islands. Bicycling is very popular on Orcas, but the hills can be a challenge. Lopez is more for the average bicycler.

DEER HARBOR

$85-$95 **DEEP MEADOW FARM BED & BREAKFAST**, P. O. Box 321, Deer Harbor, WA 98243, phone 360-376-5866. The country setting of this 40 acre farm provides tranquility away from the main roads. There are two nonsmoking guest rooms upstairs with private facilities, furnished with antiques and iron double beds. Enjoy your morning coffee on the spacious front porch that extends around to the south. Soak in the hot tub after the days activities. Hearty "farm" breakfast with fresh fruits and vegetables grown on the farm. Children over 12, by arrangement only, no pets. **Rates**: *4/01 to 10/31 two night minimum stay -* double occupancy $95; *Nov. to March*, $85. No credit cards. **Directions:** from ferry turn left onto Horseshoe Hwy, go 2.4 miles to Deer Harbor Rd., turn left and continue past Crow Valley Rd. junction, 3 miles to Cormorant Bay Rd., turn right and go to green gate, go through the gate to the house. Park to the right of the garage.

Deep Meadow Farm Bed & Breakfast

$89 **DEER HARBOR INN**, P. O. Box 142, Deer Harbor, WA 98243, phone 360-376-4110. Situated on a knoll overlooking Deer Harbor, this modern log cabin has 8 quality, nonsmoking guest rooms with private facilities. There are two sitting/reading rooms and two view decks. The rooms have coffee/tea making facilities and are provided with a breakfast basket in the mornings. The restaurant is open for dinner May through October and features fresh seafood, steaks, and homemade bread. Adults only, no pets. **Rates**: double occupancy $89; extra person $15. MasterCard, Amex, & Visa. **Directions:** from ferry turn left, after 3 miles turn left on the paved road, after one more mile you will drive by West Sound, continue 4 miles. Check in at the office in the restaurant.

$60-$70 **PALMER'S CHART HOUSE,** Box 51, Deer Harbor, WA 98243, phone 360-376-4231. Two double, nonsmoking guest units (maximum four guests) with private bath, deck, and entrance. Coffee/tea making facilities in the rooms. Spacious deck overlooks the harbor. Many activities available: kayaking, sailing, biking, fishing, etc. Hosts - Don & Majean Palmer also offer day sails on their private yacht *"Amante"* for a minimal fee when the skipper is available. Full breakfast is included. No pets, but arrangements can be made at a local kennel. **Rates:** single (1 person) $60; double occupancy $70. No credit cards. **Directions:** take the state ferry from Anacortes to Orcas Island, follow the signs to Deer Harbor. The Deer Harbor upper road overlooks the harbor; a Chart House sign is on your right.

EASTSOUND

$39-$145 **BARTWOOD LODGE,** Rt. 2 Box 1040, Eastsound, WA 98245, phone 360-376-2242 or 376-2243. Located on the North Shore, this waterfront lodge has recently been remodeled. There are 16 units, 1 nonsmoking. All rooms have private bath and cable TV. There are 3 suites with fireplaces, wet bars, and water views. Guest facilities include beach access and tennis court. Bartholomew's Bar & Grill offers waterfront dining. Children welcome, no pets. **Summer Rates:** *5/01 to 9/15* - patio rooms $80; water view rooms $90; suites $125-$145; extra person, all ages $8. **Winter Rates:** $39, $49, & $79. MasterCard & Visa. **Directions:** exit the ferry to the left, follow signs to Eastsound, in the center of town turn left, and proceed for 1.5 miles north to the beach.

$90-$190 **BEACH HAVEN,** Enchanted Forest Rd. on Orcas Island, Rt. 1 Box 12, Eastsound, WA 98245, phone 360-376-2288. *Recommend reservations 1 month in advance.* Log cabins, modern apartment, or a large A-Frame to choose from. There are 1500 feet of private beach and an old growth forest on this 10 acre resort. 13 waterfront cabins with porch, picnic table, fully furnished kitchen, electric heat, and wood stove. Six cabins in the adult section of the resort include a honeymoon cabin. The honeymoon cabin has its own private beach, knotty pine and cedar interior, and skylights to look at the stars from the 4 poster bed. The lodge has 4 modern upstairs apartments with sliding glass doors onto a shared deck, adults only. The family section has two 3 and 4 bedroom cabins and sleeps from 2 to 10 people. Behind the family section is a large playground area. No phone or TV; a quiet, family resort. Boat rentals. Children welcome, no pets. *July & August one week minimum stay.* **Rates:** one bedroom cabin $90-$100; 2 bedroom cabin $110; 3 bedrooms

$135; A-Frame $190; extra person $10. Discount rates in January and February. Checks, Visa, & MasterCard. **Directions:** exit the ferry to the left, proceed 6.6 miles, go left on Crow Valley Rd. for 1/2 mile, go right on West Reach Rd., 1.5 miles to Beach Haven, signs on both sides of the road.

$65-$75   **JOY'S INN**, Rt. 1 Box 76, Eastsound, WA 98245, phone 360-376-4292. This modern farm house overlooks a private pond with ducks and 8.5 acres of pasture. There are two nonsmoking guest rooms with shared facilities. Common living room for guests with wood stove, kitchenette, deck, and barbecue. Children welcome, no pets. **Rates:** double occupancy $65-$75; extra person $10; taxes included. No credit cards. **Directions:** 7 miles north from the ferry landing, across the road from the end of the golf course.

$55-$110   **KANGAROO HOUSE BED & BREAKFAST**, Rt. 1 Box 76, Eastsound, WA 98245, phone & fax 360-376-2175. This stately home was once owned by a sea captain who returned from one of his voyages with a kangaroo. It didn't take the island children long to name it the Kangaroo House. There are 5 nonsmoking rooms available, two with private facilities and 3 with shared facilities. The house is surrounded by expansive decks adorned with wisteria, a large yard with numerous flowers, and herb gardens. Garden hot tub. Centrally located, within walking distance of village shops and restaurants in Eastsound. In winter, the large stone fireplace offers a cozy place to snuggle up and read a book. Full breakfast is provided. Children welcome, infants free, no pets. **Rates:** double occupancy $70-$110; extra person $20. **Winter Special:** *11/01 to 4/30* - Sunday to Thursday nights $55-$85. MasterCard & Visa. **Directions:** from the ferry, follow road signs to Eastsound, turn at the 2nd left, continue for 3/4 mile, B&B on the left.

$34-$120   **OUTLOOK INN**, P. O. Box 210, Eastsound, WA 98245, phone 360-376-2200 or 1-800-767-9506, fax 360-376-2256. Stroll to shopping from this cozy country inn. There are 42 rooms total, 27 have private facilities, 15 share facilities. The original, two story historic Inn, circa 1888, provides a charming Victorian conference/reception room, full restaurant and lounge, all the guest rooms are upstairs. Room #4 is a large room with queen bed, day bed, and private balcony. The east wing, completed in 1980, has private facilities, TV, and is furnished in the period style. One room in the east wing has a balcony and bay view. 16 suites are also available, check with staff regarding price. Children welcome in east wing and suites, no pets. **Summer Rates**: shared bath $74-$79; east wing with private baths $110-$120. **Winter Rates:** $34, $44, & $99. Visa, Amex, & MasterCard. **Directions:** from the ferry, turn left, follow signs to Eastsound, 8.5 miles, second building on the left.

$63-$220 **ROSARIO RESORT & SPA,** 1 Rosario Way, East-sound, WA 98245, phone 360-376-2222 or 1-800-562-8820. This premier resort offers more than guest rooms. The opulence would indicate this is not "affordable", but timing is everything. Discounted rates apply Sunday through Thursday in the spring 04/9-6/22 and fall 9/24-4/04. All 179 rooms have coffee makers and cable TV. Some rooms have refrigerators and there are 14 equipped kitchen units. Amenities include indoor pool, spa salon, 2 outdoor pools, full service marina, dining room, lounge, boutique, and group accommodations for up to 300 people. Children welcome, no pets. Friday night seafood buffet and Sunday champagne brunch. Shuttle provided to and from the ferry. **Summer Rates:** *6/23 to 9/23 and all weekends* - double occupancy $95-$220. **Discounted Rates:** $63-$145. Also, special packages are offered throughout the year. Major credit cards. **Directions:** exit the ferry to the left, follow Horseshoe Hwy through Eastsound to Rosario.

$70-$160 **TURTLEBACK FARM INN BED & BREAKFAST,** Rt. 1 Box 650, Eastsound, WA 98245, phone 360-376-4914. Seven rooms with individual charm, all are nonsmoking and have private facilities. No phones or TV to bother you. Full breakfast is served in the dining room or on the deck overlooking the valley. The farmhouse was originally constructed in the late 1800's and renovated in 1985. Children 8 and older by special arrangement, no pets. *Two night minimum stay May 1 through October 31, plus all weekends and holidays throughout the year.* **Summer Rates:** single room $70-$150; double room $80-$160; extra person $25. **Winter Rates:** *midweek only* - double $80-$110. Visa & MasterCard. **Directions:** 6 miles from the ferry landing, 4 miles from Eastsound on Crow Valley Road.

$80-$95 **WEST BEACH RESORT,** Rt. 1 Box 510, Eastsound, WA 98245, phone 360-376-2240, fax 360-376-4746. 15 beach cabins, 7 nonsmoking. All cabins have private facilities, equipped kitchens, and fireplaces/woodstoves. The beach is safe for children and great for exploring tide pools, beachcombing, or just relaxing in the evening with a spectacular sunset. Children welcome, pets allowed. Fish and crab off the dock, boat and kayak rentals, moorage and launch. Kayak tours, RV hookups, and tent sites. Shuttle provided to ferry and airport; restaurant within 5 minutes. **Summer Rates:** *6/18 to 9/23* - cabin, 4 people $95; extra person $15; pets $8. **Winter Rates:** *excluding holidays* - $80. Call for "winter specials". MasterCard & Visa. **Directions:** west side of Orcas Island. 3 miles west of Eastsound Village, at end of Enchanted Forest Road.

$65-$85   **The WHALE WATCH HOUSE,** P. O. Box 729, Eastsound, WA 98245, phone or fax 360-376-4793. The Whale Watch House offers one very large nonsmoking room with private facilities, cable TV, VCR, refrigerator, microwave, toaster oven, and coffee/tea making facilities. On the water facing the Canadian islands, deck, barbecue, and path to the beach. Continental breakfast is provided. Two miles to the nearest restaurant. Shuttle provided to the airport and ferry. Children - 1 only, no pets. **Summer Rates:** *2 day minimum stay* - double occupancy $85; extra person $10. **Winter Rates:** *9/15 to 5/15* - $65. No credit cards accepted. **Directions:** from ferry follow Horseshoe Hwy. to Eastsound, left on No. Beach Rd. to water, turn right on Sunset Ave. to "Whale Watch House".

OLGA

$15-$91   **DOE BAY VILLAGE RESORT,** St. Rt. Box 86, Olga, WA 98279, phone & fax 360-376-2291. This bohemian type resort offers a variety of lodgings: open air tree house, rustic cabins, tent cabins, and hostel. There are 22 rustic cabins, 10 with private facilities, 12 with shared. Enjoy the waterfront views overlooking Blakely and Cypress Islands. A turn-of-the-century general store and post office now house the Doe Bay Cafe, a natural foods restaurant, and the Doe Bay Store. Behind the building, deep-set Otter Cove provides exquisite views for diners, campers, and guests. Relax in the clothing optional, mineral springs hot tubs or sauna. Children welcome, pets discouraged. **Rates:** double room $41-$91; tent cabins $46; hostel bed $15; extra person $11; pets $10. Credit cards accepted. **Directions:** from the ferry follow Horseshoe Hwy. to Eastsound, continue through town, turn right and drive through Moran State Park, continue 5 miles past the park on the main road.

ORCAS

$50-$170   **ORCAS HOTEL BED & BREAKFAST,** P. O. Box 155, Orcas, WA 98280, phone 360-376-4300, fax 360-376-4399. Be one of the thousands of guests that have stayed at this historic hotel since 1904. The hotel sits on a knoll and greets visitors to the island as they leave the ferry. The hotel's 12 nonsmoking guest rooms have been furnished with a fascinating collection of antiques, books, curios, and island

Orcas Hotel

art. Three rooms have half baths, 7 have shared. The two jacuzzi suites have private facilities and feather beds. A full breakfast is included in the room rates. The Expresso Cafe is open for breakfast and lunch. Dining room and small lounge is on the main floor. Children by arrangement (must be quiet and mature), no pets. **Summer Rates:** double occupancy $69-$110; suites $170; extra person $15. **Winter Rates:** *10/01 to 6/15, excluding weekends and holidays* - rooms that range from $69-$110 will be offered at $50, suites $85, no breakfast included. Major credit cards. **Directions:** at the ferry landing.

$85-$140 **WINDSONG BED & BREAKFAST**, P. O. Box 32, Orcas, WA 98280, phone 360-376-2500, fax 360-376-4453. Built in 1917, the stately WindSong served as the original Westsound schoolhouse, then as the American Legion Hall. In 1981, it was refurbished as the first registered bed and breakfast on Orcas Island. Located on 3 acres of meadows and trees, the WindSong offers splendid tranquility. There are 4 guest rooms available. All rooms are spacious, have private baths, and their own seating areas. Outdoor hot tub. The noted 4 course breakfast may include poached pears in chardonnay, northwest eggs benedict with smoked salmon and chives hollandaise, plus homemade granola. Adults only, no pets. **Summer Rates:** double occupancy $115-$140; extra person $25. **Winter Rates:** *11/01 to 4/30* - $85-$95. MasterCard & Visa. **Directions:** from the ferry, go to the left, 2.5 miles north on Horseshoe Hwy., left on Deer Harbor Rd. to the first house on the left.

SAN JUAN

(pop. 4,962) is the most popular of the islands. The peak tourist season is in August and advance lodging reservations are essential. The hub of commerce and industry are in Friday Harbor, the county seat. This port is active all year with a multitude of pleasure and fishing boats. Cyclists enjoy the rolling roads through pasture lands, into the woods, breaking out to a magnificent view of the water. The roads have narrow shoulders, but traffic is respectful of the cyclist. It's a different attitude, life on the islands.

$55-$125 **BLAIR HOUSE BED & BREAKFAST INN**, 345 Blair Ave., Friday Harbor, WA 98250, phone 360-378-5907. Centrally located, just blocks from the ferry landing. This home, built in 1909, is surrounded by wooded and landscaped grounds. There are 7 guest rooms, one with private facilities, 2 with half bath, and 4 with shared. There is also one cottage with private facilities. Seasonal outdoor pool and year-round hot tub. Full breakfast is provided. The entire Inn is nonsmoking. Children over 12, pets and children of all ages acceptable in the cottage. **Summer Rates:** *6/01 to 10/15* - double occupancy, guest rooms $75-$95; cottage $125; extra person, 6 and older $20, ages one to five $10; pets free. **Winter Rates:** $55-$75 & $105. Major credit cards. **Directions:** from the ferry go up Spring St., third street on the right, 2nd house on the left.

$70-$95 **DUFFY HOUSE BED & BREAKFAST**, 760 Pear Point Rd., Friday Harbor, WA 98250 phone 360-378-5604 or 1-800-972-2089. Conveniently located on a scenic jogging and bicycling loop that begins and ends at the ferry terminal. This fully-restored, 1920's Tudor style home has 5 nonsmoking guest rooms, all with private facilities. A full breakfast, featuring freshly baked goods, is provided. The Duffy House has a commanding view of Griffin Bay and the Olympic Mountains. Each room is individually decorated. Children over 8, no pets. **Summer Rates:** *5/01 to 10/30, 2 night minimum on weekends in July and August* - double occupancy $80-$95; extra person $20. **Winter Rates:** $10 less. MasterCard & Visa. **Directions:** from the ferry go up Spring St., turn left on Argyle Ave., 1/2 mile to Pear Point Rd., turn left.

$60-$155 **FRIDAY'S**, 35 First St., Friday Harbor, WA 98250, phone 360-378-5848 or 1-800-352-2632. The restoration of this 1891, three story historic building is a visual work of art. There are 9 individually decorated rooms with an assortment of antiques, leaded glass, and wildlife art. Three have private facilities and 6 have shared. Some rooms have private decks and/or views of the harbor, 2 rooms have jacuzzi tubs, one room has a TV & VCR. Children in rooms with private facilities only, no pets. Continental breakfast is provided. **Summer Rates:** *5/01 to 10/30* - double occupancy $70-$155; extra person (all ages) $20. **Winter Rates:** $60-$125. MasterCard, Amex, & Visa. **Directions:** 2 blocks from the ferry, on 1st & West.

$65-$155 **HILLSIDE HOUSE BED & BREAKFAST,** 365 Carter, Friday Harbor, WA 98250, phone 360-378-4730 or 1-800-232-4730. This is a 4,000 square foot contemporary home with 7 distinctive guest rooms. Five rooms have private facilities and 2 have dedicated bathrooms across the hall. Most rooms have window seats with great views of the harbor, ferries, Mt. Baker, or the bird aviary. A full-flight bird aviary, stocked with exotic birds, is the focal point of the gardens. Full country-style breakfast. Children over 10, no pets, no smoking. **Summer Rates:** *6/01 to 10/15* - double occupancy $85-$155; extra person $25. **Winter Rates:** $20 less. MasterCard, Amex, & Visa. **Directions:** from the ferry go up Spring St. two blocks to 2nd, turn right, 1/2 mile to Carter Ave., turn right for one block.

$48-$125 **HOTEL DE HARO,** Roche Harbor Resort, P. O. Box 4001, Roche Harbor, WA 98250, phone 360-378-2155 or 1-800-451-8910. *Closed November 1 to March 15.* Situated beside a picturesque harbor, this hotel is 107 years old and has 4 types of rooms to choose from. The Standard Room - sleeping room with sink and shared bath; Harbor View Suites - double bed, small sitting room, and private bath; Bridal Suite - king bed, sitting room, verandah overlooking the harbor, and private bath; Presidential Suite - double bed, sitting room, verandah with harbor view, fireplace, and private bath. The resort offers a full service restaurant and lounge in the summer months, Olympic size pool, tennis courts, boat rentals, full service marina, general store, and post office. The hotel is nonsmoking, children okay, no pets. **High Season Rates:** *5/12 to 10/14* - double occupancy, standard room $70-$75; suites $100-$125; rollaways $7. **Low Season:** *3/16 to 05/11 & 10/15 to 11/01* - standard room $48; suites $80-$100. Amex, MasterCard, & Visa. **Directions:** from the ferry go up Spring St. to 2nd, turn right, 3/10ths of a mile to Tucker Ave., turn right, proceed for 9 miles.

$59-$188 **The INN AT FRIDAY HARBOR & The INN AT FRIDAY HARBOR SUITES,** 410 Spring St., Friday Harbor, WA 98250, phone 360-378-4351 or 1-800-752-5752, fax 360-378-5800. Located in the heart of Friday Harbor, the Inn has 72 rooms, 50% nonsmoking. In-room amenities include coffee/tea making facilities, remote control cable TV, and direct dial phones. Two units have equipped kitchens. Enjoy the heated indoor pool, sauna, exercise room, and jacuzzi. Courtesy shuttle to the airport or ferry terminal. Children 6 and under free, no pets. **The Inn Suites** is two blocks further up Spring St. These units are condo style with living rooms and kitchens. There are some 2 bedroom units and some units allow pets. **Summer Rates:** *5/01 to 9/30* - double occupancy

$75-$125; Inn Suites - studio $89; 1 bedroom $108; 2 bedroom $188; extra person $5. **Winter Rates:** $59; Inn Suites $69. Major credit cards. **Directions:** 4 blocks from the ferry, on Spring St.

$54-$125   **ISLAND LODGE**, 1016 Guard St., Friday Harbor, WA 98250, phone 360-378-2000 or 1-800-822-4753. Island Lodge is a balance between the village and the country with just the right amount of seclusion. 20 motel rooms and 8 apartment suites, 15 nonsmoking. All units have coffee/tea making facilities and TV, no phones. Eleven units have equipped kitchens. There is a spacious hot tub, cedar sauna, sundeck, barbecues, flower gardens, and two llamas that enjoy watching guests. Located just 3/4 mile from shops and restaurants. Children 12 and over welcome, no pets. **Summer Rates:** *5/25 to 9/30* - double occupancy $80-$85; suites $100-$125; extra person $4; kitchen units $4 more. **Fall Rates:** $60-$64. **Winter Rates:** $54. MasterCard, Visa, & Discover. **Directions:** from the ferry, on Spring St. turn right at the drug store on 2nd, this street becomes Guard at the high school, go three more blocks to the lodge.

Island Lodge

$80-$100   **The MEADOWS BED & BREAKFAST**, 1980 Cattle Point Rd., Friday Harbor, WA 98250, phone 360-378-4004. Quiet and relaxation are the keynotes here. There is one guest house with 2 large bedrooms, each with a queen and twin bed, one shared bathroom, wall to wall carpeting, and dressing rooms. A delicious home-baked breakfast is provided in the 1892 farmhouse. Mountain and water views. The Meadows is a no smoking area. Children over 10 by arrangement, no pets. **Rates:** *check regarding 2 night minimum from July through*

September - double occupancy $80; 3 people $100. Check or cash preferred; MasterCard & Visa accepted. **Directions:** from the ferry follow Spring St. for 1 mile, turn left on Mullis, (this becomes Cattle Point Rd.) continue for 2 miles.

$70-$105 **OLYMPIC LIGHTS BED & BREAKFAST,** 4531-A Cattle Point Rd., Friday Harbor, WA 98250, phone 360-378-3186, fax 360-378-2097. This 1895 Victorian farmhouse sits in an open meadow, and looks out to the sea and the Olympic mountain range. There are 5 nonsmoking rooms available. The four upstairs rooms all have queen beds with goose down comforters and share two full baths. The Garden Room on the main floor has a king bed and private bath. Full breakfast is provided. Children by special arrangement only, no pets. **Rates:** double occupancy $70-$85; suite $105. No credit cards. **Directions:** from the ferry follow Spring St. for 1 mile, turn left on Mullis, this becomes Cattle Point Rd., continue 5.5 miles to Olympic Lights.

$55-$65 **ORCINUS INN,** 3580 Beaverton Valley Rd., Friday Harbor, WA 98250, phone 360-378-4060. This rustic farmhouse, built in 1912, is surrounded by rolling hills and pasture land. There are 5 guest rooms, 2 with private facilities and 3 with shared. The Inn is oriented to divers, water sports enthusiasts, and cyclists. Special areas for soaking, rinsing, and handling scuba and water sports equipment. The lodge living room, with its large stone fireplace, is a place to gather and discuss events of the day, read, or relax. The decor is a mix of nautical and antiques. Nearest restaurant 3 1/2 miles. Coffee/tea provided in the lobby. Children welcome, pets by arrangement, no smoking. **Rates:** shared facilities $55; private facilities $60-$65; extra person $5-$10. MasterCard & Visa. **Directions:** from the ferry follow Spring to 2nd, turn right, 2nd turns into Beaverton Valley Rd., proceed past Egg Lake Rd. on the right.

$70-$135 **SAN JUAN INN BED & BREAKFAST,** 50 Spring St., P. O. Box 776, Friday Harbor, WA 98250, phone 360-378-2070 or 1-800-742-8210, fax 360-378-6437. The original hotel on the island opened in 1873 and has operated continuously as a hotel to this day. Centrally located just half a block from the ferry, the Inn is in the heart of the shopping district. There are 8 rooms and 2 suites, 3 have private facilities and 1 room has a half bath. One suite has a jacuzzi tub, fully equipped kitchen, TV, and hide-a-bed. Bicycle storage and spa in the back yard. Continental breakfast provided. **Summer Rates:** *5/01 to 10/15* - double occupancy $70-$95; suite $135. **Winter Rates:** 10-15% less. Major credit cards. **Directions:** from the ferry go 1/2 block up Spring St., on the right in the middle of the block.

$80-$175 **STATES INN BED & BREAKFAST**, 2039 West Valley Rd., Friday Harbor, WA 98250, phone 360-378-6240, fax 360-378-6241. The Inn is located on a 44 acre horse boarding ranch. The nine nonsmoking rooms are decorated with a slight flavor of each of the states for which they have been named. All rooms have private facilities. A full, hearty breakfast is served with menu changes on a daily basis. Children over 10, no pets. **Rates:** double occupancy $80-$110; family rooms & suites $95-$175. MasterCard & Visa. **Directions:** from the ferry go up Spring St. to 2nd, turn right, continue on this road for 7 miles, the B & B is one mile past British Camp.

Tower House Bed & Breakfast

$95-$115 **TOWER HOUSE BED & BREAKFAST**, 1230 Little Rd., Friday Harbor, WA 98250, phone 360-378-5464. This Queen Anne style home rests on ten acres overlooking the San Juan Valley. The Tower House features 2 suites with queen beds. Each room has a private bathroom and sitting area. A full breakfast is served in the formal dining room on china and crystal, dietary requests honored with advance notice. Adults only, no pets, and no smoking. **Rates:** double occupancy $95-$115. Amex, Discover, MasterCard, & Visa. **Directions:** from the ferry go up Spring St., continue on Spring/San Juan Valley Rd. to Douglas, turn left, corner of Douglas and Little, 3.5 miles from ferry.

$70-$100 **TRUMPETER INN BED & BREAKFAST**, 420 Trumpeter Way, Friday Harbor, WA 98250 phone & fax 360-378-3884 or 1-800-826-7926. Forests and rolling hills surround this pastoral estate. There are 5 nonsmoking guest rooms, all with private facilities. Gourmet farm-style breakfast. Children by arrangement, no pets. **Summer Rates:** double occupancy $90-$100; extra person $15. **Winter Rates:** *11/01 to 3/30* - $70-$80. MasterCard & Visa. **Directions:** from the ferry go up Spring St. continue for less than 2 miles, look for sign.

$90-$125 **TUCKER HOUSE BED & BREAKFAST**, 260 B St., Friday Harbor, WA 98250, phone 360-378-2783 or 1-800-965-0123, fax 360-378-6437. There are 2 guest rooms in this 1898 Victorian, both on the 2nd floor - share one bath. Three individual cottages are set up for 2 people. One has a woodstove and the other two have equipped kitchens. Full breakfast is provided. Children 5 and older in the house, all ages in the cottages, pets in the cottages only. Two blocks from the center of town. **Summer Rates:** *5/01 to 10/15* - guest rooms $90; cottages $105-$125; extra person $25; pets $15 per night. **Winter Rates:** 10-15% discount. Amex, Discover, MasterCard, & Visa. **Directions:** from the ferry go up Spring St., turn left on Harrison, go to B St., turn right.

$80-$85 **WHARFSIDE BED & BREAKFAST**, Port of Friday Harbor Marina, P. O. Box 1212, Friday Harbor, WA 98250, phone 360-378-5661. What could be more romantic or unique than a stateroom on a 60 foot yacht, the "Jacquelyn"?

Two staterooms are available. Forward stateroom features one double bed and two bunks, a shared head with tiled tub and shower, perfect for a family. Aft stateroom is the romantic, low-beamed, captain's cabin, complete with private entrance in the stern, queen bed, settee, private head and sink, shared shower. The rooms are equipped with electric heaters, and there is a fireplace in the salon. A full gourmet breakfast is prepared in the galley each morning. Parking is available at the head of the dock and deck space for safe bicycle stowage. Children welcome, pets allowed, smoking on deck only. *Two night minimum stay 6/01 to 9/30 and holiday weekends.* **Rates:** double occupancy $80-$85; extra person $10. MasterCard & Visa. **Directions:** leaving the ferry turn right, follow Front St. 2 blocks to Port of Friday Harbor, street turns into parking area. Take Main Dock to Slip K-13.

SEABECK is located on the eastern shore of Hood Canal, 18 miles northwest of Bremerton, and 9 miles west of Silverdale.

$79 **SUMMER SONG BED & BREAKFAST**, P. O. Box 82, Seabeck, WA 98380, phone 360-830-5089. One private, waterfront cottage completely furnished that will accommodate up to 4 guests. Features include: bath, bedroom, living room, dining room, kitchen, fireplace, private decks, gas barbecue, cable TV, and VCR. A gourmet breakfast featuring wild huckleberry pastry will be served on the beach or at your cottage. Boat launch one mile away. Children limited, pets by arrangement only, smoking allowed. **Rates:** double occupancy $79; extra person $10; taxes 8.1%. MasterCard & Visa. **Directions:** 2 miles from downtown Seabeck, directions given when reservations are made.

$63-$73 **WALTON HOUSE BED & BREAKFAST**, 12340 Seabeck Hwy NW, Seabeck, WA 98380, phone 360-830-4498. This three story country home was built in 1904 and is filled with antique family treasures. There are 2 guest rooms, both have private facilities. Rooms face the Hood Canal and have a magnificent view. The guest room on the 2nd floor has a second bedroom available. Full breakfast provided; ask about the "oyster breakfast". Children 15 and older, no pets, smoking outdoors. **Rates:** double occupancy $63-$73; taxes 8.1%. No credit cards. **Directions:** from Hwy 3 take Newberry Hill Rd. to Seabeck Hwy, turn right and proceed 3 miles.

•SEATTLE (pop. 518,000) is situated on the east shore of Puget Sound. I-5 runs through the center of Washington's largest city.

Known as the *Emerald City*, the city covers 92 square miles in the shape of an hourglass between Puget Sound's Elliott Bay on the west and Lake Washington on the east. Seattle-Tacoma International Airport (Sea Tac) is south of the city center. Downtown Seattle is a mixture of skyscrapers, historic cobblestone streets at Pike Place Market, and the new basket-weave streets of Westlake Center. Seattle has an abundance of interesting places to visit and explore, and the lodging choices are also varied and numerous. In this book, lodgings are grouped by area (north, central/downtown, and south). Reference the index for lodgings available in the vicinity of different hospitals and the University of Washington.

Located in King County the sales/use taxes are 8.2%. Lodging tax of 7% applies to 60 or more units, for a total of 15.2% taxes.

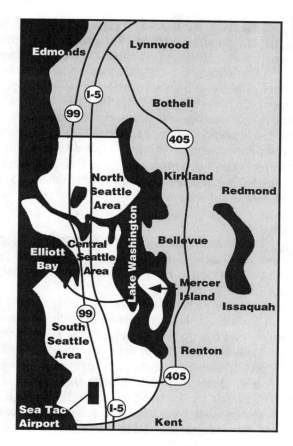

NORTH SEATTLE

Communities in North Seattle include: Ballard, Crown Hill, Greenwood, Lake City, North Gate, North Park, Ravenna, Sunset Hill, University, View Ridge, and Wallingford. Most lodgings are located either around the University of Washington or along Aurora Avenue.

$45-$65 **AURORA SEAFAIR INN,** 9100 Aurora Ave. N., Seattle, WA 98103, phone 206-522-3754, reservations 1-800-445-9297, fax 206-523-2272. 63 rooms, 24 nonsmoking. Phones and TV in all the rooms. Complimentary coffee in the lobby, no coffee/tea making facilities in the rooms. There are 27 non-equipped kitchen units. Children welcome, infants free, pets allowed. **Rates:** single room (1 bed) $45-$55; double room (2 beds) $52-$65; extra person $3-$5; pets $5; local phone calls free. Major credit cards. **Directions:** from I-5 take Exit 172 west to Hwy 99 (Aurora Ave.), turn right, proceed 6 blocks north.

$48-$78 **BLACK ANGUS MOTOR INN,** 12245 Aurora Ave. N., Seattle, WA 98133, phone 206-363-3035. 53 rooms, 50% nonsmoking. Phones and cable TV in all the rooms. Complimentary coffee in the lobby, no coffee/tea making facilities in the rooms. Seasonal outdoor pool. The adjacent restaurant and lounge is open for lunch and dinner. Children 18 and under free with parents, small dogs allowed in some rooms with deposit. **Summer Rates:** *6/01 to 9/15* - single (1 bed) $56; double (2 beds) $68; suite (3 beds) $78; local phone calls 30¢; pets $25 non-refundable deposit. **Winter Rates:** $48-$64. All major credit cards. **Directions:** from I-5 northbound take Exit 174 west to Hwy 99 (Aurora Ave.), turn left, proceed 2 blocks to 125th; southbound take Exit 175 west to Hwy 99, turn left, 1 mile to 125th.

$79-$105 **CHAMBERED NAUTILUS BED & BREAKFAST,** 5005 22nd Ave. NE, Seattle, WA 98105, phone 206-522-2536. Close to Children's Hospital, University Hospital, and within walking distance of the University of Washington. This 3 story Georgian Colonial home has 6 guest rooms, 4 with private facilities, and 2 with shared. Four rooms have porches. This is a relaxed family atmosphere with tons of books in the library and tea making facilities in the living room. All of the rooms are individually decorated with antiques and period furniture. Full breakfast provided. Children welcome with restrictions, no pets, and no smoking in the house. **Summer Rates:** *5/01 to 10/15* - double occupancy, shared facility $79; private facility $83-$105; extra person $15; local phone calls free. Winter rates available, check when making reservations. Most major credit cards. **Directions:** from I-5 take Exit 169, turn east on 50th, left on 20th Ave. NE, right on 54th, right on 22nd Ave. NE.

$39-$65 **The COLLEGE INN GUEST HOUSE**, 4000 University Way NE, Seattle, WA 98105, phone 206-633-4441. A European style bed & breakfast, housed in a 1909 Tudor style building, one block from the University of Washington campus. One hostel room with 3 beds and 25 guest rooms (with sinks) occupy the 2nd and 3rd floors; separate men's and women's bathrooms are in the hall. The office, sitting area, and TV area are on the fourth floor in a renovated attic. A generous breakfast is provided, with coffee and tea available all day. The rates are affordable to independent travelers who prefer value over an excess of luxury. Children 5 and under free, no pets. Parking is on the street or at the UW Visitors pay parking lot. **Rates:** single (1 twin) $39; double bed, 1 person $45, 2 people $55; suite (2 beds, 2 people) $65; extra person $5-$10; phone calls 25¢. MasterCard & Visa. **Directions:** from I-5 take the 45th St. Exit, east to 15th, turn right and go to 40th, take a right, in the first block.

CONTINENTAL PLAZA Best Western, 2500 Aurora Ave. N., Seattle, WA 98109, phone 206-6284-1900 or 1-800-528-1234, fax 206-283-5298.

$48-$85 **EMERALD INN**, 8512 Aurora Ave. N., Seattle, WA 98103, phone 206-522-5000. This 6 year old motel has 44 rooms, 25 nonsmoking. Phones and TV in all the rooms. Complimentary coffee in the lobby, no coffee/tea making facilities in the rooms. Six non-equipped kitchen units each have one bed. Within walking distance of restaurants. Children 12 and under free, pets by arrangement. On site security from 7:00 p.m. to 5:00 a.m. **Summer Rates:** *5/16 to 9/30* - single room $54-$58; double room $60-$66; suites $80-$85; kitchen units $6 extra; extra person $4; local phone calls free. **Winter Rates:** $48-$65. Major credit cards. **Directions:** from I-5 take Exit 172 west to Hwy 99 (Aurora Ave.), at the intersection of 85th and Aurora.

$74-$105 **MEANY TOWER HOTEL**, 4507 Brooklyn Ave. NE, Seattle, WA 98105, phone 206-634-2000 or 1-800-899-0251. Close to Children's Hospital, University Hospital, and within walking distance of the University of Washington. The tallest lodging in the University District has 15 floors with 155 rooms; 7 of the floors are nonsmoking. The corner rooms all have views of the mountains or Lake Union and the city. Phones and TV in all the rooms. Complimentary coffee in the lobby, no coffee/tea making facilities in the rooms. Restaurant/ lounge on the floor below the lobby, restaurant hours 6:30 a.m. to 10:00 p.m. Guest parking available, no charge. Children 14 and under free, no pets. Rates vary by room location. **Summer Rates:** *5/01 to 10/31* - double occupancy $88-$105; extra person $10; local phone calls 35¢. **Winter Rates:** $74-$84.

Major credit cards. **Directions:** from I-5 north take the 45th St. Exit, stay in the right lane, turn right on 45th, proceed to Brooklyn (6 blocks).

$39-$85 **QUEST INN, 14817 Aurora Ave. N., Seattle, WA 98133, phone 206-367-7880, fax 206-368-8839.** This new, clean motel was rebuilt in January of 1993. It has 29 rooms, 11 nonsmoking. Phones, refrigerators, and cable TV with HBO in all the rooms. Complimentary coffee in the office, no coffee/tea making facilities in the rooms. Restaurants within walking distance. 15-20 minutes from downtown. Children 5 and under free, no pets. **Summer Rates:** single room (1 bed) $45-$49; double room (2 beds) $55; jacuzzi suite $85; extra person $4; local phone calls free. **Winter Rates:** single $39-$42; double $52; suite $85. MasterCard, Discover, & Visa. **Directions:** from I-5 take Exit 174 west to Hwy 99 (Aurora Ave.), turn right, proceed north.

SEATTLE UNIVERSITY TRAVELODGE, 4725 25th Ave. NE, Seattle, WA 98105, phone 206-525-4612 or 1-800-578-7878, fax 206-524-9106.

$70-$104 **UNIVERSITY INN, 4140 Roosevelt Way NE, Seattle, WA 98105, phone 206-632-5055, reservations 1-800-733-3855, fax 206-547-4937.** Located adjacent to the University of Washington campus and less than 3 miles from downtown. There are 102 deluxe guest rooms, 90 nonsmoking. Phones and cable TV with Showtime in every room. Complimentary continental breakfast and newspaper in the lobby from 5 a.m. to 10 a.m. Coffee makers in 15 rooms and the coffee pot is on in the lobby 24 hours. Spa, fitness center, and year-round outdoor pool, restaurant, and two conference rooms. Children 18 and under free with parents, no pets. **Summer Rates:** *6/01 to 9/30* - single $74-$94; double $84-$104; local phone calls 25¢. **Winter Rates:** $4 less. Major credit cards. **Directions:** from I-5 take the 45th St. Exit, stay in the right lane, turn right on 45th, go to Roosevelt, turn right and go 3 blocks.

$55-$62 **UNIVERSITY MOTEL, 4731 12th Ave. NE, Seattle, WA 98105, phone 206-522-4724 or 1-800-522-4720.** Located in a quiet district, just 4 blocks to the University of Washington. This 3 story motel was built in 1962 and has 21 spacious suites, no designated nonsmoking. The rooms accommodate 1-7 people. Phones, TV, and 21 equipped kitchens. Guest laundry facilities and free parking garage. Children welcome, no pets. **Summer Rates:** *5/01 to 9/31* - single suite (1 bed) $59; double suite (2 beds) $62; extra person $6; local phone calls 25¢. **Winter Rates:** $55-$58. Major credit cards. **Directions:** from I-5 take the 50th St. Exit, stay in the right lane, turn right on 50th, proceed 5 blocks, turn right on 12th.

$84-$165 **UNIVERSITY PLAZA HOTEL**, 400 NE 45th St., Seattle, WA 98105, phone 206-634-0100, reservations 1-800-343-7040, fax 206-633-2743. Located just 8 blocks west of the University of Washington and adjacent to I-5. This 3 story motor hotel has 135 spacious rooms, 88 nonsmoking. Phones, cable TV, and some view rooms. There are coffee/tea making facilities in two king suites and room service is available. Excalibur's Restaurant on the main floor is open from 6:30 a.m. to 10:00 p.m. The lounge has nightly entertainment. Seasonal, heated swimming pool and fitness room. Banquet facilities for up to 300 people, hair salon, barber, and free on site parking. Children 12 and under free, pets allowed with deposit. **Summer Rates:** single room (1 bed) $92; double (2 beds) $96; suite $165; extra person $6; local phone calls 25¢. **Winter Rates:** $84, $90, & $165. Major credit cards. **Directions:** from I-5 northbound, take the 45th St. Exit, stay in the left lane, turn left on 45th, go across the freeway, on the corner.

UNIVERSITY SILVER CLOUD INN, 5036 25th Ave. NE, Seattle, WA 98105, phone 206-526-5200 or 1-800-551-7207.

CENTRAL SEATTLE

Communities in Central Seattle include: Beacon Hill, Capitol Hill, First Hill, Madrona, Magnolia, Mont Lake, Mt. Baker, and Queen Anne Hill.

The First Hill area is better known as "Pill Hill" due to the high density of medical facilities. In this area are Virginia Mason Medical Center, Swedish Hospital, Providence Hospital, Harbor View Medical Center, St. Cabrini Hospital, and the Fred Hutchinson Cancer Research Center.

$64-$125 **BACON MANSION BED & BREAKFAST**, 959 Broadway Ave. E., Seattle, WA 98102, 1-800-240-1864 or 206-329-1864. There are 9 spacious rooms in this Tudor style mansion. Seven have private facilities, 2 with shared. Phones and TV in all the rooms, some have equipped kitchenettes. Expanded continental breakfast provided. Children and pets by arrangement, no smoking. Located in an historic district of large homes, but still within walking distance of restaurants and shops. **Summer Rates:** 5/01 to 10/20 - double occupancy $74-$125; extra person $20; local phone calls free. **Off-season Rates:** $64-$125. Most major credit cards. **Directions:** northbound on I-5 take the Olive/Denny Exit to Broadway, turn left on Broadway, left on Prospect; southbound from I-5 take the Roanoke Exit, turn left over freeway, right at 10th, right on Prospect, follow Prospect west 1 block.

$47-$62   **BARONESS APARTMENT HOTEL,** 1005 Spring, Seattle, WA 98104, phone 206-624-0787. This ivy covered, brick complex, located on "pill hill", is a convenient and moderately priced lodging dedicated to out-patients and their visitors. There are a total of 58 units, no designated nonsmoking, but smoking is discouraged. 56 units have equipped kitchens. All rooms have TV and phones. Children by arrangement, no pets. Limited parking for a minimal fee. **Rates:** per night $47-$62; local phone calls 25¢; monthly rates available. MasterCard & Visa. **Directions:** from I-5 take the James/Madison St. Exit, follow Madison to Terry, turn left and go 1 block.

$75-$95   **BED & BREAKFAST AT MILDRED'S,** 1202 15th Ave. E., Seattle, WA 98112, phone 206-325-6072. Across the street from 44 acre Volunteer Park, this 100 year old Victorian with the wrap-around front porch is in the right neighborhood. There are 3 guest rooms on the 2nd floor, all with private facilities. TV in all the rooms. Phone and coffee/tea making facilities located just outside the door in the hall sitting area. Full breakfast provided. Shuttle to Sea Tac Airport. An electric trolley (no noise and no odor) stops at the front door. Fireplace and grand piano in the parlor. Children welcome, no pets, and no smoking. Parking on the side street. **Rates:** single room $75-$80; double room $85-$95; extra person $15; local phone calls free. MasterCard, Amex, & Visa. **Directions:** going north on I-5, Exit 166 (Olive Way), go 1 mile to 6th, turn left at stoplight, go 1 mile (north), large white house on the NE corner; going south on I-5, Exit 168A to light, turn left to 2nd stoplight, turn right to 2nd stoplight, turn left (E. Boston), follow arterial to park entrance, go 1 block.

$49-$139   **BEECH TREE MANOR BED & BREAKFAST,** 1405 Queen Anne Ave. N., Seattle, WA 98109, phone 206-281-7037. Located on historic Queen Anne Hill, minutes from the city center, restaurants, and opera. This turn-of-the-century mansion has six guest rooms on the 2nd floor, 3 with private facilities, 3 with shared. One suite on the 3rd floor sleeps up to 5 people. Scrumptious breakfasts - Virginia is chef-trained. Children welcome, pets by arrangement. Comfortable outdoor areas are provided for people who wish to smoke. On-street parking is usually available within a few steps of the Manor. **Rates:** single room (1 twin) $49; double room $59-$79; suite $95-$139. MasterCard & Visa. **Directions:** from downtown, follow 1st Ave. north to Roy St., turn left on Roy 1 block, right on Queen Anne, go up the hill, to corner of Lee.

$85-$165 **CAPITOL HILL INN BED & BREAKFAST**, 1713 Belmont Ave., Seattle, WA 98122, phone 206-323-1955. This 1903 Victorian has 6 guest rooms, 4 with private facilities, 2 with 1/2 baths and shared bathroom. Two of the rooms are double jacuzzi suites and called the "wild west rooms". Rooms are furnished with brass beds, down comforters, antiques, and chandeliers. Scrumptious full breakfast. Within walking distance of Convention Center, Broadway, and downtown. Children over 12, no pets. There are 3 off-street parking spots, occupied on a first come basis, other parking on the street. **Rates:** double occupancy $85-$115; suites $140-$165. MasterCard, Amex, & Visa. **Directions:** from I-5 take Exit 166 uphill, at 2nd light make a right on Bellevue, go 1 block, left on Olive, go 2 blocks, left on Belmont.

$79-$109 **CLAREMONT HOTEL**, 2000 4th Ave., Seattle, WA 98121, phone 206-448-8600 or 1-800-448-8601, fax 206-441-7140. This older hotel is centrally located downtown. 115 rooms, 75% nonsmoking. Phones and TV in all the rooms. Coffee pots in the rooms by request and half the rooms have small equipped kitchens. Parking available for a fee. Children 16 and under free with parents, no pets. Restaurant on the premises, Assaggio Ristorante. **Summer Rates:** 7/01 to 10/01 - standard room $79; double room or king bed $99; kitchen suite $109; extra person $10; parking $12 for 24 hours. Winter rates vary, midweek and weekends, check with desk. Major credit cards. **Directions:** downtown 4th & Stewart, park in front to check in.

$12-$49 **COMMODORE MOTOR HOTEL**, 2013 2nd Ave., Seattle, WA 98121, phone & fax 206-448-8868. Family owned and operated, this European style hotel has hostel accommodations for the value-minded traveler. Centrally located downtown, close to bus station and the Airporter. 100 rooms, no designated nonsmoking, 60 have private facilities, 40 with shared. Phones and TV in all the rooms. No coffee/tea making facilities in the rooms, but many restaurants are within walking distance, and there is a coffee machine in the lobby. Two hostel rooms, one male and one female, each have 4 beds. Guest laundry. Free covered parking available across the street. Children welcome, no pets. **Rates:** single room $27-$44; double room $31-$49; hostel beds $12; local phone calls 50¢. MasterCard, Amex, & Visa. **Directions:** downtown 2nd & Virginia - 6 blocks west, 2 blocks north of bus station.

$49-$89   **EASTLAKE INN,** 2215 Eastlake Ave., Seattle, WA 98102, phone 206-322-7726. This small motel has 12 nonsmoking rooms, some rooms have views of the Space Needle and Lake Union. All rooms have phones, basic cable TV, and non-equipped kitchens. Children welcome, pets by arrangement. **Summer Rates:** *Memorial Day through Labor Day* - single room $69; double $89; pets $10; local phone calls free. **Winter Rates:** single (1 bed) $49; double $69; weekly rates $250. MasterCard & Visa. **Directions:** northbound on I-5 take the Lakeview Exit, go under freeway to Lynn, turn left 2 blocks to Eastlake Ave., turn left.

$85-$180   **EXECUTIVE COURT SUITES,** 300 10th Ave., Seattle, WA 98122, phone 206-223-9300 or 1-800-906-6226, fax 206-233-0241. Located on "pill hill", this is a convenient lodging for out-patients or visitors. There are 76 fully equipped apartments, 30 nonsmoking. Units have phones, cable TV, washer/dryers, equipped kitchens, and microwaves. Daily maid service on short term stays, weekly on long term. Free, secure parking, shuttle provided to downtown Monday-Friday. Weekly and monthly rates. Children welcome, no pets. **Summer Rates:** studio, 1 & 2 bedrooms $130-$180; extra person $10; local phone calls 35¢. **Winter Rates:** $85-$145. Major credit cards. **Directions:** from I-5 take the James St. Exit, go up James to Broadway, turn right, one block to Jefferson, turn left, proceed 1 block to 10th Ave., turn right.

$68-$118   **GASLIGHT INN BED & BREAKFAST,** 1727 15th Ave., Seattle, WA 98122, phone 206-325-3654, fax 206-328-4803. This turn-of-the-century home has been restored to meet the needs of todays traveler. There are 15 rooms available, 12 with private facilities and three on the third floor share facilities. Nine of the guest rooms have double or queen beds, refrigerators, and TV. Six suites offer views, fireplaces, kitchens, and living rooms. Seasonal outdoor pool with several decks. Continental breakfast is provided in the dining room, or guests may choose to have it served in the privacy of their room. Located just a few blocks away from the bustle of Broadway with its popular night clubs, restaurants, and fine shops. Adults only, no pets. Eight off-street parking spots, 6 reserved for the suites. **Rates:** double room $68-$98; suites $88-$118; local phone calls free. MasterCard, Amex, & Visa. **Directions:** southbound on I-5 take the Olive/Denny Way Exit 166 toward Broadway to 15th, turn right and proceed to 1727. Northbound, take Exit 165, follow Madison to 15th.

$59-$140 **GEORGETOWN INN,** 6100 Corson Ave. S., Seattle, WA 98108, phone 206-762-2233, fax 206-763-6708. Close to Kingdome and downtown. New 52 unit, 3 story motel, 40 nonsmoking units. Phones and remote control cable TV in all the rooms. Six equipped kitchen units, microwaves available. Jacuzzi suites. Complimentary coffee in the lobby 24 hours, continental breakfast provided. Sauna, exercise room, and guest laundry. Children free, maximum of 2 per family, no pets. **Rates:** single room $59; double room $74-$77; kitchen units $82; suite $130-$140; local phone calls 25¢. Most major credit cards. **Directions:** from I-5 take Exit 162 to Michigan & Corson Ave.

$13-$40 **GREEN TORTOISE BACKPACKER'S GUEST HOUSE,** 715 2nd Ave. No., Seattle, WA 98109, phone 206-282-1222, fax 206-282-9075. Located 3 blocks from the Seattle Center and Space Needle. 17 rooms, 10 have private facilities, 7 share. Seven private rooms, 4 with private facilities, claw foot tubs or tiled showers. 10 hostel rooms sleep 6 people, 6 have private facilities. Three stories, nice view of the city, landscaped back yard area with vegie garden, picnic tables, and covered area. Laundry room in the basement, locked bicycle storage, 2 kitchens, library, and common rooms. All you can eat, cook-it-yourself breakfast of eggs, English muffins, and coffee/tea. Children under 7 allowed in the private rooms, smoking outside. Parking on the street, no problem in the evening, difficult during the day. **Rates:** private rooms (2 people) $30-$40; extra person $10; hostel rooms $13-$14 per person. MasterCard & Visa. **Directions:** from downtown, follow 4th Ave. north to Denny, turn left on Denny to 5th, turn right, proceed to Roy, turn left, continue to 2nd Ave. N., turn right.

$60-$95 **HILL HOUSE BED & BREAKFAST,** 1113 E. John St., Seattle, WA 98102, phone 206-720-7161 or 1-800-720-7161. Capitol Hill location, 2 1/2 blocks off Broadway for shops and restaurants. This 1903 Victorian home has recently been restored and decorated in a Victorian theme. There are 5 guest rooms, 3 with private facilities and 2 with shared. Two rooms have phones and TV. Full gourmet breakfast. Off-street parking for guests. This is a nonsmoking home, with no pets, and no children. **Summer Rates:** *5/01 to 10/12, 2 night minimum on weekends, 3 nights on holidays* - double occupancy, shared facilities $66-$75; private facilities $85-$95. **Winter Rates:** $60-$70 & $80-$90. Amex, Discover, MasterCard, & Visa. **Directions:** northbound from I-5 take the Olive/Denny Way Exit 166 toward Broadway for 8 blocks. Southbound, take Roanoke St. Exit, stay in left lane, cross bridge to 10th, turn right, 16 blocks to John St., turn left off Broadway.

$16-$19   **HOSTELLING INTERNATIONAL - SEATTLE,** 84 Union St., Seattle, WA 98101, phone 206-622-5443 or 1-800-444-6111, fax 206-682-2179. Centrally located downtown, walking tours available from the hostel. 140 beds in 23 rooms, family rooms available. All rooms have shared facilities. Guest amenities include baggage storage/lockers, bicycle storage, laundry facilities, fully equipped kitchen, and TV in the lounge. Half block to Metro bus stop; one block to Pike Place Market, waterfront, and art museum; 5 minutes to Pioneer Square and ferry terminal. Most major attractions provide discounts to Hostelling International members. **Rates:** dorm room $16 members; non-members $19; family room surcharge $5; local phone calls 25¢. JCB, MasterCard, & Visa. **Directions:** downtown, Union & Western.

$72-$76   **HOTEL SEATTLE,** 315 Seneca, Seattle, WA 98101, phone & fax 206-623-5110, 1-800-421-6662 (WA), 1-800-426-2439 (other). Centrally located downtown, this eleven story hotel has 81 rooms, 9 nonsmoking. Phones and TV in all the rooms. Restaurant and bar on the premises. Parking 1/2 block away in the Olympic Parking Garage. Children 12 and under free, no pets. **Rates:** double occupancy $72-$76; extra person $6; parking $12 for 24 hours; local phone calls 35¢. Major credit cards. **Directions:** northbound on I-5 take the Seneca St. Exit 2 blocks to Seneca and 4th; southbound take the 7th Ave./Union St. Exit, go to 5th, turn left 2 blocks to Seneca.

$55-$80   **INN AT QUEEN ANNE,** 505 First Ave. N., Seattle, WA 98109, phone 206-282-7357 or 1-800-952-5043. Located at the foot of Queen Ann Hill, across the street from the Seattle Center, Space Needle, and monorail. 50 rooms, 50% nonsmoking. The studios are fully furnished apartments with queen beds or queen and twin. Phones, cable TV, equipped kitchens, and microwaves. Maid service and laundry facilities. Parking is available at the Diamond Lot. Children welcome, no pets. **Summer Rates:** *5/15 to 9/15* - single (1 person) $70; double (2 people) $80; extra person $10; local phone calls 50¢. **Winter Rates:** $55 & $65. Diners Club, MasterCard, Amex, & Visa. **Directions:** from downtown, take 3rd, 4th, or 6th Avenues north to Denny Way, turn left onto Denny Way and right onto First Ave. N., on the northwest corner of First Ave. N. and Republican, just west of the Seattle Center.

$90-$200 **INN AT VIRGINIA MASON,** 1006 Spring, Seattle, WA 98104, phone 206-583-6453 or 1-800-283-6453, fax 206-223-7545. This 1920 European style building was remodeled in 1988. Located next to Virginia Mason Hospital and within easy walking distance of downtown, the area medical centers, and hospitals. There are 79 rooms available on 9 floors, one floor is a designated nonsmoking floor. No coffee/tea making facilities in the rooms, but available in the lobby. Restaurant and courtyard are on the premises. Parking available for a fee. Standard rooms have either twin beds or queen. There are a variety of suites to choose from, two with views of the city, and two with fireplaces. Children 18 and under free with parents, no pets. **Rates:** standard room $90-$110; suites $135-$200; parking $4-$5; local phone calls 35¢. Major credit cards. **Directions:** northbound on I-5 take the Madison St. Exit, right to Terry, turn left and go one block to Spring; southbound on I-5 take Stewart St. Exit, turn left onto Boren, then right onto Spring.

$50-$90 **KING'S INN,** 2106 5th Ave., Seattle, WA 98121, phone 206-441-8833 or 1-800-546-4760, fax 206-441-0730. Centrally located downtown, close to the financial district, restaurants, theaters, monorail, and shopping. 69 rooms, 24 nonsmoking. All rooms have phones, remote control cable TV with HBO, and coffee/tea making facilities. Free parking. Special "shopping package" offered periodically during the winter provides reduced rates. Children 18 and under free with parents, pets by arrangement. **Summer Rates:** 6/01 to 9/15 - single room (1 bed) $55 & $60; double (2 beds) $70-$90; extra person $5; local phone calls 30¢; parking free. **Winter Rates:** single $50-$55; double $65-$90. Major credit cards. **Directions:** downtown at 5th & Lenora.

$42-$80 **LA HACIENDA MOTEL,** 5414 1st Ave. S., Seattle, WA 98108, phone 206-762-2460, reservations only 1-800-553-7531. Located 2.8 miles from the Kingdome and Pioneer Square. 34 rooms, 7 nonsmoking. All rooms have phones and TV. There are 14 equipped kitchen units and two large family suites. A complimentary continental breakfast is available from 6 a.m. to 11 a.m. Children welcome for a fee, no pets. **Rates:** single room (1 bed) $42-$45; double room $57; suites $65-$80; extra person $10; local phone calls 25¢; parking free. Major credit cards. **Directions:** from I-5 take Exit 162, follow to light, turn right, follow to 4th Ave., turn right, go to Lucile St., turn left, go 3 blocks to 1st Ave.

$72-$105 **LOYAL INN Best Western**, 2301 8th, Seattle, WA 98121, phone 206-682-0200 or 1-800-528-1234, fax 206-467-8984. Within walking distance of the Seattle Center. Four stories, 91 rooms, 50% nonsmoking. Phones and TV in all the rooms. Morning coffee is provided in the lobby. There are 12 non-equipped kitchen units available with microwave, coffee pot, and wet bar. The jacuzzi and sauna are open 24 hours a day. Children 12 and under free; small, supervised pets allowed. **Rates:** single room (1 bed) $72-$90; double room (2 beds) $84-$84; deluxe king $88-$105; extra person $6; refrigerator $5; rollaway $8; crib $5; local phone calls 35¢. Discounts in off-season. Most major credit cards. **Directions:** southbound on I-5 take the Stewart/Denny Exit, right on Denny to 8th; northbound take Madison St. Exit, right on Madison to 8th, follow to Denny, take a left on Denny to 8th.

$34-$39 **The MOORE HOTEL**, 1926 2nd Ave., Seattle, WA 98101, phone 206-448-4851 or 1-800-421-5508. Located in the heart of downtown Seattle, this historic 1909 hotel has 135 large rooms, 12 nonsmoking. 50% have private facilities, 50% shared. Phones and TV in all the rooms. Restaurant, coffee shop, and bar on the premises. Budget rooms, no frills, and no air conditioning. Parking is not provided, but there are several pay parking lots in the area. Children 15 and under free with parents, no pets. **Rates:** single (1 person) $34; double $39; extra person $5; local phone calls 50¢. MasterCard & Visa. **Directions:** 1900 block of 2nd Ave. downtown; cross streets: Stewart to the south, Virginia to the north.

$45-$60 **O'BRIEN HAUS**, 2031 Dexter Ave. N., Seattle, WA 98109, phone 206-285-3144. Located 1.5 miles from downtown Seattle at the foot of Queen Anne Hill, the O'Brien Haus offers one spacious accommodation. A second story suite with a Lake Union view has a fully-equipped kitchen, living room, bath, private entrance, phone, TV, and access to laundry facilities. Breakfast provided is heart healthy and home style. Children welcome, no pets, and no smoking. Parking is on the street. **Rates:** one night $60; 2 nights $50 per night; 3 nights or more $45 per night; extra bed $5; local phone calls free. No credit cards. **Directions:** from I-5 take Exit 167 (Mercer St.), right on Fairview (1st light), left at next light (Valley St.), take a soft right at 2nd light onto Roy St., go 2 blocks, turn right onto Dexter, proceed 3/4 mile.

$77-$97   **PACIFIC PLAZA HOTEL,** 400 Spring St., Seattle, WA 98104, phone 206-623-3900 or 1-800-426-1165, fax 206-623-2059. In the heart of Seattle's business and financial districts and just blocks from the Convention Center. Within walking distance to shopping, Pike Place Market, Art Museum, theaters, and the waterfront.

This charming boutique hotel has 160 rooms, 71 nonsmoking. The tastefully decorated rooms all have phones and TV. A generous continental breakfast is provided in the breakfast lounge. Restaurant, coffee shop, and bar on the premises. Children free with parents, no pets. Parking at the Olympic Parking Garage for a fee. **Rates:** single/double occupancy 1 double bed $77; king bed $97; 2 double beds $87; queen bed $87; local phone calls 50¢; parking $10 for 24 hours. Major credit cards. **Directions:** from I-5 north take Union St. Exit, go straight on Union to 5th, turn left, go up 3 blocks; I-5 south, take Seneca St. Exit, go to 5th Ave., turn left, go up 3 blocks.

$60-$160   **PENSIONE NICHOLS BED & BREAKFAST,** 1923 1st Ave. #300, Seattle, WA 98101, phone 206-441-7125 or 1-800-440-7125. This European style brick building is just above Pike Place Market overlooking Elliott Bay. There are 12 rooms available; 2 suites with private facilities and 2 rooms with shared facilities are on the 2nd floor. 8 guest rooms on the 3rd floor share 3 baths. Continental breakfast is served in the dining room. Parking is not furnished, but there are many pay parking lots in the area. Restaurants within walking distance. Young children by arrangement, small dogs allowed, no smoking. **Rates:** single (1 person) $60; double $85; suite $160; extra person $15. Major credit cards. **Directions:** downtown between Virginia and Stewart, on 1st Ave.

$75-$110 **PRINCE OF WALES BED & BREAKFAST**, 133 13th Ave. E., Seattle, WA 98102, phone 206-325-9692 or 1-800-327-9692. This cozy 1903 Victorian offers charm and a friendly atmosphere in Seattle's lively Capitol Hill area. There are 4 guest rooms, all with private facilities. The Prince's Retreat, on the 3rd floor, has a private rooftop deck complete with telescope. Each room has individual, unique decor. The breakfasts are home-style and hearty. Within walking distance of restaurants and shopping. Bus stops at the door. Children over 3, no pets, smoking outdoors only. Three parking spaces available. **Summer Rates:** *5/01 to 10/01 two night minimum* - queen room $85; king room $90; suites $100-$110; extra person $15, children $5-$10. **Winter Rates:** $75-$100. MasterCard, Amex, & Visa. **Directions:** from I-5 take the Madison St. Exit, north to 12th Ave. E., right on John to 13th.

QUALITY INN, 2224 8th, Seattle, WA 98121, phone 206-624-6820 or 1-800-437-4867, fax 206-467-6926.

$60-$89 **QUEEN ANNE HILL BED & BREAKFAST**, 1835 7th Ave. W., Seattle, WA 98119, phone 206-284-9779. Perched on top of Queen Anne Hill, this 3 story B & B takes advantage of the panoramic views from a number of decks. The interior is adorned with art, antiques, and unique collectibles. 5 guest rooms are available, 1 with private facilities, and one queen bed room with a private deck. 4 rooms share 3 baths. Full breakfast is provided. Children 8 and older, no pets, and no smoking. House phone available and a TV is in the parlor. Summer weekends, two night minimum preferred. **Rates:** double occupancy, 2 rooms $89 each; other rooms $60-$79. MasterCard & Visa. **Directions:** from I-5 take Exit 167, left on Fairview, right on Denny, right on 1st Ave. N., left on Roy, right on Queen Ann, left on Galer, right on 7th Ave. W., 3 blocks to Howe. Corner of 7th & Howe.

$85-$105 **ROBERTA'S BED & BREAKFAST**, 1147 16th Ave. E., Seattle, WA 98112, phone 206-329-3326, fax 206-324-2149. This classic two story Victorian is located in the historic Capitol Hill neighborhood. Five guest rooms are available, 4 with private facilities. All rooms have queen-size beds. Guests may relax in the living room or on the wide, covered front porch. Hearty, homemade breakfast provided. Morning coffee/tea served to your door by request. Central location, next to Volunteer Park. **Rates:** double occupancy $85-$105. MasterCard & Visa. **Directions:** from I-5 northbound take Exit 166, follow

Olive to 15th, turn left, proceed to E. Prospect, turn right, proceed to 16th Ave. E., turn left. Southbound, take Exit 168A, go over freeway, turn right on 10th, turn left on E. Boston, follow to E. Highland, turn left to 16th, then right.

Roberta's Bed & Breakfast

$70-$105 **SALISBURY HOUSE BED & BREAKFAST**, 750 16th Ave. E., Seattle, WA 98112, phone 206-328-8682, fax 206-720-1019. Located on Capitol Hill close to Volunteer Park. Situated on a tree-lined residential street, this 1904 home has been renovated with comfort in mind. Four guest rooms on the 2nd floor are individually decorated and all have private facilities. Corner rooms have bay windows and views of the garden. The house has a wrap-around porch, large entry, library, living room, sun porch, and secluded garden. Full breakfast is served in the sunny dining room. Children over 12 welcome, no pets. Parking on the street. **Summer Rates:** *July/August two nignt minimum* - double occupancy $79-$105; extra person $15. **Spring & Fall:** *May/June & Sept. /Oct.* - $75-$97. **Winter Rates:** *11/01 to 4/30* - $70-$88. MasterCard, Amex, Diners, & Visa. **Directions:** from the north, take Exit 168A, turn left over the freeway to 10th Ave. E, turn right, proceed 1 mile to Aloha, turn left, continue to 16th; from the south, take Exit 164A, turn right on Madison, proceed to 15th Ave., turn left, continue 1 mile to Aloha, turn right and go 1 block.

$46-$78   **SEATTLE INN**, 225 Aurora Ave. No., Seattle, WA 98109, phone & fax 206-728-7666 or 1-800-255-7932. Located just 3 blocks east of the Space Needle. This 1950's motel is updating the 159 rooms. 105 of the rooms are now nonsmoking. All rooms have phones and TV. No coffee/tea making facilities in the rooms, but a continental breakfast is provided. Indoor pool, jacuzzi, game room with microwave, and sundeck with playground. Restaurants within walking distance. Children 15 and under free with parents, pets allowed. Two parking garages. **Summer Rates:** *5/01 to 9/30 2 night minimum on 3 day holidays* - double occupancy, single room (1 bed) $56-$68; 2 beds $59-$78; extra person $6; local phone calls 50¢; parking free. **Winter Rates:** single (1 bed) $46-$62; double $46-$68. Major credit cards. **Directions:** from I-5 northbound take Exit 167 (Mercer St.), stay in the left lane, turn left onto Fairview Ave., go 5 blocks, turn right onto Denny Way. At 6th Ave. turn right, go 1 block to John St., turn right again, entrance is on the left.

$69-$115   **SHAFER-BAILLIE MANSION**, 907 14th Ave. E., Seattle, WA 98112, phone 206-322-4654 or 1-800-922-4654, fax 206-329-4654. Located on "Old Millionaire's Row" a block away from Volunteer Park. Ornate woodwork, chandeliers, and large windows adorn the 3 floors of this mansion. A total of 13 nonsmoking guest rooms, 11 have private facilities and refrigerators. Three rooms on the third floor share facilities. One central suite has a private balcony, and smoking is allowed outside. All rooms have TV, phones, and elegant antique/

Shafer-Baillie Mansion

Victorian furnishings. There are 5 rooms on the 2nd floor, 6 on the 3rd floor, and 2 studio apartments with equipped kitchens in the carriage house. Weddings and special parties fill the weekend calender for the main floor and lower level, but all is quiet by 11 p.m. Continental breakfast provided at 8:30 a.m., coffee earlier. Children welcome, pets by arrangement. Parking on the street. **Rates:** double occupancy $69-$115; extra person $15. Amex & Discover. **Directions:** from I-5 take Exit 168A, at the stop sign turn right, proceed to the next stop sign, turn left on Belmont, continue up to Broadway and Roy, turn left onto Roy, go 1 block, turn right on Aloha, continue to 14th, on the corner.

$80-$160 **SIXTH AVENUE INN,** 2000 6th, Seattle, WA 98121, phone 206-441-8300 or 1-800-648-6440, fax 206-441-9903. Centrally located downtown. Five stories, 166 rooms, 140 nonsmoking. Phones and TV in all the rooms. Restaurant, bar, and coffee shop on the premises. Room service is available starting at 7 a.m. Children 18 and under free with parents, no pets. Parking spaces for 80 vehicles on a first come basis. **Summer Rates:** *6/01 to 9/15* - double occupancy $96-$99; suite $160; extra person $12; local phone calls 50¢; parking free. **Winter Rates:** $80; suite $110. Major credit cards. **Directions:** from I-5 take the Stewart/Denny Exit, 6th and Virginia.

TRAVELODGE by the Space Needle, 200 6th Ave. N., Seattle, WA 98109, phone 206-441-7878 or 1-800-578-7878.

$55-$165 **TUGBOAT CHALLENGER,** 1001 Fairview Ave. N., Seattle, WA 98109, phone 206-340-1201, fax 206-621-9208. Two yachts and a 1944 tugboat have been converted to floating "bunk & breakfast" lodgings at the south end of Lake Union, The Challenger is fully equipped for both luxury and comfort. Of the 12 cabin rooms, 9 have

double beds and private facilities. Two bunk rooms have 2 beds and shared facilities. Main salon sitting area with TV, fireplace, and working bar that provides mixers, guests BYOB. There is a full buffet breakfast in a solarium that looks out over Lake Union. Rates are based on the room and view. Children 7 and up, no pets. Although popular with couples, guests who travel on business find this a relaxing home-like retreat. Valet free parking at the head of the dock. **Summer Rates:** *2 night minimum on weekends* - cabins with private facilities $90-$165; bunk rooms (shared facilities) $55 per person or $75 for two. MasterCard, Amex, & Visa. **Directions:** from I-5 take the Mercer St. Exit, stay in the right lane to Fairview, turn right, 3 blocks on the left.

WESTCOAST VANCE, 620 Stewart, Seattle, WA 98101, phone 206-441-4200 or 1-800-426-0670.

$85-$99 **WILLIAMS HOUSE BED & BREAKFAST,** 1505 Fourth Ave. N., Seattle, WA 98109, phone 206-285-0810 or 1-800-880-0810. Located atop historic Queen Anne Hill. Five guest rooms on the 2nd floor, 2 with private facilities, 2 with shared, 1 with 1/2 bath. Most rooms have views of Puget Sound, downtown skyline, and surrounding mountains. TV in the parlor, phone in the hallway. Decorated with antiques and Victorian furniture. Full "home away from home" breakfast. Children welcome by arrangement, no pets, limited smoking. Parking on the street. **Rates:** *2 night minimum* - shared facilities $85; private facilities $99; extra adult $10; small child $5. MasterCard & Visa. **Directions:** from I-5 follow signs to Seattle Center, turn right onto 5th Ave. N., go 6 blocks to Highland, left 2 blocks to stop sign, right onto 3rd Ave. N., 2 blocks to Galer, right 1 1/2 blocks to 4th Ave. N.

SOUTH SEATTLE

Communities in South Seattle include: Beverly Park, Boulevard Park, Burien, Columbia, Dunlap, Georgetown, Highland Park, Holly Park, Junction, Rainier Valley, South Park, West Seattle, White Center, and Youngstown. Cities included in the South Seattle listings are Sea Tac and Tukwila.

$60-$85 **AIRPORT PLAZA HOTEL,** 18601 Pacific Hwy S., Seattle, WA 98188, phone 206-433-0400 or 1-800-356-1000, fax 206-241-2222. 123 rooms, 63 nonsmoking. Phones and TV in all the rooms. In-room coffee service available upon request and provided in the lobby 24 hours. Shuttle provided to the airport. Restaurant, bar, and coffee shop on the premises. Guest laundry, men's and women's hair salon, meeting and banquet facilities, business services available. Children 12 and under free, small pets allowed at no charge. Ample parking. **Rates:**

single room $60; double room $65; suites start at $85; extra person $5; local phone calls 40¢. Major credit cards. **Directions:** from I-5 take Exit 152, west to 28th Ave. S., turn right, then take the 2nd entrance into Airport Plaza, follow signs to the front of the building.

COMFORT INN SEA TAC, 19333 International Blvd., Seattle, WA 98188, phone 206-878-1100 or 1-800-826-7875.

DAY'S INN SEA TAC AIRPORT, 19015 International Blvd., Seattle, WA 98188, phone 206-244-3600 or 1-800-DAYS-INN.

ECONO LODGE, 13910 International Blvd., Seattle, WA 98168, phone 206-244-0810 oe 1-800-446-6661.

HAMPTON INN HOTEL SEATTLE-AIRPORT, 19445 International Blvd., Seattle, WA 98188, phone 206-878-1700, reservations 1-800-HAMP-TON, fax 206-824-0720.

HERITAGE INN SEATTLE, 16838 International Blvd., Seattle WA 98188, phone 206-248-0901 or 1-800-845-2968, fax 206-242-3170.

HOLIDAY INN Boeing Field, 11244 International Blvd., Seattle, WA 98168, phone 206-762-0300 or 1-800-HOL-IDAY, fax 206-762-8306.

HOWARD JOHNSON, 20045 International Blvd., Seattle, WA 98198, phone 206-878-3310 or 1-800-USA-0202.

$38-$70   **JET INN MOTEL,** 3747 S. 142nd, Tukwila, WA 98188, phone 206-431-0085. Close to the airport, this two story motel is only 7 years old and very tidy. There are 32 rooms, 50% nonsmoking. All rooms have phones and TV, remote controls and refrigerators available. Morning coffee is available in the lobby. Children 5 and under free, no pets. **Summer Rates:** *6/01 to 10/01* - single room (1 bed) $55; double room $70; local phone calls 35¢. **Winter Rates:** single $38; double $55-$60. MasterCard, Amex, & Visa. **Directions:** from I-5 take Exit 151 west one mile to International Blvd., turn right, proceed to the Jet Inn.

LA QUINTA INN, 2824 S. 188th St., Seattle, WA 98188, phone 206-241-5211 or 1-800-531-5900.

QUALITY INN, 17101 International Blvd., Seattle, WA 98188, phone 206-246-7000 or 1-800-221-2222, fax 206-246-1715.

$36-$70 **SANDSTONE INN,** 19225 International Blvd., Seattle, WA 98188, phone 206-824-1350 or 1-800-223-4476. Close to Sea Tac Airport, and two blocks to an 18 hole golf course. The Inn has 98 rooms, 80 nonsmoking. All rooms have phones and TV. Kitchenettes available, cookware and dishes require a deposit. Morning coffee and pastries are available in the lobby at 5 a.m. A conference room and restaurant/lounge on the premises. "Park and fly package" provides 7 days of free parking with one nights lodging. 24 hour shuttle to Sea Tac Airport. Children 12 and under free, pets allowed by arrangement. **Rates:** single room $36-$48; double room $48-$58; suite $50-$70; extra person $5; local phone calls 40¢. Most major credit cards. **Directions:** from I-5 take Exit 152 west one mile to International Blvd., turn left, go 2 blocks, on the right side.

$39-$55 **SEA-TAC CREST MOTOR INN,** 18845 Pacific Hwy S., Seattle, WA 98188, phone 206-433-0999 or 1-800-554-0300, fax 206-248-7644. Close to Sea Tac Airport. 46 rooms, 40 nonsmoking. All rooms have phones and TV, some with remote control. No coffee/tea making facilities in the rooms, but complimentary coffee and donuts are available in the lobby. "Park and fly package" provides 7 days of free parking with one nights lodging. 24 hour shuttle to Sea Tac Airport. Children welcome, small pets allowed with deposit. **Rates:** single room $39-$45; double room $48-$55; rollaway $5; crib $4; refrigerator $5; local phone calls 25¢. Most major credit cards, no checks. **Directions:** from I-5 take Exit 152 west one mile to International Blvd., turn left, proceed for 1/2 block, on the right side.

SILVER CLOUD INN at Tukwila, 13050 48th Ave. S., Tukwila, WA 98168, phone 206-241-2200 or 1-800-551-7207, fax 206-246-0222.

TRAVELODGE SEA TAC NORTH, 14845 International Blvd., Seattle, WA 98168, phone 206-242-1777.

SEAVIEW see Long Beach Peninsula.

SEDRO WOOLLEY (pop. 6,550) is located on the Skagit River six miles east of I-5, just north of Mt. Vernon.

(SEE-droh-WOO-lee) Although the economic base has diversified over the years, timber-related industries are still major employers of many of the residents. Parks in the area are Riverfront Park, Memorial Park, Bingham Park, and Lion's Park.

$30-$42 **SKAGIT MOTEL,** 1977 Hwy 20, Sedro Woolley, WA 98284, phone 360-856-6001 or 1-800-582-9121. 47 units, 20 nonsmoking. Phones and TV in all the rooms. Complimentary coffee is available in the lobby. Restaurant next door. Children 12 and under free, small pets allowed. **Rates:** single room (1 bed) $30-$35; double room $42; extra person $5; pets $5; taxes 7.8%. MasterCard, Discover, Amex, & Visa. **Directions:** 4 miles east of Burlington on Hwy 20, 1 mile west of Sedro Woolley.

$54-$88 **THREE RIVERS INN,** 210 Ball St., Sedro Woolley, WA 98284, phone 360-855-2626 or 1-800-221-5122, fax 360-855-1333. Two story modern facility with 42 units, 20 nonsmoking. In-room movies and phones in all the rooms. The suites have a living room, 2 TVs, hide-a-bed, refrigerator, and coffee makers. Upstairs rooms have balconies and main floor rooms have patios. Complimentary coffee is available in the lobby. Outdoor heated pool and spa, restaurant/lounge, and banquet facilities. Continental breakfast provided at 6 a.m. Children 18 and under free with parents, pets allowed. **Summer Rates:** single room (1 bed) $54; double room $62; suite $88; extra person $6; pets $10 non-refundable deposit; taxes 7.8%. MasterCard, Discover, Amex, & Visa. **Directions:** from I-5 take the Cook Rd. Exit to the stoplight, turn left onto Hwy 20.

SEKIU is located in the northwest corner of Washington, 17 miles east of Neah Bay and 31 miles north of Forks.

(SEE-kyoo) is a small fishing village that attracts scuba divers, beachcombers, and people serious about sport fishing for salmon, bottom fish, and halibut.

Located in Clallam County the sales/use taxes are 7.9%.

$35-$49 **BAY MOTEL**, P. O. Box 10, Sekiu, WA 98381, phone 360-963-2444. Open year-round. Located on the Strait of Juan de Fuca, along the highway going into Sekiu. This motel has 16 rooms, 6 nonsmoking. Rooms have phones, TV, coffee/tea making facilities, equipped kitchens, and microwaves. Children free with parents, pets by arrangement. **Summer Rates:** single (1 person) $35; double occupancy $40; family room $49; extra person $5; pets $5. Major credit cards. **Directions:** 15562 Hwy 112 west.

$33-$70 **HERB'S MOTEL & CHARTERS**, P. O. Box 175, Sekiu, WA 98381, phone 360-963-2346. Open year-round. This motel has 12 rooms, no designated nonsmoking. Phones and TV. No coffee/tea making facilities, but 8 units have equipped kitchens. Some rooms have views of the Strait of Juan de Fuca. The motel is within easy walking distance of marinas and beach. Children welcome, pets by arrangement in designated rooms. **Rates:** single room $33; double room $40-$55; suite $65-$70; pets $10; local phone calls free. Amex, MasterCard, Discover, & Visa. **Directions:** located on the main waterfront road at the west end of Sekiu.

$50-$125 **VAN RIPER'S RESORT**, P. O. Box 246, Sekiu, WA 98381, phone 360-963-2334. *Open February through September.* This waterfront resort has 16 rooms, no nonsmoking. Six rooms have views of the Strait of Juan de Fuca. All rooms have cable TV and equipped kitchens, no phones in the rooms. One large family unit has 3 queen beds and 2 twin beds with living room and kitchen. The penthouse sleeps 6 comfortably. Children welcome, no pets. Prices are per individual unit. **Rates:** single room (1 bed) $50-$55; double room (2 beds) $55-$65; penthouse suite $75; family unit $125. MasterCard, Discover, & Visa. **Directions:** on Front and Rice streets.

SEQUIM (pop. 3,780) is located on the northern rim of the Olympic Peninsula in the Dungeness Valley.

(SKWIM) recreation includes year-round salt water fishing, hunting, beachcombing, golfing, and attending community concerts or the aquatic recreation center. Just north of Sequim is the Olympic Game Farm, a multi-acre complex that is home to movie star animals including bears, buffaloes, llamas, and others in a natural habitat.

Located in Clallam County the sales/use taxes are 7.9%.

$75-$90 **BRIGADOON BED & BREAKFAST,** 62 Balmoral Court, Sequim, WA 98382, phone 360-683-2255 or 1-800-397-2256. This 1920 farmhouse is tastefully decorated with English antiques. There are 3 guest rooms, all with private facilities. Two rooms have TV and there is also one in the parlor. Coffee/tea making facilities in one room. A full hearty breakfast is provided. Enjoy the garden spa after a day of fishing, golfing, or exploring the Dungeness Spit. Adults only, no pets, and no smoking. **Rates:** double occupancy $75-$90; extra person $20. No credit cards. **Directions:** go north on Sequim-Dungeness Way, past Sunland to Brigadoon Blvd., then turn left and make another immediate left at the mailbox.

$30-$75 **GRANNY SANDY'S ORCHARD BED & BREAKFAST**, 405 W. Spruce, Sequim, WA 98382, phone 360-683-5748 or 1-800-841-3347. This is a comfortable place that encourages guests to be at home. Coffee, tea, and ice are provided free. There are 5 rooms, 2 with private facilities and 3 with shared. All breakfasts are served family style - first one in chooses the menu item, 2nd one chooses the time to eat! This is a quiet location within walking distance of downtown. Well-behaved children welcome, no pets, and no smoking. **Summer Rates:** 5/15 to 9/30 - rooms with shared facilities $40-$55; private facilities $75; extra person $15. **Winter Rates:** $30-$45 & $65. MasterCard & Visa. **Directions:** go north on 4th from Hwy 101 for 2 blocks, corner of 4th & Spruce.

$52-$160 **GREYWOLF INN Bed & Breakfast**, 395 Keeler Rd., Sequim, WA 98382, phone 360-683-5889, fax 360-683-1487. Tucked between field and forest on a hilltop overlooking Sequim, Greywolf provides peaceful seclusion with easy access to all the attractions of the northern Olympic Peninsula. Six rooms all have private facilities. Each room is theme decorated, Bavaria to Japan, east meets west. Relax by the large fireplace in the sitting room or enjoy the Japanese style hot tub house in the enclosed courtyard. Full four course breakfast is served in the French country breakfast room. Gift shop with unique gifts and collectibles for wolf lovers. Children 12 and older welcome, no pets, and no smoking. **Summer Rates:** *6/15 to 9/15* - double occupancy $65-$110; suite $160; extra person $20. **Winter Rates:** $52-$98; suite $140. Major credit cards and personal checks. **Directions:** one mile east of Sequim, turn north on Keeler Rd., go 4/10 mile to the bottom of the hill, driveway on the left.

$59-$125 **MARGIE'S INN ON THE BAY BED & BREAKFAST**, 120 Forest Rd., Sequim, WA 98382, phone 360-683-7011 or 1-800-730-7011. A spacious, contemporary, ranch-style home, with 180 feet of water frontage on Sequim Bay. Within walking distance of John Wayne Marina. There are 5 guest rooms, all with private facilities. The deluxe room has its own private patio and the master suite has a fireplace. Panoramic views are enjoyed on the rear patios and breakfast room. A full breakfast is provided from an ever changing menu. Children 12 and older welcome, no pets, smoking outdoors. **Summer Rates:** *5/16 to 10/14* - double occupancy $69-$125; extra person $15. **Winter Rates:** $59-$114. MasterCard, Discover, & Visa. **Directions:** turn right off of Hwy 101 onto W. Sequim Bay Rd., go 2 miles, turn right on Forrest Rd.

$65 **RANCHO LAMRO BED & BREAKFAST**, 1734 Woodcock Rd., Sequim, WA 98382, phone 360-683-8133. Previously a working dairy farm, there are 2 guest rooms available with private facilities. The rooms "in the barn" are decorated with farm objects and artifacts. The Daisy Room has a queen bed, VCR/TV, kitchenette, woodstove, and patio. Lulabelle has twin beds, coffee/tea making facilities, and patio. Well-behaved children welcome, pets by arrangement, smoking outdoors. Continental breakfast provided. Antique and classic car collection tour available for interested people. Golf course across the road. **Rates:** double occupancy $65. No credit cards. **Directions:** turn right off Hwy 101 onto Sequim/Dungeness Way, follow to Woodcock, turn left.

$50-$100 **RED RANCH INN**, 830 W. Washington, Sequim, WA 98382, phone 360-683-4195 or 1-800-777-4195, fax 360-683-1546. This two story, country ranch style motel has 55 rooms, 19 nonsmoking. In-room amenities include extra big beds, direct dial phones, and cable TV. No coffee/tea making facilities in the rooms. There is a restaurant, coffee shop, and lounge on the premises. Children 12 and under free, small dogs by arrangement. Golf packages year-round. **Summer Rates:** *5/01 to 8/31* - single room (1 bed) $70; double room $80 suite $90-$100; pets $6; local phone calls free. **Off-Season:** single $50-$60; double $60-$70; suite $70-$90. Major credit cards. **Directions:** Hwy 101, west side of town.

$57-$135 **SEQUIM BAY LODGE Best Western,** 268522 Hwy 101 , Sequim, WA 98382, phone 360-683-0691 or 1-800-622-0691. This two story motel has 54 rooms, 21 nonsmoking. Phones, TV, and coffee/tea making facilities in all the rooms, some rooms have non-equipped kitchenettes. Suites have fireplaces, wet bars, and hot tubs. Restaurant, bar, and 9 hole putting course on the premises. A continental breakfast is provided in the winter when the restaurant is closed. Children 12 and under free, pets allowed. **Summer Rates:** *5/01 to 9/30* - single (1 person) $67; double (2 people) $77; suite $97-$135; extra person $6; local phone calls 35¢. **Winter Rates:** $57-$67; suites $87-$120. Major credit cards. **Directions:** on Hwy 101, east side of town.

SEQUIM ECONO LODGE, 801 E. Washington, Sequim, WA 98382, phone 360-683-7113 or 1-800-488-7113.

$52-$140 **SEQUIM WEST INN,** 740 W. Washington, Sequim, WA 98382, phone 360-683-4144 or 1-800-528-4527. This two story, New Orleans style lodging has 21 rooms, 16 nonsmoking, plus 13 fully equipped modular homes that sleep 4 to 6 people. In-room amenities include coffee/tea making facilities, microwave, fridge, hair dryer, phone, king or queen bed, and cable TV. Within walking distance of restaurants and shopping mall. RV park and facilities adjacent. Children 12 and under free, no pets. **Summer Rates:** *5/01 to 10/01* - single (1 bed) $64-$71; double (2 beds) $75; suite $95; modular homes $125-$140; first 6 local phone calls free. **Winter Rates:** single $52-$59; double $62; suite $72; modular homes $65-$85. MasterCard, Amex, Discover, & Visa. **Directions:** on Hwy 101, west side of town.

$70-$90 **SIMONE'S GROVELAND COTTAGE Bed & Breakfast Inn,** 4861 Sequim Dungeness Way, Sequim, WA 98382, phone 360-683-3565 or 1-800-879-8859. This turn-of-the-century Inn retains much of its original decor. There are 5 guest rooms, 3 with private facilities and 2 with shared. The rooms have king or queen beds, 3 have TV/VCR and the Secret Room, a detached cottage behind the Inn, has a small kitchen area. Morning newspaper and beverage is brought to your door prior to a complete and satisfying breakfast. Children

12 and older welcome, no pets, no smoking. **Rates:** double occupancy $70-$90; extra person $15. Major credit cards. **Directions:** turn right off of Hwy 101 onto Sequim Ave., this becomes Sequim Dungeness Way, 1/2 mile from the beach on the west side of the road.

$45-$80   **SUNDOWNER MOTEL**, 364 W. Washington, Sequim, WA 98382, phone 360-683-5532 or 1-800-325-6966. The two story units are 6-7 years old, and the older units towards the back are on one level but have been remodeled.   There are 34 units, 11 nonsmoking. Phone, cable TV with remote, and coffee/tea making facilities in all the rooms. Seven units have kitchens, with basic cookware and dishes available at the office.   Adjacent restaurant.   Near the Aquatic Center. Children welcome, small pets allowed. **Summer Rates:** *5/01 to 9/30* - single (1 bed) $59; double $69; suite $80; extra person $5; pets $4; local phone calls free. **Winter Rates:** $45-$75. Major credit cards. **Directions:** on Hwy 101, west side of town.

SHELTON (pop. 7,600) is located 20 miles north of Olympia on Hwy 101.

The area around Shelton has 44,000 acres of commercial Christmas trees. The timber industry has been the major source of employment in Shelton since 1850. For two days in October, the West Coast Oyster Shucking Championship and Seafood Festival gets underway with entertainment, exhibits, and all types of seafood.

Located in Mason County the sales/use taxes are 7.8%.

$34-$43   **CITY CENTER BEST RATES MOTEL**, 128 E. Alder, Shelton, WA 98584, phone 360-426-3397. Centrally located, this motel has 13 units, 3 nonsmoking. Rooms have queen, double, or twin beds and TV. No coffee/tea making facilities in the rooms. Children welcome, infants free, pets allowed. **Rates:** single room (1 person) $34-$38; double room $38-$43; crib $5; pets $8.   MasterCard & Visa. **Directions:** coming into town from the south, continue past the stoplight 2 blocks.

$38-$55   **HALLMARK MOTEL**, 628 Railroad Ave., Shelton, WA 98584, phone 360-426-4468 or 1-800-451-4560, fax 360-426-7927. This two story motel has 30 rooms, 60% nonsmoking. In-room amenities include phones, refrigerators, coffee/tea making facilities, and basic cable TV with HBO, some with remote controls. Coffee is also provided in the lobby and there are two equipped kitchen units. Seasonal outdoor pool, restaurant adjacent. Children 12 and under free, small house-pets allowed. **Summer Rates:** *6/01 to 10/31* - single room (1 bed) $40-$48; double room $50-$55; kitchen unit $46-$54; extra person $5; pets free. **Winter Rates:** $2-$3 less. Major credit cards. **Directions:** on the main street of town.

$55 **TWIN RIVER RANCH BED & BREAKFAST**, E. 5730 Hwy 3, Shelton, WA 98584, phone 360-426-1023. Located on a saltwater bay and stream, this 140 acre cattle ranch (Black Angus) has wildlife, woods, and picturesque old buildings. The old manor house is decorated with antiques and has 2 guest rooms with shared facilities. Full ranch style breakfast. Shuttle provided to Shelton, Olympia, or Bremerton. Adults only, no pets, and no smoking in the rooms. **Rates:** double occupancy $55. MasterCard & Visa. **Directions:** 5.7 miles north of Shelton on Hwy 3.

SILVER CREEK is located 14 miles east of I-5 on Hwy 12.

$35-$40 **LAKE MAYFIELD MOTEL**, 2911 Hwy 12, Silver Creek, WA 98585, phone 360-985-2484. Close to fishing on the Cowlitz River, boating and swimming in Lake Mayfield and Riffe Lake. This motel has 8 units, no designated nonsmoking. Phone in the office, TV in the rooms. Restaurant on the grounds for morning coffee. Children welcome, pets allowed. **Rates:** single room (1 bed) $35; double room (2 beds) $40; extra person $5; pets free; taxes 7.6%. MasterCard & Visa. **Directions:** 13 miles east of I-5, Exit 68 on Hwy 12, across from the Lake Mayfield Dam.

SILVER LAKE is located 5 miles east of I-5 on the Spirit Lake Hwy going to Mt. St. Helens.

$45-$75 **SILVER LAKE MOTEL & RESORT**, 3201 Spirit Lake Hwy, Silver Lake, WA 98645, phone 360-274-6141. This lakeside motel has 6 motel rooms, 5 cabins, RV park, and tent sites. The motel units are spacious with full kitchens, limited cookware, and TV. Fish from the balcony and enjoy the view of Mt. St. Helens. The waterfront cabins also have kitchens, no TV. Complimentary coffee available in the office/store. Many varieties of boats to rent, volleyball, horseshoes, convenience store, and tackle shop. Fish include large mouth bass, perch, and crappie. Children 5 and under free, pets allowed. **Rates:** motel units, single room (2 people) $65; double room (4 people) $75; cabins, 1 bedroom (2 people) $45; two bedroom (4-6 people) $75; taxes 9%. MasterCard, Discover, & Visa. **Directions:** 6.5 miles east of I-5, Exit 49.

Silver Lake Motel & Resort

SILVERDALE (pop. 13,000) is located on Dyes Inlet, north of Bremerton.

Silverdale is a modern day boom town due to the Navy's decision to build a base for Trident nuclear submarines at Bangor.

Located in Kitsap County the sales/use taxes are 8.1%.

$45-$55 **CIMARRON MOTEL,** 9734 Silverdale Way NW, Silverdale, WA 98383, phone 360-692-7777, fax 360-692-0961. Located in the city center, this motel has 63 units, 36 nonsmoking, and 9 equipped kitchen units. The rooms have recently been remodeled with all new furnishings. In-room amenities include phones, queen beds, and cable TV. Coffee and rolls are provided in the lobby. Children welcome, no pets. Kitsap Mall and waterfront are 2 blocks away. Many restaurants nearby. **Rates:** single room (1 bed) $45; double room $55; local phone calls free. Most major credit cards. **Directions:** go to city center.

$49-$66 **POPLAR'S MOTEL,** 9800 Silverdale Way NW, Silverdale, WA 98383, phone 360-692-6126, reservations 1-800-824-7517. This motel has 53 units, 36 nonsmoking. In-room amenities include phones, remote control cable TV, and VCR. Coffee is provided in the lobby. Other amenities include outdoor pool and spa. Restaurant adjacent. Children welcome, no pets. Kitsap Mall 1 block away. Three golf courses and a boat marina/beach are nearby. **Rates:** single room $49-$55; double room $66; extra person, all ages $9; local phone calls free. MasterCard, Diners Club, Amex, & Visa. **Directions:** city center.

SKYKOMISH (pop. 275) is located east of Seattle on Hwy 2.

(skeye-KOH-mish) is the closest lodging to the Stevens Pass ski area. This spectacular wilderness area offers hiking, fishing, river rafting, kayaking, biking, swimming, alpine skiing, and cross country skiing.

Located in King County the sales/use taxes are 8.2%. Lodgings with 60 or more units have a 2.8% lodging tax for a total of 11%.

$20-$32 **CASCADIA INN BED & BREAKFAST,** 210 Railroad Ave. E, Skykomish, WA 98288, phone 360-677-2356. This older hotel is downtown on the main street. The main floor has a restaurant and bar. The 2nd floor has 14 basic sleeping rooms, 1 with private facilities, 13 share 4 bathrooms, no designated nonsmoking rooms. Breakfast certificates of $5 for a single room, $10 for double, restaurant opens at 7 a.m. Children welcome, small pets allowed. 1/2 block from the river. **Rates:** single room $20; double room $32. MasterCard & Visa. **Directions:** from Hwy 2 turn into town, cross the bridge to the main street, turn left, at the end of the block.

$50-$90 **SKYRIVER INN,** P. O. Box 280, Skykomish, WA 98288-0280, phone 360-677-2261, reservations 1-800-367-8194 (WA). Perched on the bank of the Skykomish River, this family oriented motel offers 18 rooms. In-room amenities include king, queen, or double beds, refrigerator, coffee/tea making facilities, phones, AC, and TV. There are 4 equipped kitchenette units and 2 kitchens. Most rooms have a view of the Skykomish River. Many of the rooms have a sliding glass door that opens to the river's grassy bank. There is also a spacious deck and picnic area. Children welcome, well-mannered family pets allowed. **Winter Rates:** *11/01 to 2/28* - single room $55-$58; double room $70; family apartment $90; extra person $3; pets $3; kitchen units $6 extra. **Summer Rates:** $5 less. MasterCard, Discover, & Visa. **Directions:** from Hwy 2 turn into town, cross the bridge, take a left at the end of the bridge.

SNOHOMISH (pop. 6,550) is located about 7 miles east of Everett.

(snoh-HOH-mish) the "Antique Capitol of the Northwest" has 250 antique dealers and other shops for antique hunters. Many homes are on the National Historic Register. Tour the Victorian homes on Avenues A-E. The Snohomish-to-Everett 5 mile bicycle route covers flat terrain, with moderate traffic, good visibility, varied landscapes, and pleasing river views.

Located in Snohomish County the sales/use/lodging taxes are 10.2%.

$40-$65 **CABBAGE PATCH BED & BREAKFAST,** 111 Ave. A, Snohomish, WA 98290, phone 360-568-9091 or 1-800-290-9091. This B & B has 3 nonsmoking guest rooms, one with private facilities and two with shared. TV in the parlor, restaurant and bar on the premises. Full breakfast provided. Within walking distance of antique stores and restaurants. Children welcome, small pets by special arrangement. **Rates:** shared facilities $40-$45; private facilities $65; children $5; extra person $10; taxes included. MasterCard & Visa. **Directions:** five miles east of Everett on Hwy 2.

$55-$65 **COUNTRYMAN BED & BREAKFAST**, 119 Cedar St., Snohomish, WA 98290, phone 360-568-9622 or 1-800-700-9622, fax 360-568-3422. This 1896 Queen Anne Victorian has three guest rooms with private baths. Your stay includes a full breakfast, your choice from the menu. Centrally located, 1/2 block to antique shops. Children 9 and under free, small pets by arrangement. **Rates:** single (1 person) $55; double $65; extra person $10; continental breakfast $5 less per person. Major credit cards. **Directions:** from Hwy 2 take the Snohomish Exit to 2nd St., turn left on Cedar.

$53-$80 **INN AT SNOHOMISH**, 323 Second St., Snohomish, WA 98290, phone 360-568-2208 or 1-800-548-9993, fax 360-568-6292. This new motel has 21 rooms, 14 nonsmoking. Phones, TV, two queen beds, and coffee/tea making facilities in the rooms. Refrigerators available. Access to public school swimming pool across the street. Restaurants within walking distance, maps in the rooms. Ample free parking. Honeymoon suite with 2 person jetted soaking tub. Children 18 and under free with parents, no pets. **Rates:** single (1 person) $53; double (2 people) $59; suite $80; extra person $5; fridge $5. MasterCard, Discover, & Visa. **Directions:** on Hwy 2 going towards Monroe, take the 88th St. Exit 1/2 mile to the motel.

SNOQUALMIE (pop. 1,500) is approximately 30 miles east of downtown Seattle and 3 miles north of North Bend.

(snoh-KWAHL-mee) Snoqualmie Falls is one of the most popular attractions in the state. The cascading falls, 100 feet higher than Niagara, may be viewed from a special observation deck overlooking the oldest hydroelectric plant in the Pacific Northwest.

Located in King County the sales/use taxes are 8.2%. Lodgings with 60 or more units have a 2.8% lodging tax for a total of 11%.

$65-$185 **RIVER INN SNOQUALMIE VALLEY**, 4548 Tolt River Rd., Carnation, WA 98014, phone 206-333-6000. This bed and breakfast country retreat is located on a secluded bend of the Tolt River, on seven lush acres. There are 6 rooms available, 4 nonsmoking; 4 suites with private facilities, 2 with shared. A European style, solar villa in a panoramic river setting with a wild bird sanctuary. Amenities include heated indoor pool, sauna, steamroom, soaking tub, and country breakfast. Two suites have equipped kitchenettes. Children and pets by arrangement. **Rates:** *midweek* - rooms $65-$95, suites $125-$155; *weekends* - rooms $75-$95, suites $155-$185; extra person $25. MasterCard, Discover, & Visa. **Directions:** from Carnation take Entwhistle St. east 2 miles, look for sign.

$75-$125 **The OLD HONEY FARM COUNTRY INN**, 8910 384th Ave. SE, Snoqualmie Falls, WA 98065, phone 206-888-9399 or 1-800-826-9077, fax 206-888-9399. In a pastoral setting with a full view of Mt. Si and the Cascades. The Inn features 10 rooms with private baths, 1 is wheelchair accessible. It is decorated in country style with a cozy fireplace area and outside deck. The Inn is open to the public for breakfast, lunch, and dinner. Brunch is offered Saturday and Sunday. Service bar and wine cellar are available. Guests are provided with a complimentary full breakfast. Children over 14 welcome, no pets, no smoking. Reservations are recommended. **Rates:** double occupancy $75-$125. MasterCard, Discover, & Visa. **Directions:** from I-90 Exit 27, go one mile downhill, take a sharp left at Snoqualmie sign onto 384th Ave. SE, go 1/2 mile; from North Bend westbound, take Exit 31 to the light, turn left and go up a long hill to Snoqualmie turnoff, right lane, from stop sign continue ahead on 384th for 1/2 mile.

SNOQUALMIE PASS

Snoqualmie Pass is at the summit of I-90 going over the Cascades.

Snoqualmie Pass is best known as a ski area. It can be reached in less than 20 minutes from the town of Snoqualmie. Both alpine and cross country skiing are geared to all levels of ability.

$69-$89 **SUMMIT INN**, P. O. Box 163, Snoqualmie Pass, WA 98068, phone 206-434-6300. Located at the top of Snoqualmie Summit 47 miles from Seattle. The Inn has 82 rooms, 62 nonsmoking. Phones and cable TV in all the rooms. Two suites have coffee/tea making facilities, otherwise coffee is available in the lobby or restaurant. Outdoor pool, hot tub, sauna, and heated indoor pool open year-round. Ski storage, mountain bike storage, and guest laundry facilities. Children welcome, small pets allowed with deposit. **Spring/Fall Rates:** *04/01 to 05/31 & 9/01 to 10/31* - king bed $69; two queens $75; refundable pet deposit $200; rollaways $8; cribs $5; taxes 11%. **Summer Rates:** *6/01 to 8/31* - king $79; double queen $85. **Winter Rates:** *11/01 to 3/31* - king $69 midweek, $85 weekends; double queen $75 midweek, $89 weekends. MasterCard, Discover, Amex, & Visa. **Directions:** on I-90 at the top of the pass.

SOAP LAKE

(pop. 1,215) is centrally located, 120 miles west of Spokane and 180 miles east of Seattle.

Local Indians long ago named this area "Smokiam" which means "Healing Water". Soap Lake's water contains 16 minerals. Bathing in the water is said to relieve arthritis, muscular pains, nervousness, and skin conditions such as psoriasis. The lake water is piped into many of the town's hotels and motels. When you're not soaking in the mineral water, take time for excellent fishing, hunting, or browsing in antique shops on the main street of town.

Located in Grant County the sales/use taxes are 7.5%.

$40-$105   **The INN AT SOAP LAKE**, 226 Main Ave. E., P. O. Box 98, Soap Lake, WA 98851, phone 509-246-1132 or 1-800-557-8514. This historic building was constructed in 1905 and completely restored in 1993. The exterior of the building is faced with round, water-worn stones which were exchanged by local farmers for stock in Jane's Soap Lake Product Co. The Inn is decorated in country Victorian and sits on beach front property in the heart of town. Guest accommodations include 17 rooms and 3 cottages, 11 nonsmoking. They are decorated with antiques, brass beds, and oversized soaking tubs with Soap Lake mineral water. All rooms have phones, remote cable TV, microwaves, and instant

coffee. The cottages sleep 6 and have fully equipped kitchens, fireplaces, and private patios. A bridal suite is tucked away on the upper level and has a fresh water jacuzzi tub for two. Children 5 and under free, no pets. **Rates:** single room $40-$75; suite $95; cottage $105; extra person $7; local phone calls free. Discover, MasterCard, & Visa. **Directions:** in the center of town.

$38-$90 **NOTARAS LODGE**, 241 E. Main, P. O. Box 987, Soap Lake, WA 98851, phone 509-246-0462. Five large log buildings with 20 theme-decorated guest rooms, e.g. John Wayne, Chief Joseph, Norma Zimmer, etc., 3 are nonsmoking. All rooms have phones, cable TV, mineral water tubs, microwave, instant coffee, and small refrigerators. Restaurants within walking distance, one block to the beach. Children 5 and under free, pets allowed with a deposit. **Rates:** single room (1 person) $38; double (2 people) $45; jacuzzi suite $90; extra person $7; local phone calls 25¢; pet fee $10 per night, $50 deposit. MasterCard & Visa. **Directions:** downtown Soap Lake, one block west of Hwy 17.

$39-$45 **ROYAL VIEW MOTEL**, P. O. Box 968, Soap Lake, WA 98851, phone 509-246-1831. 16 units, 4 nonsmoking. All rooms have equipped kitchens and TV. Children welcome, small pets allowed. Located across the road from East Beach. **Rates:** double occupancy weekdays $39, weekends $45; children 12 and under $3; extra person $7. MasterCard & Visa. **Directions:** 436 4th.

$44 **TOLO VISTA MOTEL**, 22 Daisy N., P. O. Box 386, Soap Lake, WA 98851, phone 509-246-1512. Six cozy log cabins with knotty pine interior and screened porches. All cabins have equipped kitchens, TV, and mineral water tubs. Some microwaves available and 2 cottages have phones. Children 12 and under free, small pets allowed. **Rates:** double occupancy $44; extra person $5. MasterCard & Visa. **Directions:** Hwy 17, just past Main St.

SOUTH BEND (pop. 1,545) is located in the southwest corner of the state on coast Hwy 101.

This small community has one of the most prestigious court houses in the state; it is two blocks south of Hwy 101. The Willapa Bay Oyster Company sells fresh oysters at a very reasonable price.

Located in Pacific County the sales/use taxes are 7.8%.

$34-$44 **H & H MOTEL**, E. Water & Pennsylvania, South Bend, WA 98586, phone 360-875-5523. This basic motel has 16 units, 2 nonsmoking. TV in the rooms and two kitchen units available. No phones or coffee/tea making facilities, but there is a restaurant and bar on the premises. Children welcome, pets allowed. Shuttle provided to Raymond or Astoria. **Rates:** single room $34; double room $44. MasterCard & Visa. **Directions:** north end of town on Hwy 101.

$55-$70 **MARING'S COURTHOUSE HILL BED & BREAK-FAST,** 602 W. 2nd St., South Bend, WA 98586, phone 360-875-6519 or 1-800-875-6519. Your hosts - Ed & Frances Maring offer comfort and warm hospitality in this tastefully decorated home with views of the Willapa River, the wooded hills, and picturesque South Bend. There are 3 nonsmoking rooms, 1 spacious room on the main floor has private facilities and 2 on the 2nd floor share. Two rooms have queen beds and one room has twin beds, all rooms have TV. Full breakfast served. Adults only, no pets. **Rates:** double occupancy $55-$70; extra person $15. MasterCard & Visa. **Directions:** turn off Hwy 101 on Memorial Dr., proceed up the hill and follow signs, one block east of the historic Pacific County Courthouse.

$35-$48 **SEAQUEST MOTEL,** 801 W. 1st St., P. O. Box 309, South Bend, WA 98586, phone 360-875-5349. View of Willapa River and mountain range. 16 units, 2 nonsmoking available. Phones, TV, coffee/tea making facilities, and equipped kitchens. Hot tub. Excellent seafood restaurant within walking distance. Children 11 and under free, no pets. **Rates:** single room $35; double room $38; suite $48. MasterCard & Visa. **Directions:** turn off Hwy 101 at SeaFirst Bank, towards Pacific County Courthouse.

SPOKANE (pop. 178,500) is located 18 miles from the Idaho border and 110 miles south of the Canadian border.

(spoh-CAN) Spokane is known as the "Lilac City" and is the largest city in the Inland Northwest. Downtown Spokane has a unique skywalk system connecting the downtown businesses and shopping district. The Riverfront Park was the site of Expo '74 World's Fair. This 53 acre park has year-round events. The Centennial Trail is a paved trail designed for walking, jogging, or cycling; it extends from downtown to the Idaho border. Spring and early summer is the time to take the gondola ride over Spokane Falls or view the falls from the Monroe Street bridge. In the Spokane Valley, the Walk in the Wild Zoo provides homes for native and exotic animals on a 240 acre preserve.

Lodgings for Spokane are listed in five sections: north, downtown, south, east, and west. The airport is west of town.

Located in Spokane County the sales/use taxes are 8%. Lodging tax on 40 or more units is 2% for a total of 10%.

NORTH

$46-$71 **APPLE TREE INN MOTEL**, 9508 N. Division, Spokane, WA 99218, phone 509-466-3020, reservations 1-800-323-5796. This two story motel has 71 rooms, 45 nonsmoking. Phones, coffee/tea making facilities, and TV in all the rooms. Spacious two and three bedroom suites have fully equipped kitchens. The single units with mini-kitchens are not equipped with cookware or dishes. Outdoor pool. Children welcome, no pets. Located within walking distance of five restaurants and Rosauers Grocery. Close to Wandermere Golf Course and the Holy Family Hospital. **Rates:** single room, double occupancy $46; double room (2 beds) $56; suite (4 people) $71; local phone calls free. Most major credit cards. **Directions:** from I-90 take Division St. Exit, proceed for 8 miles, on the right.

$15-$40 **KIRK'S LODGE - MT. SPOKANE**, Rt. 1 Box 340, Mead, WA 99021, phone 509-238-9114. Lodging includes private rooms, dorm, RV hookups, and tent sites. There are 13 rooms, 2 with private facilities, that sleep 1-6 people; 4 rooms have 1/2 baths (toilet, sink, and shower across the hall); other rooms share 3 bathrooms with 2 showers. One dorm room, with full bath, sleeps up to 24 people. *Winter and spring open Wednesday thru Sunday.* Activities include: cross country skiing, snowmobiling, sledding, and innertubing. Snowmobile and xc ski rentals. Four miles away from the ski hill. *Summer and fall open Friday thru Sunday.* Activities include hiking, horseback riding, picnicking, and huckleberry picking. Restaurant on the premises. **Rates:** private rooms, 1-6 people $35-$40; dorm room, includes breakfast $15. Amex, Discover, MasterCard, & Visa. **Directions:** from I-90 take Division St. Exit, proceed toward Newport on Hwy 2, travel for 10.4 miles, turn right on Mt. Spokane Park Dr., continue on SR 206, 15 miles to the lodge.

$75-$98 **LOVE'S VICTORIAN BED & BREAKFAST**, N. 31317 Cedar Rd., Deer Park, WA 99006, phone 509-276-6939. This 1886 Victorian has 3 guest rooms, all with private facilities. TV and VCR in common area. A romantic getaway furnished with antiques. The turret suite has a balcony overlooking the pond and waterfall. A full breakfast is provided; cider in the evenings. Children and pets by arrangement. **Rates:** double occupancy $75; turret suite $98; extra person $10. MasterCard & Visa. **Directions:** provided with reservations.

$55-$75 **MARIANNA STOLTZ HOUSE BED & BREAKFAST**, 427 E. Indiana, Spokane, WA 99207, phone 509-483-4316 or 1-800-298-6587. Five blocks from Gonzaga University and 5 minutes from downtown Spokane. This classic, American foursquare home was built in 1908 and is listed on the Spokane register of historic homes. There are 4 guest rooms on the second floor, 2 with private facilities, 2 with shared. The rooms have king, queen, or single beds, family quilts, lace curtains, and TV. Full gourmet breakfast provided. Children by arrangement, no pets, smoking outside. **Rates:** single room $55-$65; double room $65-$75; extra person $10. Major credit cards. **Directions:** from I-90 take Exit 282 (Trent/Hamilton), go north to 4th traffic light, turn left on Indiana, go 5 blocks.

QUALITY INN, Oakwood, N. 7919 Division, Spokane, WA 99208, phone 509-467-4900, reservations 1-800-221-2222.

$38-$69 **ROYAL SCOT MOTEL**, W. 20 Houston, Spokane, WA 99208, phone 509-467-6672. Close to Holy Family Hospital and VA Hospital. This 2 story motel has 39 rooms, 26 nonsmoking. Phones and cable TV with HBO in every room. No coffee/tea making facilities in the rooms, but coffee is available in the lobby. Outdoor pool. Children welcome, no pets. **Rates:** single bed $38-$65; double bed $60-$69; extra person $5; local phone calls free. Major credit cards. **Directions:** from I-90 take Division St. Exit, go north on Division St. 4 miles, across from K-Mart.

$33-$38 **SHADOWS MOTEL & RV PARK**, 9025 N. Division, Spokane, WA 99218, phone 509-467-6951. This tidy motel has 12 rooms, 5 nonsmoking. In-room amenities include phones and cable TV. Within walking distance of restaurants. Children welcome, no pets. 40 RV sites available. **Rates:** single room $33; double room $38; local phone calls 25¢. MasterCard & Visa. **Directions:** from I-90 take Division St. Exit, proceed north on Division 5 miles, at the north Division "Y".

$60-$80 **WAVERLY PLACE BED & BREAKFAST**, W. 709 Waverly Pl., Spokane, WA 99205, phone 509-328-1856. This turn-of-the-century Queen Anne Victorian is across the street from Corbin Park. There are 4 guest rooms available, 1 with private facilities,

3 share two bathrooms. All rooms are on the 2nd floor. The main floor has two parlors, a fireplace, and a wrap-around verandah. Seasonal outdoor pool. A full breakfast and afternoon snacks are provided. Children welcome, no pets, smoking outside. **Rates:** double occupancy $60-$70; suite $80; extra person $15. Discover, MasterCard, Amex, & Visa. **Directions:** from I-90 take the Division St. Exit, follow Division St. to N. Foothills Dr., turn left, go to Washington, turn right, 2 blocks to Waverly Place, turn left.

DOWNTOWN

$30-$38   **CALKINS' CLINIC CENTER MOTEL,** S. 702 Mc-Clellan, Spokane, WA 99204, phone & fax 509-747-6081. Located in the heart of the hospital/medical district, just one block away from Sacred Heart Hospital and the Heart Institute. This motel has 31 rooms, no designated nonsmoking. The rooms were refurbished 4 years ago. In-room amenities include queen beds, phones, and remote control TV. Morning coffee is available at 6:00 a.m. **Rates:** single room (1 bed) $30-$32; double room $38; local phone calls 25¢. MasterCard, Amex, Discover, & Visa. **Directions:** from I-90 take Exit 281, follow the signs to Sacred Heart Hospital, up to 7th, turn right, go two blocks, then left on McClellan.

$59-$89   **The COBBLESTONE BED & BREAKFAST INN CAFE, S. 620 Washington, Spokane, WA 99204, phone 509-624-9735.** The Inn is near Sacred Heart Hospital, Deaconess Hospital, and many other professional offices. It was built in 1900. The Inn's architecture features a large granite block foundation, large front porch, detailed woodwork, parquet wood floors, and stained glass. There are 2 second floor guest rooms with private facilities and large bay windows. Common rooms include a spacious living room with TV and dining room. Nights lodging includes morning breakfast highlighted by fresh baked breads and pastries. Children 10 and under free, no pets, smoking on the front porch only. **Rates:** single room (1 bed) $59-$69; double room $79-$89; extra person $10. MasterCard & Visa. **Directions:** from I-90 take Exit 281 south to 7th, turn right, proceed 4 blocks to Washington.

$70-$85   **FOTHERINGHAM HOUSE BED & BREAKFAST, 2128 W. 2nd Ave., Spokane, WA 99204, phone 509-838-1891, fax 509-838-1807.** Built in 1891, this was the original home of the first mayor of Spokane. Located in the historic Browne's Edition next to Patsy Clark's Restaurant. The current owners have worked hard for two years to completely restore this great old house inside and out, which earned them the 1994 residential historic preservation award. There are three guest rooms, 1 with private facilities, 2 with shared. The second floor has an area to conduct business - phone, fax, and work area. Guests in the rooms that share one large bath are furnished with robes. Full breakfast with menu changing daily. Children 13 and older, no pets, smoking on the verandah only. **Rates:** double occupancy $70-$85. MasterCard & Visa. **Directions:** from I-90 take Exit 280 north 3 blocks to 2nd, turn left, stay in the right lane, proceed to 2128 W. 2nd Ave.

Fotheringham House Bed & Breakfast

$34-$44 **SUNTREE 8 INN,** S. 123 Post, Spokane, WA 99204, phone 509-838-8504, reservations 1-800-888-6630. This 3 story motor inn has 47 rooms, 31 nonsmoking. All rooms have outside entrances, phones, and remote control cable TV. Morning coffee is available with a continental breakfast in the lobby. Other amenities include below ground parking and downtown location. Children 14 and under free with parents, pets allowed. **Rates:** double room $34-$44; local phone calls 35¢; pets $35 refundable deposit. Major credit cards. **Directions:** from I-90 take Lincoln St. Exit to 1st Ave., to Post.

THUNDERBIRD INN Best Western, W. 120 3rd, Spokane, WA 99204, phone 509-747-2011, reservations 1-800-57T-BIRD.

$40-$66 **TRADEWINDS Best Western,** W. 907 3rd., Spokane, WA 99204, phone 509-838-2091, reservations 1-800-586-5397. This 4 story motor inn has 59 rooms, 17 nonsmoking. In-room amenities include phones, coffee/tea making facilities, remote control cable TV with HBO and Showtime. Morning coffee is also available with a continental breakfast in the lobby. Other amenities include seasonal pool, year-round spa, rec room with pool table and weights. Located just 2 blocks from the Deaconess Hospital, 5 blocks from downtown and Shriner's Hospital, and 6 blocks from the park. Children 12 and under free, no pets. **Rates:** single room $40-$58; double room $45-$66; extra person $5; local phone calls free. Major credit cards. **Directions:** from the east on I-90 take the Lincoln Exit 280B, make a loop around the block to the left; from the west take Exit 280, left to 1st light (3rd Ave.), take a right and go 6 blocks.

$36-$52 **VALU-INN by Nendels,** W. 1420 2nd, Spokane, WA 99204, phone 509-838-2026, reservations 1-800-246-6835. 54 rooms, 34 nonsmoking. In-room amenities include phones, refrigerators, and cable TV/VCR. Morning coffee and rolls are available in the lobby. Other amenities include seasonal pool, 24 hour restaurant, and truck parking. Centrally located: 5 blocks to city center, close to Opera House, Coliseum, Convention Center, Riverfront Park, and hospitals. Children welcome, pets by arrangement. **Rates:** single room (1 bed) $36-$48; double room $42-$52; extra person $5; local phone calls free. Most major credit cards. **Directions:** from the east on I-90 take the Maple Street Bridge Exit 280A, follow Walnut to 2nd; from the west take Exit 280.

$34-$68 **VALUE INNS by Cavanaughs,** W. 1203 Fifth Ave., Spokane, WA 99204, phone 509-624-4142, reservations 1-800-843-4667, fax 509-325-7324. Close to Sacred Heart Hospital, Deaconess Hospital, and St. Luke's Hospital. This motor inn has 55 rooms, 51 nonsmoking. In-room amenities include phones and TV, some with remote controls. Morning coffee is available in the lobby, or make your own in one of the 48 equipped kitchen units. Shuttle to the airport, downtown, and some of the hospitals when the shuttle is available. Children under 18 free with parents, pets allowed. **Rates:** single room (1 bed) $42-$45; double room $45-$48; suite $68; hospital rates $34-$45; local phone calls 25¢. Major credit cards. **Directions:** from I-90 eastbound take Exit 280 thru 2 lights to first cross street (Jefferson), turn right to Value Inns. Westbound, take Exit 280B to 2nd Ave., west 3 blocks to Jefferson, turn left, go to 5th, turn right.

$85-$105 **WestCoast RIDPATH HOTEL** W. 515 Sprague, Spokane, WA 99204, phone 509-838-2711 or 1-800-426-0670. This large complex has 350 recently renovated rooms, 6 nonsmoking floors. All rooms have phones and remote control cable TV. Morning coffee is available in the coffee shop. Other amenities include year-round pool, exercise equipment, parking, restaurant, two bars, liquor store, gift shops, beauty salon, coffee shop, and shuttle to the airport, bus, or train station. Centrally located, close to hospitals, business district, and downtown. Children 18 and under free with parents, no pets. **Rates:** single or double room $85-$95 & $105; local phone calls 50¢. Major credit cards. **Directions:** from I-90 take Division St. Exit 281, north on Division, third light will be Sprague, turn left and go 5 blocks.

SOUTH

$85-$95 **ANGELICA'S MANSION BED & BREAKFAST,** West 1321 9th Ave., Spokane, WA 99204, phone 509-624-5598. This 1907 foursquare house on the South Hill has two spacious suites on the 2nd floor. Both rooms have private baths, queen beds, walk-in closets, and sitting areas. One room has a fireplace. A full breakfast is served in the dining room or on the large verandah. Can accommodate special events like weddings, receptions, or business meetings. Adult guests, no pets, and no smoking. **Rates:** double occupancy $85 & $95; three night minimum $75. MasterCard & Visa. **Directions:** from I-90, east, take Exit 280, west, Exit 280A, proceed to Maple St., turn south to 9th Ave., and proceed two blocks.

$47-$55 **HILLSIDE HOUSE BED & BREAKFAST,** 1729 E. 18th Ave., Spokane, WA 99203, day phone 509-534-1426, evenings and weekends 509-535-1893. This custom designed house, built in the early 1930's, is in a quiet neighborhood three miles from downtown. There are two guest rooms with shared bath. The Lace Room has two lace-draped twin beds and TV. The Blue Room has a double bed and a hillside view. A full hearty breakfast is served in the dining room or sundeck. Airport pickup by arrangement. Children 2 and under free, no pets, and no smoking. **Rates:** single $47; double occupancy $50-$55; extra person $15. MasterCard & Visa. **Directions:** from I-90 take the Thor-Freya Exit 283, south on Thor 3/4 mile, right on 17th 3/4 mile, left on Martin 1 block, right on 18th to E. 1729, street parking.

$10-$25 **HOSTELLING INTERNATIONAL,** S. 930 Lincoln, Spokane, WA 99204, phone 509-838-5968. Located in a beautiful residential neighborhood on the South Hill and 10 blocks south of downtown. Five rooms share 2 1/2 bathrooms and sleep 1 to 4 people. 20 person capacity in 10 sets of double bunks. A private room can be arranged if space is available. Kitchen, bath, laundry facilities, linen rental, equipment storage area, on-site parking, and large dining room. The hostel furnishes 1 top sheet, pillow case, blankets, mattress cover; bring your own sheet sleeping bag. Supermarket is 1 block west. **Rates:** dorm room $10 members; $13 nonmembers; private room $25; family of four $25; group rates $7 per person. Major credit cards. **Directions:** from I-90 take Division St. Exit north, turn left on 2nd, 10 blocks, left on Monroe, left on 17th, then left on Lincoln.

$50-$60 **OSLO'S BED & BREAKFAST,** 1821 E. 39th Ave., Spokane, WA 99203, phone 509-838-3175. An attractive South Hill home with a Norwegian atmosphere. Two guest rooms, both have private facilities. One room has a queen bed, the other a double bed. A large terrace overlooking the garden may be enjoyed with a full breakfast of Scandinavian cuisine, if desired, when weather permits. A small park is located 1/2 block away, with tennis courts, exercise stops, and paths for walking. Adults only, pets by arrangement, smoking outside. **Rates:** double occupancy $50-$60; extra person $15. **Directions:** from I-90 east take the Thor-Freya Exit 283, south on Thor to Ray, turn right on 37th, proceed to Napa, turn left, go to 39th, turn right.

EAST

COMFORT INN, Valley, 905 N. Sullivan Rd., Veradale, WA 99037, phone 509-924-3838 or 1-800-221-2222.

WEST

$28-$45 **CEDAR VILLAGE MOTEL,** W. 5415 Sunset, Spokane, WA 99204, phone 509-838-8558 or 1-800-700-8558, fax 509-624-2450. In a quiet, park-like setting with a large front lawn. This motel has a log cabin design with some individual cabins. There are 28 units, 10 nonsmoking. In-room amenities include phones and TV. Morning coffee is complimentary in the office and 10 units have fully equipped kitchens. Shuttle provided to the airport, bus, and train station. Close to the airport and downtown. Children welcome, pets allowed.

Rates: single room (1 bed) $28-$34; double room (2 beds) $45; queen deluxe $42; local phone calls 25¢; pets $3 per night. Most major credit cards. **Directions:** from I-90 west Exit 277B, then Business 90 to the right, one mile from exit; from the east, take the Airport Exit, then Business 90 to the right.

$32-$75   **EL RANCHO MOTEL,** W. 3000 Sunset, Spokane, WA 99204, phone 509-455-9400. Close to community college, this motel has 28 rooms, 23 nonsmoking. In-room amenities include phones and TV. Morning coffee is available in the lobby. There are 10 equipped kitchen units. Other amenities include seasonal outdoor pool, and self-contained RV parking. Close to the airport and downtown. Children welcome, no pets. **Rates:** single room $32-$39; double room $42-$50; family room $55-$75; extra person $5-$7; local phone calls free. MasterCard, Amex, Discover, & Visa. **Directions:** from I-90 use Exits 280 & 280A, follow Business Loop 90, west to Sunset Blvd.

$49-$75   **FRIENDSHIP INN,** W. 4301 Sunset, Spokane, WA 99204, phone 509-838-1471, reservations 1-800-424-4777. This 5 story motel has a view of the city. There is a restaurant and bar on the premises. 89 rooms, 30% nonsmoking. In-room amenities include phones and cable TV. Morning coffee is available at the restaurant. Other amenities include indoor spa, sauna, and seasonal outdoor pool. Shuttle provided to the airport, bus, and train station. Children 18 and under free with parents, pets allowed in some rooms. **Rates:** single (1 person) $49; double (2 people) $54; jacuzzi suite $75; local phone calls 25¢. Major credit cards. **Directions:** from I-90 take the Garden Springs Exit 277, go to stop sign, turn left.

HAMPTON INN Spokane, 2010 S. Assembly Rd., Spokane, WA 99204, phone 509-747-1100 or 1-800-HAM-PTON, fax 509-747-8722.

$37-$50   **WEST WYNN MOTEL,** W. 2701 Sunset Blvd., Spokane, WA 99204, phone 509-747-3037, fax 509-747-9123. 33 rooms, 14 nonsmoking. In-room amenities include phones, cable TV with HBO. Morning coffee is available at Mary Ann's Restaurant on the premises. Other amenities are indoor pool, sauna, laundry facilities, and jacuzzi. One equipped kitchen apartment available. Children welcome, no pets. **Rates:** single room (1 bed) $37-$42; double room $$45; family room (4 people) $50; extra person $5; local phone calls 25¢. Discover, MasterCard, Amex, & Visa. **Directions:** from I-90 westbound take Exit 280A straight down 4th Ave. to Sunset, turn left; eastbound, take Exit 280, turn left at 2nd light, go 1 block and turn left on 4th, proceed 5 blocks to Sunset, left on Sunset and over the bridge.

STEHEKIN (steh-HEE-kin) see Lake Chelan.

STEILACOOM see Anderson Island for lodging.

STEVENSON (pop. 1,150) is in the Columbia River Gorge, approximately 42 miles east of Vancouver.

The sternwheeler *Columbia Gorge* departs from Stevenson twice daily from mid-June to early October. Narrated tours of the Columbia River are provided. Visit the new Columbia Gorge Interpretive Center to appreciate the history and the evolution of the region.

$38-$60　**ECONO LODGE**, 40 NE 2nd St., Stevenson, WA 98648, phone 509-427-5628 or 1-800-553-2666. There are 29 rooms, 16 nonsmoking. Phones, TV, and hair dryers in every room. Kitchen units with basic cookware are available. No coffee/tea making facilities in the rooms, but a continental breakfast is provided in the lobby at 7 a.m. Children 18 and under free with parents, pets allowed. Within walking distance of restaurants, downtown, and the river front. **Summer Rates:** *5/ 01 to 9/30* - single room (1 bed) $45-$50; double (2 beds) $55-$60; extra person $5; pets $5 per night; local phone calls free; taxes 7%. **Winter Rates:** single $38-$42; double $45. Major credit cards accepted. **Directions:** east end of Stevenson, on Hwy 14, 3 miles from the Bridge of the Gods.

•SULTAN (pop. 2,300) is located approximately 23 miles east of Everett on Hwy 2. Sultan lies at the confluence of the Sultan and Skykomish rivers.

$44-$59　**DUTCH CUP MOTEL**, P. O. Box 369, Sultan, WA 98294, phone 360-793-2215, reservations 1-800-844-0488, fax 360-793-2216. 20 air-conditioned units, 11 nonsmoking, plus 2 one bedroom kitchenettes. In-room amenities include phones, cable TV with Movie Channel, and refrigerators. Get your complimentary morning coffee and hot drinks in the office. Adjacent Dutch Cup Restaurant and Lounge. Children welcome, pets allowed. **Rates:** single room (1 bed) $44-$51; double room (2 beds) $59; extra person $5; pets $5; local phone calls free; taxes 8.2%. Major credit cards accepted. **Directions:** Hwy 2 and Main Street.

SUMAS (pop. 767) is located approximately 20 miles east of Bellingham on the Canadian border.

$35-$48 **B & B BORDER INN MOTEL**, 121 Cleveland, P. O. Box 178, Sumas, WA 98295, phone 360-988-5800. 21 rooms, no designated nonsmoking. All rooms have phones and TV. Twelve upstairs rooms have air conditioning. Restaurant and lounge on the premises. Get your morning coffee with the continental breakfast provided in the restaurant. Children 10 and under free, small pets allowed with refundable deposit. **Rates:** single room $35-$40; double room $48; extra person $5; pet deposit $25; local phone calls free; taxes included. MasterCard & Visa. **Directions:** on the main street of Sumas, 1 1/2 blocks to the border.

$35-$60 **SILVER LAKE PARK CABINS**, 9006 Silver Lake Rd., Sumas, WA 98295, phone 360-599-2776. Six individual rustic cabins, all nonsmoking. Cabins contain stove/oven, refrigerator, gas heater, cold water sink, two or three double beds. Three large cabins have fireplaces. Restrooms are outhouses. Cooking utensils and bedding are not provided. Bathhouse with showers open 8:00 a.m. to dark, April through October only. Cabins operate year-round. Boat rentals, swimming area, fishing, etc. Children welcome, pets on a leash. **Rates:** small cabin $35-$55; large cabin $45-$60; extra person $5; taxes included. MasterCard & Visa. **Directions:** from I-5 take Hwy 542, 28 miles east to Maple Falls, turn left on Silver Lake Rd., and follow signs 3 miles to park.

$50-$110 **SUMAS MOUNTAIN VILLAGE**, 819 Cherry St., Sumas, WA 98295, phone 360-988-4483. The design of this lodge is a replica, in a smaller scale, of the Mt. Baker Hotel that was destroyed by fire in 1931. The observation tower offers a view of Mt. Baker and the surrounding countryside. All 9 rooms feature wooden floors, braided rugs, antique furniture, hand-stripped log beds, phones, TV, and pictures of the old Mt. Baker Lodge. Six rooms have jetted tubs and two rooms have stone fireplaces. Children welcome, no pets, and no smoking in the rooms. **Rates:** double occupancy, 6 rooms range in price from $50-$80; cabin $80; 2 suites $95-$110; extra person $5; local phone calls free; taxes 7.5%. MasterCard, Amex, & Visa. **Directions:** on the main street of Sumas.

SUMNER (pop. 7,190) is located approximately 10 miles east of Tacoma.

$48-$61 **SUMNER MOTOR INN**, 15506 E. Main St., Sumner, WA 98390, phone 206-863-3250. This 5 year old, two story motel has 39 rooms, 30 nonsmoking. In-room amenities include phones and TV. Complimentary morning coffee in the lobby. Eight units have small kitchens. Cookware and dishes provided at the office. Children 12 and under free, no pets. **Rates:** single room $48; double room $57; family room $61; extra person $5; local phone calls 50¢; taxes 9.9%. MasterCard, Amex, Discover, & Visa. **Directions:** from I-5 take Exit 512 onto Hwy 410, take 2nd Sumner Exit, left onto Valley Ave., right on E. Main.

SUNNYSIDE (pop. 11,600) is located off Hwy 82, 30 miles southeast of Yakima and 42 miles west of Richland.

Sunnyside is known as the asparagus capital of the Northwest. It is also a major trade center for cattle and farm crops. Local wineries include Tucker Cellars and Washington Hills Winery. Sportsmen enjoy fishing and bird hunting; rock hounds find jasper, opal, and petrified wood in the surrounding hills.

Located in Yakima County the sales/use taxes are 7.6%.

NENDELS INN, 408 Yakima Valley Hwy., Sunnyside, WA 98944, phone 509-837-7878 or 1-800-547-0106, fax 509-837-5254.

$49-$85 **SUNNYSIDE INN BED & BREAKFAST**, 800 E. Edison Ave., Sunnyside, WA 98944, phone 509-839-5557 or 1-800-221-4195. Eight nonsmoking rooms, all with private facilities, including double-wide jacuzzi tubs, king and queen beds, and two rooms have gas fireplaces. Unlike most B & Bs, there are phones and TV in every room. Guests are provided with fresh popcorn, juice, ice cream and cookies on request, as well as a full country breakfast. One common kitchen is open for the guests. Dinner is also available Monday through Saturday for an extra charge. Children welcome, well-behaved pets by arrangement. **Summer Rates:** *March to November* - double occupancy $49-$85; extra person $5; local phone calls free. **Winter Rates:** $49-$70. Major credit cards. **Directions:** from the north, take Exit 63 off I-82 or Exit 69 from the south and follow City Center signs to Edison.

Sunnyside Inn Bed & Breakfast

$35-$47 **TOWN HOUSE MOTEL**, 509 Yakima Valley Hwy., Sunnyside, WA 98944, phone 509-837-5500 or 1-800-342-4435, fax 509-837-8534. 21 units, 9 nonsmoking. All rooms have phones, TV, and refrigerators. No coffee/tea making facilities in the rooms, but there are 2 equipped kitchenettes. Microwave available with extended stays. Restaurant/bar within walking distance. Children welcome, pets allowed. **Rates:** single room $35-$38; double room $38-$47; extra person $3; pets $3; kitchen units $6 extra; no charge for local phone calls. Major credit cards. **Directions:** take Exit 63 or 67 off I-82.

$55-$100 **VON HELLSTRUM INN BED & BREAKFAST**, 51 Braden Rd., Sunnyside, WA 98944, phone 509-839-2505 or 1-800-222-8652. Six nonsmoking rooms, all with private facilities. One anniversary suite with a small refrigerator, jacuzzi garden tub, and patio. TV in the parlor. Full breakfast provided. Quiet, relaxed country atmosphere in this fully restored, 1909 Victorian farm home with beautiful gardens, ponds, and a gazebo. Children over 12 welcome, no pets. **Rates:** single $55; double $65; suite $100. Visa & MasterCard. **Directions:** take Exit 69 off I-82, turn right onto Waneta, proceed to Alexander Rd., turn left, go 1/2 mile to Braden.

• TACOMA (pop. 177,500) is located in western Washington, 31 miles south of Seattle on I-5.

(tuh-KOH-muh) is situated on the shores of Puget Sound and offers an abundance of recreational opportunities for sports and nature enthusiasts. Miles of waterfront parks offer access to every imaginable water activity. Attractions include the Tacoma Art Museum, Point Defiance Park, and the Tacoma Dome. See Fife for additional lodging.

Located in Pierce County the sales/use/lodging taxes are 9.9%.

$65-$75 **BAY VISTA BED & BREAKFAST**, **4617 Darien Dr. N., Tacoma, WA 98407, phone 206-759-8084.** Bay Vista offers sweeping views of Puget Sound, Mt. Rainier, and the Cascade Mountains. One suite with a private bath has a queen bed, sitting room, wet bar, hot pot for coffee and tea, TV/VCR, fireplace, private entrance, and patio. Another bedroom, with a double bed, is available if there are more than two in the party. Continental breakfast. 14 blocks from the Point Defiance Park in north Tacoma. Children 12 and older welcome, no pets. **Rates:** suite $65 & $75; extra room $50 & $55. MasterCard & Visa. **Directions:** available with reservations.

$75-$105 **COMMENCEMENT BAY BED & BREAKFAST**, **3312 N. Union, Tacoma, WA 98407, phone 206-752-8175, fax 206-759-4025.** This colonial style home with a view, located in north Tacoma, offers 3 guest rooms, all with private facilities. The rooms are large and beautifully decorated. Phones in all the rooms, 2 have TV and one has a VCR. A work area with modem hookup is available for business travelers. Game room, hot tub, fireplace room, deck area, and view of the bay. Full breakfast and gourmet coffees provided. Children 12 and older, no pets, and no smoking. **Summer Rates:** double occupancy, weekends $85, $95, & $105. **Winter Rates:** double occupancy $75-$95. Discover, MasterCard, Amex, & Visa. **Directions:** from I-5 take the Bremerton Exit

(Hwy 16), proceed to the 2nd exit (Union Ave.) to the first stop sign, turn left on 26th to Proctor, right to N. 34th, turn right, then another right on Union, 2nd house on the right.

DAYS INN, 6802 Tacoma Mall Blvd., Tacoma, WA 98409, phone 206-475-5900, reservations 1-800-325-2525, fax 206-475-3540.

ECONO LODGE at Port of Tacoma, 3518 Pacific Hwy E., Tacoma, WA 98424, phone 206-922-0550 or 1-800-424-4777.

HOWARD JOHNSON LODGE, 8702 S. Hosmer, Tacoma, WA 98444, phone 206-535-3100, reservations 1-800-446-4656, fax 206-537-6497.

$50-$60 **INGE'S PLACE BED & BREAKFAST U.S.A.,** 6809 Lake Grove SW, Tacoma, WA 98499, phone 206-584-4514. This ranch style home is in the residential area of Lakewood, a quiet area with several lakes. There are 3 rooms available. One suite has private facilities, and two rooms share facilities. TV and hot tub. Full breakfast. Children welcome, pets by arrangement. Hostess - Inge Deatherage speaks German and English. **Rates:** double occupancy $50; suite $60. No credit cards. **Directions:** from I-5 take the Gravelly Lake Exit 124, follow to Lakewood (3 miles), turn left on Alfaretta SW, go to the end of the street and turn right onto DeKoven, go 2 blocks, stay to the right on Lake Grove.

$50-$65 **KEENAN COUNTRY HOUSE BED & BREAKFAST,** 2610 N. Warner, Tacoma, WA 98407, phone 206-752-0702. This Victorian Tudor house has 4 guest rooms, 2 with private facilities and 2 with shared. The rooms are decorated in a country style. Full breakfast, featuring fresh baked breads and rolls. Children welcome, no pets, smoking permitted on the porch and balconies. Located 7 blocks from the University of Puget Sound; 10 minutes by car, to the Point Defiance Park and Vashon Island ferry. **Rates:** single $50-$55; double occupancy $55-$65. No credit cards. **Directions:** from I-5 take the Bremerton Exit, follow Hwy 16 to the Union Exit, take Union north to N. 26th, turn right onto N. 26th, follow 2 blocks to Warner.

$55-$110 **LAKEWOOD MOTOR INN Best Western,** 6125 Motor Ave. SW, Tacoma, WA 98499, phone 206-584-2212, reservations 1-800-528-1234. Conveniently located in the suburban Lakewood area, this colonial style motel has 78 rooms, 65 designated nonsmoking. All rooms have phones, TV with HBO, and coffee/tea making facilities. Continental breakfast provided in the lobby. Suites have microwaves and refrigerators. Close to Western State Hospital and V.A. Medical Center. Children 12 and under free, small pets allowed. **Rates:** single room $55-$66; double room $59-$66; suite $90-$110; extra person $7; local phone calls free; pets $6. Major credit cards. **Directions:** from I-5 take Exit 125 west onto Bridgeport 1.8 miles to Gravelly Lake Dr., turn left, go 1/4 block, turn right onto Motor Ave.

$28-$60 **ROTHEM INN,** 8602 S. Hosmer, Tacoma, WA 98444, phone 206-535-0123, fax 206-539-1169. This new, three story motel has 37 rooms, 9 nonsmoking. In-room amenities include phones and TV with HBO - remote controls available with a deposit. Morning coffee is available in the office and there are 6 equipped kitchen units available. Children 5 and under free, no pets. **Rates:** single (1 bed) $28-$50; double (2 beds) $45-$55; kitchen unit $60; extra person $5; rollaway $5; first 10 local phone calls free, then 25¢ each; taxes included. MasterCard, Amex, & Visa. **Directions:** from I-5 southbound take Exit 129; from I-5 northbound take Exit 128, go east to Hosmer.

$65-$75 **SALLY'S BEAR TREE COTTAGE BED & BREAKFAST,** 6019 W. 64th St., Tacoma, WA 98467, phone 206-475-3144. One private, cozy cottage located on 5 acres with old-growth fir and cedar trees. The cottage overlooks a salmon spawning creek, and the property intertwines with an adjoining public golf course. The cottage is located behind the main house. It has a queen bed, fireplace, cable TV, full bath, and mini-kitchen. Continental breakfast provided the night before. Adults only, no pets. **Rates:** single $65; double $75. No credit cards. **Directions:** from I-5 take the 56th St. Exit, west to Orchard St., turn left and follow to 64th St., go to the end of the golf course and through Springwater Estates.

$39-$59 **SHERWOOD INN,** 8402 S. Hosmer, Tacoma, WA 98444, phone 206-535-2800 or 1-800-362-4296, fax 206-535-2777. 118 large guest rooms, 50% nonsmoking. Phones and basic cable TV in the rooms. No coffee/tea making facilities in the rooms, but provided in the lobby. Restaurant/lounge on the premises. Seasonal outdoor pool, business services, meeting and banquet facilities. Children 12 and under free, pets allowed in smoking rooms. **Summer Rates:** single room (1 bed) $39-$59; double room $59; family unit, double occupancy $59; local phone calls free; extra person $5; pets $5. **Winter Rates:** $39-$49. Major credit cards. **Directions:** from I-5 southbound take Exit 129, left to S. 84th; from I-5 northbound take Exit 128, go east to Hosmer.

$58-$80 **TACOMA INN Best Western**, 8726 S. Hosmer, Tacoma, WA 98444, phone 206-535-2880 or 1-800-528-1234, fax 206-537-8379. This two story complex has 149 rooms, 75% nonsmoking. Phones, remote control TV with HBO, drip coffee makers, and room service. Full service restaurant on the premises opens at 6:30 a.m. Outdoor pool, 2 jacuzzis, exercise gym, courtyard, putting green, laundry room, and playground. 8 equipped kitchen units available and some rooms have balconies. Meeting facilities for large groups. Children 12 and under free, small pets allowed. **Rates:** single room $58-$70; double room $64-$70; kitchen unit $69-$80; local phone calls 30¢; extra person $6; rollaway $10; pets $20 one time charge. Major credit cards. **Directions:** from I-5 southbound take Exit 129 to Tacoma Mall Blvd., follow directions to 84th, turn left, turn right at Hosmer; from I-5 northbound take Exit 128 to Hosmer, turn right.

Tacoma Inn

TRAVELERS INN, 4221 Pacific Hwy E., Fife, WA 98424, phone 206-922-9520 or 1-800-633-8300.

•TOKELAND *is located on the north side of Willapa Bay.*

This small community occupies storm-swept and salt-bleached Toke Point, which juts south into oyster-rich Willapa Bay. The point and the settlement were both named after Chief Toke of the Shoalwater Bay Tribe. This is the nation's smallest Indian reservation, approximately one square mile, and is at the base of the peninsula.

Located in Pacific County the sales/use taxes are 7.8%.

$44-$95   **The TOKELAND HOTEL & RESTAURANT**, 100 Hotel Rd., Tokeland, WA 98590, phone 360-267-7006. This 102 year old, historic hotel has 18 nonsmoking guest rooms on the second floor. 17 of the rooms share nearby bathrooms that contain all the modern conveniences, one room has private facilities. The rooms are furnished in a turn-of-the-century decor. Enjoy the panoramic view of Willapa Bay from the casual, but quaint, Tokeland dining room, serving 3 meals a day. A basic breakfast is included in the price of lodging. Children welcome, no pets. Just 15 minutes away from Westport for charter fishing, golfing at the 9 hole golf course in Raymond, or spending the day on the beach. **Summer Rates:** *3/15 to 10/15* - single room (1 bed) $55-$65; double (2 beds) $95; extra person $10. **Winter Rates:** single $44-$49; double $65. MasterCard, Discover, & Visa. **Directions:** turn off Hwy 105 at the Tokeland Exit, continue for two miles. The hotel is a large grey structure on the left.

$45-$70   **TRADEWINDS on the BAY MOTEL**, P. O. Box 502, Tokeland, WA 98590, phone 360-267-7500. This two story motel has 17 units, 10 nonsmoking. In-room amenities include equipped kitchen, queen bed, queen hide-a-bed, and TV. One room has a fireplace. Phone in the office. Other amenities include outdoor pool, play equipment, and the beach. Children 10 and under free, pets allowed. **Summer Rates:** *5/01 to 10/01* - single or double occupancy $60-$70; extra person $5; pets $5. **Winter Rates:** $45-$60. MasterCard & Visa **Directions:** turn off Hwy 105 at the Tokeland Exit, 4305 Pomeroy Ave.

TONASKET (pop. 880) is located in north central Washington, approximately 20 miles south of the Canadian border.

(tuhn-AS-kuht) This area is a sportsman's paradise, with plenty of hunting, fishing, hiking, and snow sports. Downhill ski at Sitzmark Ski Area, cross country ski on over 25 km of groomed trails at Highland Sno Park, or snowmobile over hundreds of miles of trails.

Located in Okanogan County the sales/use taxes are 7.6%.

$22-$38   **BONAPARTE LAKE RESORT**, 615 Bonaparte Rd., Tonasket, WA 98855, phone 509-486-2828. This back country resort has 10 rustic log cabins nestled in the trees at Lake Bonaparte. There are also tent, camper, and trailer sites available. Three cabins have private facilities and 7 share. Bathrooms, showers, and the laundromat are together in one building. Bedding, towels, and kitchen equipment are not furnished. Two cabins have 2 double beds, refrigerator, and wood stove. The cabins have no running water in the winter. Morning coffee is available at the lakeside cafe open 7 days a week from April to October, Saturdays and Sundays in the winter. Rowboat rentals, ice-skating, fishing, hunting, and snowmobiling. Children welcome, pets allowed on a leash. **Rates:** cabins $22-$38; extra person $2; pets free; campsites and RV facilities $7-$11. MasterCard & Visa **Directions:** 20 miles east of Tonasket and 20 miles west of Republic, turn off Hwy 20 to Bonaparte Lake, proceed for 6 miles.

$65-$95 **HIDDEN HILLS RESORT**, 104 Fish Lake Rd., Tonasket, WA 98855, phone 509-486-1890 or 1-800-468-1890. This quiet, isolated resort gives you an 1890's experience with 1990's convenience. There are 10 nonsmoking guest rooms all with private facilities, a queen bed, and adorned with Victorian antiques. A restaurant is attached to the hotel. A full breakfast is provided to hotel guests, dinner available by reservation. One mile from Fish Lake. There are walking trails, horses, and numerous wildlife around the ranch. Children 12 and older, no pets. **Rates:** double occupancy $75-$95; single $10 less. MasterCard & Visa. **Directions:** 12 miles north of Omak, from Hwy 97 turn left on Pine Creek So., go 7 miles to resort gate, turn right 1 1/2 miles up the hill to the hotel.

$37-$42 **RAINBOW RESORT**, 761 Loomis Hwy, Tonasket, WA 98855, phone 509-223-3700 or 1-800-347-4375. Located on Spectacle Lake, this resort is *open from April 1st to October 31*. There are four cabins with private facilities and equipped kitchens. Closest restaurant is 4 miles away. Amenities include good fishing, a game of horseshoes, large grassy area, club house, small store, RV hookups, and camping. Children welcome, pets on a leash and cleaned up after. **Rates:** cabin (2 people) $37; cabin (4 people) $42; extra adult $5; children $3. MasterCard & Visa **Directions:** 16 miles northwest of Tonasket, take Loomis Hwy off Highway 97.

$37-$53 **RED APPLE INN**, Hwy 97 & 1st St., P. O. Box 453, Tonasket, WA 98855, phone 509-486-2119. 21 units on one level, 6 nonsmoking. Phones, TV, and 3 non-equipped kitchen units are available. Morning coffee is available in the lobby. Children 5 and under free, pets by approval. **Rates:** single room $37-$47; double room $44-$47; kitchen units $53; extra person $4; pets $2. Major credit cards. **Directions:** on Hwy 97 at the north end of town.

$25-$100 **SPECTACLE LAKE RESORT**, 10 McCammon Rd., Tonasket, WA 98855, phone & fax 509-223-3433. 12 motel style units, open year-round, are located on the waterfront. These are cabin-like rooms with equipped kitchens.   Also, one completely furnished house on the waterfront and one rustic, cold water cabin next to the campground bath house. Amenities include heated pool, horseshoe pits, play area, boat and motor rental, docks, volleyball, swings, boat launch, and small store. The campground has RV hookup sites, tent sites, and two cookout shelters. Children welcome, pets welcome if on a leash and cleaned up after. **Rates:** motel (2 people) $45; house (2-6 people) $80-$100; cabin (2 people) $25; extra person $3-$5. Discover, MasterCard & Visa. **Directions:** 12 miles NW of Tonasket, take the Many Lakes turn-off at the Texaco station in Tonasket and follow the signs.

TOPPENISH (pop. 7,500) is located 20 miles southeast of Yakima off Hwy 97.

(TAH-puhn-ish) is the central headquarters of the Yakima Indian Nation. The Yakima Nation Cultural Center is just off Hwy 97. There you can learn Indian history from exceptional exhibits with special audio-effects. Take time to see the western art murals painted on the outside walls of several buildings, promoting Toppenish as the "City of Murals".
    Located in Yakima County the sales/use taxes are 7.6%.

$34-$39 **EL CORRAL MOTEL**, 61731 Hwy. 97, Toppenish, WA 98948, phone 509-865-2365. 16 units, 3 nonsmok- ing. All rooms have phones, queen beds, cable TV, and AC. Some rooms have refrigerators and microwaves. No coffee/tea making facilities in the rooms. A shady, grassy area with a large fountain is located in the front. Children welcome, pets by arrangement. Truck and trailer parking. **Rates:** single (1 person) $34; double (2 people) $39; local phone calls free. Discover, Amex, MasterCard & Visa. **Directions:** just off Hwy 97 at Toppenish.

$39-$69 **TOPPENISH INN MOTEL,** 515 S. Elm, Toppenish, WA 98948, phone 509-865-7444, reservations 1-800-222-3161, fax 509-865-7719. 41 units, 31 nonsmoking. In-room amenities include phones, queen or king beds, TV, AC, microwaves, refrigerators, and hair dryers. Suite has jacuzzi spa and king bed. Morning coffee is available in the lobby with a complimentary continental breakfast 7 a.m. to 10:30 a.m. Meeting room, indoor pool and spa. Children 12 and under free, small pets allowed. **Rates:** single (1 bed) $39-$46; double (2 beds) $56; suite $69; pets $10; extra person $5; local phone calls free. Major credit cards. **Directions:** located on the east side of junction Hwy 97 and Hwy 22.

$30 **YAKIMA NATION RESORT & RV PARK,** 280 Buster Rd., P. O. Box 151, Toppenish, WA 98948, phone 509-865-2000 or 1-800-874-3087. Experience the "old west" at the Yakima Indian Nation Cultural Center and Resort. There are 14 authentic tepees that sleep 7-10 people. The tepees are akin to glorified tents with concrete floors, no bedding furnished, but cots can be rented. The grounds offer 95 RV spaces, swimming pool, hot tub, game room, restrooms, showers, laundry, one mile walking/jogging path, picnic area, basketball court, volleyball court, tenting area, play area, and meeting room. The Cultural Center features a gift shop, restaurant, museum, movie theater, lodge, and library. Children 3 and under free, pets on a leash. **Rates:** tepee, 5 people or less $30; cot $2.50; extra person $2.50. Major credit cards. **Directions:** 22 miles south of Yakima on Hwy 97.

TRI CITIES

is located in south central Washington just 30 miles north of Oregon at the intersection of State Highways 182, 240, and I-82.

Kennewick, Pasco, and Richland are clustered together at the confluence of the Snake, Columbia, and Yakima Rivers.

KENNEWICK

(pop. 42,780) has an economy revolving around light industry, food processing, and retail businesses. Columbia Center Mall is the largest covered mall in eastern Washington. Located in Benton County the sales/use taxes are 7.8%.

$65 **The DOGWOOD COTTAGE A Bed & Breakfast,** 109 N. Yelm, Kennewick, WA 99336, phone 509-783-5337. Located across the street from the golf course. One large suite, with queen bed, private bath, and a sitting room with TV/VCR, desk and phone. Breakfasts during the week are light, weekends a full health breakfast is prepared. Within walking distance of restaurants. Limited to two guests per night, no pets, and no smoking. **Rates:** $65. MasterCard & Visa. **Directions:** follow Kennewick Ave. east to Yelm, turn left.

$43-$51 **NENDEL'S INN,** 2811 W. 2nd Ave., Kennewick, WA 99336, phone 509-735-9511 or 1-800-547-0106. 106 rooms, 53 nonsmoking. In-room amenities include phones and TV. Morning coffee is available in the lobby with a complimentary continental breakfast. Outdoor pool. Children 12 and under free, small pets in certain rooms. **Rates:** single room (1 bed) $43-$48; double room (2 beds) $51; extra person $5; local phone calls free. Major credit cards. **Directions:** from the east and west take Umatilla Exit up the hill; from the south come straight into town on Hwy 395 to 2nd Ave.

RAMADA INN on Clover Island, 435 Clover Island, Kennewick, WA 99336, phone 509-586-0541 or 1-800-272-6232.

$44-$52 **SHANIKO SUITES MOTEL,** 321 N. Johnson, Kennewick, WA 99336, phone 509-735-6385, fax 509-736-6631. This 3 story motel has 47 efficiency studios, each with 440 square feet, 30 nonsmoking. All units have equipped kitchens, queen bed(s), phones, and cable TV with HBO. There are 24 units with one bed and 23 with 2 beds. Rates include a continental breakfast. Outdoor pool, barbecue, and picnic area. Within walking distance of restaurants. Children under 12 free, pets allowed. Shuttle provided to the airport. **Rates:** single room (1 bed) $44-$49; double room $52; extra person $5; pets $4; local phone calls free. Major credit cards. **Directions:** in Kennewick on Hwy 395 take Clearwater west, turn north on Johnson, 200 feet north of Clearwater.

SILVER CLOUD INN, 7901 W. Quinault Ave., Kennewick, WA 99336, phone 509-735-6100 or 1-800-551-7207.

TAPADERA BUDGET INN, 300-A North Ely, Kennewick, WA 99336, phone 509-783-6191 or 1-800-722-8277, fax 509-735-3854.

PASCO

(pop. 20,660) is primarily an agricultural town. It is the gateway city to the Columbia Basin and is the largest city in the million-acre Columbia Basin Irrigation Project.
Located in Franklin County the sales/use taxes are 7.8%.

RED LION INN, 2525 N. 20th Ave., Pasco, WA 99301, phone 509-547-0701 or 1-800-RED-LION.

$34-$43 **TRIMARK MOTEL**, 720 W. Lewis St., Pasco, WA 99301, phone 509-547-7766, fax 509-545-5306. 63 units, 30 nonsmoking. In-room amenities include phones and cable TV with HBO. Morning coffee is available in the lobby. Heated outdoor pool. Children 12 and under free, pets allowed. **Rates:** single room (1 bed) $34-$37; double room (2 beds) $43; extra person $3; pet deposit $10; local phone calls free. MasterCard, Amex, Discover, & Visa. **Directions:** from Kennewick cross over the Blue Bridge to Lewis St., turn right and proceed for 1 mile.

$39-$54 **VINEYARD INN**, 1800 W. Lewis, Pasco, WA 99301, phone 509-547-0791 or 1-800-824-5457. 165 units, 50% nonsmoking. In-room amenities include phones, cable TV, and queen or king beds. In-room movies and VCR available. Morning coffee and a continental breakfast are provided in the lobby. Heated indoor pool, jacuzzi, and guest laundry facilities. Children under 12 free, pets allowed. **Rates:** single room $39-$46; double room $44-$54; extra person $5; pets $5; local phone calls free. Major credit cards. **Directions:** from Hwy 395 south take Lewis Street Exit through 2 lights; from Hwy 395 north take 20th Ave. Exit, turn right, go to Lewis, turn left.

RICHLAND

(pop. 32,740) In 1943-44 the Hanford Nuclear Project expanded the population of this small town from 240 to 11,000. Today there are several manufacturing firms in the community. Principal products are nuclear-oriented and scientific in nature. Richland is home to numerous parks and beaches.
Located in Benton County the sales/use taxes are 7.8%.

$35-$45 **BALI HI MOTEL**, 1201 George Washington Way, Richland, WA 99352, phone 509-943-3101, fax 509-943-6363. Two story motel with 44 units, 14 nonsmoking. In-room amenities include phones, cable TV with HBO, microwaves, coffee/tea making facilities, and refrigerators. Other amenities include an indoor spa, seasonal outdoor pool, sun deck, and eating area. Restaurant next door. Children welcome, infants free, pets allowed. **Rates:** single room $35-$39; double room $41-$45; extra person $5; pets $25 deposit, $5 per night; local phone calls free. Major credit cards. **Directions:** take George Washington Way Exit off I-82 or I-182; from SR 240 one block over, towards the river is George Washington Way.

$33-$48 **COLUMBIA CENTER DUNES MOTEL,** 1751 Fowler, Richland, WA 99352, phone 509-783-8181 or 1-800-638-6168, fax 509-783-2811. Two story motel with 89 units, 18 nonsmoking. Phones, cable TV, and coffee/tea making facilities. Some rooms have refrigerators and there are 2 equipped kitchen units. Sauna and seasonal outdoor pool. Several restaurants within walking distance. Children under 3 free, pets allowed. **Rates:** single room (1 bed) $33-$37; double room $38-$48; kitchen units $37-$42; extra person $5; pets $5 per night; local phone calls free. Major credit cards accepted. **Directions:** on SR 240 at Columbia Center Blvd.

RED LION INN, 802 George Washington Way, Richland, WA 99352, phone 509-946-7611 or 1-800-RED-LION.

$39-$47 **RICHLAND NENDELS,** 615 Jadwin Ave., Richland, WA 99352, phone 509-943-4611 or 1-800-547-0106. Two story motel with 98 rooms, 58 nonsmoking. In-room amenities include phones and TV. There are 13 equipped kitchen units available. Morning coffee is available in the lobby with a complimentary continental breakfast. Seasonal outdoor pool. Children 12 and under free, pets allowed. Shuttle provided to the airport. Close to Columbia River recreation area, Hanford Science Center, and Columbia Center Mall. **Rates:** single room $39-$44; double room $47; extra person $5; pets $5; local phone calls free. Major credit cards. **Directions:** I-182 to George Washington Way (Exit 5B), left on Jadwin Ave.

SHILO INNS, 50 Comstock, Richland, WA 99352, phone 509-946-4661 or 1-800-222-2244.

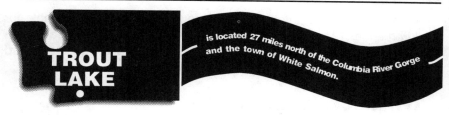

TROUT LAKE is located 27 miles north of the Columbia River Gorge and the town of White Salmon.

Trout Lake offers a unique getaway experience in the shadow of Mt. Adams. Bicycle, fish, hike, cross country ski in the winter, or just take in the spectacular scenery.

Located in Klickitat (KLIK-i-tat) County the sales/use taxes are 7%.

$60-$85   **The FARM A Bed & Breakfast**, 490 Sunnyside Rd., Trout Lake, WA 98650, phone & fax 509-395-2488. Two nonsmoking rooms with shared facilities are available in this farmhouse. Quiet and eclectically decorated, the Quilt Room is furnished with a double bed adorned with antique quilts. The 1890 Room has a queen bed, one twin and a Victorian love seat. Full "farm" breakfast is provided. Children free in the 1890 Room, no pets. **Summer Rates:** double occupancy $70-$85. **Winter Rates:** $60-$72. No credit cards. **Directions:** from Hwy 14 take Hwy 141 north toward Trout Lake. At mile marker 21, turn east on Warner Rd., go to the end, go north, it is the second house on the right.

$60-$135   **MIO AMORE PENSIONE**, 53 Little Mountain Rd., P. O. Box 208, Trout Lake, WA 98650, phone 509-395-2264. A European bed & breakfast inn with 4 nonsmoking guest rooms decorated with memorabilia from around the world. Three rooms with shared facilities and one with private. Each room has its own unique character. A generous breakfast is provided, and dinners featuring a Northern Italian menu are available by reservation. Enjoy the spa, swimming in the creek, hiking, bicycling, fishing, and more. Not suitable for children under 15, no pets. **Rates:** double occupancy $60; suite $135; extra person $20. MasterCard & Visa. **Directions:** from Hwy 14 take Hwy 141 toward White Salmon, north to Trout Lake (23 miles), take a sharp right turn immediately after passing the small church, on the right-hand side.

$60   **TROUT LAKE COUNTRY INN BED & BREAKFAST**, 15 Guler Rd., Trout Lake, WA 98650, phone 509-395-2894. There are 2 nonsmoking rooms with shared facilities in this combination restaurant, bed and breakfast. In the summer, from May to September, it is also a Dinner Theatre; call for mailing list. Built in 1904, next to Trout Lake Creek, the Inn is rustic and decorated with antiques. One room has two double beds and the other has a queen bed. Full breakfast is provided and the restaurant opens at noon for lunch. Not suitable for children under 12, no pets. **Rates:** double occupancy $60; extra person $15. MasterCard & Visa. **Directions:** from Hwy 14 take Hwy 141 toward White Salmon north to Trout Lake (23 miles).

TUKWILA see South Seattle.

TUMWATER see Olympia.

TWISP (pop. 880) is located in north central Washington, 11 miles south of Winthrop.

Twisp and Winthrop have become popular recreation towns since the North Cascade Highway opened in 1972, providing a northern route through the Cascades to the Methow Valley. Activities include downhill skiing, cross country skiing, river and lake fishing, snowmobiling, bicycling, horseback riding, mountaineering, rafting, canoeing, hiking, and all the other outdoor sports. Even though the valley is no longer isolated, the rural life-style is still the essence of the community.

Located in Okanogan County the sales/use taxes are 7.6%.

$42-$56 **IDLE-A-WHILE-MOTEL**, P. O. Box 667, Twisp, WA 98856, phone 509-997-3222. Located on the Cascade Loop, this motel has 25 units, 12 are nonsmoking. Nine individual cabins with equipped kitchens and four equipped kitchenette units. Phones and TV in all the units. Large grassy area with picnic tables and barbecue pits. Tennis court, hot tub, and sauna. VCR and movie rentals. Restaurant within walking distance. Children welcome, dogs allowed. **Rates:** single room (1 bed) $42-$55; double room (2 beds) $45-$56; extra person $4; pets $1 each. MasterCard, Visa, & Discover. **Directions:** on Hwy 20, it is ten miles south of Winthrop, and 35 miles west of Omak.

$79-$89 **METHOW VALLEY INN BED & BREAKFAST**, P. O. Box 668, Twisp, WA 98856, phone 509-997-2253. This historic Inn is undergoing a restoration and plans to reopen in the summer of 1996. The Inn has 7 guest rooms on the 2nd floor, 3 with private facilities, and 4 share 2 baths. Antique pedestal sinks in all the rooms, furnished with European antiques and queen beds. Expanded continental breakfast is served in the dining room. Access to the Methow and Twisp rivers is one and a half blocks away. Children and pets by arrangement, no smoking in the Inn. **Rates:** double occupancy $79-$89. MasterCard & Visa. **Directions:** centrally located in Twisp, turn east at the first intersection.

$31-$120 **SPORTSMAN MOTEL**, 1010 E. Hwy 20, Twisp, WA 98856, phone 509-997-2911. This clean, older motel has 9 units, 2 nonsmoking, and one fully equipped house trailer. All the motel units have knotty pine interiors, equipped kitchens, air conditioning, and TV. The house trailer has 2 bedrooms, equipped kitchen, and sleeps 2-7 people. Step outdoors to shade trees and lawn. Within walking distance of the Methow River, restaurants, and the shopping center. Children welcome, dogs allowed. **Summer Rates:** single room (1 bed) $31-$36; double room (2 beds) $39; trailer $50-$120; extra person $4; pay phone 25¢. MasterCard & Visa. **Directions:** on Hwy 20, 8 miles south of Winthrop.

$28-$35 **WAGON WHEEL CAFE & MOTEL**, HCR 73 Box 57, Twisp, WA 98856, phone 509-997-4671. This small, family owned motel is adjacent to the cafe. There are 4 rooms available, all with private facilities, queen beds, and TV. No coffee/tea making facilities in the rooms, but available at the cafe. Cafe is open from 11 a.m. to 8 p.m., 7 days a week. Children welcome, pets allowed. **Rates:** single (1 person) $28; double (2 people) $35; pay phone 25¢. No credit cards. **Directions:** on Hwy 20, 3 miles south of Twisp.

UNION

in located on the southern hook of the Hood Canal, north of Olympia and south of Bremerton.

Union is in a fiord-like inlet of Puget Sound, framed by the towering, snowcapped Olympic Mountains and the the wooded terrain of the Olympic Peninsula.
Located in Mason County the sales/use taxes are 7.8%.

$79-$189 **ALDERBROOK RESORT Golf & Conference Center**, E. 7101 Hwy 106, Union, WA 98592, phone 360-898-2200 or 1-800-622-9370. Located on the shores of Hood Canal, this 525 acre resort features 78 guest rooms, two 3 bedroom suites, and 18 two bedroom cottages with kitchens and fireplaces. There are 32 nonsmoking units. In-room amenities include phones and remote control cable TV. Morning coffee is available at the Beachside Restaurant, open for breakfast, lunch, and dinner. Other amenities include an 18 hole golf course, Olympic-sized indoor pool, jacuzzi, marina, two swimming docks, playground, volleyball court, horseshoe pit, and nine meeting and conference rooms. The lounge, overlooking the canal, features live entertainment. Children 16 and under free with parents, pets allowed with deposit. **Summer Rates:** 6/ 01 to 9/30 - guest rooms, double occupancy $89-$99; cottages (1-4 people) $149-$189; suite (2 people) $149-$189; pets $8 one time charge, $25 deposit. **Winter Rates:** guest rooms $79-$89; cottages $109-$179; suite $129-$169. Major credit cards. **Directions:** E. 7101 Hwy 106 in Union.

$75-$155 **ROBIN HOOD VILLAGE**, E. 6780 Hwy 106, Union, WA 98592, phone 206-898-2163. Situated on the Hood Canal Inlet, the Robin Hood Village has 4 cottages that sleep from 2 to 10 people. No designated nonsmoking cottages. Each cottage has equipped kitchens, cable TV, and bathrooms. Cottages 1 and 2 share a hot tub and three cottages have fireplaces. One large cottage sleeps 2-10 people. Children welcome, pets allowed. RV and tent sites available. **Rates:** 3 cottages $75, $85, & $100; large cottage $155, 2 night minimum; extra person $5. Major credit cards. **Directions:** E. 6780 Hwy 106 in Union.

UNION GAP see Yakima for lodging.

USK •

(USHK) is located in the northeast corner of the state at the crossroads of Hwy 20 and Hwy 211.

Usk is just 16 miles north of Newport on the Pend Oreille (PAHN-do-RAY) River.

$25-$35 **The INN AT USK**, 410 River Rd., Usk, P. O. Box 100, WA 99180, phone 509-445-1526. This wonderful old country Inn is loaded with atmosphere and cozy rooms, each individually decorated in country charm. All 10 rooms are on the second floor. Three have private facilities, 1 with half a bath, and 6 with shared facilities; no designated nonsmoking rooms. All rooms have overhead fans. Phone in the lobby, TV in the living room with VCR and movies. Coffee/tea and juice in the dining room with microwave and toaster. Picnic area, barbecue, canoe rental, upstairs sun deck, and 5 tent sites. Children and pets welcome. The Inn at Usk is a popular spot for hunters and cross country cyclists. **Rates:** $25-$35; tent sites $8; taxes 7.5%. Amex, Discover, MasterCard, & Visa. **Directions:** center of town.

VANCOUVER (pop. 47,190) is located in the southwest corner of the state, across the Columbia River from Portland, Oregon.

Vancouver is primarily a residential area with nice waterfront parks and access to the Columbia Gorge. The small city center has historical buildings with turn-of-the-century architecture.

Located in Clark County the sales/use taxes are 7.6%.

COMFORT INN, 13207 NE 20th, Vancouver, WA 98686, phone 360-574-6000 or 1-800-221-2222.

$50-$80 **COUNTRY HEART BED & BREAKFAST**, 7507 NE 51st, Vancouver, WA 98662, phone 360-896-8316 or 1-800-636-8316 (WA). Located in the heart of Vancouver on a park-like acre, this B & B offers the convenience of the city and the atmosphere of the country, with chickens, ducks, and geese. The 1900's farmhouse has 4 guest rooms, 2 with private facilities, and 2 with shared. Phones available in two rooms on request. The "friendship room" has a fireplace. All rooms are decorated in cozy country. Full breakfast with a new menu daily. Well-behaved children welcome, no pets. Easy freeway access, close to the Vancouver Mall. **Rates:** double occupancy $50-$70; suite $80; taxes included. Amex, MasterCard & Visa. **Directions:** brochure with map available with reservations.

$54-$68 **FERRYMAN'S INN Best Western**, 7901 NE 6th Ave., Vancouver, WA 98665, phone 360-574-2151. This two story motel has 134 rooms, 47 nonsmoking. The spacious rooms all have phones, cable TV, and air conditioning. Morning coffee is available with a complimentary continental breakfast in the lobby. Eight equipped kitchen units, on site laundry, and seasonal outdoor pool. Conference room for 10 to 200 people. Special "Race Package" to Portland Meadows: admission, parking, and program is included with the price of the room. Children 12 and under free, pets allowed. **Rates:** single room (1 bed) $54-$59; double room (2 beds) $63-$68; kitchen units $60-$65; local phone calls free; extra person $5; pets $3. Major credit cards. **Directions:** from I-5 take Exit 4 (78th St.) to the west side of freeway, turn on 6th.

$37-$44 **FORT MOTEL**, 500 E. 13th St., Vancouver, WA 98660, phone 360-694-3327. This motel with a family atmosphere has 28 rooms, 2 nonsmoking. In-room amenities include phones and TV. Morning coffee is available in the office where the pot is always on, usually with some kind of homemade goodies. Three equipped kitchen units. Children 18 and under free with parents, pets allowed. **Rates:** single room (1 bed) $37; double room $44; extra person $7; pets $20 per night; local phone calls free. MasterCard & Visa. **Directions:** I-5 and Mill Plain Rd.

$40-$52 **GUEST HOUSE MOTEL**, 11504 NE 2nd St., Vancouver, WA 98684, phone 360-254-4511. 47 rooms, 24 nonsmoking. In-room amenities include phones and TV. Morning coffee is available in the snack room. Restaurants within walking distance. Ten minutes to Portland Airport and Vancouver Mall. Children welcome, no pets. **Rates:** single room $40; double room $42; family room $48-$52; rollaway $5; local phone calls free. Major credit cards. **Directions:** I-205, to Exit 28 east, left turning lane to motel.

$45-$58 **MARK 205 INN & Conference Center**, 221 NE Chkalov Dr., Vancouver, WA 98684, phone 360-256-7044 or 1-800-426-5110, fax 360-256-1231. Located near shopping, restaurants, and theaters. The Mark 205 has 116 rooms, 57 nonsmoking. In-room amenities include phones and cable TV with Showtime. Morning coffee is available in the lobby with breakfast rolls. Indoor swimming pool and jacuzzi. Free shuttle to the airport, train, and bus station. Children 16 and under free with parents, pets allowed. **Summer Rates:** *6/01 to 8/31* - single room $52; double room $58; extra person $5; pets $15 per stay; local phone calls free. **Winter Rates:** Singlt $45; double $50. Major credit cards. **Directions:** exit I-205 at Mill Plain.

$55-$65 **PHEASANT RUN BED & BREAKFAST**, 27308 NE 182nd Ave., Battleground, WA 98604, phone 360-687-0942. A Cape Cod style home located in the quiet country side. The inn is secluded on tree-shaded grounds just minutes from Battle Ground Lake. Two guest rooms with shared facilities are furnished with many lovely antiques. The sitting room, between the rooms, is stocked with books and games. Well-behaved children over 12 welcome, no pets, and no smoking in the rooms. Bountiful breakfast with gourmet coffee and fresh fruits. **Rates:** queen bed, double occupancy $65; double bed $55. MasterCard & Visa. **Directions:** take the Battleground Exit off I-5, follow Main St. thru town, left on 182nd, proceed one mile past the lake.

$34-$48 **RIVERSIDE MOTEL**, 4400 Lewis & Clark Hwy, Vancouver, WA 98661, phone 360-693-3677. This one level motel has 17 rooms, 4 nonsmoking. The brick construction of the motel blocks out the highway noise. In-room amenities include phones, TV, and refrigerators. No coffee/tea making facilities in the rooms. There are 9 non-equipped kitchen units. Children 5 and under free, pets allowed with overnight guests only. **Rates:** single room (1 bed) $34-$36; double room (2 beds) $42-$48; kitchen unit by the week $165; extra person $8; pets $5; local phone calls free. Major credit cards. **Directions:** two miles east of downtown Vancouver on Camas Hwy 14.

$45-$55 **SALMON CREEK MOTEL**, 11901 NE Hwy 99, Vancouver, WA 98686, phone 360-573-0751. This one level motel has 18 rooms, 5 nonsmoking. All rooms have phones and TV. No coffee/tea making facilities in the rooms. Some units have non-equipped kitchenettes. Children 2 and under free, no pets. One block from Salmon Creek Lake. **Rates:** single room $45-$50; double room $55; extra person $6; local phone calls 25¢. Most major credit cards. **Directions:** from I-5 take the 134th St. Exit, 1/2 mile from the exit on left-hand side of Hwy 99.

$40-$48 **SUNNYSIDE MOTEL**, 12200 NE Hwy 99, Vancouver, WA 98686, phone 360-573-4141. This one level motel has 16 rooms, 3 nonsmoking. All rooms have phones and TV. No coffee/tea making facilities in the rooms. Some units have non-equipped kitchenettes. Children 5 and under free, no pets. Two blocks from Salmon Creek

Lake for swimming, fishing, and picnicking. Parking outside the door. **Rates:** single room $40; double room $48; extra person $6; local phone calls 25¢. Most major credit cards. **Directions:** from I-5 take the 134th St. Exit, to 2nd traffic light, turn left, proceed 1/2 mile, motel on the right.

$40-$72 **VANCOUVER LODGE,** 601 Broadway, Vancouver, WA 98660, phone 360-693-3668. A red brick, two story lodge that was orginally a Red Lion, 45 rooms, 18 nonsmoking. All rooms have phones, TV, and refrigerators. No coffee/tea making facilities in the rooms. Located in downtown Vancouver, within one block of restaurants and bus service. Children 10 and under free, pets allowed. **Rates:** single room (1 bed) $40-$54; double room (2 beds) $58-$65; family room $72; extra person $6; pets $5 per night; local phone calls free. Major credit cards. **Directions:** northbound take Exit 1B (City Center) from I-5; southbound Exit 1C (Mill Plain) from I-5, take a right to Broadway, then left.

VANTAGE is located where I-90 crosses the Columbia River, just above Wanapum Dam.

Vantage is just north of I-90 on the Columbia's west bank. Vantage is the home of the Ginkgo Petrified Forest State Park. Ginkgoes (ging koh), or Maidenhair Trees, are slender trees with fan-shaped, fernlike leaves that grow on the end of shoots. Outside the park's center, a grove of living ginkgoes can be seen.

$34-$100 **VANTAGE KOA & MOTEL,** P. O. Box 135, Vantage, WA 98950, phone 509-856-2230. 14 motel units, 3 nonsmoking; 4 houses, 1 nonsmoking. All have private facilities and TV, no phones. All 4 houses have 3 bedrooms and kitchens, but do not furnish cooking utensils. Seasonal outdoor pool. Children welcome, pets allowed. This is the closest lodging for people attending a concert at the Gorge amphitheater; make your reservations early. No reservations taken for the KOA during the summer concert season - it's on a first come basis. **Winter Rates:** motel units, single $34; double $39; houses, double occupancy $45; pets $4; extra person $4; taxes 7.5%. **Summer Rates:** motel units, single $44-$49; double $49; houses $75. **Concert Weekends:** motel, single $75; double $79; houses $100. MasterCard & Visa. **Directions:** west side of the bridge.

VASHON ISLAND

(pop. 5,470) is located in Puget Sound, north of Tacoma and south of Seattle.

(VASH-ahn) Island is accessible by a 15 minute ferry ride from either Seattle or Tacoma. The downtown Seattle-Vashon Ferry is a passenger only ferry and takes 25 minutes. To get to the Fauntleroy Ferry in West Seattle by auto, take Exit 163A off I-5; by bus, catch the 118-119 Express or 54. The island stretches north to south for 13 miles over pastoral land and forest. Located in King County the sales/use taxes are 8.2%.

$75-$95   **ALL SEASONS LODGING**, 12817 SW Bachelor Rd., Vashon, WA 98070, phone 206-463-3498. A waterfront cottage with views of both Tacoma and Mt. Rainier. Located on the south end of Vashon Island, this cottage is a complete house with kitchen, phone, TV, fireplace, and a large sundeck. Stroll on the beach, storm watch, suntan, or just relax; there is something for all seasons. Adults only, no pets. **Rates:** double occupancy $95, *two night minimum;* $75 a night for a week or more. No credit cards. **Directions:** available with reservations.

$65-$85   **ARTIST'S STUDIO LOFT BED & BREAKFAST**, 16529 91st Ave. SW, Vashon, WA 98070, phone 206-463-2583. Three guest rooms available, all with private facilities. Each room is uniquely decorated, oak parquet floors, cathedral ceiling, skylights, stained glass windows, sundeck, patio with barbecue, picnic table, and a hot tub. The studio loft features a queen size bed, TV-VCR, stereo, refrigerator, microwave, Mr. Coffee, and a shower. Adults only, no pets. Expanded continental breakfast includes coffee/tea, baked goods, and orange juice. **Rates:** *2 night minimum on weekends* - double occupancy $65-$75 & $85. Amex, MasterCard & Visa. **Directions:** go to Vashon, in the middle of the island, 1/4 mile north of town turn east on Gorsuch Rd., proceed 3/4 mile, make a hard left onto 91st St.

$9-$55   **VASHON ISLAND RANCH & SUMMER HOSTEL**, 12119 SW Cove Rd., Vashon Island, WA 98070, phone 206-463-2592. The AYH Ranch has a unique western facade with covered wagons, teepees, and a log lodge on 10 pastoral acres surrounded by forest. When the hostel is open, *May 1 to Oct. 31,* 40 beds are available, one with private facilities, 39 with shared. The room with private facilities in the lodge is a bed and breakfast room in the winter. There are 6 Indian teepees, ideal for couples or families, equipped with beds; or sleep in the covered wagons. The lodge sleeps 14 in bunk rooms, has 2 bathrooms with showers, and a fully equipped kitchen. Free do-it-yourself pancake breakfast. Campfire wood is provided. Old bikes available for use. Children welcome at half price, no pets. Groups can reserve the entire lodge and grounds, private room extra. **Rates:** hostel $9 members, $12 non-members; private room summer, members $35, non-member $45; winter $55; group rates for 7 or more; taxes included. MasterCard & Visa. **Directions:** once on the Island, take bus 118 or 119 to Vashon, go to the Thriftway Grocery Store, call the hostel free, and someone will pick you up.

WALLA WALLA (pop. 28,874) is located in the southeast corner of the state.

(WAH-luh-WAH-luh) is the home of the Walla Walla sweet onion. The lure of rural living is enriched by the cultural and academic flavor found at three colleges: Whitman College, Walla Walla College, and Walla Walla Community College. The Blue Mountains bordering the Walla Walla Valley provide a paradise for outdoor activities.

Located in Walla Walla County the sales/use taxes are 7.8%.

$32-$56 **CAPRI MOTEL**, 2003 Melrose, Walla Walla, WA 99362, phone 509-525-1130 or 1-800-451-1139, fax 509-525-1465. 39 rooms, 19 nonsmoking. Phones, remote control cable TV with HBO, and coffee/tea making facilities in every room. One kitchen unit, with basic cookware, is available and some units have mini refrigerators and microwaves. Seasonal pool. Children welcome, infants free, pets allowed. Restaurants within walking distance. Close to Pioneer Park and bus service. **Summer Rates:** *5/01 to 9/30* - single (1 bed) $32-$42; double (2 beds) $46; family room $56; rollaway $8; pets $5; local phone calls free. **Winter Rates:** single $32-$39; double $43; family room $52. Major credit cards accepted. **Directions:** Wilbur St. Exit off Hwy 12, 3 blocks to Melrose.

$32-$55 **COLONIAL MOTEL**, 2279 E. Isaacs, Walla Walla, WA 99362, phone 509-529-1220. Tidy, one level motel with 17 rooms, 60% nonsmoking. Phones, cable TV with Showtime, and coffee/tea making facilities in every room. Half the rooms have refrigerators, and microwaves are available. Restaurants within walking distance and close to jogging trail. Children welcome, infants free, small pets allowed. **Rates:** single room (1 bed) $32-$38; double room (2 beds) $46; suite $55; local phone calls 25¢; extra person $2; pets free. Major credit cards. **Directions:** from the west take the Wilbur St. Exit off the freeway, left on Isaacs; from the east Exit Business Route 12.

COMFORT INN, 520 N. Second Ave., Walla Walla, WA 99362, phone 509-525-2522 or 1-800-221-2222, fax 509-522-2565.

ECONO LODGE, 305 N. Second Ave., Walla Walla, WA 99362, phone 509-529-4410 or 1-800-446-6900, fax 509-525-5777.

$75-$100 **GREEN GABLES INN BED & BREAKFAST**, 922 Bonsella, Walla Walla, WA 99362, phone 509-525-5501. This arts and crafts style mansion was built in 1909 and remained in the same family until 1950. For 3 decades the mansion served as a home for nurses and later administrative offices. Today, the Inn is a delightful blend of antique furnishings and modern conveniences. Guests may chose from 5 spacious bedrooms, each with private facilities. All rooms are equipped with mini refrigerators and cable TV. The master suite has a jacuzzi tub, fireplace, and outside deck. On the main level enjoy living room comfort with the warmth of two fireplaces, or the wrap-around porch. Full breakfast served in the dining room or on the front porch, weather permitting. Children over 12, no pets, and no smoking. **Rates:** double occupancy $75-$85; suite $100. MasterCard, Discover, & Visa. **Directions:** from Hwy 12 bypass take the Clinton St. Exit to Bonsella, then turn right for 1 block; from downtown take E. Rose or E. Main to Isaacs, turn left on Clinton, then turn left on Bonsella for 1 block.

$49-$58 **NENDELS WHITMAN INN**, 107 N. Second Ave., Walla Walla, WA 99362, phone 509-525-2200 or 1-800-237-1495 (WA), 1-800-237-4436 (nationally). 70 rooms, 39 nonsmoking. In-room amenities include phones and cable TV. Morning coffee is available in the restaurant on the main floor. The newly remodeled restaurant and lounge serves excellent food. Outdoor pool. Children 12 and under free with parents, no pets. **Rates:** single room $49-$54; double room $58; extra person $5; local phone calls free. Major credit cards. **Directions:** from Hwy 12 take Exit 2 to Second Ave., proceed 4 blocks.

PONY SOLDIER INN, 325 E. Main, Walla Walla, WA 99362, phone 509-529-4360 or 1-800-634-7669 (25).

$75 **STONE CREEK INN Bed & Breakfast,** 720 Bryant Ave., Walla Walla, WA 99362, phone 509-529-8120. A three story mansion, once owned by the territorial governor, is situated on 4 acres of park-like grounds. The 2 guest rooms available have private facilities, cable TV, and refrigerators. The Governor's Suite is on the main floor and the Eastlake Room, with a fireplace, is on the second floor. Breakfast is served in the dining room. Children over 12 by arrangement, no pets, and no smoking. **Rates:** double occupancy $75. No credit cards. **Directions:** given with reservations.

TAPADERA BUDGET INN, 211 N. Second, Walla Walla, WA 99362, phone 509-529-2580 or 1-800-722-8277.

TRAVELODGE, 421 E. Main, Walla Walla, WA 99362, phone 509-529-4940 or 1-800-578-7878, fax 509-529-4943.

WAPATO

(pop. 3,760) is in the Yakima Valley Wine Country; Staton Hills Winery is located here. (WAH-puh-toh) see Yakima, Toppenish, or Sunnyside for lodging.

WASHOUGAL

(pop. 4,240) is just east of Vancouver, Washington along the Columbia River.

(waw-SHOO-guhl) and Camas host the industrial firms of James River Corp. (pulp/paper), Hewlett-Packard (laser jet printers), Pendleton Woolen Mills, Sharp Microelectronics (integrated circuit design), Fiberweb North America (surgical gown materials), and Tidland Corp. (pneumatic shafts).

$40-$52 **ECONO LODGE,** 544 6th St., Washougal, WA 98671, phone 360-835-8591, fax 360-835-0240. 26 rooms, 12 nonsmoking. Phones, cable TV with Showtime, refrigerators, coffee/tea making facilities, and hairdryers in every room. Four kitchen units with basic cookware are available. Children under 5 free, pets allowed. Close to restaurants and the Pendleton Outlet Store. **Rates:** single (1 bed) $40-$44; double (2 beds) $52; kitchen units $7 extra; pets $3-$5; extra person $5; local phone calls free; taxes 7.6%. Major credit cards. **Directions:** 3 blocks off Hwy 14 on 6th Street.

$45 **GILDERSLEEVE HOME BED & BREAKFAST**, SW 140 Cooper, P. O. Box 657, Washtucna, WA 99371, phone 509-646-3417. This home has 2 guest rooms with shared facilities. One block from the shopping district, easy walking to park and swimming pool and access to the BNRR bicycle path. The B & B provides a homey atmosphere and has good bird watching. Full breakfast provided. Children welcome, no pets, and no smoking in the rooms. **Rates:** double occupancy $45; extra person $10; taxes 7.6%. No credit cards. **Directions:** D & Cooper streets, half a block from City Hall in the middle of town.

(wuh-NACH-ee) and East Wenatchee are in different counties and separated by the Columbia River. The two communities have a combined population base of about 50,000. Wenatchee is best known for its apple industry, sunshine, skiing, and recreation. The busiest weekends of the year are during the Ridge to River Relay Race (3rd weekend in April) and the Apple Blossom Festival. The festival occurs the last weekend in April and the first weekend in May. Lodging is at a premium during these times and reservations made well in advance are recommended. Mission Ridge Ski Area has four chairlifts and is just 13 miles from town. Many area motels offer ski packages.

Wenatchee is located in Chelan County sales/use/lodging taxes are 10%. E. Wenatchee is in Douglas County, their sales/use/lodging taxes are 9.9%.

$40-$75 **AVENUE MOTEL**, 720 N. Wenatchee Ave., Wenatchee, WA 98801, phone 509-663-7161, reservations 1-800-733-8981. Mature landscaping shelters this 39 unit motel. There are 20 nonsmoking units available. All rooms have a phone, TV, and coffee/tea making facilities. Other amenities include outdoor pool, hot tub, and a restaurant next door. There are 12 equipped kitchen units. Children 5 and under free, pets allowed. **Summer Rates:** *5/01 to 10/15* - single room (1 bed) $45; double room (2 beds) $55; suite $65-$75; kitchen units $5 extra;

extra person $5; pets free. **Winter Rates:** single $40; double $50. Major credit cards. **Directions:** between 7th & 9th on Wenatchee Ave.

$75-$85 **The CHERUB INN BED & BREAKFAST,** 410 N. Miller, Wenatchee, WA 98801, phone 509-662-6011, fax 509-664-8050. A romantic, elegant atmosphere permeates this 3 story Dutch Tudor mansion. Four nonsmoking rooms on the 2nd floor are adorned with many collectibles. All rooms share two full bathrooms. One room, decorated in a nautical theme, has a private balcony, double bed, and king bed in a loft. Two rooms have queen beds, and the other room has a double and twin bed. All rooms have overhead fans. Amenities include a 30 seat theater on the 3rd floor with a 100" screen, outdoor seasonal pool, year-round hot tub, fountain in the garden, and a full breakfast on weekends. Can host groups of up to 25 people with advance notice. Off-street parking. Children welcome, pets by arrangement at no charge. **Rates:** *weekends* - double occupancy $85; *midweek* - $75; extra person $15. MasterCard, Visa, & Amex. **Directions:** follow Wenatchee Ave. to 5th St., turn west, proceed 7 blocks to Miller St., turn left, 2nd house on the right.

$60-$85 **CHIEFTAIN MOTEL RESTAURANT,** 1005 N. Wenatchee Ave., Wenatchee, WA 98801, phone 509-663-8141 or 1-800-572-4456 (WA), fax 509-663-8176. Noted for its quality food and service, the Chieftain has faithfully served Wenatchee and visitors since 1956. There are 105 rooms, 67 nonsmoking. In-room amenities include phones and cable TV with HBO. Morning coffee is available in the restaurant that opens at 6:00 a.m. Other amenities are a covered outdoor pool and hot tub. The lounge features a "midnight raid" five nights a week (starts at 11 p.m.). Children free with parents, pets allowed in some smoking rooms. **Rates:** single room (1 bed) $60; double room (2 beds) $70; suite $85; pets free; local phone calls free. Major credit cards. **Directions:** centrally located on Wenatchee Ave., north of 9th Street.

$55 **COVENTRY INN BED & BREAKFAST,** 519 King, Wenatchee, WA 98801, phone 509-662-6771. This vintage home was built in 1915. The verandah has a park view. Two nonsmoking rooms are furnished with antique queen beds and share one bath with shower and vanity. Victorian furnishings throughout the Inn. Continental breakfast of juice, fruit, and baked goods. Adults only, no pets. **Rates:** double occupancy $55. No credit cards. **Directions:** from the north follow Wenatchee Ave. to Orondo St., turn west, go uphill to Idaho St., turn right, go 2 blocks to King, turn right; from the south bridge, go to the stoplight and turn right onto Mission St., get in the left lane, proceed to Orondo St.

$44-$85 **FOUR SEASONS INN**, 11 W. Grant Rd., E. Wenatchee, WA 98802, phone & fax 509-884-6611 or 1-800-223-6611. Located in East Wenatchee on the Columbia River. There are 100 rooms, 40 nonsmoking. In-room amenities include phones and TV. Morning coffee is available in the 24 hour coffee shop. Other amenities include restaurant/lounge, outdoor pool, spa, and sauna. Also, an 18 hole, par 3 putting course by the river with a pro shop. Children 13 and under free, small dogs allowed. There is a small park just to the south of the motel with many resident groundhogs. Ample parking for large trucks or RVs. **Summer Rates:** *3/15 to 10/15* - single room (1 bed) $54-$65; double room (2 beds) $67; suite $85; extra person $5; pets $5. **Winter Rates:** single $44; double $56; suite $65. Major credit cards. **Directions:** located off Hwy 2 in E. Wenatchee.

HERITAGE INN Best Western, 1905 N. Wenatchee Ave., Wenatchee, WA 98801, phone 509-664-6565 or 1-800-528-1234.

$32-$55 **HILL CREST MOTEL**, 2921 School St., Wenatchee, WA 98801, phone 509-663-5157 or 1-800-245-5157. This one level motel has 16 rooms, 6 nonsmoking, and 7 equipped kitchen units. Amenities include phones, TV, coin-op laundry, and outdoor pool. Morning coffee is available in the lobby after 8 a.m. Family oriented, children welcome, pets allowed. Outdoor play area for children, picnic tables, and barbecue. RV spaces with hookups. **Summer Rates:** *5/01 to 10/01* - single room (1 bed) $40-$45; double room (2 beds) $55; extra person $5; pets free. **Winter Rates:** *excluding festivals and holidays* - single $32-$36; double $45. Most major credit cards. **Directions:** 1 mile north of Wenatchee on Hwy 97.

HOLIDAY LODGE, 610 N. Wenatchee Ave., Wenatchee, WA 98801, phone 509-663-8167 or 1-800-722-0852.

$28-$70 **LYLES MOTEL**, 924 N. Wenatchee Ave., Wenatchee, WA 98801, phone 509-663-5155 or 1-800-582-3788. This motel was completely remodeled in 1993. All 25 rooms are newly decorated, 13 nonsmoking rooms available. In-room amenities include phones and TV. Morning coffee is available in the lobby. Other amenities include outdoor pool and indoor hot tub. There are 5 apartment units with equipped kitchens. Children under 10 free, pets allowed. **Summer Rates:** single room (1 bed) $28-$44; double room (2 beds) $42-$50; kitchen units $50-$70; extra person $5; pets $5-$20. Check on winter rates. MasterCard,

Amex, Discover, & Visa. **Directions:** centrally located on Wenatchee Ave. just north of 9th St.

$48-$74 **ORCHARD INN,** 1401 N. Miller Ave., Wenatchee, WA 98801, phone 509-662-3443 or 1-800-368-4571 (WA), fax 509-663-1665. This 3 story motel has 103 guest rooms, 57 nonsmoking. In-room amenities include phones, TV with HBO, and some with micro/fridges. Morning coffee is available in the lobby and Denny's is just across the street. Covered year-round pool and hot tub. Children 12 and under free, pets allowed with a refundable deposit. **Summer Rates:** *5/01 to 10/01* - single room (1 bed) $48-$58; double room (2 beds) $58-$61; suites $69-$74; extra person $3; pet deposit $50. **Winter Rates:** single $48-$52; double $58; suite $69. Major credit cards. **Directions:** north end of Wenatchee, turn east (towards the river) at Maple, proceed 1 block.

$50 **PITCHER CANYON BED & BREAKFAST,** 1402 Pitcher Canyon Rd., Wenatchee, WA 98801, phone 509-662-0130. Close to Mission Ridge ski area. This two year old home has 2 guest rooms that share one bathroom. One room has a double bed and the other 2 twins. The rooms are at ground level in the daylight basement, have large windows and private entrance. Full breakfast provided, closest restaurant is 3-4 miles. Children by arrangement, no pets, smoking outside. **Rates:** double occupancy $50, tax included. No credit cards. **Directions:** follow the signs to Mission Ridge, proceed 2 1/4 miles on Squilchuck Rd., turn right on Pitcher Canyon Rd., 1/2 mile up the canyon.

RED LION INN, 1225 N. Wenatchee Ave., Wenatchee, WA 98801, phone 509-663-0711 or 1-800-RED-LION.

$57-$62 **RIVERS INN,** 580 Valley Mall Pkwy., E. Wenatchee, WA 98802, phone 509-884-1474 or 1-800-922-3199 (WA). Located in East Wenatchee across from Wenatchee Valley Mall shopping center. There are 55 rooms with king or queen beds, 35 nonsmoking. In-room amenities include phones and TV. Some rooms also have micro/fridges. Morning coffee is available in the lobby with a complimentary continental breakfast. Other amenities include an outdoor pool and year-round jacuzzi. Pool-side rooms with patios and balconies are available. Adjacent restaurant and sports bar. Shuttle provided to airport and Amtrak. Children 11 and under free, no pets. **Rates:** single room (1 bed) $57; double room (2 beds) $62; extra person $5. Major credit cards. **Directions:** on East Wenatchee's main street, Valley Mall Pkwy, across from the Mall.

$50-$95 **ROSE MANOR BED & BREAKFAST**, 156 S. Emerson, Wenatchee, WA 98801, phone 509-662-1093. Located in the heart of Wenatchee, this four story, 5,000 plus square foot home was originally constructed in 1904. There are 5 nonsmoking guest rooms, 3 with private facilities and 2 with shared. Two rooms have phones, one has TV. Each room has an individual color theme. Panoramic view of the mountains from any of the five comfortable porches. In-house gift shop and within walking distance of downtown. Full gourmet breakfast. Children welcome, no pets. Shuttle provided to airport or train. **Rates:** double occupancy $50-$65; suite $95; extra person $5-$10. MasterCard & Visa. **Directions:** from the north, Wenatchee Ave., right on Miller, proceed to Idaho St., turn left to Emerson; from the south, cross bridge to light, turn right on Mission, to Orondo, turn left, proceed to Emerson, turn right.

$32-$65 **STARLITE MOTEL,** 1640 N. Wenatchee Ave., Wenatchee, WA 98801, phone 509-663-8115. 34 units, 8 nonsmoking. In-room amenities include phones, TV, and coffee/tea making facilities. 12 units have equipped kitchens. Coffee available in the lobby. Seasonal outdoor pool. Children 12 and under free, no pets. **Summer Rates:** *5/01 to 10/01* - single room $40; double room $50; kitchen unit $65; family room $50-$65. **Winter Rates:** $32-$55. Major credit cards. **Directions:** first motel on the west side of Wenatchee Ave., coming into town from the north.

TRAVELODGE, 1004 N. Wenatchee Ave., Wenatchee, WA 98801, phone 509-662-8165 or 1-800-578-7878.

$54-$66 **UPTOWNER MOTEL,** 101 N. Mission, Wenatchee, WA 98801, phone 509-663-8516 or 1-800-288-5279. 22 rooms, all with equipped kitchenettes, 7 nonsmoking. Phones, TV, queen beds, coffee/tea making facilities in every room. Outdoor swimming pool and sauna. Restaurants within walking distance. One block from convention center and downtown shopping. Children 5 and under free, pets with deposit. **Rates:** single room (1 bed) $54; double room (2 beds) $60; family room (3 beds) $66; extra person $10; local phone calls free. Major credit cards. **Directions:** 1 block west of Wenatchee Ave. on Mission & 1st.

VAGABOND INN, (formerly the Econo Lodge) 700 N. Wenatchee Ave., Wenatchee, WA 98801, phone 509-663-8133 or 1-800-522-1555.

$75 **WARM SPRINGS INN BED & BREAKFAST,** 1611 Love Lane, Wenatchee, WA 98801, phone 509-662-8365 or 1-800-543-3645. Located just west of Wenatchee in the foothills of Warm Springs Canyon, this plantation style home offers four spacious guest rooms. All have private baths and fabulous views of the Wenatchee River. Full breakfast provided. Older children by arrangement, no pets, smoking outside. The Inn is available for day retreats, wedding receptions, and holiday parties, can accommodate up to 80 people. **Rates:** double occupancy $75; extra person $18. Visa & MasterCard. **Directions:** from the west on Hwy 2, go past Monitor 3/4 mile and turn right on Lower Sunnyslope Rd., turn right on Love Ln., proceed to the end of the road; coming from the east go 1 mile west of Wenatchee, turn left on Lower Sunnyslope Rd. to Love Ln., turn right.

Warm Springs Inn Bed & Breakfast

WELCOME INN, 232 N. Wenatchee Ave., Wenatchee, WA 98801, phone 509-663-7121 or 1-800-561-8856.

WESTCOAST WENATCHEE CENTER HOTEL, 201 N. Wenatchee Ave., Wenatchee, WA 98801, phone 509-662-1234 or 1-800-426-0676.

WESTPORT

(pop. 1,890) is located on the southwest shore of Grays Harbor, about 20 miles west of Aberdeen.

Westport is primarily a working man's fishing port. Serious fishermen come here to take advantage of the numerous charter boats and to learn from the experienced crews. Tourists also flock to Westport for whale watching.

Located in Grays Harbor County the sales/use/lodging taxes are 10.9%.

$47-$72 **CHATEAU WESTPORT**, 710 West Hancock, P. O. Box 349, Westport, WA 98595, phone 360-268-9101 or 1-800-255-9101. Built in 1968, this year-round resort is a destination for pleasure and business. 108 rooms, 20 nonsmoking. In-room amenities include phones and TV. Morning coffee is available in the lobby with a complimentary continental breakfast. Select from a variety of rooms, some have fireplaces, equipped kitchens, balconies, and ocean views. Suites available, ask management about price. Children under 1 free, no pets. **Summer Rates:** 5/01 to 9/30 - double room $67; studio with kitchen $72; extra person $7; local phone calls free. **Winter Rates:** *excluding holidays* - $47-$50. Major credit cards. **Directions:** going into Westport on Hwy 105 Spur (Forest St.), turn left on Hancock Ave.

$47-$85 **COHO CHARTERS MOTEL & RV PARK**, 2501 N. Nyhus, P. O. Box 1087, Westport, WA 98595, phone 360-268-0111 or 1-800-572-0177 (WA). Open year-round, this three story motel has 28 rooms, 7 nonsmoking. Newly refurbished rooms have phones, TV, and instant coffee/tea pots. Coffee is available in the lobby, and restaurants are within walking distance. One block to the beach, shops, and harbor. Meeting facility seats approximately 80 people. Charter facilities have 4 boats for salmon, tuna, halibut, bottom fishing, and whale watching. Crab pots for rent, bait for sale. **Summer Rates:** single room $57; double room $62; suite $70; family room (4 people) $85; extra person $5; local phone calls free. **Winter Rates:** single $47; double $50; suite $65; family room $80. Major credit cards. **Directions:** follow Hwy 105 into Westport, go to Dock St., turn left on Nyhus and proceed to the Coho.

$40-$65 **FRANK L. AQUATIC GARDEN RESORT,** 725 S. Montesano, Westport, WA 98595, phone 360-268-9200. Open year-round, this updated 1950's motel has 13 rooms, 2 nonsmoking. In-room amenities include phones and cable TV. Morning coffee available in the lobby. Three full kitchen units and 5 equipped kitchenettes. Large patio, barbecue, clam and crab cooking facility. Relax in the gardens amidst Koi ponds, creeks, waterfalls, and the wildlife bird sanctuary. Children welcome, pets allowed. **Summer Rates:** *6/01 to 10/01* - single room $47; double room $51; kitchen units $53-$65; extra person $10; pets $5; local phone calls free. **Winter Rates:** $40-$60. MasterCard & Visa. **Directions:** follow Hwy 105 into Westport, turn right on Montesano.

$50-$150 **GLENACRES INN BED & BREAKFAST,** 222 N. Montesano, P. O. Box 1246, Westport, WA 98595, phone 360-268-9391. Eight rooms in the Inn and 4 cottages. Secluded among stately evergreens on eight wooded acres, this 1898 Inn offers 8 rooms, all with private facilities, 5 nonsmoking. Some rooms open onto a large deck. Centered on the deck is a gazebo-covered hot tub. A complete breakfast is provided to guests in the Inn. The cottages are nestled among the trees surrounding the Inn. Cottages will accommodate four to eleven people, all have completely furnished kitchens. Children free with parents, pets allowed in cottages only. **Rates:** Inn rooms $50-$72; cottages $45-$150. Major credit cards. **Directions:** from the east follow Montesano to 1st stoplight, go thru light, 1st driveway on the right; from the south, go to stop sign, turn right to stoplight, turn left at the 1st driveway.

$43-$98 **ISLANDER CHARTERS & MOTEL,** P. O. Box 488, Westport, WA 98595, phone 360-268-9166 or toll free *May to Sept.* 1-800-322-1740. 31 ocean view units, no designated non-smoking. In-room amenities include phones and TV. Morning coffee is available at the coffee shop on the premises. There are 4 non-equipped kitchen units available. Other on site amenities include a charter fishing office, gift shop, outdoor pool, news stand, beauty salon, meeting facilities, restaurant, and lounge. Karaoke in the lounge 7 nights a week. Children welcome, pets allowed. **Summer Rates:** *6/01 to 10/01* - single room $62-$69; double room $76; kitchen units $98; extra person $5; pets $10 one time fee; local phone calls free. **Winter Rates:** single $43-$46; double $50; kitchen unit $73. Major credit cards. **Directions:** corner of Westhaven and Neddie Rose Dr., overlooking the marina.

$37-$55 **MARINERS COVE INN,** 303 Ocean Ave., Westport, WA 98595, phone 360-268-0531. This 4 year old motel is all on one level and has 9 queen size units, 5 nonsmoking. In-room amenities include phones, bar refrigerators, coffee/tea making facilities, and TV. There is 1 equipped kitchen unit available and a gazebo-covered barbecue area with picnic tables. Adjacent restaurant. Children welcome, pets by arrangement. **Summer Rates:** single room $49-$52; double room $59; kitchen unit, 1 bed $55; extra person $5; local phone calls free. **Winter Rates:** $37-$50. MasterCard, Diners Club, & Visa. **Directions:** at the stoplight on Montesano turn left, 1/2 block.

$36-$48 **McBEE'S SILVER SANDS MOTEL,** 1001 S. Montesano St., Westport, WA 98595, phone 360-268-9029. This is a two story motel with 19 units, 4 nonsmoking. In-room amenities include 2 double beds, phones, and cable TV. Morning coffee is available in the lobby. Children welcome, no pets. Close to restaurants and within five minutes of ocean beaches and marina. **Summer Rates:** double occupancy $48; extra person $5-$6; local phone calls free. **Winter Rates:** $36. MasterCard & Visa. **Directions:** on Montesano Ave., south of town.

$38-$125 **OCEAN AVENUE INN,** 275 W. Ocean Ave., P. O. Box 571, Westport, WA 98595, phone 360-268-9400 or 268-9278. 12 units, 1 nonsmoking. In-room amenities include phones and cable TV. Nine equipped kitchenette units. There is also one 2 bedroom guest cottage. Morning coffee is available at the cafe across the street. 1 block to public transportation; shuttle provided to dock area and Aberdeen. Children welcome, small pets allowed. **Summer Rates:** single room $45-$55; double room (2 beds) $75; 3 bedroom suite (maximum 8 people) $125; small pets $5 per night; local phone calls free. **Winter Rates:** $38-$68. Major credit cards. **Directions:** coming into town from the east, turn right on Montesano, proceed to Ocean Ave., turn left, go 1 1/2 blocks - on the left.

$44-$59 **PACIFIC MOTEL & TRAILER PARK,** 330 S. Forrest St., Westport, WA 98595, phone 360-268-9325. 12 units, 7 nonsmoking. In-room amenities include TV, queen beds, and 6 equipped kitchenette units. Some rooms have coffee/tea making facilities. Pay phone by the office. There is also a large recreation room with a kitchen. Seasonal, heated outdoor pool. 80 full trailer hookups and large tent sites. Children welcome, no pets. 80 RV and tent sites. **Rates:** single room $44-$49; double room $54-$59; extra person $5. MasterCard & Visa, cash discounts. **Directions:** coming into town from the south, go to the stop sign, take a right.

$32-$42 **SANDS MOTEL & R.V. PARK**, 1416 S. Montesano, P. O. Box 2044, Westport, WA 98595, phone 360-268-0091. Quiet location, fresh sea air, and only 5 minutes to the docks and fishing fleet. This motel has 12 units, 6 nonsmoking. All rooms with private bath and remote control cable TV. Morning coffee is available at local restaurants within walking distance. Newly remodeled RV park adjoins the motel. Fish and crab cleaning area with cooking facilities. Children welcome, pets by arrangement. **Rates:** single room (1 bed) $32-$38; double room $42; extra person $4. MasterCard & Visa. **Directions:** coming from the east on Hwy 105 take the first Westport Exit, go one mile; from the south, turn right just past Twin Harbors State Park, go to Montesano, turn left, go one mile.

$35-$45 **WINDJAMMER MOTEL**, 461 E. Pacific, P. O. Box 655, Westport, WA 98595, phone 360-268-9351. Located on a quiet, dead-end street, this motel has 12 units, 4 nonsmoking. Cable TV in all the rooms, 4 equipped kitchenette units have coffee/tea making facilities. Complimentary coffee is also available in the office from 7 a.m. to 11 a.m. Within walking distance of restaurants. The bay can be seen from the back lawn, which has a large grassy area, picnic tables, and barbecue. Sea creature cleaning area. Children welcome, no pets. **Summer Rates:** *6/01 to 10/01* - single (1 person) $40; double (2 people) $45; extra person $5. **Winter Rates:** $35-$40. MasterCard & Visa. **Directions:** in the middle of town, 3 blocks from the police station and main through street.

WHIDBEY ISLAND is located approximately 20 miles north of Seattle. From the south, take the Mukilteo/Clinton Ferry or drive Hwy 20 from the north over Deception Pass.

(WHID-bee) Island is the longest island in the continental United States at 50 miles in length. Major towns are Clinton, Coupeville, Freeland, Greenbank, Langley, and Oak Harbor. The Whidbey Island Naval Air Station is the primary employer on the island. There are three approaches to Whidbey Island. From the north, take Hwy 20 across Deception Pass Bridge; from the west, take the Keystone Ferry from Port Townsend; from the south, follow I-5 north to Exit 189, follow the signs to the Mukilteo Ferry, take the ferry to Whidbey Island.

Located in Island County the sales/use taxes are 7.9%.

COUPEVILLE

(KOOP-vil) is located approximately 28 miles from the Clinton ferry dock. This is the second oldest town in the state. The Victorian frame houses, quaint shops, and old churches make your stop here worthwhile.

$65-$90 **ANCHORAGE INN BED & BREAKFAST**, 807 N. Main St., Coupeville, WA 98239, phone 360-678-5581. This 5 year old Victorian replica was built as a bed and breakfast. There are 5 guest rooms, all with private facilities and TV. Phone in the office. Four course gourmet breakfast is provided in the dining room. The Inn is located in the historic district of Coupeville wihin walking distance of shops and restaurants. The guest lounge, the "Crow's Nest" offers TV, VCR, games, books, excercise bike, videos, and cookies. Children 14 and older, no pets. **Rates:** midweek $65; weekends and holidays $75-$90; extra person $10; local phone calls free. Major credit cards. **Directions:** coming into Coupeville, at the traffic light turn onto Main Street, go 9 blocks to the Anchorage Inn. Look for the big white Victorian house with the red roof.

$65-$95 **COLONEL CROCKETT FARM BED & BREAKFAST**, 1012 S. Fort Casey Rd., Coupeville, WA 98239, phone 360-678-3711. Five nonsmoking rooms, all with private facilities. Full hot breakfast provided. Step back 135 years into the serenity and comfort of this Victorian farm house, which is on the National Register of Historic Places. Nearby, guests can browse through the small shops of historic Coupeville. Children over 14, no pets. **Rates:** double occupancy $65-$95; extra person $10. Visa & MasterCard. **Directions:** from the north on Hwy 20, turn right at the Coupeville light, in 3.3 miles turn left on Ft. Casey Rd., in 1/2 a mile turn right into driveway. From the south on Hwy 525, turn left onto Hwy 20W, in 1.4 miles turn right onto Wanamaker Rd., in 1.7 miles turn left onto Ft. Casey Rd., proceed for two blocks.

The Colonel Crockett Farm Bed & Breakfast Inn

$56-$105 **The COUPEVILLE INN**, 200 Coveland St., P. O. Box 370, Coupeville, WA 98239, phone 360-678-6668, reservations 1-800-247-6162 (WA). 24 guest rooms, 3 nonsmoking. In-room amenities include TV and phones. Morning coffee is available with a complimentary continental breakfast in the dining room overlooking Penn Cove Bay. Restaurants are within walking distance. Children welcome, infants free, pets allowed in the off-season. Rooms with private balconies overlook the historic seaport. Panoramic views of Coupeville, Penn Cove, and the Cascade Mountains. **Summer Rates:** *5/01 to 9/30* - double occupancy $56-$105; extra person $10; local phone calls free. **Winter Rates:** $56-$85; small pets $5, medium $10 per night. Major credit cards. **Directions:** located at Penn Cove in the center of Whidbey Island.

$60-$125 **The INN AT PENN COVE**, 702 N. Main, P. O. Box 85, Coupeville, WA 98239, phone 360-678-8000 or 1-800-688-2683. Two Victorian houses built in 1889 and 1891 just three blocks from the water. 6 nonsmoking guest rooms, 4 with private facilities, 2 with shared. Five rooms have queen beds, one suite has a jacuzzi and king bed. TV, pump organ, and fireplace in the common rooms. Full breakfast is provided. Children welcome under most circumstances, no pets. **Rates:** double occupancy $60-$105; suite $125. Major credit cards accepted. **Directions:** turn right onto Main St., go down the hill until you see the sign.

$65-$100 **The VICTORIAN BED & BREAKFAST**, 602 N. Main, P. O. Box 761, Coupeville, WA 98239, phone 360-678-5305. This beautiful old Victorian is 106 years old and is listed on the National Historic Register. There are 2 rooms in the main house and one cottage. All have private facilities and queen beds. TV and VCR in the tea room. The cottage has a kitchen, trundle bed, TV, and VCR. Full breakfast is provided. Children 6 and under free, pets allowed only in the cottage. **Summer Rates:** guest rooms, double occupancy $80; cottage $100; extra person $20; pets $20. **Winter Rates:** rooms $65; cottage $85. MasterCard, Discover, & Visa. **Directions:** on 6th and Main St.

FREELAND

is located on the southern end of Whidbey Island, where Holmes Harbor and Mutiny Bay are separated by less than one mile of land. Freeland is an "off highway" delight that offers beautiful panoramas of the Cascade Mountains on one side and the Olympic Mountains on the other.

$85-$95 **BUSH POINT WHARF BED & BREAKFAST**, 229 E. Main St., P. O. Box 1042, Freeland, WA 98249, phone 360-331-0405 or 1-800-460-7219. Two guest rooms overlooking the water. One room is nonsmoking, both have private facilities with jacuzzi, living room, coffee/tea making facilities, refrigerator, TV, and VCR. Continental breakfast is provided. Located next to the Bush Point Restaurant (open April to October). Adults only, no pets. **Rates:** double occupancy, midweek $85; weekends $95. MasterCard, Amex, & Visa. **Directions:** from Freeland go north to Bush Point Rd., turn left, proceed to Scurlock Rd. all the way to the waterfront.

$47-$76 **The HARBOUR INN,** 1606 E. Main, P. O. Box 1350, Freeland, WA 98249, phone 360-331-6900. 20 units, 13 nonsmoking. In-room amenities include phones, radios, and cable TV. Most rooms have refrigerators. Morning coffee is available in the lobby with a continental breakfast. Four equipped kitchen units available. Within walking distance of a restaurant. Large lawn with outdoor furniture; 1/4 mile from the water, beach, and boat launch. Children welcome, pets in some rooms. **Rates:** single room (1 bed) $47-$69; double room $69; kitchen units $76; children $3-$6. MasterCard & Visa. **Directions:** 10 miles from the ferry, the Inn is on the left side of the road coming into town from the east.

$50-$115 **MUTINY BAY RESORT MOTEL**, 5856 S. Mutiny Bay Rd., P. O. Box 249, Freeland, WA 98249, phone 360-331-4500. Chalets, cabins, and trailer pads. The four chalets have two story glass walls facing Puget Sound and the beach. Fireplace, TV, 2 bedrooms downstairs, a loft upstairs, plus a fully equipped kitchen, and front porch (sleeps 7). The 5 cabins are smaller (sleep 3-5 people), 1 has private facilities, 4 have 1/2 baths, all have fully equipped kitchens. Private dock for fishing; crab pot and fishing pole rentals; bait and ice available. Children welcome, no pets. **Summer Rates:** chalets, double occupancy $115; cabins $60 & $65; extra person $5. **Winter Rates:** chalet $100; cabins $50 & $55. MasterCard & Visa. **Directions:** at Freeland, turn west on Fish Road off Hwy 525, proceed 1 mile to end of road, turn right, then left at the sign.

$60-$95 **SEASIDE COTTAGE BED & BREAKFAST**, 213 E. Sandpiper Rd., P. O. Box 970, Freeland, WA 98249, phone 360-331-8455, fax 360-331-8636. Two 1 bedroom units. The cottage is on the beach with magnificent mountain and water views. Queen bed, sleeper sofa, TV/VCR, fireplace, fully equipped kitchen, washer/dryer. The suite has a garden view, fully equipped kitchen, sleeper sofa, TV, and piano. Breakfast provided in the cottage only, by request in the suite. Smoking allowed on the decks. Other amenities include Weber BBQ, beach buckets, firewood, and kites. Children by arrangement, no pets. **Rates:** cottage $95; suite $60; both units together $135. Discover card. **Directions:** from ferry go north on Hwy 525 to Bush Point Rd. (10.6 miles), turn left, go 2.7 miles to Scurlock, turn left, follow yellow line to bottom of hill, turn left in front of restaurant, go 1 block, turn right on Sandpiper, turn right into 1st driveway on the right.

$80-$90 **UNCLE JOHN'S COTTAGE BED & BREAKFAST,** 1762 E. Lancaster Rd., Freeland, WA 98249, phone 360-321-5623 or 1-800-779-5623, fax 360-331-7129. Two complete guest cottages with beautiful views. This country setting is on 10 acres with beaches nearby. Each cottage has 2 bedrooms, fully equipped kitchen, TV, and fireplace. The refrigerator is stocked for a complete breakfast. Nonsmokers preferred. Children welcome, infants free, pets by arrangement. Group lodging for up to 16 people. **Summer Rates:** *5/15 to 9/15* - double occupancy $90; extra person $15; children $5; group rates $25 per person. **Winter Rates:** $80; extra person $10. MasterCard & Visa. **Directions:** from ferry go north on Hwy 525 , turn left at Double Bluff Rd., go 1/2 mile to first cross road, turn right on Lancaster, proceed 1 mile to top of hill, left side.

LANGLEY

This "Village by the Sea" is a charming place to visit. Enjoy art galleries, unique shops, good restaurants, friendly people, and, of course, the magnificent waterfront setting. Take the beach access stairwell at Seawall Park for a stroll on the beach.

$85-$110 **COUNTRY COTTAGE OF LANGLEY,** Bed & Breakfast, 215 6th Street, Langley, WA 98260, phone 360-221-8709. This restored farmhouse has 5 separate guest cottages, all nonsmoking. Old World charm with modern comforts. All the cottages have private facilities, coffee/tea making facilities, and refrigerators. A full breakfast is provided and restaurants are within walking distance. Adults only, no pets. **Summer Rates:** *5/15 to 10/15* - double occupancy $95-$110. **Winter Rates:** $85-$95. MasterCard & Visa. **Directions:** from the Clinton ferry dock follow Hwy 525 north 3.9 miles to Maxwelton Rd., turn right, follow signs to Langley, on 6th Street.

$45-$55 **DRAKE'S LANDING,** 203 Wharf St., P. O. Box 613, Langley, WA 98260, phone 360-221-3999. Located directly across the street from the boat harbor. Five rooms available, all with private facilities, no designated nonsmoking. The queen bedroom has an outside entrance and roll top desk. One upstairs room has a full bed, windows to the water, and access to the deck. Two other rooms have outside entrances and full beds. No TV or phones in the rooms, just tons of books and lots of pillows. Morning coffee is provided in the lobby and restaurants are within walking distance. Children and pets by arrangement. **Rates:** single or double room $45-$55; extra person $15; pets $5-$10. MasterCard & Visa. **Directions:** in Langley, go downhill off 1st Street, across the street from the boat harbor.

$95-$115   **EAGLES NEST INN Bed & Breakfast**, 3236 E. Saratoga Rd., Langley, WA 98260, phone 360-221-5331. Perched high on a hill with spectacular views of Saratoga Passage, Camano Island, and Mt. Baker, this elegant home has 4 nonsmoking guest rooms, all with private facilities. Each room has a TV and VCR. A library is located on the third level with many books and video selections. Outdoor hot tub. Full breakfast is provided. Children 12 and older, no pets. **Rates:** double occupancy $95-$115; extra person $15. MasterCard, Discover, & Visa. **Directions:** from the Clinton ferry dock follow Hwy 525 for 2.7 miles and turn right on Langley Rd., go 3.7 miles to Langley, follow 2nd Street 1.5 miles, turn left into driveway and go up the hill.

$80-$100   **The GALLERY SUITE**, 302 First St., Langley, WA 98260, phone 360-221-2978. This suite is a completely furnished apartment. The living room has an unobstructed view of Saratoga Passage and Camano Head. A spacious deck provides a place to breathe the fresh sea air or catch the afternoon sun. A deluxe continental breakfast is provided and the kitchen is equipped with basic dishes. Adults only, no pets, and no smoking. Located in the rear of the Proctor/Childers Art Gallery. **Rates:** *two night minimum on weekends and holidays* - double occupancy, first night $100; 2nd night $90; third night $80. Major credit cards. **Directions:** from the Clinton ferry dock take Hwy 525 for 2.7 miles, turn right on Langley Rd., proceed to Langley's main street.

$80-$150   **The GARDEN PATH INN,** 111 First St., P. O. Box 575, Langley, WA 98260, phone 360-221-5121. Two serene, elegant suites let you know the owner is an interior decorator; shop downstairs. The smaller suite in the back has a living room, bedroom, bath and kitchenette equipped with a toasteroven, sink and refrigerator. The larger suite in front has a view of Saratoga Passage and Langley's colorful First Street. Continental breakfast provided. Adults only, no pets, and no smoking. **Rates:** double occupancy, small suite $80; large suite $150. MasterCard & Visa. **Directions:** in Langley, on the main street.

$65-$90   **ISLAND PALMS BED & BREAKFAST**, 619 First St., P. O. Box 62, Langley, WA 98260, phone 360-221-8173. Located on a hill overlooking Langley, this Victorian home offers 3 guest rooms, two with private facilities. One room has a balcony with views of the Cascades. Another spacious room looks towards Mt. Baker. Choose from twin beds, double bed, or queen bed. Two of the rooms are on the 2nd floor and one on the main floor. A continental breakfast is provided. Children welcome, no pets, smoking outside. **Rates:** double occupancy $65, $75,& $90; extra person $10. No credit cards. **Directions:** 1.5 blocks west of downtown Langley.

$90-$115   **LOG CASTLE BED & BREAKFAST**, 3273 E. Saratoga Rd., Langley, WA 98260, phone 360-221-5483. This magnificent, hand-crafted log home brings up images of hobbits and wizards. All four rooms are unique and different with great views. All have private facilities. The main floor of the lodge is warm and inviting with a large stone fireplace. Breakfast includes homemade bread and warm cinnamon rolls. Canoe or rowboat available. Fish for perch, cod, and sole directly in front of the lodge. Children over 10, no pets, no smoking, and no alcohol. **Rates:** double occupancy $90-$115; extra person $25. MasterCard, Discover, & Visa. **Directions:** from the Clinton ferry dock follow Hwy 525 for 2.7 miles and turn right on Langley Rd., go 3.7 miles to Langley, on 2nd St. to Saratoga Rd., proceed 1.5 miles and turn right.

Log Castle turret room

$95-$110 **LONE LAKE COTTAGE & BREAKFAST**, 5206 S. Bayview Rd., Langley, WA 98260, phone 360-321-5325. "On Golden Pond", the Terrace Cottage, Garden Cottage, Lakeside Suite, and the Whidbey Queen. Each cottage has a fireplace, kitchen, lovely china, TV-VCR, gas barbecue, double jacuzzi tubs, and view of the lake. The Whidbey Queen is a tiny stern-wheel houseboat permanently moored at its own private dock. The bird aviary on the grounds has many species to watch. Amenities include a rowboat, canoe, pickle ball court, private beach, lawn chairs, bicycles, and picnic tables. A deluxe continental breakfast is placed in the cottages the first two days of your stay. Adults only, no pets. Smoking is permitted on the outside covered deck areas. **Summer Rates:** double occupancy $110; extra person $15. **Winter Rates:** midweek $95. No credit cards. **Directions:** from the Clinton ferry dock follow Hwy 525 for 5.5 miles, turn right on Bayview Rd., proceed 1 mile, entrance on the left.

$75 **PINE COTTAGE BED & BREAKFAST**, 3827 McKay Dr., Langley, WA 98260, phone 360-730-1376. One nonsmoking cottage. Private facilities, TV, coffee/tea making facilities, wood stove, and French doors that open onto a deck. Private patio with barbecue, lawn chairs, and picnic table just below the deck; large yard; walk to the beach. Continental breakfast provided. Children welcome, but space is limited, no pets. **Rates:** double occupancy $75; extra person $10. Credit cards for reservations only. **Directions:** in Langley follow Saratoga 3.5 miles to McKay, turn right at the white rock.

$99-$110 **PRIMROSE PATH COTTAGE**, 3191 E. Harbor Rd., Langley, WA 98260, phone 360-730-3722 or 1-800-333-4724. One nonsmoking cottage. Private facilities, two bedrooms, phone, and fully equipped kitchen. This is an authentic Whidbey Island cottage built in 1928 that offers true period charm. Nestled on a wooded acre, this private cottage can accommodate up to four people. There is a water view, private beach access, and a hot tub. Continental breakfast provided. Children welcome, no pets. **Summer Rates:** *5/01 to 11/30* - double occupancy $110; 4 people $135. **Winter Rates:** *weekends* $99; *midweek* first night regular price, consecutive nights 1/2 price. Discover card. **Directions:** from the Clinton ferry go north on Hwy 525 for 8 miles, turn right onto Scott Rd., follow into Freeland, turn right at stop sign onto E. Harbor Rd., go for 6.2 miles, last house on the right.

$75-$85 **SARATOGA SUNRISE GUEST HOUSE**, 3770 S. Bells Beach Rd., Langley, WA 98260, phone 360-730-8407. A one bedroom cottage that overlooks Saratoga Passage and is within easy walking distance of a secluded beach. Roomy enough for two couples, the knotty pine living room has a fireplace and a queen size sleeper sofa. The fully equipped kitchen is stocked with breakfast for the first morning of your stay. Phone, TV, VCR, lots of books, and a great view. Children over 12 welcome, no pets, and no smoking. **Rates:** *Fridays & Saturdays* - double occupancy $85; *Sunday - Thursday* - $75; extra person $15. No credit cards. **Directions:** in Langley follow 2nd St. north for 4 miles to Center St., turn right, go two short blocks to Bells Beach Rd., turn right, look for the 4th house on the right.

$85-$120   **TWICKENHAM HOUSE BED & BREAKFAST INN,** 5023 Langley Rd., Langley, WA 98260, phone 360-221-2334. This romantic getaway is adult-oriented for peace, quiet, and relaxation. Six nonsmoking guest rooms all have private facilities and are decorated in French Canadian and European pine furniture. The two suites on the main floor both have private decks to catch sun rays and to enjoy the animals in the front pasture. A 3 course gourmet breakfast is provided. The living room has a brick fireplace and baby grand piano. In the "Britannia" room you will find an authentic English pub with draft beer on tap, pub food, darts, stone fireplace, TV/VCR for watching sports events and old movies. **Rates:** double occupancy $85-$90; suite $110-$120; extra person $15. MasterCard & Visa. **Directions:** from the Clinton ferry dock follow Hwy 525 north 4 miles to Maxwelton Rd., turn right and proceed to the end of the road.

OAK HARBOR

is the largest of Whidbey Island's towns with a population of 13,400. In April, the Holland Happening festival celebrates the heritage of Whidbey Island's Dutch immigrants. The temperate climate and favorable flying weather (96% of the time) are why the U. S. Navy decided to build a seaplane base here in 1941. More people would probably join the Navy if they were guaranteed to be stationed here.

$44-$88   **ACORN MOTOR INN,** 8066 80th NW, Oak Harbor, WA 98277, phone 360-675-6646 or 1-800-280-6646. 32 rooms, 9 nonsmoking. Phones, TV, coffee/tea making facilities, and refrigerators in every room. Some equipped kitchenettes available. Complimentary continental breakfast. Shuttle provided to Oak Harbor Airport and U. S. Naval Air Station. Within walking distance of city beach and restaurants. Children welcome, pets allowed. **Summer Rates:** *6/15 to 9/15* - single room (1 bed) $52; double room (2 beds) $58; suites $78-$88; extra person $4; pets $5 one time charge; local phone calls free. **Winter Rates:** $44-$65. Major credit cards. **Directions:** south end of town on Hwy 20, across the street from Safeway.

$45-$135 **AULD HOLLAND INN**, 5861 Hwy 20, Oak Harbor, WA 98277, phone 360-675-2288 or 1-800-228-0148, fax 360-675-2817. A unique "old-world" Dutch atmosphere. The office and deluxe suites are located inside a windmill. A total of 34 rooms, 17 are nonsmoking. In-room amenities include phone, TV, and refrigerator. Some rooms have fireplaces. Morning coffee is available with a complimentary continental breakfast. There are 6 equipped kitchen units. Outdoor heated pool, hot tub, sauna, tennis, basketball, and children's play area. The restaurant, Kasteel Franssen, specializes in French and Dutch cuisine. The lounge has entertainment on Friday and Saturday nights. Children welcome, pets allowed in select units. **Summer Rates:** *6/15 to 10/31* - double occupancy $55-$75; fireplace/jacuzzi suites $85-$135; extra person $5; pets $10; local phone calls free. **Winter Rates:** $10 less. Major credit cards. **Directions:** north end of town on Hwy 20.

Auld Holland Inn

$54-$90 **COACHMAN INN**, 5563 Hwy 20, Oak Harbor, WA 98277, phone 360-675-0727 or 1-800-635-0043. A variety of deluxe suites, 100 rooms, 40 nonsmoking. Kitchenettes, 2 bedroom units, and 10 private jacuzzi suites. Phones, TV, and coffee/tea making facilities. Restaurant, spa, outdoor pool, and workout room. Continental breakfast provided. Shuttle to marina, airport, and U. S. Naval Air Station. Children 18 and under free with parents, no pets. **Summer Rates:** *5/15 to 10/15* - single room (1 bed) $60; double $70; suites $80-$90; extra person $5; local phone calls free. **Winter Rates:** $54-$84. Major credit cards. **Directions:** intersection of Goldie Rd. and Hwy 20.

$37-$68 **NORTH WHIDBEY INN,** 1175 Midway Blvd., Oak Harbor, WA 98277, phone 360-675-5911. This one level motel has 17 units, 5 nonsmoking. In-room amenities include phones and TV. Morning coffee is available in the lobby and 13 units have equipped kitchenettes. Children welcome, no pets. **Rates:** single room $37-$58; double $41-$68; extra person $5-$10; local phone calls 25¢. Major credit cards. **Directions:** business loop on Midway Blvd.

$44-$62 **QUEEN ANN MOTEL,** 1204 W. Pioneer Way, Oak Harbor, WA 98277, phone 360-675-2209. 22 motel rooms and one 2 bedroom cottage, no designated nonsmoking. Phones, cable TV, and instant coffee/tea makers in the rooms. Indoor pool and hot tub, open year-round. Four equipped kitchen units available. Children 12 and under free, no pets. Adjacent restaurant, one block to city beach. Near U. S. Naval Air Station and golf course. **Rates:** single room $44-$47; double $51-$58; cottage (4 people) $75; kitchen units $62; extra person $5; local phone calls free. Major credit cards. **Directions:** downtown.

WHITE PASS see Naches.

WHITE SALMON (pop. 1,870) is located just off Hwy 14 in the Columbia River Gorge across the river from Hood River, Oregon.

Visit the Charles Hooper Winery just north of town or the Mont Elise Winery in Bingen. There are many activities in this area, but the most popular is boardsailing in the Gorge, followed by river rafting on the White Salmon River.

Located in Klickitat (KLIK-i-tat) County the sales/use taxes are 7%.

$89-$115 **INN OF THE WHITE SALMON,** 172 W. Jewett, P. O. Box 1549, White Salmon, WA 98672, phone 509-493-2335 or 1-800-972-5226. This bed and breakfast was once a hotel. It offers guests 16 rooms, 14 are nonsmoking. All rooms have private facilities, phones, TV, and are decorated with antiques. There is a large outdoor hot tub, a parlor with a fireplace, and lots of books to read. A full breakfast is provided. Children welcome, pets allowed at no charge. **Rates:** double occupancy $89; suites $99-$115; children $1 per year up to 12; extra person $20; local phone calls free. Major credit cards accepted. **Directions:** from Hwy 14 take Hwy 141 to White Salmon, this becomes Jewett, follow to the end of the town.

$55-$75 **LLAMA RANCH BED & BREAKFAST**, 1980 Hwy 141, White Salmon, WA 98672, phone 509-395-2786 or 1-800-800-LAMA. Here is the place for all you llama fanciers. This unique bed and breakfast has 7 nonsmoking guest rooms. Two rooms have private facilities, five share two baths. Enjoy the view of Mt. Adams on one side and Mt. Hood on the other. A full breakfast is provided. Take a llama walking through the woods. Children 3 and under no charge, pets by arrangement. Llama boarding free. Nearest restaurant 3 miles. **Rates:** double occupancy $55-$75; extra person $10; local phone calls free. Amex, MasterCard, Visa, & Discover. **Directions:** go through White Salmon, proceed north on Hwy 141 for approximately 19 miles.

WILBUR (pop. 860) is on Hwy 2 west of Spokane, 19 miles east of Grand Coulee Dam.

$28-$38 **SETTLE INN MOTEL**, 303 NE Main St., Box 607, Wilbur, WA 99185, phone 509-647-2100. This motel is in a quiet area on a creek. There are 11 rooms, 8 nonsmoking. Rooms all have phones, TV, and coffee/tea making facilities. Restaurants within walking distance. Children welcome, no pets. **Rates:** single $28-$32; double $28-$38; extra person, all ages, $6; local phone calls free; sales taxes 7.6%. Amex, MasterCard, Visa, & Diners. **Directions:** on Hwy 2, east side of town.

WINTHROP (pop. 322) is located in north central Washington in the Methow Valley.

Winthrop is a playground in the mountains. Numerous activities include: world-class cross country skiing, mountain biking, hiking, relaxing, fishing, hunting, golf, and canoeing, etc. The town itself is small with a western, cowboy facade; after all, this is cowboy country. As many as 10,000 people can pack in here for Memorial Day/Rodeo weekend, and there are all types of accommodations to meet their needs. The Methow Valley Central Reservations is very helpful for booking vacation rentals 1-800-422-3048. The North Cascades Highway, Hwy 20, leads into the Methow Valley from the west and is usually closed during the winter.

Located in Okanogan County the sales/use taxes are 7.6%.

$60-$100 **BROWN'S FARM**, 887 Wolf Creek Rd., Winthrop, WA 98862, phone 509-996-2571. The Browns have three types of cabins available, all have TV and equipped kitchens. Two of the cabins have 1 queen size bed, and optional sleeping on hide-a-bed or futon for guests with their own sleeping bags. One 2 bedroom cabin sleeps six in beds. Close to ski trail system. Horseback riding at Rocking Horse Ranch and horse lodging. Closest restaurant is 9 miles away. Children 4 and under free, dogs allowed, no smoking in cabins. **Rates:** double occupancy, one room cabin $60; small cabin $70; large cabin $100; extra person $10; pets $10 per night. MasterCard & Visa. **Directions:** 5 miles east of Mazama, mile post 184, turn at Wolf Creek Rd.

$55 **DAMMANN'S BED & BREAKFAST**, 716 Hwy 20, Winthrop, WA 98862, phone 509-996-2484 or 1-800-423-0040. Located on the banks of the Methow River and just a short walking distance to downtown. Three guest rooms, 1 with private facilities, 2 with shared. Queen bed, double bed, or twins. Use of rec room with pool table and piano. Full continental breakfast. Adults only, no pets, and no smoking. **Rates:** double occupancy $55. No credit cards. **Directions:** south side of town, before the bridge when approaching from the east.

$56-$66 **DUCK BRAND HOTEL & CANTINA**, P. O. Box 238, Winthrop, WA 98862, phone 509-996-2192 or 1-800-996-2192. Downtown Winthrop. The hotel has 6 rooms above the Cantina, all are nonsmoking with private facilities, small balconies, air conditioning, and TV. Morning coffee is available in the restaurant, it is open from 7 a.m. to 9:30 p.m. Children welcome, no pets. **Rates:** double occupancy, single room $56; double room $66; rollaway $6. Major credit cards. **Directions:** downtown.

$37-$66 **FARMHOUSE INN**, 709 Hwy 20, Winthrop, WA 98862, phone 1-800-996-2192. The Inn has 6 non-smoking guest rooms, 3 with private facilities and 3 rooms share two bathrooms. Queen beds or extra long double beds. TV in all the rooms. Outdoor hot tub. Children welcome, no pets. **Rates:** double occupancy $37, $56 & $66. Major credit cards. **Directions:** check in at Duck Brand Hotel.

$55-$85 **HOTEL RIO VISTA**, 285 Riverside, Box 815, Winthrop, WA 98862, phone 509-996-3535. 16 cozy rooms all have private decks overlooking the confluence of the Methow and Chewuch Rivers. Located on the main street of town, within walking distance of shops and restaurants. All rooms are nonsmoking, with phones, TV, and air conditioning. Morning coffee is available in the lobby. Hot tub. Children welcome, infants free, no pets. **Summer & Holiday Rates:** single room $80; double $85; extra person $5. **Winter Rates:** weekends - $65-$75; midweek - $55-$60. MasterCard & Visa. **Directions:** on the south end of the main street, 285 Riverside.

$58-$80 **MARIGOT MOTEL**, 960 Hwy 20, Box 813, Winthrop, WA 98862, phone 509-996-3100 or 1-800-468-6754. This two story motel has 65 units, 43 nonsmoking. All rooms have phones, basic cable TV, and a choice of king or 2 double beds. Morning coffee is available with a complimentary continental breakfast in the lobby. Outdoor hot tub. Children 12 and under free, pets allowed in 4 rooms. **Summer Rates:** double occupancy $70-$80; extra person $10; pets $10 per night. **Winter Rates:** $58-$67. Major credit cards. **Directions:** south of town on Hwy 20.

$54-$260 **PATTERSON LAKE CABINS**, P. O. Box 1000, Winthrop, WA 98862, phone 1-800-572-0493, ext. 713. Eight one-room cabins (no designated nonsmoking), each have equipped kitchenette, wood burning fireplace, queen bed, queen hide-a-bed, full bath, and deck. Five 2 bedroom suites sleep up to 6 people. Guests share all of Sun Mountain Lodge's amenities. The lodge is 1 mile up the road. Lakefront activities include rental rowboats, canoes, paddleboats, and sailboats. Fishing and swimming are also an option. The rates vary, depending on the season, midweek, weekend, or holiday. The special value time is spring, 3/12 to 4/13, or fall, 11/03 to 12/14, when midweek rates are $54 for a cabin or $100 for a 2 bedroom suite, double occupancy. **Rates:** 2 night minimum on weekends, 3 nights on holidays - double occupancy, cabins $54-$160; suites $100 to $260; extra person $16. Major credit cards. **Directions:** follow the road to Sun Mt. Lodge.

$55-$85 **RIVER RUN INN**, P. O. Box 157, Winthrop, WA 98862, phone 509-996-2173. The Inn is directly on the river. Six guest rooms in the Inn are furnished with new log furniture and queen beds. Five rooms upstairs share facilities, one riverview suite on the main floor has private facilities. The rooms in the Inn are provided with a continental breakfast. Common area with TV/VCR, indoor pool open year-round. A new wing has an additional 6 large suites, with private facilities, TV, and riverfront decks. Children 13 and over in the Inn, all ages in the Riverhouse suites, no pets, smoking outside. Located on the Methow River and surrounded by mountains, this is a secluded, private retreat; the only noise is the river. **Rates:** double occupancy, Inn rooms $55, $65, & $75; Riverhouse suites $85; extra person $15. MasterCard & Visa. **Directions:** on Hwy 20, west of Winthrop 1/4 mile.

$49-$260 **SUN MOUNTAIN LODGE**, P. O. Box 1000, Winthrop, WA 98862, phone 509-996-2211 or 1-800-572-0493. This world class resort offers 91 guest rooms, 22 nonsmoking, all with spectacular views. Choose from single, double, or triple bed rooms. The

Gardner rooms have fireplaces, wet bars, and private decks. Lodge amenities include restaurant/lounge, swimming pool, 2 hot tubs, exercise room, gift shop, and library. Mid-April through October there is horseback riding, mountain bike rentals, and 2 tennis courts. Winter activities include xc skiing, sleigh rides, and ice skating. Children 12 and under free, no pets. The rates vary, depending on the season and day. The most "affordable" stay would be in the lodge with a valley view, mid-week in the spring, 3/12 to 4/13, or fall, 11/03 to 12/14, double occupancy $49. **Rates:** *2 night minimum on weekends, 3 nights on holidays* - valley view, lodge $49-$155; mt. view, lodge $54-$160; lodge deluxe or Gardner $59-$185; suites $100-$260; extra person $16. Major credit cards. **Directions:** from Hwy 20, just south of Winthrop, follow the signs to the top of the mountain, approximately 8 miles.

Sun Mountain Lodge

$60-$180 **SUNNY MEADOWS INN & GOLF COURSE**, 280 W. Chewuch Rd., Winthrop, WA 98862, phone 509-996-3103 or 1-800-433-3121. Two completely remodeled farmhouses are perched on a hill overlooking 80 acres of rolling meadows, the Chewuch River, a 9 hole golf course, and an ice skating pond. Building A is a complete 2 bedroom apartment with a living room, kitchen, and two baths. Building B has 3 guest rooms with private facilities, a sitting room with TV, kitchen area with microwave and refrigerator. The upstairs, a 1300 square foot apartment, has two bedrooms with queen beds, one bath, private deck and entry. Located just 5 minutes from downtown Winthrop. Children and pets by arrangement, no smoking. **Rates:** Building A, 4 people $180; Building B, double occupancy, rooms 1-3 $60-$80; Apt., 4 people $170. No credit cards. **Directions:** on the west side of Winthrop, turn up the W. Chewuch Rd. at the Red Barn, proceed for 2.7 miles.

$40-$65 **TRAIL'S END MOTEL**, P. O. Box 189, Winthrop, WA 98862, phone 509-996-2303. On the main street of Winthrop, this motel has 12 rooms, 6 nonsmoking. All rooms have phones, TV, VCR, and coffee/tea making facilities. Sauna, bookstore, coffee shop, and video rental store on the premises. Continental breakfast provided from November through May. Children welcome, no pets. **Summer & Holiday Rates:** double occupancy $55-$65; children 15 and under $7; adults $10. **Off-Season Rate:** double occupancy $40-$52; extra person $8; local phone calls free. MasterCard, Amex, & Visa. **Directions:** on the main street, 1 block from Hwy 20 intersection.

$55-$75 **The VIRGINIAN**, 808 Hwy 20, Winthrop, WA 98862, phone 509-996-2535 or 1-800-854-2834. River-view rooms and individual cabins. There are 39 units, 28 nonsmoking. The 7 log cabins sleep 4 people. They look rustic, but have modern conveniences, color TV, kitchenettes, and air conditioning. The deluxe motel rooms sleep two to six people; two have wet bars and coffee makers. The upper level rooms have balconies facing the mountains or river. Standard rooms have two double beds and TV. Morning coffee is available in the lobby or at the restaurant on the premises, 7 a.m. to 9:30 p.m. Courtesy phone in the office. Heated outdoor pool, volleyball, and horseshoes. Children 5 and under free, pets allowed in some units. **Summer Rates:** double occupancy, cabins $75; motel $55-$75; extra person $10; pets $5. Winter rates are less, check when making reservations. MasterCard, Amex, Discover, & Visa. **Directions:** on Hwy 20 just south of Winthrop.

$50-$150 **WESTAR LODGE & RETREAT**, 390 W. Chewuch, Winthrop, WA 98862, phone 509-996-2697. The Westar caters to groups of 30 or less. The lodge has 5 sleeping rooms with 23 beds, 4 with private facilities, 1 with shared. A separate cottage sleeps a maximum of 7 in 2 bedrooms, has equipped kitchen, washer/dryer, and private hot tub. Complimentary tea, coffee, and hot chocolate are provided. Guests have use of the kitchen and hot tub on the deck of the lodge. Conference and meeting facilities on the lower floor of the lodge. Children welcome, no pets. **Rates:** cottage $150 first night, $112 for each additional night; lodge, double occupancy $50; extra person $10; group rates $330. No credit cards. **Directions:** turn onto the W. Chewuch Rd. at the Red Barn west of town, proceed for 3.9 miles.

$65-$75 The **WINTHROP INN MOTEL**, P. O. Box 265, Winthrop, WA 98862, phone 509-996-2217 or 1-800-444-1972. Located on 10 park-like acres, this motel offers 30 rooms, 26 nonsmoking. Units have one or two queen size beds, TV, balconies on the second floor, and air conditioning. No coffee/tea making facilities in the rooms, but available in the lobby. Hot tub and heated outdoor pool. The Winthrop Inn is just a stone throw away from the Methow River, bring your fishing poles or kayak. Children 12 and under free, small pets allowed. **Rates:** single room (1 bed) $65; double room $75; extra person $8; pets $10, one time charge. MasterCard & Visa. **Directions:** on Hwy 20 south of Winthrop 3/4 mile.

$63 **WINTHROP MOUNTAIN VIEW CHALETS**, P. O. Box 936, Winthrop, WA 98862, phone 509-996-3113 or 1-800-527-3113. Six cozy cabins, all nonsmoking. The cabins have a country decor, queen beds, TVs, air conditioning, microwaves, and coffee/tea making facilities. Courtesy phone at the office. The cabins are for two people, no pets. **Rates:** double occupancy $63. MasterCard & Visa. **Directions:** on Hwy 20 at the south edge of town.

$59-$149 **WOLFRIDGE RESORT**, Rt. 2 Box 655, Winthrop, WA 98862, phone 509-996-2828 or 1-800-237-2388. This resort has 3 log duplex townhouses with a variety of combinations and one new individual log cabin. There are 4 hotel style rooms, upstairs, with a queen bed, trundle, and balcony; two deluxe hotel style rooms, upstairs, with queen bed, queen sofa sleeper, mini kitchen, and balcony; 6 one-bedroom suites with separate equipped kitchen, living/dining room, private deck with barbecue; 6 two-bedroom, two bath townhouses with equipped kitchens, living/dining rooms, balconies upstairs, and private decks with barbecues. All units have phones and TV. Resort amenities include heated outdoor pool, spa, log playground area, log recreation/conference building with pool table and woodstove, and groomed xc ski track. Children welcome, pets by arrangement. **Rates:** double occupancy, hotel style rooms $59-$69; one bedroom suite $93; 2 bedroom townhouse $149; children $5; extra person $10. Discount rates offered in early spring and late fall. MasterCard & Visa. **Directions:** south of Winthrop, turn off Hwy 20 onto Twin Lakes Rd., proceed 1.5 miles to Wolf Creek Rd., turn right, proceed for 3 miles until the pavement ends, continue on this road for 1 mile, on the right.

WOODINVILLE is located northeast of Seattle, 1 mile off Hwy 405. It is the home of the Chateau St. Michelle Winery.

$58

BEAR CREEK INN Bed & Breakfast, 19520 NE 144th Pl., Woodinville, WA 98072, phone 206-881-2978. This shingle-clad Inn is in a park-like setting. There are two guest rooms with shared facilities. The rooms are decorated with oak, brass, and ornate iron. Queen beds have fluffy comforters. Soft robes are furnished to guests for the hot tub or the tiled bath with shower-tub. Warmth and charm are reflected in the river rock fireplaces and polished wood beams of the gathering rooms. Breakfast has a varied menu of delights. Children by arrangement, no pets, and no smoking. **Rates:** double occupancy $58; taxes 8.2%. No credit cards. **Directions:** given with reservations.

WOODLAND (pop. 2,592) is located just 20 miles north of Vancouver at the junction of I-5 and Highway 503.

Woodland is the southern gateway to Mt. St. Helens. The Lewis River and lower Columbia provide excellent fishing. Colorful displays of tulips, daffodils, and iris bloom each spring on the Woodland bottomlands. Bicyclists are attracted year-round by the flat roadways winding through pastoral scenes. Meadows and marshes are a favorite haunt of bird watchers.

Located in Cowlitz County the sales/use/lodging taxes are 9.5%.

$39-$55 **GRANDMA'S HOUSE BED & BREAKFAST**, 4551 Old Lewis River Rd., Woodland, WA 98674, phone 360-225-7002. Over the meadow and through the woods to grandmother's house we go! A quaint farmhouse on 35 acres overlooking the north fork of the Lewis River. There are 2 nonsmoking guest rooms that share one bathroom, full kitchen, living room, and dining room. Full breakfast included. Mature landscaping includes an enormous Monkey Pod Tree. Children welcome, pets by arrangement. **Rates:** single occupancy $39; double occupancy $55; taxes included. MasterCard & Visa. **Directions:** Woodland Exit off I-5, east on Hwy 503 eight miles to Fredrickson Rd., turn right, another immediate right on Old Lewis River Rd., continue to the house.

$34-$44 **HANSEN'S MOTEL**, 1215 Pacific, Woodland, WA 98674, phone, 360-225-7018. All 6 units have knotty pine interior and are on one level. No designated nonsmoking, but the owners purchased a machine that keeps the rooms smelling very fresh. TV and phones in the rooms. No coffee/tea making facilities, but a restaurant is within walking distance. Children welcome, dogs allowed, no cats. **Rates:** single (1 bed) $34-$38; double (2 beds) $38-$44; extra person $4. MasterCard & Visa. **Directions:** Exit 21 off I-5 to west side of freeway, follow access road to the right.

$30-$40 **LAKESIDE MOTEL**, 785 Lakeshore Dr., Woodland, WA 98674, phone 360-225-8240. Across the street from the lake and park. Fishing, swimming, and picnic area. 13 rooms, 4 nonsmoking. Rooms have phones and cable TV. No coffee/tea making facilities in the rooms. Children welcome, infants free, pets allowed. **Summer Rates:** single (1 bed) $36; double (2 beds) $40; extra person $3; pets $5. **Winter Rates:** $30-$35. MasterCard & Visa. **Directions:** Exit 21 off I-5 to west side of freeway, turn left, across the street from the park.

$46-$60 **LEWIS RIVER INN**, 1100 Lewis River Rd., Woodland, WA 98674, phone 360-225-6257 or 1-800-543-4344, fax 360-225-9515. 49 rooms on two levels, 50% nonsmoking. Queen beds, phones, remote cable TV, and river-view rooms with balconies. No coffee/tea making facilities in the rooms, but available in the lobby. Children 16 and under free with parents, pets allowed. **Rates:** single (1 bed) $46; double (2 beds) $50; river-view rooms $56-$60; extra person $5; pets $5. Major credit cards. **Directions:** Exit 21 off I-5 east of freeway.

$44-$50 **WOODLANDER INN**, 1500 Atlantic St., Woodland, WA 98674, phone 360-225-6548 or 1-800-444-9667. 61 rooms, 80% nonsmoking. In-room amenities include phones, cable TV, and queen size beds. Indoor pool and spa. Morning coffee is available in the lobby. Six units have micro/fridges, no utensils. Restaurants within walking distance. Children 6 and under free, pets allowed. **Rates:** single room (1 bed) $44-$48; double room (2 beds) $50; extra person $6; micro/fridge $1 extra; pets $3-$5. Major credit cards. **Directions:** Exit 21 off I-5, go east of freeway, turn left 4 blocks.

YAKIMA (pop.57,660) is located in the south central region of Washington along Hwy 97.

(YAK-i-maw) is an agricultural community with diverse crops of fruit, hops, grapes, and many vegetables. The Yakima Valley is currently the second largest wine-producing region in the nation. Area attractions include visits to the Thurston Wolfe Winery, horse racing at Yakima Meadows, and tours of historic sites on the Yakima Electric Trolley.

Located in Yakima County the sales/use taxes are 7.9%.

$70-$140 **'37 HOUSE BED & BREAKFAST**, 4002 Englewood Ave., Yakima, WA 98901, phone 509-965-5537. Five nonsmoking rooms all have private facilities, phones, and TV. The grounds offer an English garden. Three floors of accommodations for overnight guests, meetings, retreats, and special events. The paneled lower level, complete with stone fireplace, is especially adaptable for all-day meetings. Full gourmet breakfast is provided and arrangements can be made for other meals. Supervised children welcome, no pets. **Rates:** double occupancy $70-$90; suite (2 to 4 people) $140; extra person $10; local phone calls free. MasterCard, Visa, & Amex. **Directions:** off I-82 take Hwy 12 west; off Hwy 12 west take 40th Ave. Exit; located at the top of the hill on the corner of 40th Ave. and Englewood.

$70-$100 **BIRCHFIELD MANOR BED & BREAKFAST**, 2018 Birchfield Rd., Yakima, WA 98901, phone 509-452-1960 or 1-800-375-3420. Five nonsmoking rooms, all have private facilities. TV. Coffee/tea making facilities in the lounge area, outdoor pool, and sauna. Restaurant on the grounds. Full breakfast is provided to guests. Children over 8 years old, no pets. Located in a country setting only two miles from Yakima. An ideal location for touring the wine country. Award winning dinners prepared by chef/owner. **Rates:** double $70-$100; extra person $15; local phone calls free. Diners, MasterCard, Visa, & Amex. **Directions:** Exit 34 from I-82, east 2 miles, turn right onto Birchfield Rd., first house on the right.

CAVANAUGH'S at YAKIMA CENTER, 607 E. Yakima Ave., Yakima, WA 98901, phone 509-248-5900 or 1-800-THE-INNS.

$43-$52   **COLONIAL MOTOR INN,** 1405 N. 1st St., Yakima, WA 98901, phone 509-453-8981. 53 units, 28 nonsmoking. In-room amenities include phones, TV, and air conditioning. Morning coffee is available in the lobby and a continental breakfast is provided. Other amenities include indoor pool and two hot tubs. Several restaurants within walking distance. Children 6 and under free, small pets allowed. Trolley to downtown 6 days a week. **Rates:** single (1 bed) $43-$49; double (2 beds) $52; extra person $6; local phone calls free; pets $6. Major credit cards. **Directions:** take Exit 31 off I-82, 2 1/2 blocks south on the left side of the street, just past the Red Lion.

HOLIDAY INN, 9 N. 9th St., Yakima, WA 98901, phone 509-452-6511 or 1-800-465-4329, fax 509-457-4931.

$52-$66   **HUNTLEY INN, 12 Valley Mall Blvd., Yakima, WA 98903, phone 509-248-6924, or 1-800-448-5544, fax 509-575-8470.** 86 units, 35 nonsmoking. In-room amenities include phones, TV, AC, and small refrigerators. Morning coffee is available in the lobby along with an extensive continental breakfast. Other amenities include a guest laundry and seasonal outdoor pool. Children 12 and under free, pets allowed. Shuttle provided to the airport. Located directly across the street from Valley Mall. **Rates:** single room (1 bed) $52-$59; double room (2 beds) $66; rollaway $10; local phone calls free; pets $10 one time charge. Major credit cards. **Directions:** Union Gap Exit 36 off I-82.

$60   **IRISH HOUSE BED & BREAKFAST, 210 S. 28th Ave., Yakima, WA 98901, phone 509-453-5474.** Three nonsmoking guest bedrooms are located on the second floor, off the central hallway, and share a full bath. Comfortable double or queen size beds occupy the rooms. All rooms are graciously decorated in nineteenth century style with today's comfort. Children over 12, no pets. Continental plus breakfast is served in the dining room. This Victorian farmhouse is typical of the era; oriel windows, ornate woodwork, stained and beveled glass. **Rates:** double occupancy $60. Amex. **Directions:** Exit 33 from I-82, west on Yakima Ave. to 28th, south two blocks.

Irish House Bed & Breakfast

$35-$59 **RED APPLE MOTEL**, 416 N. 1st St., Yakima, WA 98901, phone 509-248-7150. 60 units, 18 nonsmoking. In-room amenities include phones, TV, and air conditioning. Morning coffee is available in the lobby. Black Angus restaurant next door. Seasonal outdoor pool. Children welcome, pets allowed. **Rates:** *weekdays* - single room (1 bed) $35; double (2 beds) $52; *weekends* - single $46; double $59; pets $20 deposit, $4 per night; local phone calls free; taxes included. Major credit cards. **Directions:** Exit 31 off I-82, first intersection with light, next to the Black Angus Restaurant.

$57-$67 **SUN COUNTRY INN**, 1700 N. 1st St., Yakima, WA 98901, phone 509-248-5650 or 1-800-559-3675. 70 units, 18 nonsmoking. Phones, TV, AC, seasonal outdoor pool, sauna, and laundry facilities. Morning coffee and continental breakfast is available in the lobby. There are 6 equipped kitchenette units. Some units have microwaves and refrigerators for an additional charge. Children 18 and under free with parents. Small pets, no charge, in smoking rooms only. **Rates:** single room (1 bed) $57; double room (2 beds) $66; kitchen units $67; microwaves/refrigerators $5. Major credit cards. **Directions:** off I-82, Exit 31.

$53-$65 **RIO MIRADA MOTOR INN**, 1603 Terrace Ht. Dr., Yakima, WA 98901, phone 509-457-4444, 1-800-521-3050, fax 509-453-7593. 96 units, 65 nonsmoking. In-room amenities include phones, TV, and air conditioning. Morning coffee is available in the lobby. Other amenities include 6 equipped kitchenette units, seasonal outdoor pool, adult indoor jacuzzi, shuttle to the airport, and the city bus stops out front. All rooms have decks or balconies that overlook the Yakima River. Seven miles of the Greenway Trail is just outside the door. Children 6 and under free, no pets allowed. **Rates:** single $53-$58; double (2 people) $63; kitchen units (2 people) $65; extra person $8; local phone calls free. Major credit cards. **Directions:** Exit 33 off I-82.

ZILLAH

(pop. 1,950) is located in the Yakima Valley Wine Country. Zillah (ZIL-uh) wineries include Bonair Winery, Covey Run Vintners, Horizons Edge Winery, Hyatt Vineyards, Portieus Winery, and Zillah Oakes Winery. See Yakima, Union Gap, Toppenish, or Sunnyside for lodging.

Need Another Copy?

Number of books you would like → | | x **$12.95** = |

Shipping and Handling			SALES TAX*	
Quantity	Cost			
1	$2.00	→	SHIPPING	
2	$3.00			
each additional	$0.50		TOTAL	

* Washington State residents only - add 8% sales tax.

A D D R E S S

Name _____
First   Last

Address _____

City _____ State ____ Zip ____

Daytime Phone (____) _____

Delivery Time

Please allow 3 to 4 weeks, shipped via U.S. Mail

S H I P T O

(if different than above)

Name _____

Address _____

City _____ State ____ Zip ____

Phone (____) _____

Canadian Orders

$17.95 and $3.00 shipping and handling

Extra "Ship To" Addresses

Add $2.00 for each address

P A Y M E N T

☐Check or Money Order $ _____

Make checks payable to: Direct Book Service

☐VISA ☐Master Card ☐Discover

_____
Account Number   Expiration Date

Volume Orders

Quantity price discounts available, call us!

		$12.95
	SubTotal	
	SHIPPING	
	TOTAL	

Washington State residents only, please add 8% sales tax.